Uncertain power

DATE			

uncertain POWER

Pergamon Titles of Related Interest

Related Journals*

*Free specimen copies available upon request.

uncertain POWER

The Struggle for a National Energy Policy

Edited by

Dorothy S. Zinberg

John F. Kennedy School of Government
Harvard University

Pergamon Press

New York   Oxford   Toronto   Sydney   Paris   Frankfurt

Pergamon Press Offices:

U.S.A.	Pergamon Press Inc., Maxwell House, Fairview Park, Elmsford, New York 10523, U.S.A.
U.K.	Pergamon Press Ltd., Headington Hill Hall, Oxford OX3 0BW, England
CANADA	Pergamon Press Canada Ltd., Suite 104, 150 Consumers Road, Willowdale, Ontario M2J 1P9, Canada
AUSTRALIA	Pergamon Press (Aust.) Pty. Ltd., P.O. Box 544, Potts Point, NSW 2011, Australia
FRANCE	Pergamon Press SARL, 24 rue des Ecoles, 75240 Paris, Cedex 05, France
FEDERAL REPUBLIC OF GERMANY	Pergamon Press GmbH, Hammerweg 6, D-6242 Kronberg-Taunus, Federal Republic of Germany

Copyright 1983 Pergamon Press Inc.

Library of Congress Cataloging in Publication Data

Main entry under title:

Uncertain power.

    Includes bibliographical references and index.
    1. Energy policy – United States – Congresses.
I. Zinberg, Dorothy S.
HD9502.U52U43 1983   333.79′0973   83-6277
ISBN 0-08-029388-3
ISBN 0-08-029387-5 (pbk.)

Printed in the United States of America

The great significance of a change in the cost of energy arises from the fact that energy is a part of the cost of achieving all values. It takes energy even to dream.

William F. Cottrell, Energy and Society (New York: McGraw-Hill, 1955) p.113.

CONTENTS

PREFACE

Spawned in 1973 in the aftermath of the first Arab oil embargo, energy studies proliferated during the 1970s. By 1980 they had shaped a significant public policy literature. For the most part, the studies addressed problems of supply, usually of oil and natural gas; the technology of producing energy from solar and nuclear sources, and synthetic fuels; and above all, the economics of these resources. As predictions failed and ambitious projects foundered, the limitations of some of these studies became apparent. The price of oil, which quadrupled in the aftermath of the 1973 Arab-Israeli War, was not expected to rise again significantly by 1980.[1] The fall of the Shah of Iran in 1979 demolished such optimistic predictions as prices almost tripled, making the second oil shock even more debilitating than the first.[2] Nuclear power plants, expected to provide some 40 percent of United States' electricity in the 1980s, were by 1982 contributing less than 12 percent, and there was no likelihood that earlier goals could be achieved. The production of oil by oil-shale extraction, which by some estimates was to have provided 5 million barrels of oil per day by 1984, is languishing on the brink of extinction; while the boom towns hastily created in anticipation of a vigorous, new industry, are already beginning to resemble the deserted silver-mining towns of the nineteenth century. The classical tools of economic analysis and forecasting had proven inadequate.

Many of the early studies paid scant attention to what have rapidly come to be recognized as crucial factors in national and international energy policy planning, namely, the social, psychological, and political dimensions of energy problems. Conversely, the relatively few studies written by social scientists (after a flurry of interest in the peaceful uses of the atom had paled) usually ignored technological innovations and economics. When social scientists did address technology or economics, their work was most often published in journals read only by other social scientists. For example, the article, "Sociologists Should Reconsider Nuclear Energy," a plea for "cogent analyses of the social costs and benefits of alternative energy futures, soundly based in sociological theory," was published in *Social Forces,* a publication not likely to be read by specialists in the Department of Energy, or the Atomic Industrial Forum (AIF), or even by nonsocial scientists in universities.[3] Other studies such as *A Time to Choose,* which did examine several social issues, appeared in 1974 before the social aspects of the energy problem had gained national prominence. Consequently, it failed to attract the public's attention.[4]

Rapid growth in the antinuclear movement beginning in the 1970s further illuminated the social-political dimensions of energy problems and made clear the need for a new brand of professional—one who could analyze the social, psychological, and political aspects of energy problems, but with due reference to the technologies involved. The new problems demanded experts who could assess metal stress in aging nuclear power plants while also considering the significance of mental stress among residents of Three Mile Island (TMI) following the accident.[5,6] This new breed of analyst has evolved over the past decade, in part from recycled, traditionally trained physical and social scientists, in part from the first-generation graduates of university energy programs, and to a lesser extent from the rare and valuable autodidacts.

Three interdisciplinary research programs at Harvard University's John F. Kennedy School of Government have abetted the development of these specialists during recent years. For a decade the Center for Science and International Affairs, whose major concern is arms control and international security problems, has been studying the links between energy security (as an aspects of national and international security) and nuclear proliferation as they relate to issues of civilian nuclear power, waste disposal, nuclear weapons, and terrorism.[7] More recently, the Energy and Environmental Policy Center has carried out research on allocation, development, regulation, and conservation of energy and environmental resources. The Program for Science, Technology and Public Policy for more than 15 years has been training students in the policy aspects of science and technology-related problems. The director of this program chaired the most comprehensive U.S. energy study group to date, the Committee on Nuclear and Alternative Energy Systems (CONAES), whose report was published in 1979.[8] By bringing together social and physical scientists, CONAES made a significant contribution to the development of a new network of specialists addressing energy issues. The rapidly changing scene in energy policy, which called for greater multidisciplinary efforts, suggested that the CONAES approach should be adopted and broadened. Drawing on both the CONAES and the Kennedy School's networks of energy policy experts, the Kennedy School held a workshop in May 1981. The participants were:

Mr. Alvin L. Alm
Director, Harvard Energy Security Program
Kennedy School of Government

Prof. Ian Barbour
Director, Program in Science, Ethics and Public Policy
Carleton College

Mr. James Bishop, documentary producer
President, Bishop Associates

Prof. Kenneth Boulding
Director of the Program of Research on General Social and Economic Dynamics,
Institute of Behavioral Science
University of Colorado

Prof. Harvey Brooks
Benjamin Peirce Professor of Technology and Public Policy
Harvard University

Dr. Benjamin S. Cooper
Professional Staff Member, Senate Committee on Energy and Natural Resources

Prof. Paul Doty
Director, Center for Science and International Affairs Kennedy School of
Government

Prof. Roger Kasperson
Director, Center for Technology, Environment and Development
Clark University

Prof. Sanford Lakoff
Professor of Political Science, University of California,
San Diego; Fellow, National Humanities Center

Dr. Rodney Lay
Department Head, Renewable and Advanced Energy Systems
The MITRE Corporation

Dr. Douglas MacLean
Research Associate, Center for Philosophy and Public Policy
University of Maryland

Mr. Alan McGowan
President, Scientists' Institute for Public Information

Prof. Allan Mazur
Professor of Sociology, Syracuse University

Prof. Linda B. Miller
Professor of Political Science, Wellesley College

Prof. Laura Nader
Professor of Anthropology
University of California, Berkeley

Ms. Dorothy Powers, Chairperson
League of Women Voters Education Fund

Mr. Michael Rice
Senior Fellow, Aspen Institute for Humanistic Studies

Mr. Richard Sclove
Research Associate, Center for International Studies, M.I.T.

Prof. Frank Von Hippel
Princeton University

Ms. Margaret Bush Wilson
National Chairperson—NAACP; Attorney at Law

Mr. Daniel Yankelovich
Chairman, Yankelovich, Skelly & White, Inc.
President, Public Agenda Foundation

Dr. Daniel Yergin
Adjunct Lecturer, Kennedy School of Government

Dr. Dorothy S. Zinberg
Director of Seminars and Special Projects, CSIA;
Lecturer on Public Policy, Kennedy School of Government

Mr. Charles Zraket
Executive Vice President, MITRE Corporation

The workshop was originally convened to discuss "energy and social adaptation." The title of the book that has resulted, *Uncertain Power: The Struggle For A National Energy Policy,* reflects the change of emphasis that evolved largely from intense discussions during the workshop. Despite the agenda the group found itself returning repeatedly to the subjects of political process, public opinion and participation, the subtle issue of consensus, and the, as yet, unresolved problems of energy supply and national security.

Because of the significance of the United States in world affairs, its own national security and even its energy consumption are major international concerns. That decisions regarding these issues can no longer be made in isolation has been recognized for many years. Pollution, resource depletion, conservation efforts, food production, and population growth are all globally, inextricably linked. These long-range problems and challenges reveal the necessity for new forms of international cooperation, and in turn, presage the need for new perspectives, values, and behavior. The group concluded that gaining further clarification of certain national problems before embarking on the international implications would provide a more solid base from which to conduct future research and policy studies.

More important, on rereading the papers and subsequent commentaries on the workshop it became evident that social adaptation was no longer a suitable rubric for what the workshop had brought into prominence. The stalemates that we had repeatedly confronted in energy policy making were not of adaptation, but of a continuing struggle in the political and public arenas as witnessed by the inequities in the distribution of burdens borne by different groups in society, the need for political action, the importance of coalition building, and, perhaps, the linchpin—the role of the public. Thus the title and concern of this volume: the struggle for a national energy policy. To place these new topics in context we have had several additional papers written on federal, state, and local interactions, and also on conservation. We hope that the resulting collection will provide a broader framework within which to integrate social, economic, political, and technical variables so that their interdependence will become obvious to all who strive to create workable national energy policies.

ACKNOWLEDGMENTS

I wish to thank the many colleagues and friends who have read, and in several instances reread, different chapters in this book. During the successive stages of the book's preparation from workshop drafts to final essays, I have benefited from correspondence, conversation, and, often, heated discussions with Professors Ian Barbour, Harvey Brooks, Albert Carnesale, Paul Doty, William Hogan, Sanford Lakoff, Laura Nader, and Norman Zinberg. As the book's chapters will reveal once more, consensus is not easily achieved on energy issues.

The hallmarks of several energy problems changed drastically during the period the book was being written. For example, the cost of oil decreased as did the number of barrels imported daily into the United States; nuclear power plant cancellations increased; the American public's concerns shifted from energy to the economy; and the synthetic fuel program suffered innumerable vicissitudes. Accordingly, the work of several research assistants was crucial for up-dating of the data through 1982. At an early stage, Fredie Kaye helped plan the format and substance of the workshop, while Andrea Larson prepared the background material for the workshop and carried out the research for the section on the history of public participation. Later, David Kissinger ferreted out the sources of obscure references and compiled additional bibliographies, and Christopher Gates searched the final drafts for anachronisms and inaccuracies.

The administrative and organizational underpinnings of the workshop were ably provided by Daryl Battin while the arduous task of transliterating the papers to a newly installed and often dysfunctional word processor was carried out very professionally by Diane Asay. Woodward Wickham's unique editorial skills provided all of us with new insights into the possibilities for translating 'energese' into English. The lapses, which I hope are few, result from our intractability, not his lack of guidance.

Not insignificant in the book's becoming a reality was the contribution made by many of my colleagues at the Center for Science and International Affairs who stepped in and performed the chores that were ordinarily mine during the time the conference and book were in process. They have set a model for collaboration upon which it would be hard to improve.

The MITRE Corporation and the Rockefeller Family Foundation generously contributed funds for the project, while the Center for Science and International Affairs at Harvard University's Kennedy School of Government provided space, staff time, and its most highly coveted privilege, access to the new word processor. I am most appreciative for all of their support—financial, institutional, and collegial.

NOTES

1. See "Limits to Models" in Robert Stobaugh and Daniel Yergin, eds., *Energy Future: Report of the Energy Project at the Harvard Business School* (New York: Random House, 1979), p.245.
2. For a discussion of the impact of the oil price increases see Robert Dohner, "The Bedeviled American Economy" in *Global Insecurity: A Strategy for Energy and Economic Renewal*, ed. Daniel Yergin and Martin Hillebrand (Boston: Houghton Mifflin Co., 1982).
3. Sociologists should reconsider Otis Dudley Duncan, "Nuclear Energy," *Social Forces*, 57 (Sept. 1978):1.
4. Energy Policy Project of the Ford Foundation, *A Time to Choose* (Cambridge, MA: Ballinger Publishing Co., 1974).
5. See interview with Sir Alan Cottrell, "PWRs Unlikely To Be Safe, Says Metallurgist," *Nature*, 283 (Feb. 1980).
6. On mental stress, see "Mental Stress Given Environmental Status," *Nature*, 295, (21 Jan. 1982); "Psychological Stress: New Factor in TMI-1 Restart," *Nuclear Industry*, 29 (Feb. 1982).
7. Frederick Williams and David Deese, *Nuclear Proliferation* (New York: Pergamon Press, 1979); David Deese and Joseph Nye, eds., *Energy and Security* (Cambridge, MA: Ballinger Publishing Co., 1981); Derek Leebaert, ed. *European Security in the 1980s* (Lexington, MA: Lexington Books, 1979); Michael Mandelbaum, *The Nuclear Question: The United States and Nuclear Weapons: 1946–1976* (New York: Cambridge University Press, 1979).
8. CONAES Report, Supporting Paper 7, *Energy Choices in a Democratic Society* (Washington, DC: National Academy of Sciences, 1980).

INTRODUCTION

Dorothy S. Zinberg

OVERVIEW

In the past decade, policy planning has rapidly become both the subject and object of political, technical, and social debate. American presidents and politicians are elected, in part, because they appear to be responding to the country's wish to be guided by rational policies for health, social welfare, education, employment, local-state-and-federal balance of power, economic growth, foreign affairs, and national defense. They have proposed ambitious plans only to be stymied by the vastness of the problems and, more significantly, by the lack of sustained consensus in the country as to the relative weight each policy should receive. As Lester Thurow illuminated even in the title of his provocative book, *The Zero Sum Society,* the size of the economic pie isn't changing, only the size of the portions. For each decision on defense spending, social benefits, and taxation, there are winners and losers; redistribution, not net gains, results. In a utopian society a comprehensive public policy would contribute to improving the lot of every citizen. In the real world, particularly one in which economic growth has slowed and unemployment soared, each decision is at the expense of a competing interest. Accordingly, at every organizational and institutional level of society and in every nook and cranny of the country, groups coalesce around a shared interest to protect themselves from becoming one of the losers in this redistribution of influence, power, and money.

A quick look at the political fate of recent presidents (none has been elected for two terms) and the disappearance from the Congress of familiar figures once considered permanent fixtures suggests that the public's disappointment in the failure of leaders to carry out acceptable national policies has made incumbency a potential impediment to reelection. As pressure grows for more rational, comprehensive planning, the many diverse, conflicting interests of this heterogeneous, pluralistic, decentralized, fiercely competitive society crash noisily into each other, and the promised policy implementation is shattered. Only partial policies can then be enacted. The public, consequently, becomes increasingly disaffected and cynical, and responds by voting for a change, or as is often the case, passively, by not voting. Successive governments also respond by creating or expunging departments, boosting or slashing budgets, and emphasizing what they perceive to be their mandate from the public.

Stalemates result and paradoxes abound. For example, the American public has stated firmly that the federal government is bloated and too powerful. Both Presidents Carter and Reagan came into office committed to carrying out the public's wish to cut federal spending programs. Nevertheless, the public has continued to want the federal government to be the employer of last resort; 74 percent of them believe that we should have a federal program to create jobs for the unemployed, even if the result increases the budget deficit.[1]

All of these contradictions in the struggle among competing interests and goals have crystalized in the struggle to develop a national energy policy. As the authors of *Uncertain Power* make clear, the struggle is a reflection not just of the problems of energy, but of many other tensions and issues in American society.

As we noted in the preface, the very notion of an energy policy is relatively new—a product of a growing awareness of the links between the economy and energy and the sharp rise in oil prices which began with the 1973 Arab oil embargo. As the interrelatedness of energy resources became more apparent and efforts to arrive at balances among oil, coal, natural gas, nuclear, renewables, and conservation began to emerge, the search for an energy policy began in earnest. The National Academy of Sciences spent the largest sum of money in its history to design a proposal for a national energy policy;[2] policy studies began to appear and, like the struggle itself, covered a spectrum of views many of which were less part of a spectrum than mutually exclusive propositions.

Whereas the need for energy policy crystalized the problems besetting the country as well as the difficulties of designing and implementing policy, nuclear energy policy provided an even sharper focus. It quickly became the single lens through which much of the overall energy debate was refracted. Nuclear power is unique and some would argue that as a consequence nuclear-related policy cannot serve as a model for decision making or as an illumination of policy formulation in general. Yet as the authors of *Uncertain Power* explain, the questions that penetrate to the core of democratic process (questions about equity, the distribution of risk, and representative government) are embodied in nuclear-related issues.

Since World War II the spectacular growth of high technology with its attendant benefits and risks has pushed technology into the spotlight of public admiration tempered by concern. Each time a satellite fails and threatens to disintegrate on some undetermined part of the earth's surface or an airplane disaster creates a tragedy of unprecedented dimensions, the gains these technologies have brought are questioned by the public. Though committed to new advances in high technology, particularly in medicine, agriculture, and industry, they nevertheless retain serious reservations about how the quality of life is being adversely affected by technologies that threaten to outstrip our capacity to control them.

Nuclear power continues to be enthusiastically endorsed for the long-term energy needs of the world by the majority of scientific and engineering elites.[3] The general public is less certain. Because the near-term economics remain unfavorable for the industry, there is less publicity about the public's attitudes. However, recent revelations of fraud in the industry (the steel used in construction of many light-water reactors is defective) combined with the underlying fear about the relationship of radiation to cancer (now being tested in several class action suits filed by 1950s veterans of above-ground weapons testing in southwestern U.S. deserts and by nuclear weapons production personnel at Rocky Flats, Colorado) and the residual anxiety from the Three Mile Island accident have deprived nuclear power of majority public support.[4] The percentage favoring the further development of nuclear power, as opposed to those who think it is too dangerous, has dropped from 50 percent in 1979 to 41 percent in 1982.

These concerns pale in comparison with growing public anxiety about the upward spiral of the arms race. Despite years of effort by industry and government to separate civilian and military nuclear power in the mind of the public, the 1981 U.S. government announcement that it was contemplating the use of commercial reactor fuel for the new generation of nuclear warheads destroyed the credibility of earlier assurances.[5,6]

Policy for national security is inextricably linked to nuclear weapons which in turn are linked to the generation of nuclear fuel at home and the proliferation of power plants around the world. A wary, pro-civil-nuclear power physicist has written that nuclear power's "weapons connection" does not "manifestly render its use intolerable" but rather that:

> a realistic appraisal of the weapons liability must be included—along with the best information about the other costs and benefits of nuclear power and of the alternatives—in any sensible evaluation of energy strategies.[7]

In the short space of a decade, the United States has striven to develop a comprehensive energy policy to subsume all of the concerns identified above. The authors of *Uncertain Power* contend that the aim of achieving such comprehensiveness was misguided and unrealistic. Because the issues are ultimately political and the country so diverse, a more realistic approach is to explore the assumptions and the values underlying policy planning and choices. The aim should be to develop incremental, flexible policies that reflect the realities of resource availability, the potential for technological development, and, above all, the political will of the public.

The research agenda is full. An evaluation of energy decision making in the 1970s concludes that:

> Perhaps the most striking conclusion from this review is that so little systematic research is available on the topic of energy decision making in the American political system. Despite frequently repeated condemnations of pre-embargo government organization and policy, most reports and book-length studies proceed to offer recommendations without having analyzed the existing decision-making apparatus or its product.[8]

Accordingly, there is still much to be learned about *how* policy is made, how it is implemented, and how it can be evaluated.

The authors of *Uncertain Power* believe that the emphasis on the economics and technology camouflaged the major issues of the role of social values and different goals among those who influence the political process. As we noted in the introduction, the problems call for a new cadre of experts conversant in many languages and skills who can begin to create and evaluate policy.

The issues vary in complexity. A number of papers in the book will be readily understood by neophytes in energy policy. Others such as those on risk are more difficult to grasp, but, because they are integral to an understanding of the trade-offs, compromise, and ethical demands involved in virtually all policy making, are worth the struggle.

The energy crisis has receded for the moment, but we believe that what we can learn from trying to resolve energy problems is applicable to resolving other policy problems. Not unimportantly, continuing to struggle for more understanding of energy issues themselves will provide insurance that will pay substantial dividends in the not-too-distant future.

It is not surprising, however, that the American public has gratefully accepted the latest news that the energy crisis is over. For nearly a decade the imminence of an energy catastrophe was made vivid by gasoline lines, escalating prices, and supply interruptions. Just when we as a country were beginning to believe the energy crisis real (in 1980, 70 percent according to one poll called energy "one of the two most important concerns facing the country"), optimists began to proclaim the good news.[9] Articles in the *New York Times* and the *Wall Street Journal* heralded a more relaxed era, while a *Harper's* cover boomed, "The Energy Crisis Is Over!"[10] That the once-fearsome OPEC was now choking on its self-produced oil "glut" and would soon expire, a victim of its own greed, compounded the pleasure these announcements gave us.[11] Those who believed that the energy crisis was a myth supported by "a propaganda war of startling dimensions" appeared to be exonerated.[12] Usually skeptical Americans accepted the good news with relief; there were other problems—inflation, unemployment, and, for some, national security—of more immediate concern.

The authors of *Uncertain Power* contend that the country is being seriously misled if it believes that the energy problem, in the words of one writer in the *New York Times,* has "joined global famine, the limits of growth, and the population bomb as ideas whose inevitability has mercifully passed."[13] We attempt to demonstrate that energy is an integral aspect of the many problems facing society. The economic and national security concerns now crowding energy off center stage, while not a result solely of energy problems, require that concerted energy plans be formulated. The market has failed to solve the many dimensions of the energy problem because it cannot accommodate national security needs and more subtle ethical problems with the responsibilities of this generation to future generations. Nor can it balance profits with equity, health risks, and threats to the environment.

Long-term guidance is needed if the country is to produce and deliver, in an equitable fashion, resources adequate to meet national needs and to satisfy international responsibilities that the United States has assumed under an agreement with the International Energy Agency, to share oil in times of emergency with its allies. Without appropriate planning, the news that the predicted crises of famine, no-growth, and overpopulation are past is, as Mark Twain remarked on reading his obituary, "greatly exaggerated."

The United States' de facto policies or decisions have international repercussions, whether they be the amount of oil to import, the price of natural gas, the amount of coal to mine, or under what conditions nuclear fuels can be exported. As the authors of *Uncertain Power* have written here and elsewhere, energy problems do not exist in isolation. Environmental hazards—acid rain that results from the burning of fossil fuels, or fallout from a nuclear power plant accident, or carbon dioxide buildup in the atmosphere that can lead to warming the earth's surface—do not recognize geographical boundaries and often create political hazards. Rising temperatures threaten the agricultural productivity of those parts of the globe that currently provide food for less-arable areas. Acid-rain production has already led to friction between traditional allies, Canada and the United States, as well as between Great Britain and the Scandinavian countries. Denmark and Austria, both without active commercial nuclear power plants, worry about the impact of nuclear accidents and wind-borne radioactivity issuing from plants in Sweden and Germany.

The alliance between the United States and its West European allies was severely tested in 1982 because of an energy project that was singled out by President Reagan to express his disapproval of the Soviets' behavior in Poland. The USSR had begun work on a 3700-mile natural gas pipeline, which, when finished, will provide Western Europe with approximately 2.5 percent of its total energy supply. In late 1981 the Reagan administration, reversing a promise made earlier to the NATO allies, ordered an export ban on equipment, manufactured in Europe under American licenses, that was needed for construction in the USSR. Claiming that the pipeline would provide the Soviets with hard currency with which to increase their military spending and, in addition, would make the European countries politically vulnerable to supply cut-offs, the Reagan administration threatened draconian measures against the first American company to disregard the embargo. That the United States continued to sell grain to the Soviets made the American rhetoric and action appear hypocritical in the extreme to its allies, who needed not only the natural gas from the pipeline, but also the thousands of additional jobs the construction would provide. The United States' stance also seemed short-sighted to its many critics at home. On November 13, 1982, President Reagan, under heavy pressure from critics at home and abroad, lifted the sanctions he had previously imposed. The natural gas pipeline project vividly illustrates the intertwining of domestic and foreign policy, the lack of consensus within the United States, and the political-economic tensions between the United

States and its allies. A policy made to satisfy ideological commitments at home creates new energy-supply and political problems abroad, threatens traditional alliances, and deepens the rift between the United States and the Soviet Union.

These problems cannot be resolved without international collaboration. Nevertheless, in order for the United States to work effectively on these and other related problems, it must have its own house in order. To do so entails establishing some greater measure of consensus than exists at present. For this reason, the authors of *Uncertain Power* are focusing on the internal tensions and struggles that have impeded the development of a national consensus. This lack of agreement has prevented the country from adopting a set of of rational, flexible energy policies. In this book, the authors examine a number of the gains, losses, and missed opportunities that mark energy-policy struggles of the past decade. A few of the more adventurous contributors offer, somewhat tentatively, guidelines for the possible resolution of energy problems and, even more tentatively, hope for the future.

The book is divided into four parts:

I. Energy and the Public
II. Energy and The Evaluation of Risk
III. Energy and Government
IV. Toward A Solution

The reader will note, however, that the book, like the energy issue itself, resists precise, analytically distinct categorization. A number of themes arise in many of the chapters: the dilemma of whether consensus can or should be achieved; the unique symbolic significance of nuclear power; the impingement of nontechnical factors on technology-related decisions; the tension among federal, state, and local governments; the growing significance of public opinion polls; the surge in public participation, particularly in special interest groups; and the public's expectation that it has the right, if not the duty, to shape and implement energy policy decisions. The authors examine these issues from a shared assumption of the importance of strengthening democratic values and the political process. The discovery that this group (homogeneous when compared with the general public) has such widely divergent views on so many of the issues, including what constitutes democratic practices, should not discourage the reader who seeks synthesis. Rather, we hope that the diversity itself will provide a deeper understanding of the interlocking complexities of the issues of equity, national security, productivity, and the preservation of democracy as they relate to energy and the environment.

THE FADING-CRISIS CRISIS

As the media and the federal government, by its inaction, have pronounced, the energy crisis is over. The Cassandras, who for a decade captured the public's attention with warnings about the likelihood of escalating oil prices and supply interruptions, have begun to fade from public view. Like aging movie stars, they have been relegated to minor roles on TV (the major source of the public's information), while their publications have been overshadowed by others mirroring the current national concern, the threat of nuclear war. Even Israel's invasion of Lebanon evoked relatively little comment about the likelihood of triggering an oil-supply cutoff in a conflict-torn Middle East. And the problems of nuclear power, though still reported in the media, have lost some of their steam since Three Mile Island in 1979.

The public's concern about energy has plummeted from 70 percent in 1980 to 3 percent in the fall of 1982 and most polls no longer include questions about energy. How can any problem so complex and onerous have been resolved so quickly? The answer in the opinion of our authors is that it has not; only the diagnosis has changed.

A crisis, real or psychological, cannot by definition be maintained indefinitely. It is a critical situation or a decisive state of affairs that has to be resolved imminently. If not, the response changes. In a visible crisis, such as war, the resources of a country are organized against an outside enemy. When President Carter announced that the energy crisis was the moral equivalent of war, he was attempting to mobilize the public as it had been mobilized in World War II. He failed because he did not follow through with concerted action, and the public inferred that the energy crisis had been fabricated by those who stood to benefit from it. A crisis mentality serves neither an individual nor a country well. When, for example, individuals are faced with a protracted crisis that promises no resolution, the anxiety that, in part, provides the energy to deal with the crisis can turn into depression—an overwhelming sense of hopelessness or helplessness. If sufficiently severe, these feelings, in turn, give rise to fears of an impending catastrophe about which the individual can do nothing. The response is apathy. For others, the mechanism is different. They respond by isolating themselves from the anxiety and deem the crisis inconsequential or meaningless. Depression and apathy, in one instance, and denial and isolation, in the other, interfere with the ability to effect rational and constructive planning. Although the body politic functions neither as an individual nor as the sum of individual psychological dispositions, there are similarities—the initial national anxiety and depression following the first Arab oil embargo (1973), for example, and the current sense of indifference and isolation from the problem beginning after oil prices declined (1981). The "energy crisis" mentality could not be maintained for a decade. The country had not been drawn into an all-out war, and, fortunately, the feared demise of democracy as predicted by staunchly pro- and antinuclear energy groups had not materialized.

In addition, conservation and efficiency practices began to show results, and oil consumption dropped by 8.5 percent between 1978 and 1981. Oil prices decreased, in part, because of a persistent world-wide economic recession, which had been brought on in some degree by the cost of energy resources. OPEC appeared to have lost its fangs, and concerns began to shift to the international repercussions that would occur if oil-producing nations, such as Mexico and Nigeria, could not rely on revenues to pay their debts. As economists predicted, the high price of oil had indeed generated the momentum to develop once-uneconomic oil resources, natural gas, and coal reserves.

The authors of *Uncertain Power* believe that as the oil glut did not signal the end of the energy crisis, neither did the recent declaration of an energy "victory" end the need for further examination of energy problems. Obviously, we think there is a need for further analysis and discussion, because the gains of the decade (conservation and efficiency) are only partial solutions, because other gains are likely to be transitory (lower oil prices), and because the major threats of war and the erosion of democracy are still with us and looming larger. Energy supplies and prices play a major role in maintaining relations among allies and in changing the likelihood of war, while at home they directly affect the social stability of the country.

It may be (as the former Secretary of Energy, James Schlesinger, warned) that the energy crisis is past until the next crisis occurs. The public is justifiably skeptical about the yo-yo behavior of government and industry. From the declaration of the moral equivalent of war (1977) to the apathy and isolation born of the failure to resolve the crisis on a long-run basis, the United States has lost valuable time in solving a long-term problem.

If the crisis mode of reacting can be abandoned, and a steadier pace substituted, perhaps this new period, a respite from the acute crisis—like the calm in the eye of a hurricane—will foster a fundamental reexamination of policy, and planning for a future that promises to be little like the halcyon years following World War II.

THE AMBIGUITIES OF CONSENSUS

Perhaps consensus exists only in retrospect, like the contemporary vision of an earlier, more wholesome, small-town America. Distance lends enchantment; "restorationist sentiment" romanticizes the past as healthier and saner.[14] Many citizens living in the early part of the twentieth century—blacks (enslaved in all but name); exploited mill workers (children, men, and women); uneducated, underpaid immigrants; migrant farm workers and tenant farmers, and grindingly poor urban and rural whites—would hardly recognize the roseate society that has come to be idealized by many Americans today. The stereotype did exist: small towns, neat clapboard houses kept clean by virtuous, hard-working, God-fearing families, and a political way of life that featured town meetings and, with the exception of presidential elections, little incursion of Washington into citizens' lives. But novelists Theodore Dreiser and Upton Sinclair revealed the realities of the putative simple life, and, later, social scientists showed that small-town living produced more alcoholism and mental illness than did urban life. Things were seldom as they seemed.

So it is with energy policy, the further one is removed from it or the higher the level at which it is generalized, the more consensus there is about it and its antecedents. When, however, the issue is current or examined in depth, the consensus vanishes.

For example, there has been a general agreement that the country should reduce its dependence on foreign oil. Yet, the attempt to implement such a goal generates new tensions, and the consensus crumbles as government, industry, special interest groups, and different geographical areas of the country propose mutually exclusive solutions.

Nuclear power has become the symbol for much of this disagreement. The authors of *Uncertain Power* express differing opinions that include all but the most die-hard commitment to the technology. Ranging from crucial, through necessary-but-flawed (a question of who bears the risks, now and in the future), to undemocratic and, consequently, unacceptable, the diverse opinions within even a relatively homogeneous group reveal the complexities of attempting to create an energy policy for even one resource.

Energy experts have, by and large, agreed on several points in their recommendations during the past decade: the need for conservation and efficiency; reduction of oil imports; and decontrol of oil and, less unanimously, gas prices as necessary first steps toward establishing a more stable and secure energy situation. Each of the major energy policy studies of the past decade has defined the energy problem somewhat differently, or, at least, with a different emphasis. The majority emphasize economics, supply problems, and technology.[15] More recently studies have begun to identify the energy problem as "a crisis of our political system" and a question of values and ethics.[16] Although the definitions are not mutually exclusive—economic, political, and social values are to varying degrees part of each definition—the way in which each balances the variables determines the emphasis and the consequent policy recommendations.

RECENT HISTORY OF UNITED STATES ENERGY CONSUMPTION

Throughout the middle years of this century, pessimists were predicting the end of fossil fuel supplies. Being out of tune with the optimism of an ever-expanding economy that promised unending prosperity, they received little attention. After World War II, the American public assumed that abundance would continue to increase. Oil and gas were cheap and readily available. Besides, the atom had been harnessed in the 1940s and would provide electricity "too cheap to meter," a promise that, even if apocryphal, conveys the certainty with which nuclear technology was launched. American technology, after proving itself gloriously in World War II, could be counted on to provide for the future.

Energy policy was not an issue; the country was booming. Unravaged by war, possessed of high technological competence and a work force that was mobile, both geographically and socially, and united in its belief in hard work, the United States prospered dramatically between 1950 and 1970. The economic growth was unprecedented (average family, real income in constant dollars rose from $5600 to $12,000), and the majority of the population became comfortably middle class. Only a minority, 10 to 20 percent of the population, remained poor, yet Presidents Kennedy and Johnson were confident that the fiscal dividend from the "Great Society" would end poverty.[17] Highways proliferated, suburbs mushroomed, and the automobile became the backbone of the economy and the symbol of individual success.

With the exception of the period of the Great Depression, each generation of Americans had improved its lot over that of its parents. As American technology dominated world markets and incomes continued to rise, there was little reason to believe that this golden age would not continue. The social science literature of the 1950s mirrored the optimism. Writers such as David Riesman and John Kenneth Galbraith took for granted the limitless resources of oil and water and believed that, as in World War II, technology would create the substitutes for scarce resources.[18] The only problems left would be how to improve technology and managerial policy, and their solution would yield a fiscal surplus that would provide the measure of tranquility needed to reconcile social fragmentation in a rapidly growing society noted for its "fierce individualistic energies."[19] A national mood of rising expectations gave way to one of rising entitlements. What had been the hallmark of affluence before the war (e.g. home ownership, an automobile, summer vacations, and college educations) came to be expected by those recently arrived in the middle class.

No small amount of this prodigious growth stemmed from the availability of cheap, seemingly unlimited supplies of oil and gas, which were being consumed at a rate increasing by 3.4 percent each year (4.5 percent annually between 1965 and 1973).

Throughout the postwar decades, oil imports began to rise steeply as the real price continued to fall. The Organization of Petroleum Exporting Countries (OPEC), which had been organized in 1960 with little international attention, was for its first 10 years unable to change the downward direction of oil prices. The 1947 price was $2.17 per barrel; in 1969 it reached a low of a little more that $1.00 per barrel.[20] By 1969, the United States was consuming six times as much energy per capita as the world average. Demand continued to grow, but domestic oil production had reached its peak in 1970 and began to decline. Domestic production could no longer compete with cheaper imports. By 1973, the United States was importing 35 percent of its oil, and the price had quadrupled by 1974.

Though the real price of oil declined from 1974 to 1978, inflation continued to rise. Its origins were not solely in the OPEC-induced price rises, but also in the legacy of the Vietnam War. Misled in the 1960s by President Johnson, who tried to conceal the war's costs, the public was not fully aware that "guns *and* butter," his policy that proclaimed the country's ability to support both a war abroad and "The

Great Society" at home, would along with energy costs lead to double-digit inflation.

The first Arab oil shock in 1973 produced panic and a blinding, if brief, flash of insight. Informed citizens and government officials were aware that the party was over—cheap, reliable oil was soon to be a relic of the past. More importantly, they realized that in a rush to economic growth, much needed energy policies had not been formulated. Not even a serious conservation policy was in practice, and the media were focusing their attention elsewhere.

Because of its energy-dependent economy, the United States had become vulnerable to supply interruptions and price manipulations. The country's non-oil-producing allies were even more critically affected. Japan was virtually 100 percent dependent on imports for oil, which constituted 70 percent of its total energy consumption; for France and Germany, imported oil constituted 75 percent and 60 percent, respectively, of their total energy consumption. The implications were inescapable. The Arabs, troubled by American aid to Israel, had turned oil into a potent political weapon and threatened further disruptions. In addition, the allied nations became aware of their interdependence; an oil shortage in one strained the economic and political relations of all.

The majority of the American public, however, was still convinced that the real problems had to do with pricing, and that once the producers had exploited the consumers by raising the prices of domestic natural gas and oil, the problem would go away. Accordingly, there was little sustained impetus to forge a comprehensive energy plan and reduce oil imports. Imports continued to rise. Between 1972 and 1978, imports almost doubled, from 4.7 million barrels per day (mbd) to 8.4 mbd, or, more tellingly, from 29 percent to 47 percent of all oil consumed.[21] The annual expenditure for foreign oil was $40 to $50 billion.

It was not until the overthrow of the Shah in 1979 and the consequent sharp rise in oil prices that a once indifferent public was truly shaken. Only then did significant conservation measures begin to take hold. Decidedly less exciting than the technology of nuclear power or breakthrough visions of nuclear fusion and outer space solar satellites, conservation got off to a grudgingly slow start. Had the government mounted a concerted conservation effort in 1973, after the OPEC oil embargo, oil imports would likely have decreased. Instead, by 1979 imports had almost doubled, while prices had tripled.

Between 1978 and 1979 alone, the world price of a barrel of oil more than doubled (from $13 to $30 per barrel), and the dollar declined sharply. Even all-powerful American technology, which had been counted on to deliver the country from a precarious oil supply to safe, clean, and inexpensive nuclear power, seemed to falter when the accident at Three Mile Island in March 1979 shook American complacency about the ease of an energy transition.

The apparent refusal of American government and industry to reduce the country's oil imports provoked resentment among U.S. allies, who interpreted this as arrogance and indifference. A number of state and local agencies were able to introduce energy conservation programs, aided by modest federal funding, with varying degrees of success.

During the late 1970s, increasing numbers of citizens became actively involved in energy conservation efforts by insulating their homes, replacing electric appliances with more efficient models, driving less and more slowly, turning out the lights, and, like President Carter, investing in warm sweaters. American business organizations became the leaders in retrofitting buildings and instituting conservation measures.

New ideas also received a hearing. As Richard Sclove writes in Chapter 3, "Amory Lovins, a young environmentalist trained in physics, achieved startling success by promoting the idea that the United States must choose between two mutually exclusive paths, hard and soft, to achieve energy self-sufficiency." According to Lovins, "A hard energy path, relying on large-scale energy supply technologies such as coal and nuclear-fired electric power plants, threatened unnecessarily to deplete nonrenewable resources, degrade the environment, jeopardize lives, eliminate jobs, squander capital, disrupt communities, and subject us all to rule by 'elitist technocracy.'"In contrast, a "soft energy path" could be chosen that would use small-scale solar technologies, improvements in the efficiency of energy use, and limited quantities of fossil fuel to avoid each of these pitfalls, while promoting cultural diversity, thrift, self-reliance, and democracy. At first politely ignored by orthodox energy analysts and industry representatives, Lovins became an acknowledged political force after he was invited to meet with Canadian Prime Minister Pierre Trudeau, former Swedish Prime Minister Olof Palme, and United States President Carter in 1977. *Energy Future: Report of the Energy Project at the Harvard Business School,* hardly a likely contender for the best-seller list, surprised its authors by its runaway success in 1979. The book was an early champion of the cause of energy conservation, even though more than one-half the public still believed the energy problem was fabricated.[22]

Conservation and efficiency, nevertheless, began to look more attractive as prices continued to rise. Even though the winter of 1980 averaged three degrees colder than 1979, the demand for home heating oil decreased by 13 percent. Price decontrol contributed to the 20 percent drop of imports from their highest point; so did efficiency, lower thermostats, and insulation. Just when conservation had taken firm enough hold so that OPEC was being paid $50 million less every day, the Reagan administration made it clear that conservation had little place in its policy. Cutting back on loans, grants, and other incentives for home insulation, being indecisive about maintaining the 55 mph speed limit, and drastically cutting funds for public education, the administration impeded the conservation momentum.

Prior to the Reagan administration, federal funding had made it possible for states and local governments to begin to shape conservation programs. A number of instances of vigorous leadership; a tradition of open government and resource management in many of the states; a belief that energy efficiency would favor the locality's long-term economic health; and an extensive public participation process introduced prior to a program's implementation combined to create an atmosphere conducive to addressing the problem of energy. Since 1980 the momentum has slowed. In the future, the readiness of state and local governments to intervene in the energy marketplace will rise and fall with energy prices. These governments will be unable to intervene as often or as efficiently in the remainder of the decade, if the incentives, especially federal funding, are withdrawn. Energy will be integrated into state and local policymaking as a resource constraint, not treated as a separate issue. The struggle between the federal government and local and state governments will increase as a result of these new tensions. The recent proclamation that the energy crisis is past is of little meaning to local officials, who are striving to cope with the energy problems of the poor, the old, and the unemployed.

During a period of 100 years, the country had moved fairly smoothly from wood to coal to oil and natural gas, each transition having been, as a rule, to a cleaner, cheaper, and more abundant source than the energy resource it replaced. The present transition away from nonrenewable resources is fraught with uncertainty (social, political, and economic) and the American public and government have been ill-prepared to deal with it.

At this point the American people have to consider a number of options. Conservation and efficiency, coal, solar (including wood, wind, tidal power, ocean thermal conversion, and photovoltaic cells), and nuclear are the most immediate choices to be developed during the transition from fossil fuels to renewable energy resources. (Nuclear fusion, which uses hydrogen isotopes and promises virtually limitless sources of energy, is still only a "noble dream.") Some of the advantages and disadvantages of these options are well known. More subtle disadvantages, such as the environmental pollution and startling increase in the incidence of fires produced by something as seemingly benign as woodburning, have yet to be adequately publicized. However, as we shall see, each resource has its price, and before discussing the political choices that have to be made, it is useful to survey some of the issues.

CONSERVATION AND EFFICIENCY

As we noted earlier, the current administration has sharply slowed the conservation momentum. At the same time, declining world demand and internal disagreements within OPEC have produced a temporary glut of oil and a cutback in prices. Oil, like gas and coal, remains a finite resource. Whether the depletion of oil, at least to the extent that it is no longer a major resource, occurs in 50 years or 100 is less significant than the fact that it is finite. Oil and natural gas account for 70 percent of U.S. energy consumption. Even with a drop in oil prices, other resources once considered uneconomical are being pursued, though at a decidedly slower pace in 1983 than in 1980 and 1981. Each has noteworthy advantages and, consequently, fervid advocates, while none of them is without drawbacks—social, political, environmental, health, or economic. The antagonists are equally passionate.

Even conservation, a relatively uncontroversial option, has begun to reveal unanticipated risks.

As we insulate our houses better to save energy we reduce the inflow of fresh air. Since at least 75 percent of most people's lives are spent indoors, indoor pollution can become a serious problem. Plant fungicides, dry cleaning fluids, carbon monoxide, cadmium from cigarette smoke, etc., may be at much higher concentrations in our better insulated houses of tomorrow than they are today. Particularly vulnerable are the children who grow up in these homes. They would have more years of exposure to these pollutants than we did and their breathing rate per unit of body weight is much greater than an adult's. The concentration of many of these heavier-than-air pollutants is greater at a child's height than at an adult's. It is possible that a well intended act of energy conservation could result in a public health hazard, only to be perceived years later.[23]

If that is not sobering enough, a recent study has demonstrated that concentration of natural background radiation products will increase to dangerous levels as the ionized particles that in the past circulated freely between the inside and the outside of the house would be trapped in well-insulated houses.[24] The level of radiation could exceed those acceptable in the area of a nuclear power plant. Fungi from inadequately dried wood have increased respiratory problems. Triple-sash windows in newly built, conservation-designed houses in Sweden have begun to rot because of inadequate ventilation and the costs of replacement are exorbitant.[25] This is not to suggest that home insulation and the search for the resolution of its problems should not continue, but, rather, that even the most benign energy option is likely to have hidden costs, and that the promise of a risk-free choice is unlikely.

COAL

Since the 1970s, Congress has tried to spur the use of coal, which it had identified as *the* transition fuel. The United States, with 31 percent of the world's reserves, has been dubbed the "Saudi Arabia of coal." The supply is sufficient to provide between one-half and two-thirds of the world's additional energy needs for the next 20 years. To do so, however, coal production would have to increase nearly 300 percent, an awesome requirement in light of the deteriorated state of trains, railroad tracks, and harbors. Coal has been promoted as the alternative to nuclear power and as the basis of the synthetic fuel that would be cost-competitive with OPEC oil by 1990. The World Coal (WOCOL) Study, directed by an MIT engineer, has identified coal as the nation's "bridge to the future."[26] However, as we mentioned earlier, a growing body of evidence shows that coal burning causes serious environmental and health problems which have yet to be adequately explored. Even promoters admit that there is probably a relationship between coal burning and at least two major environmental problems. (A Swedish environmental chemist has identified more than eight coal-induced environmental problems.[27]) One problem is acid rain and the other is the increase of carbon dioxide in the atmosphere. According to a recent study, acid rain is "an insidious but deadly pollution resulting from industrial combustion. As well as killing fish populations and aquatic vegetation, it threatens forests, crops, and soils; erodes building and automobile surfaces; and may be a danger to human health."[28] This and several other reports suggest that the damage may be irreversible.

Carbon dioxide also produced by burning coal causes the earth's surface to warm in such a way that, some scientists believe, the polar ice cap could be melted, coastal cities inundated, and once fertile agricultural regions submerged. Until recently, most assertions about carbon dioxide have been speculative. However, a study by seven scientists from the National Aeronautics and Space Administration (NASA) concludes that on a global basis carbon dioxide has already been warming the earth for a century. The study predicts that carbon dioxide will produce "unprecedented" warming in the next century.[29] This could result in the "creation of drought-prone regions in North America and Central Asia as part of a shifting of climatic zones [and] erosion of the West Antarctic ice sheet, with a consequent worldwide rise in sea level." Definitive results are not yet available, but this kind of warning from a group other than environmentalists suggests that those who want to slow the development of solar because it is too expensive, or of nuclear because it is too hazardous, will have to include these findings in their decisions.

In time, technology will likely be developed to cope with the sulfur dioxide and nitrogen oxides emitted during the combustion of fossil fuels. Many devices are already in place, but are too expensive to use routinely. However, the warming effect of burning more fossil fuels is not amenable to technological intervention, regardless of the money expended.

There are other social costs of coal mining. For example, much future coal will be strip mined, disrupting large tracts of land and forcing changes on the society and the economy of people living near the mines. Even more traumatic to residents, according to the NASA study, would be "the cultural clash when large numbers of transient mine workers move into rural communities." The combination of the damage to the soil in strip mining, the cost of reclamation, the upheaval in the lives of people living near the mines, and the larger environmental damage has led a committee at the National Academy of Sciences to predict that "coal may eventually be priced out of the fuel mix when its price includes the social costs of mining and combustion."[30]

SOLAR

For many, solar holds the greatest promise for long-term future supplies of energy. But if the Reagan administration's plans to cut the solar budget by 66 percent are carried out, the likelihood of any significant growth in solar energy production will dim markedly.

Estimates of what solar energy will actually be able to contribute to the U.S. energy mix by the year 2000 vary from 5 percent to approximately 40 percent. If we assume optimistically that, with major backing from government, solar could contribute as much as 20 percent by the year 2000, the public will still feel betrayed. In a survey reported by Roper, 57 percent of the public expressed the opinion that solar would replace oil within five years; 63 percent predicted it would replace oil by the year 2000.[31] Whether, as Roper commented, this was naivete or clairvoyance, the important point here is that the public believes solar can and will replace oil. Like the nuclear option in the 1950s, solar energy is being over-promised.

The advantages of solar energy are well known. Its current problems (e.g. high costs and insufficient research funds to develop its potential) are also well publicized. Less well understood are the potential consequences of global deployment. As the nuclear power industry learned to its dismay, only when there were few nuclear power plants was there little public concern. When numerous plants began to come on line, the antinuclear movement began to grow. What will happen to the support for solar energy if, as one scientist has pointed out,

> large areas of desert lands are covered with machines, valleys are flooded to provide hydroelectric facilities, and scenic coastlines are dotted with thousands of towers holding wind generators.[32]

In addition, it is not unlikely that "covering upwards of a million square kilometers of sunny land with solar conversion machines" will modify the climate and produce increased cloudiness and rain.

As with the other unanticipated drawbacks to energy options, these problems do not suggest that the research for solar development should lag, but, rather, that the public should become aware early in the process that even solar, the best and the brightest, will not be a panacea.

NUCLEAR ENERGY

By far the most divisive of all energy choices, nuclear energy has stimulated unprecedented hopes and unparalleled fears. It remains today a bitter national controversy muted only by the slowdown in plant construction and a surplus of electricity-generating capacity.

Despite the growing evidence of the damage that coal is likely to cause the environment (including the deposition of radioactive ash) and health (including accidents from coal mining and transportation), the general public still believes that nuclear power poses greater risks. The possibility of a catastrophe, no matter how remote, is more threatening than the likelihood of many single or clustered accidental deaths from automobiles, airplanes, or coal mines accumulating over time.[33] The history of these perceptions is complex. Radiation, which is invisible, without smell, and penetrates skin and bones, arouses powerful fears. Nuclear energy had its origins in war, destruction, and secrecy; these negative antecedents have never been dissociated from nuclear power's peaceful applications. The recent reemergence of the peace movement has reinforced the link with nuclear weapons, terrorism, and militarism. The impressive safety record of the nuclear industry is lost on those who reason, "What if?" What if there is a core meltdown? What if the disposal of high-level nuclear wastes is inadequate and radiation leaks into the groundwater? What if the transportation of these wastes is so dangerous that armed guards have to protect them and the sites at which they are stored? What if terrorists can blackmail the country with stolen plutonium? What if increasing concentrations of radiation cause genetic damage? What if this highly centralized, large-scale technology increases the social control that industry and government have over the lives of individuals? Will democracy be threatened? Every aspect of nuclear energy is fraught with controversy.

At present, the future of conventional nuclear energy is uncertain. Conservation and a slowdown in the economy, with a resulting decrease in demand for new electricity generation, have left the industry in a shambles. Electric utilities are slowly converting to coal, and no new orders have been placed for reactors in the last five years. Between 1977 and 1982 more than 80 plant construction projects were cancelled, and more than 10 plants under construction were cancelled during the past two years. Even pronuclear investors are loath to invest funds in such unpromising, risky circumstances.

Now the "What if?" question has to be reversed. What if coal proves too dangerous or solar too unwieldy? What if conservation reaches its limits and there is still insufficient energy to fuel the needs of the American economy? What if the Americans slow their technological research and are unable to provide either resources or technology for energy-depleted developing nations? Nuclear, then, might be reassessed by all but its staunchest opponents.

HARD CHOICES

The rapid rise of public interest, environmentalist, and consumer groups to do battle in the courts and in congress over controversial energy policies is as traditional as 4th of July parades and as American as the proverbial apple pie. The American citizen's right to "fight city hall" is shocking to some of its European allies. A French energy bureaucrat viewed the process as "democracy run amok," while a former French cabinet official stated that "in France, democracy stops at technology, thank God. Otherwise we would never have had nuclear power or the bomb."[34] To the dismay of many American industrialists and government officials, who would like to have more control over decision making, democracy does not stop at technology in the United States, but, rather, technology increasingly has come under public scrutiny. Many factors account for the differences between the two countries. Tradition, national character, trust in authority, and the availability of energy resources contribute to the mode of public participation in democratic countries. Two of the most important differences are the organizational structure of the government (for example, centralized versus decentralized; open versus closed decision making) and the legal institutions. In France, they mitigate against public participation (or even the participation of experts outside the government).

In the United States, public participation is encouraged by the traditional tensions among federal, state, and local governments; the general availability of many government documents; the rise in the number of experts and public interest groups; and a multitiered, open judicial system (and not insignificantly, an exponential increase in the numbers of lawyers). Some critics argue that this participation boom can lead to a paralysis of decision making, while others argue that because the public involved in these activities is not sufficiently representative of the broader society, the process cannot be considered democratic.

As the authors of *Uncertain Power* argue, there is a solid measure of consensus on the need for broad public education and an airing of the issues. They do not agree on how much public participation is healthy for the system, crucial for democracy, or an actual threat to the resolution of pressing problems.

Because each decision that is made often conflicts with the values or perceived needs of equally significant groups, there are no simple answers. Those who believe that strengthening national security is the highest priority will recommend answers different from those offered by groups predominantly concerned with the protection of the environment. Those who believe that the country must be geared to producing the greatest number of goods and services will differ in their recommendations from those who believe that a major energy goal should be to conserve resources for future generations. Each of these beliefs or values contributes to the definition of the problem and the options available to achieve specific goals. Where at one time economic costs and profits were the only significant factors used to determine energy options, now increasingly an informed public, aided by recent legislation (National Environmental Policy Act and the Freedom of Information Act), insists that social costs and benefits be included in the decision making processes. Each option, then, reflects a system of values and an image of what society should be.

These choices among conflicting values and special interests can be made only in the political arena. But political leadership has failed to produce coherent policies. In a dismal-sounding analysis, the economist William Nordhaus describes United States energy policy of the past decade as

a drain down which we have poured enormous legislative, analytical and political efforts, yet it produced mostly noise and fury.[35]

The authors of *Uncertain Power* argue that now is the time to begin to improve on this sad record. The temporary oil glut could easily mask the reality of the country's vulnerability to oil-supply interruptions. Rather than waiting for severe problems among the Western nations as U.S. and North Sea oil production declines, we should forego the crisis mode of management as the way to ease the transition from fossil fuels to renewable resources of energy.

In a rush to solutions, short-term decisions (if any) are being made by legislators who worry about reelection every other year or every four years. It is difficult to campaign on a promise of rising prices. No president has been able to convince the public that the energy crisis is real and public concern has shifted to more immediate problems. Scientists trained in empirical methods often disregard qualitative factors—human response, fears, and expectations—in their calculations and are surprised by the hostility their omissions arouse. Industrialists whose career success is measured by annual profits find it difficult to implement long-range plans, particularly in a severe economic recession. And the consumer, hard pressed by economic uncertainties, finds it difficult to focus on global issues of rising carbon dioxide concentrations in the atmosphere or other environmental changes not likely to occur for 100 years.

Angry and skeptical as American citizens are about the failure of government, they are, nevertheless, beginning to scale down their expectations about future personal economic gains. These decreasing expectations, so different from the attitudes of "rising entitlements" in the 1960s, create a new context, a national mood within which national goals need to be reestablished.

Social learning for governments and individuals is slow and painful. A fragmented government and public have to embark on a mutual education program to offset the consequences of crisis-mode thinking and to begin to accept conflict even when there is some measure of consensus about national goals.

There will be no quick fixes—economic, social, technological, or political. Rather, the acceptance of the reality of a less brave new world, one perilously close to George Orwell's 1984, dependent on energy in countless ways, will mark the beginning of wisdom and, perhaps, coherent if incremental policies. *Uncertain Power* (in both the political sense of government engulfed by the competing, legitimate demands of its many constituents, and the unreliable nature of future energy resources) can become somewhat less uncertain only when the unresolvable tensions in democracies are accepted as a basis from which to work toward coalitions and compromise. In 1886 an Austrian physicist declared that "available energy was the main object at stake in the struggle for existence and the evolution of the world." Almost 100 years later, his words remain prophetic.[36]

NOTES

1. *New York Times*, CBS Poll reported in *New York Times*, 25 Jan. 1983.
2. CONAES Report, Supporting Paper 7, *Energy Choices in a Democratic Society* (Washington, DC: National Academy of Sciences, 1980).
3. Stanley Rothman, and S. Robert Lichter, "The Nuclear Energy Debate: Scientists, the Media and the Public," *Public Opinion*, (Aug.-Sept. 1982), 47-52.
4. Yankelovich, Skelly, and White opinion polls, Dec. 1982.
5. Bernard Spinrad, "Nuclear Power and Nuclear Weapons: The Connection in Tennessee," in *Nuclear Energy, Weapons Proliferation, and the Arms Race*, ed. Jack Hollander, (Stony Brook, N.Y.: American Association of Physics Teachers, 1982).
6. Colin Norman, "Weapons Builders Eye Civilian Reactor Fuel," *Science*, 214 (16 Oct. 1981), 307-08.
7. John P. Holdren, "Nuclear Power and Nuclear Weapons," *Bulletin of the Atomic Scientists*, (Jan. 1983), 40-45.
8. Charles O. Jones, "American Politics and the Organization of Energy Decision Making," *Ann. Rev. Energy*, 4 (1979), 99-121.
9. *The Cambridge Report*, (1983).
10. William Tucker, "The Energy Crisis is Over," *Harper's*, (Nov. 1981).
11. William M. Brown, "Can OPEC Survive the Glut," *Hudson Communique* Supplement (Croton-on-Hudson, NY: Hudson Institute, Dec. 1981).
12. Yale Brozen, "Six Lies on Energy," *New York Times*, 6 July 1979.
13. Karl E. Meyer, "Energetic Predictions" *New York Times Book Review* 15 Aug. 1982, p.8. A review of *Global Insecurity: A Strategy for Energy and Economic Revival*, ed. Daniel Yergin and Martin Hillenbrand, (Boston: Houghton Mifflin, 1982).
14. Kevin Phillips and Paul H. Blackman, *Electoral Reform and Voter Participation: Federal Registration, A False Remedy For Voter Apathy* (Washington: American Enterprise Institute for Public Policy Research, 1975).
15. Steven C. Carhart, Assistant Director of the Mellon Institute, quoted in the *New York Times*, 6 April 1981; Wolf Haefele, *Energy In A Finite World: Paths to a Sustainable Future* (Cambridge, MA: Ballinger, 1981); Alvin M. Weinberg, "Energy: the need for technical fixes" *Nature* (31 Jan. 1980), 283, 425.
16. Robert Stobaugh and Daniel Yergin, *Energy Future: Report of the Energy Project at the Harvard Business School* (New York: Ballantine Books, 1980) p.25; Laura Nader, "The Politics of Energy: Toward a Bottom-up Approach," *Radcliffe Quarterly* (Dec. 1981) 5; Ian G. Barbour, *Technology, Environment, and Human Values* (New York: Praeger, 1980).
17. Allen H. Barton, "Fault Lines in American Elite Consensus," *Daedalus*, (Summer 1980), 1-24.
18. David Riesman, "The Dream of Abundance Reconsidered," *Public Opinion Quarterly*, (Fall 1981); John Kenneth Galbraith, *The Affluent Society* (Boston: Houghton Mifflin, 1976).
19. Riesman, "The Dream of Abundance Reconsidered."
20. Stobaugh and Yergin, *Energy Future*.
21. Ibid.
22. CBS/*New York Times* Poll, 6 Nov. 1979, p.35.
23. Herschel Specter, *Getting the West Out of the Oil Dilemma: An Energy Family Approach* (Washington, DC: Atlantic Council of the United States, 1979), p.33.

24. U.S. Department of Health, Education, and Welfare, H. Hurwitz, Jr., "Public comments on the Work Group Reports, Interagency Task Force on Health Effects of Ionizing Radiation," Doc.62 (Washington, DC: HEW, 1979).

25. Professor Torbjorn Westermark, Department of Nuclear Chemistry, The Royal Institute of Technology, 3-100-44 Stockholm, Sweden; Kerstin Nibleaus, Energy Advisor to Prime Minister Olof Palme of Sweden.

26. World Coal Study (WOCOL) *Coal—Bridge to the Future,* ed. Carroll Wilson Vols. 1 and 2 (Cambridge, MA: Ballinger, 1980).

27. Professor Westermark, op. cit.

28. Environment Canada, *Downwind* (Ottawa, Ontario: Information Directorate). Precisely what percentage of acid rain comes from coal combustion is uncertain, as it also results from the combustion of all fossil fuels, human activities, and probably from the exhaust of automobiles.

29. NASA Study, "Climate Impact of Increasing Atmospheric Carbon Dioxide," *Science,* 213, (1981) 957.

30. Committee on Soil as a Resource in Relations to Surface Mining for Coal; Board on Mineral and Energy Resources; Commission on Natural Resources, National Research Council, *Surface Mining: Soil, Coal and Society* (Washington, DC: National Academy Press, 1981).

31. Burns Roper, Speech delivered to the Atomic Industrial Forum, Washington, DC, 18 Nov. 1980.

32. J. Weingart, "Systems Aspects of Large Scale Solar Energy Conversion" (Laxenburg, Austria: International Institute for Applied Systems Analysis). Quoted in Richard Caputo, "Solar Energy for the Next 5 Billion Years," *IIASA,* (May 1981), 81-89.

33. Paul Slovic, Sarah Lichtenstein, and Baruch Fischoff, "Images of Disaster: Perception and Acceptance of Risks from Nuclear Power," *Electric Perspectives* No. 79/3, (Washington, DC: Edison Electric Institute, Inc., 1979) 8-20.

34. Author's interview with nuclear power government official in Paris, 1979; Lecture by Thierry de Montbrial, Harvard University, 1980.

35. William Nordhaus, "Energy Policy: Mostly Sound and Fury," *New York Times,* Sunday, 30 Nov. 1980 (Business Section) as quoted in Harvey Brooks' chapter in *Uncertain Power.*

36. Darcy Thompson, ed., *On Growth and Form* (New York: Cambridge University Press, 1961) p. 14.

PART I

ENERGY AND THE
PUBLIC

In this section, the authors examine the significance of public education, opinion, and participation in energy policy planning and implementation.

In the chapter, *The Public, Experts, and Government: A Delicate Balance,* Dorothy S. Zinberg identifies the many elements of the public: the "grassroots" public—groups organized to create energy policy from the "bottom up"; the affected public—those whose lives would be directly altered by local strip mining, the siting of a nuclear waste facility, or the construction of a dozen whirring windmills; and the unprotected public—the poor, for whom new policies resulting from rising costs of energy have meant "doing without." Without a concerned government they have become increasingly dependent on public consumer groups to lobby for their protection. There is also a new public, forged from a larger group of experts outside of government and industry, who because of their scientific, technical, legal, or policy training participate as professionals in public interest groups (The Sierra Club, League of Women Voters), in "professional" public interest groups (Scientists and Engineers for Secure Energy, The Union of Concerned Scientists), and as "friends of the court" in numerous lawsuits.

As the public-interest experts and general public struggle to influence local, state, and federal legislation, they highlight both the potential for public participation and the constraints on this crucial activity. As Daniel Yankelovich demonstrates in *The Failure of Consensus,* there must be some measure of consensus, a general agreement in society that there is an energy problem or more accurately, energy problems. The elements for this consensus require a sharpened public awareness of the issues, a measure of agreement about the problem and its solution among national leaders and the elites, and the existence of a potential solution around which consensus could develop. The solution, in order to attract consensus, must be simple to understand, ideologically appealing, and possible to carry out. These three elements have been absent with regard to energy policy to date.

Richard Sclove in *Energy Policy in a Democracy* argues that neither consensus building nor public participation as they currently exist are consistent with democratic theory because citizen participation, direct and through representative institutions, has not been truly reflected in political discourse and decision making. In reviewing the contributions of Amory Lovins to energy policy making in the 1970s, Sclove credits him with enunciating most clearly the proposition now generally accepted that a choice between different technologies is also a political and social choice, one in which citizens have not had an adequate role. Sclove goes on to argue (contrary to the belief often expressed by industrialists and government officials) that democratic participation is a necessary condition for true efficiency.

From three different perspectives, each of these authors argues that the energy debate is a debate about social values, which must be resolved through the political process. Identifying these social values and publicly debating their underlying significance so that they are incorporated into energy policies is as necessary as choosing the ideal mix of energy resources and technologies.

Chapter 1
THE PUBLIC, EXPERTS, AND GOVERNMENT: A DELICATE BALANCE AMONG THE PARTICIPANTS

Dorothy S. Zinberg

Public policies in the United States are forged by balancing factors that often are in direct conflict with one another. The public participates in this process by electing representatives to carry out its wishes, but in recent years the public has insisted on having a more direct involvement in national, state, and local policy making. Nowhere has this shift been more evident than in efforts to develop energy policies during the past decade. Energy policy makers have been forced to take into account (besides economic, technological, regional, and geopolitical considerations), the needs, values, sensitivities, and will of "the public."

Just how much and what kinds of public participation are needed in a democracy, how effective that participation has been, and what might be its limits are less clear.[1] What is clear, is that public participation is receiving powerful support from diverse, influential sources. Recognizing the changed social situation, former Under-Secretary of State George Ball remarked:

> The nuclear issue is being taken away from the priesthood. People are asserting themselves, and the non-experts may have a lot better judgment on this (nuclear weapons) than a bunch of mandarins.[2]

Government bureaucrats and energy industrialists, although in principle in favor of public participation, have been less enthusiastic as they have watched the public decisively influence the development of nuclear power, strip mining, solar energy, and conservation, among other areas of energy policy. The nuclear industry held the antinuclear public responsible for the industry's slowdown almost a decade before the current economic recession began. Some have even blamed the antinuclear public for the recession itself.[3]

This chapter will briefly review the history of public participation in the United States as it relates to the decline of trust in government, the subsequent plunge in political party affiliation, and the dramatic growth in single-issue politics. The failure of both the executive and legislative branches of government to reach closure on energy policy has intensified public participation and with it, the participation of scientists and a new cadre of energy policy experts. The chapter will explore this interaction and its significance for the development of workable energy policies. And, finally, because public opinion polls have become powerful analytic and political tools, providing the public, experts, and government with much of its information as well as the basis for policy decisions, their use and misuse will be examined.

The energy debate, particularly as it involves nuclear power, has become a surrogate for many issues dividing the country, issues that involve vastly different, often conflicting images of American values and goals. The debate has been sharpened by the ever-increasing impact of science and technology on society. For some, science and technology are counted on to produce a secure energy future, in much the same way as the 1933 Chicago World's Fair Guidebook proclaimed: "Science discovers, genius invents, industry applies, and man adapts to or is molded by new things." For others, the very success of that promise has weakened other American values (e.g., egalitarianism, self-sufficiency, communalism, and even democracy itself).

In this intense debate, each side has come to rely on the testimony of experts. In the interplay of the public and policy makers, scientists who had long appeared to favor nonintervention in political matters have, since World War II, increasingly taken sides in policy disputes. Acting sometimes as a part of the general public, sometimes in alliance with public interest groups or professional societies, and sometimes on behalf of industry or government, they have become a force to be reckoned with in contemporary energy policy making.

Yet the very diversity of scientists' opinions has confused a public educated to believe that science produces indisputable facts. As the internal disagreements within the scientific community have become public, the public has sought more control over issues which involve science and technology, even while sustaining its faith in most scientific evidence.

In its insistence on gaining a more potent role in decision making, the public has been encouraged by political leaders at federal, state, and local levels. In 1975 the California state legislature concluded:

> After listening to 120 learned witnesses who could not agree on the merits of the initiative or the safety of nuclear power, it is clear that no objective conclusions can be drawn. The issues are not solely resolvable through application of scientific expertise. The debate is more the result of differing views on human fallibility and human behavior than anything else. The questions involved require value judgments, and the voter is no less equipped to make such judgments than the most brilliant Nobel laureate.[4]

Several years later, President Carter in addressing the Congress about nuclear waste stated: "It is essential that all aspects of the nuclear waste management program be conducted with the fullest possible disclosure to, and participation by, the public and the technical community."[5]

As this is being written, the legitimacy of the public role is receiving increasing recognition. Debate over energy policy and military policy, particularly where they are linked with nuclear power plants and nuclear weapons, is demonstrating again the force of public opinion and participation.

THE PASSIVE PUBLIC OF THE PAST

Democratic political systems have traditionally rested on the concept of the consent of the governed, with the understanding that the wishes of the public must be taken into account. But through American history, the government's perception of the public, and the public's self-perception, have changed significantly. At the turn of the last century, the public was often characterized as omnipotent, capable of recalling elected officials at will. By mid-twentieth century, the national leadership saw the mass public as neither informed about nor interested in the political process. Today the public is perceived as fragmented, but with an activist minority, influential beyond its number, working on a broad range of issues from local to global.

The authority of the public has always been a central tenet of democratic ideology. Political scientists describe democratic systems as having an "ethical imperative" to heed the opinion of the public, out of prudence, if for no other reason.[6] In recent American history, democratic hopes and expectations, embodied in the notion of government by public opinion, reached a peak during the years before World War I. At that time strong feelings in favor of the popular will prevailed, and direct involvement of the people in the governmental process was seen as the ideal, even though, ironically, women could not vote and the majority of blacks were outside the political process.

This faith in the wisdom of the people declined after World War I, an aspect of the general erosion of Wilsonian idealism. The change is embodied in the writings of the influential journalist, Walter Lippmann, whose disdain for the public was unambivalent:

> The common interests very largely elude public opinion entirely, and can be managed only by a specialized class.[7]
> With the substance of the problem it can do nothing but meddle ignorantly or tyrannically. . . . Only the insider can make the decisions, not because he is inherently a better man, but because he is so placed that he can understand and can act.[8]

Lippmann helped to scuttle the belief that the ordinary citizenry was capable of deciding affairs of state. In its place, Lippmann presented the exhausted worker, uninterested in the pros and cons of current political matters. Average citizens, in his view, could not be mobilized to participate in public affairs, and even if they were willing to devote spare time to the study of public issues, the information available to them was inadequate and unenlightening. Lippmann's new image of the public was that of an amorphous, passive body that, even when informed, was incapable of taking action.

During the same postwar period, several developments tended to undermine the image of the public as competent to guide political affairs. New theories of human behavior characterized people as nonrational, highly susceptible creatures with barely restrained unconscious wishes. The development of the art of propaganda reinforced the belief that people could be manipulated by the mass media. Advertising and public relations organizations became all-powerful as the techniques they developed were used to sell everything from soap and cigarettes to public policies and political candidates.

After World War II, the growing audiences for radio and television reinforced the notion of mass opinion; the public was likened to a malleable giant whose opinion was subject to all-powerful manipulators able to mold attitudes and engineer consent.

Through continuing research on the nature of the public a more complex image began to emerge. In the mid-1950s, sociologist C. Wright Mills advanced the concept of the "power elite," a small inner circle comprised of wealthy corporate heads, military leaders, and key politicians who controlled national policy. An outer, somewhat less influential circle was made up of groups such as the press, broadcast media, and minor politicians. Still consistent with post-World War I views, the public was to be found farthest from the center of influence. Accordingly, it is not surprising to discover that nowhere does Mills mention the possibility that the public, by membership in political parties or by participation in elections, could affect power relations.[9]

Though varied in their emphases and directions, most social scientists studying "the public" during the fifties confirmed this image of the public as a largely passive entity.[10] A summary analysis of 1950s studies concluded that the public

- was only mildly involved in politics and thought about politics in relatively simple and narrow terms;
- allied itself with the major political parties with ties that were more habitual than rational; and
- was basically satisfied with the working of the political system.[11]

Political science literature reported that in the 1950s party affiliation was a fundamental political orientation, transmitted with regularity from generation to generation. This observation was consistent with increasing data available on the role of the party in elections during that decade. Most voters held a partisan commitment that tended to be long term and that was a strong predictor of voting decisions.[12] In the 1960s, what had been a predictable and relatively harmonious

American political public became sharply fragmented into discordant parts. This more recent, fragmented public has given rise to the new, activist public.

THE NEW ACTIVE PUBLIC

A study of the American voter published in 1979 provides a useful analysis for understanding the changes in the public. Its authors argue that democratic government depends on both the support of the citizenry and the capacity of the political process to reconcile conflicting forces.[13] In the past, reconciliation was achieved by building coalitions in order to win elections under the umbrella of one party or the other. In the sixties and seventies political parties were unable to accommodate these conflicting forces. The result has been a dramatic withdrawal of public support for the party structure and for the political process itself. In its place, the public developed a great interest in single issues and an eagerness to participate politically through new means.

A comparison of two intervals—1952 to 1964 and 1964 to 1974—illustrates those partisanship changes. From 1952 to 1964, the proportion of the population strongly identified with a major political party remained stable at one-third of the populace. A slightly larger group was weakly partisan, and 20 percent of the population labeled itself Independent.[14] During the period from 1964 to 1974, however, the proportion of Independents rose, while those identifying strongly with a party dropped. By 1974, nearly 40 percent of the public termed itself Independent, and only one voter in four could be considered strongly partisan.[15]

The decline in partisanship also meant more independent political behavior and an increase in ticket splitting. From 1960 to 1972, the proportion of the population reporting straight-party-ticket voting fell from 65 percent to 33 percent. The influence of the party on the voter's choice of candidates also declined: in 1952, 46 percent of the voters cited a party reason for candidate preference; by 1972, only 24 percent relied on party evaluation.[16]

Events since 1960 have reduced further the significance of party affiliation for those who remained identified with a party, but the behavior of new voters has been a still more telling sign of the decay of partisanship. Each cohort of new voters entering the electorate between 1952 and 1974 became increasingly independent of the party structure. In 1952, 26 percent of new voters registered as Independents; in 1960, the figure was 34 percent; in 1968, it had risen to 45 percent; by 1974, 50 percent of new voters registering chose no party identification; and the trend continues.[17]

External issues have challenged the public to make political evaluations based increasingly on issues rather than party. This change has been encouraged, also by the public's tendency to see public policy decisions as more central to citizens' lives. For example, the Department of Energy is currently exploring sites as potential locations for permanently storing nuclear wastes in deep salt deposits. At one of them in Tulia, Texas, a group of citizens has organized Serious Texans Against Nuclear Dumping (STAND). They believe that everything that is central to their well-being (i.e., productive agricultural farm land; unpolluted water; a stable, small-town population; a healthy environment in which to raise children) will be threatened by the technical failures of nuclear waste storage schemes. Road building, pressure on water supply, social problems arising from an influx of new workers, and other consequences of boom-town construction, according to STAND, would wreak havoc with their way of life and perhaps create health hazards for future generations. Not all of Tulia's citizens agree. Older citizens and business owners, more concerned about the town's economic well-being, favor the new facility. Thus, the controversy developed along two lines: the town's establishment versus local opposition, and the latter group (STAND) versus the federal government. In this way, a policy decision made in Washington about the disposal of nuclear waste generated outside the state of Texas becomes a deeply felt concern for citizens in the small town. As in many similar cases, this kind of controversy, namely, the average citizen challenging the federal government, has direct popular appeal and attracts attention in the media. A short time after STAND's creation, Tulia and its citizens were featured on a major national TV program.[18]

The decline in partisanship and the salience of single-issue politics in the sixties and the seventies are also linked to the public's ability to conceptualize issues at a more complex level.[19]

This change can be partially explained, in turn, by the significant educational gains achieved nationally since World War II. By 1972, 30 percent of the population had some college training, up from 20 percent in 1956. At the same time, the proportion of those with less than a complete high school education was falling substantially—from 52 percent in 1956, to 25 percent in 1977, and to 16 percent by 1982. By 1980, 50 percent of high school graduates were going on to some form of further training.[20]

Increased education has brought about changes in attitudes, expectations, and behavior. For example, higher education increases an individual's estimate of the value of her or his opinions and the influence they should have. While the relative economic gains of college attendance have decreased, and the quality of the education itself is thought to have deteriorated, the social gains have not. Educated citizens, because of their sense of independence and self-esteem, seek more control over the decisions that affect their lives, for example, the conditions under which they work, the quality of their environment, and the laws that govern their actions.[21] These attitudes have favored challenges to the legitimacy of traditional authority. For example, during the crisis phase of Three Mile Island (TMI), when the workers were instructed not to flee from the plant because management deemed it safe from further damage, the only discernible difference between those who remained on the job and those who did flee was in level of education. The majority of those who left, whether thinking they knew better or simply distrusting management, had been to college.[22]

Growing alienation and skepticism in the American public have also been demonstrated. Trust in government and political leaders has been on a steady downhill course since the early 1960s, when some 55 percent of the American public strongly trusted the government and another 30 percent expressed moderate trust. By 1978 the majority support had vanished.[23] Even the temporary upsurge in trust with which a new president is traditionally greeted failed to materialize for President Reagan, and the slide continues.[24]

The government's erratic behavior during the past decade on energy policy, characterized by fervent, patriotic rhetoric and pallid, ineffective policies, has served to deepen the alienation.[25]

As trust in government declined, public participation in single issues began to rise. During the 1950s Americans expressed little concern about the future of energy or the environment: their optimism paralleled the growth of the economy. There was little public controversy about nuclear energy, in part because most of the nuclear enterprise came under the aegis of the military and was, therefore, secret. Also, in the early stages of nuclear power development, its promise far outweighed concerns about safety issues (or any of the problems that have since come to plague it, such as waste disposal, terrorism, or nuclear weapons proliferation), which were only dimly perceived. Rather, the remarkable new public activism of the late twentieth century took shape in relation to another technology-related issue: the environment.

Concerns about the fragility and finite nature of the planet began to catch the public's attention. With the publication of *Silent Spring* (1962) by Rachel Carson, the national consciousness began to change. A *New York Times* book review exhorted the public to action: "It is high time for people to know about these rapid changes in their environment, and to take an effective part in the battle that may shape the future of all life on earth."[26] In 1972, the publication of *Limits to Growth* triggered intense debates, which were enlarged to include problems related to *Social Limits to Growth*.[27] By 1978, scientists raised their own concerns by raising the question of whether there should be *Limits of Scientific Inquiry*.[28] And a runaway best-seller published first in 1973, but "discovered" in the late 1970s, expounded that *Small is Beautiful*.[29]

By 1970 environmentalists' concerns were reflected in new legislation. The Freedom of Information Act in 1966 and 1967 effectively ended decades of secrecy, providing the public with access to many previously classified documents. It was followed by the Toxic Substances Control Act in 1976, the Advisory Committee Act, the Sunshine Act, and then the Clean Air Amendment Acts and the Clean Water Act in 1977.

The National Environmental Policy Act (NEPA), enacted in 1970, required that any major development project file with the newly constituted Environmental Protection Agency an environmental impact statement that would identify all anticipated environmental effects of the proposed projects. Until that time, government agency analysis and decision making were open neither to the public nor even to specialists outside an agency. As a result of NEPA, decisions on environmental and energy issues were subject to review by independent committees, and environmental impact statements were mandated. The passage of the Freedom of Information Act had stimulated increasing scrutiny of government actions by citizens and advocacy groups, who now had access to papers and proceedings previously closed to them. Agency misjudgments and misdeeds became public information. At the same time, judicial action made it possible for citizens and public interest groups to take legal action in opposition to decisions that represented dangers to the environment. In *Calvert Cliffs v. the AEC,* a landmark decision of the courts gave a monumental boost to the morale of nuclear opposition groups in the United States. The United States Court of Appeals asserted that "NEPA was not a vague testament of pious generalities but an unambiguous demand for reordering of priorities in specific decision making procedures, including, very particularly, those of the Atomic Energy Commission (AEC)."[30] The environmental movement, which was to lead the way for public involvement in energy issues, was rapidly becoming a permanent lobby with wide influence. For example, the United States Court of Appeals in Washington, in the most recent and controversial interpretation of NEPA, ruled that the undamaged TMI reactor (TMI 1) could not be restarted until the Nuclear Regulatory Commission could demonstrate that such a move would not adversely affect the mental health of local citizens. The lawsuit filed by People Against Nuclear Energy (PANE) sought to expand the interpretation of a "full environmental impact statement" as legislated by NEPA.[31] With this far-ranging interpretation of the Act, psychological and social factors, at least at TMI, have now become a significant factor in federal decision making in the licensing of nuclear power plants.[32] By shaping federal legislation the environmental movement had within a decade become a major force in American society, and this success led directly to public participation in energy issues.

As energy problems have been reflected in escalating fuel and electricity prices, a disaffected public perceives the traditional political process based on party affiliation as an inadequate vehicle for public expression. Special interest and single interest groups have multiplied. From successful grassroots movements to sophisticated, professional organizations, public interest groups have been providing a more continuous, informal, and personal route for the expression of citizens' views.

In 1973 there were 100 national public interest groups with Washington, D.C. offices.[33] Three years later, more than 450 consumer groups existed across the country.[34] By 1978 there were more than 8000 registered grassroots neighborhood organizations[35] and approximately 350 additional environmental organizations had sprung up.[36] By 1980 there were more than 1500 antinuclear groups and 200 pronuclear groups.[37] In June 1982, at the biggest demonstration in New York City's history, three-quarters of a million participants gathered to protest further development of nuclear weapons.[38]

Nuclear issues had come full circle. The bombings of Hiroshima and Nagasaki had given rise to a small but vocal American peace movement. Far more robust was its British counterpart, the Campaign for Nuclear Disarmament (CND), which in 1958 rallied 10,000 citizens to march for four days to protest against weapons development at the Atomic Weapons Research Establishment in Aldermaston. By 1960 the CND had won a vote from the Labour Party endorsing unilateral disarmament, but the signing of the Test Ban Treaty in 1963 effectively ended both groups' public visibility. Nuclear concerns began to shift to nuclear energy, and the peace movement faded as its membership divided on the nuclear energy issue. It was not until in 1980 that the antinuclear movement began to merge with a new, loose coalition that included a reenergized peace movement.[39] As a result, environmentalists, the clergy, professionals, students, previously politically inactive middle-class citizens, and a smaller number of blue collar workers have forged a new coalition of activist citizens.[40]

This energetic activity represents a significant departure from the 1950s image of a passive public that could be relied on to vote the party line, although a significant percentage of the public has remained inactive. Only 47.5 percent of those eligible voted in the 1980 presidential election. Those who do vote are more aware of political issues, more likely to rely on personal judgment on candidates and issues, and more likely to desert the party over a given issue or set of issues than they ever were in the past. The new reality is that of a minority, articulate public, interested and concerned, but, nonetheless, highly dissatisfied with the political process. By employing traditional democratic procedures—public debates and public education, public protest and litigation, the introduction of referendums on local and state election ballots, as well as coalition building—citizen activists are attempting to make political processes responsive to their perceived needs.

THE PUBLIC DISAGGREGATED

Public opinion polls and survey analyses have become commonplace in American life, pervading discussions by politicians, the media, and the citizenry of what they believe to be the reality of their society. Using well-established sampling methods, pollsters and social scientists can identify representative samples of the population and register the opinions of diverse groups within the society. When the question seeks to elicit information on past actions, such as "For whom did you vote?" the answers reliably reflect actual behavior. When the measurement is of "subjective states," such as perceptions, values, opinions, and intended behavior, the task becomes more complicated.[41] It is difficult then to evaluate a given answer and the knowledge (as opposed to opinion) it reflects, its time limitedness (would the answer be different tomorrow?), and most difficult, the relationship between an opinion and actual behavior. This task has "never surrendered easily to empirical study or quantification."[42]

In most instances, data collected over a period of years provide, if not the most valid, at least the most reliable information about public opinion trends. When the same questions are asked of statistically comparable groups at repeated intervals, the answers can reflect trends, as well as the persistence or volatility of a given opinion.

For example, a decade of comparable annual survey data reveals that nuclear-related beliefs and attitudes continue to change. From 1971 to 1979 "a plurality to a majority of the public supported the general concept of constructing more nuclear power plants."[43] After TMI, the support weakened temporarily, then returned to earlier levels. By 1982, however, the plurality had been lost.[44] These data do not identify what lies behind the shifts in attitude—fears about plant safety, changing attitudes about the need to achieve energy independence, fluctuating oil and gasoline prices, diminishing faith in American technology, and a host of other factors. They do, however, provide a background against which the issues and the public can be examined in greater detail.

Unlike nuclear power, whose history has been controversial and consequently well known to the public, energy as a larger problem has only recently come into the public consciousness, and is already fading.[45] Consequently, there is little long-term cumulative data on American attitudes toward energy. The data from many of the studies that do exist are not comparable with each other because the questions, structured differently in each case, bias the answers. Every year for more than a decade, the Gallup poll has asked the public to name the top four problems facing the country. During that period energy appeared in the top four only once, in October 1974 (after the first Arab oil embargo), and then only 3 percent of the respondents identified it as one of the top four problems.[46] However, in a survey conducted by another polling organization five years later, when respondents were presented with a list of choices and were asked to "cite the most important issues facing the country," more than 70 percent chose energy, which did not even appear in the Gallup results that year.[47] Consequently, as a first step to understanding opinion poll findings, we must know the exact wording of the question, whether the respondents were asked to choose among given problems or to suggest the answers themselves, the date the survey was conducted, and whether the sample and the methods used allow the findings to be aggregated with results from other surveys.[48]

But a well-designed public opinion poll *can* "reach a truly representative sample of the population and aggregate the feelings of those who are inarticulate as well as those who express their feelings in a variety of forms."[49] They can also be designed to elicit misleading information biased in favor of those who have commissioned the poll.[50]

In 1950, a political scientist, Gabriel A. Almond, proposed a scheme for analyzing the structure of American society and the ways in which different segments of the population mobilize for action on foreign policy isssues.[51] The scheme is a helpful format for representing public behavior on energy issues.

Briefly stated, the model, in the form of an isosceles triangle, depicts a small group, the decision makers, at the top. Underneath them are arranged, in successively larger numbers, the elites, the attentive public, and (the majority) the nonattentive public. It is within the "attentive public" that the traditional potential activists on a given issue reside. Here the difference between public opinion and public participation becomes significant. Everyone can have an opinion about virtually any subject, but to become active and effective requires knowledge, organization, a commitment of time, and an understanding of what processes— protest, litigation, negotiation, referendums—will bring about the desired goal.

This combination of requirements limits the number of activities for which any one "attentive" citizen can be mobilized. There are fiercely contested public policy debates requiring some understanding of the scientific and technological developments of countlesss complex issues, from recombinant DNA research to nuclear weapons development, pollution control, acid rain, chemical and nuclear wastes, and ozone depletion. No citizen can become expert in every area. Yet without direct citizen involvement, the political process can be "dominated by the more parochial elements of the American political elite, elements drawn from or close to the American business elite."[52]

Both of these groups are currently distrusted by large segments of the population. One study reports that "there is [also] widespread distrust of the oil and gas industry, local utilities, the President, government generally, and energy experts, coupled with disbelief, distrust, disaffection, and undertones of moral outrage."[53] The authors end with the gloomy view that "the social tension and personal insecurities accumulated as a result of the energy situation are potentially destabilizing."

However, the anger that results from a feeling of helplessness, and an inability to control one's environment can be effectively transformed through participation in citizens' groups. Of course, there are limits both to the level of tolerable frustration for a group and to public participation, which can infringe on democratic processes.

This process of turning passive into active, of challenging big business, special interests, and the government, has had its fullest expression in grassroots and consumer groups. Here the emphasis has been on "bottom-up change," where small groups, most often community based, "are beginning to experiment with self-reliant modes of energy production, such as efficiency, conservation, and passive solar. . . ."[54] Local citizens have banded together to stop the installation of electric power lines, the siting of nuclear power plants, the transportation of radioactive wastes through city streets, and (most recently in town meetings) the development of nuclear weapons.[55-58] Protest actions have led to the formulation of broader, long-range initiatives and the introduction of referendums at state and local levels, organized outside traditional power alignments. These citizens are creating an activist renaissance.[59]

For many citizens, this sense of active involvement does not have to be derived from direct participation, but can be achieved by becoming sufficiently well-informed so as to develop a sense of social identification with a particular participatory process.[60] Membership in a public interest group is one way of developing this identification. More influential than grassroots groups because of their financial base, membership, publications, and advocacy skills, public interest groups have risen steadily in numbers and influence since the early 1970s. With access to Congress, the media, and the courts, many of them have affected energy policy decisions in the courts as well as at the federal, state, and local levels of government. They have, also, been actively involved in educating the "attentive" public through their newsletters, journal articles, TV-radio appearances, and frequent letters to the editor.

Public disenchantment with the Reagan administration, whose views on energy and particularly the environment are antithetical to those of a large segment of the population, has swelled the membership lists of environmental organizations, and further diminished traditional Republican-Democratic party differences. Where at one time many public interest groups were believed to be left-liberal and, consequently, anathema to more conservative citizens, the Reagan administration's attack on the environment (e.g., wilderness lands, scenic coastal waters, endangered species, on funds for conservation and solar energy, and, most recently, on efforts to limit nuclear weapons production) has elicited a response from those moderate and conservative "attentives" for whom the protection of the environment supercedes allegiance to other political concerns.

In March 1982, 14 of these public interest groups collaborated on a critique of the Reagan administration's energy policy, *The Reagan Energy Plan: A Major Power Failure*. The 14 groups are: Center for Renewable Resources, Cousteau Society, Environmental Action, Environmental Action Foundation, Environmental Defense Fund, Federation of American Scientists, Friends of the Earth, National Audubon Society, Natural Resources Defense Council, the Nuclear Club, Nuclear Information and Resource Service, Sierra Club, Solar Lobby, and Union of Concerned Scientists.[61] Declaring the energy policy "unbearably expensive, socially disruptive, and needlessly damaging to the long-term national interest," the group attacked the Administration's indiscriminate "produce, produce, produce" philosophy in oil, gas, and coal and urged that investments be made in energy efficiency.

The groups individually have very different histories. For example, the Sierra Club, founded in 1892 to protect the wilderness, played a major role in the development of the National Park Service and the Forest Service. Often criticized early in its history as elitist and politically conservative in its efforts to protect nature for the rich rather than for the public, the organization has changed considerably, becoming a political lobby opposing "quick-fix" solutions to energy problems. In its zeal to protect the environment it has broadened its membership base, studied the environmental problems connected with nuclear waste, and, consequently, become a major critic of nuclear power.

With very different antecedents and with more overtly political aims, the Federation of American Scientists (originally Federation of Atomic Scientists) was organized by members of the Manhattan Project after World War II to lobby in the public interest for issues pertaining to science and society, particularly those concerned with nuclear weapons. Today the organization is composed of natural and social scientists and engineers.

Both of these groups, in the attack on the Reagan Energy Plan, as well as those groups who favor Reagan's policies (Scientists for Secure Energy and Americans for Energy Independence, for example) and the League of Women Voters, which attempts to educate without taking a position, agree on two premises. They believe that energy issues have a technical aspect that must be understood before appropriate economic, social, and political choices can be made. In addition, they agree with the pollster who said, "In the long run all decisions have to be acceptable to the public."[62] These beliefs have led the organizations to embark on public education programs. Various in substance, and difficult to categorize accurately as left or right politically, the programs all lean heavily on advice from scientists.

THE RISE OF THE EXPERT

As scientists have become more visible through their participation in controversial public issues, so their participation has become more controversial. The now routine appearance of scientists on both sides of an issue creates some confusion for the public, and this conflict may reduce their political impact.[63] Yet the public remains "unequivocal in recognizing the expertise of scientists and engineers on problems relating to their areas of specialization."[64]

During the past several decades, local and national public interest groups turned increasingly to experts (e.g., economists, lawyers, scientists, and science policy professionals) to learn about the issues on which they planned to challenge government and industry. Even when the group's goal was not to advocate, but, rather, to educate or to formulate ethical and religious positions, as when the World and National Council of Churches issued statements on several aspects of nuclear power production, advice from scientists became the bedrock on which the positions would be based.

The word of the scientist has not always been as commanding as it has become during the past several decades. With surprise one writer noted somewhat ironically shortly after World War II:

Physical scientists are the vogue these days. . . . No dinner party is a success without at least one physicist to explain . . . the nature of the new age in which we live.[65]

The trend would continue. Science and technology, having succeeded in bringing about an American military victory, received ever-growing funding from government and industry. Thus enriched, scientists and engineers generated new knowledge and technology at an explosive rate, which in turn created an increasing demand for specialists. Between 1950 and 1966, the employment of scientists and engineers increased 154 percent; employment in all other sectors rose only 24 percent. By 1981 there were more than three quarters of a million scientists with Ph.D. degrees. As Thorstein Veblen had predicted in 1920, America appeared to be a country governed by professional elites. Of minor significance in the first large-scale study of occupational prestige carried out in 1947, by 1966 science ranked just under medicine, the military, and education as an institution in whose leaders the public had "great confidence."[66] By 1980 it had risen to second place.[67]

Scientists had been thrust into the national consciousness by the development of the atomic bomb. Previously underpaid, with their research underfunded and their advice rarely sought outside of their laboratories, they were suddenly among the elite of the professionals. Described as "a form of established religion, and scientists its priests and ministers," science continued to grow in national esteem.[68] Although confidence in all institutions has declined since the 1960s, confidence in the leaders of science has declined relatively less, the greatest absolute decline having occurred in education, the military, and major U.S. business organizations.[69]

Part of the reason for the continuing rise of esteem for scientists can be traced to the post-World War II period, when science and technology were enlisted to achieve the social goals of society. Full employment and better nutrition and health care would result from basic science and technological innovation. The development of a safe, economical, readily available energy source was another of those goals. Nuclear energy, unleashed in its destructive capacity on Hiroshima and Nagasaki, was now to be converted into a constructive resource. Expressed in the slogan "Atoms for Peace," the optimistic 1953 vision of President Eisenhower promised a world of nuclear-fueled airplanes, automobiles, and elevators. Radioactive isotopes would advance medicine, biochemical research, and agricultural productivity. The scientists who had developed the bomb, the public was told, would spearhead the campaign to harness nuclear energy for peaceful uses.

THE EXAMPLE OF NUCLEAR POWER

Nuclear power, however, presented unanticipated problems. Unique in the fears it engendered as well as the hopes it stimulated, nulear power became a compelling symbol. For the pronuclear group it is American technology at its best—clean, efficient, safer than other resources, economical, and exportable. For those opposed, it represents the worst of big government, business, labor, science, and social control. Most often, it is perceived by antinuclear groups as a dangerous technology with the potential to produce catastrophic accidents, the damage from which will be irreversible. Each group believes that the other is threatening democracy by its unwillingness to see the error of its assumptions.

At present nuclear power contributes less than 4 percent to the United States' energy supply (12 percent to electricity), and the long-term future of the domestic industry is uncertain.[70] Yet all of the issues and players in this drama provide a model for understanding conflicts about the relative influence that experts, the public, the media, the courts, business, and the government exert in energy policy decision making where science and technology are involved.

Had the scientific community taken a stand 100 percent for or against nuclear power, there would likely have been less interest in the role of scientists. It was the dissension among the experts, the varied interpretations of similar data, and the misplaced certainty that aroused concern. The scientific community had become so large and diversified that no one voice spoke for their many different public and private interests. This was not new to science; the history of scientific discoveries reveals that controversy has frequently been a part of "scientific revolutions."[71]

What was also new by the late 1960s was that the public was listening to and became embroiled in debates about nuclear issues. An eager audience sprang up, ready to respond to each new revelation from scientists. The secrecy that had been the hallmark of war research had carried over to the Atomic Energy Commission, formed in 1954. Gradually, however, as records were declassified and the extent of radiation damage in Japan and the Pacific atolls became public knowledge, an articulate group of scientists also went public with their own doubts. Many alumni of the Manhattan Project who had gained a new-found audience in Washington were committed to ending the arms race, had serious reservations about building the hydrogen bomb, and wanted an end to above-ground testing. Others, with strong anti-Soviet ideological biases, disagreed vigorously.[72] These splits within the scientific community carried over into the nuclear power debate, but the reasons for the divisions between pro- and antinuclear power were less clear.

Several surveys illustrate the overall pronuclear power attitudes in the scientific community. One survey, addressed to elite scientists, asked respondents to react to the statement: "The benefits of nuclear power are greater than the risks involved." Seventy-four percent of the scientists agreed strongly with the statement (compared to 90 percent of the military, 83 percent of business people, 64 percent of the news media, and 58 percent of religious institutions).[73] Another survey, addressed only to scientists "dedicated to the sensible development of energy and natural resources and to the prudent use of technology," reported (not surprisingly) that 99 percent agreed that "nuclear electricity must play a crucial role in the U.S. energy future." Almost 100 percent of that group also believed the "scientific community has primary responsibility for correcting misconceptions and educating the press and public on energy issues." They were considerably less certain that "the media are capable of reasonable coverage of emotional issues such as nuclear power"(47 percent).[74] Other studies report that "elite scientists," as measured by membership in the National Academy of Sciences, are more pronuclear than non-elite scientists.[75] But majority opinion has not been as important as minority action.

On August 6, 1975, the 30th anniversary of the atomic bombing of Hiroshima, more than 2000 biologists, physicists, chemists, engineers, and other scientists sent a declaration to Congress and the president urging a "drastic reduction in new nuclear power plant construction starts . . . until major progress [was made on] controversies about safety, waste disposal, and plutonium safeguards." This petition prepared under the auspices of the Union of Concerned Scientists (UCS) also urged that the nation "suspend its program of exporting nuclear plants to other countries pending resolution of national security questions . . ." Now with more than 138,000 sponsors, the UCS, though a minority voice when compared with scientists' opinions as expressed in opinion poll surveys, has become an influential public interest group in energy policy not only in nuclear issues but also in lobbying for government support of conservation, solar, and renewables.

The usefulness of survey studies to convey the level of activity and the intensity of commitment breaks down when an issue is social, psychological, scientific, and political. The question usually taps all four (or more) variables, but the answer does not specify the relative weight of each variable in the respondent's mind. Consequently, the survey does not measure how significant the opinion is to those who hold it. The majority of the scientific community may indeed be in favor of nuclear power, but it is the minority outside of government and industry, that is, scientists without an apparent vested interest, who have serious doubts about nuclear power, who have caught the attention of the media and the public. J. Robert Oppenheimer wrote:

> For scientists it is not only honorable to doubt, it is mandatory to do that when there appears to be evidence in support of that doubt.[76]

The scientists who are doubters about nuclear power are not necessarily antinuclear (although many of them are) but often concerned about specific stages of the nuclear fuel cycle. Mining, transportation of nuclear fuel, nuclear plant siting and safety, nuclear waste disposal, and the proliferation of nuclear weapons production as a consequence of plutonium production are all serious problems. Just how serious is the argument among the experts. By questioning the adequacy of current regulations to deal with any or all of those problems, the doubters have marshalled support and increased, or at least intensified, antinuclear sentiment, even when the scientists themselves believed they were working simply to make the nuclear fuel cycle safer. By publicizing their doubts, they increased the public's knowledge about nuclear technology. When the media present technological information, even in neutral fashion, the public tends to become more opposed to the technology, nuclear or other. Once something is identified as having problems, the public increases its opposition.[77]

The nuclear doubters gained greater prominence after TMI. Although several of them have publicly announced their guarded conversion to a pronuclear position, the public has continued to become increasingly antinuclear.[78] By the spring of 1982, a majority were against nuclear power in general and against siting a nuclear power plant near their homes.[79] This sentiment is expected to change only if national security is threatened from the outside; a domestic energy shortage or coal strike will not do it.[80] The nuclear power industry, nevertheless, plans to launch a major drive to increase public support. Their advisors continue to urge the industry to employ scientists and physicians in their public "education" efforts.

At the annual meeting of the Atomic Industrial Forum, the leaders of the industry were encouraged to:

> Find people who do not appear to have a vested interest—scientists and doctors. Only they can communicate to the public about this issue. Use them and use them well.
>
> It may be rather shallow of us to think of such things but the other side is doing the same thing. The people who are believed are those with scientific credentials.[81]

Leaders of government propose much the same. South Carolina Governor Richard W. Riley, appointed by President Carter to head the State Planning Council to determine national policy on radioactive waste disposal, wrote:

> The very manner in which past decisions were made simply did not provide the opportunity for adequate critical assessments that might have encouraged new knowledge and technology to solve the questions facing us today.
>
> Therefore, if the questions are truly "Who will decide what will be done?" and "How will they decide?", those of us who are involved in these decisions must ensure that the demands of the political process are balanced with and informed by *appropriate scientific expertise*.[82] (italics added)

But how does one assess appropriateness? As the issues of energy policy, in general, and nuclear power, in particular, become more political, that is, (to paraphrase the political scientist, Harold Lasswell) related to questions of who gets what, when, and where, finding a truly disinterested scientist becomes a fruitless pursuit. The commitment of time and energy required to become an expert in the technology of nuclear issues and in the comparative questions regarding other resources results in the person's developing an opinion for or against nuclear and other options. Once an opinion is arrived at, or more likely, in the process of arriving at the opinion, a scientist's values become subtly involved.

The same data, without any conscious attempt by scientists to mislead the audience, can be interpreted variously depending on scientists' personal and professional values. Those who believe that strengthening national security is the highest priority will recommend different ways of dealing with energy problems than those who are predominantly concerned with the protection of the environment. Those who believe that the country must be geared to maximize production of goods and services will differ in their recommendations from those who believe that a major energy goal should be to conserve resources for a future generation. And those who believe that only a strong federal government can manage the country's energy policies will stress different data than those who believe that energy systems should be decentralized.

Obviously there are issues that are primarily scientific—for example, estimating the stability of a salt deposit for the burial of nuclear wastes, assessing the brittleness of the metal used to build a nuclear power plant, or predicting the impact that large solar collectors will have on rainfall. The decision on how to deal with these problems, however, is political, and the scientific "facts" are only one among many variables in the final calculation. As the chagrined chairman of the Presidential Commission to Investigate Three Mile Island, John G. Kemeny, himself a mathematician, recounted:

> In the course of our commission's work, we again and again ran into cases where emotions influenced the judgments of even very distinguished scientists. This was most disturbing to me, and I was reminded of that famous incident when Galileo was forced to recant some of his great discoveries because they ran counter to religious beliefs. Today the problem is not with religion per se, but I kept running into scientists whose beliefs border on the religious and even occasionally on the fanatical. And I hasten to add that I observed this at both extremes of the nuclear debate. These people distort their own scientific judgments and hurt their reputations by stating things with assurance that they know, deep down, could only be assigned small probabilities. They become advocates instead of unbiased advisors. This is incompatible with the fundamental nature of science and it creates an atmosphere in which there is a serious mistrust of experts: even when the hard evidence is overwhelming, if the issue is sufficiently emotional you can always get an expert to dispute it and thereby help throw all of science into national disrepute.[83]

THE GOVERNMENT AS ARBITRATOR

Even with the new congressional staff of science experts, the endless congressional hearings, government reports, expert witnesses and executive science advisory committees, the progress toward developing a coherent set of related energy policies has been dismal.

Having bemoaned the character of scientific advice, John G. Kemeny went on to make a number of stark observations about the ways in which two branches of the federal government functioned.

The Executive

> It was so disorganized during the emergency that the White House had to step in and knock heads so that the different agencies could work together. Four weeks after the accident, at our first public hearing, senior officers from

three major branches of the executive testified that they did not go out and measure radiation until two and a half days after the accident. Here we were, a brand-new commission confronting one of our most important charges— to estimate the health effects of the accident—and we were terrified that the crucial information had been lost. I went to sleep greatly worried. The next morning, a representative of the Department of Energy by the name of John Deutch (professor of Chemistry at MIT, then on leave) testified about DOE helicopters going in and measuring radiation. I interrupted, "Would you mind telling us when you started taking those measurements?" And he said, "I'm sorry, I don't have my notes here on that. It could have been 12:30 or 1:00." I said, "Sir, the question isn't at which hour, but which day?" And he answered, "Why, of course, the day of the accident. We were there within hours of the accident." And indeed DOE produced all the data we needed to make our estimate . . . Four weeks after the accident, the other three major branches of the executive that participated still had not discovered that DOE had this crucial information. So I worry greatly about whether we have a system to pull experts together from many different fields and come up with integrated plans.[84]

The Congress

I am much more worried, however, about Congress. We received a most sympathetic hearing with senators and representatives, but generally they were poorly briefed and there was no time for in-depth discussion. I do realize, of course, that the issue of Three Mile Island—overwhelming in our minds at that moment—was for them but one of a hundred issues. Representatives, moreover, are continually running for reelection—an enormous drain on their energy. But beyond all that, I had the impression that Congress has particular difficulty coming to grips with issues that involve significant input from science and technology. They cannot possibly be experts (not the way they are elected), but they seem to be confused even on the *use* of experts. I recall distinguished physicists on the commission being asked not about physics at all but to make a pure value judgment, when I thought that we elect senators and representatives to make value judgments on our behalf. At the same time, some of them very freely expressed strong opinions on scientific fact. I thought that is what we have scientists for. Indeed. I had a horrible nightmare one night in Washington: The House of Representatives, by a vote of 215 to 197, had repealed Newton's Law of gravitation![85]

Professor Kemeny is not alone in his harsh assessment of the government's fumbling actions. In 1978, even before TMI, some 50 percent of the public believed that "government officials don't know what they're doing," up from 25 percent in 1964.[86] Little has happened to reverse the trend.

The need for strong congressional leadership has been recognized by the public and political analysts because it provides the political diversity lacking in the executive. However, this diversity often leads to stalemates. A political scientist after studying the effects of internal reforms of the 1970s on the ability of the Congress to make policy, argued that because the Congress does not allow for strong, centralized leadership that this "ensures that Congressional decisions on major policy matters . . . will be incremental at best, immobilized and incoherent as a norm."[87] Another analyst reinforced this view when he wrote that few issues have been "as substantively and politically complex as energy policymaking in the mid-1970s," and suggested that the Congress could not deal with the complexity.[88] Now in the 1980s, when the oil supply problem has temporarily abated, the Congress will require concerted public pressure to force it to reexamine the energy issues which they were unable to grapple with successfully, but which remain to be confronted for the long-term welfare of the country—a very difficult assignment in the face of rising unemployment *and* decreasing oil prices.

CONCLUSIONS

No wonder the public is confused, skeptical, and disillusioned. Besides the ineptitude of government, the public has also had to acknowledge the limitations of the experts. Scientists are still regarded by the public as tɥe most reliable source for technical information, but their disputes have become a major cause of confusion for policy makers and for the public.[89] Even when expert advice aids in clarifying scientific or technical problems, it is also likely to increase conflict.[90] In a study of interest, level of information, and personal involvement, the authors report that when the conflict, as in the case of highly specific scientific questions dealing with chemical food additives or outer space, requires a great deal of information to understand the issues, the public is likely to refrain from involvement unless it believes it is well informed.[91] This does not pertain to nuclear power issues, where the number of those who would participate is greater than the number considering themselves well informed. The authors conclude: "The more public concern there is about an issue, the more the public wants to take an active part, and the less it wants to leave the decision to federal agencies or commissions."

The public also insists on a greater role in decisions about technology as scientific expertise becomes more politicized. Thus the public (e.g., individuals, grassroots groups, and special interest groups) has moved from support of science, technology, and public policy to increased demands for shaping and controlling them. As a result, the public has turned to the law, and at present, the courts have become the arbiters of which scientific opinion should prevail.

Given the new levels of educational achievement in the public and the refusal of people to give their proxy to political parties for the forging of compromises among political interests, it is no surprise that there is a vocal and increasingly intractable public attached to each position on every public question. Is there any hope that, short of restructuring our system of government, compromises can be forged and coherent policies adopted and implemented on complex technological issues?

Yes, but only when certain circumstances prevail. The most important and most difficult to achieve is to reverse the downward trend in public trust in government. This can be brought about only by the government itself. Among the many prerequisites for such a shift are increased accessibility to government, and greater openness, sensitivity, integrity, and accountability on the part of government. Government must have a greater awareness of the need for public education and participation, not just for the elite or "attentive public," but throughout the society. Participation, eventually, must be channeled into voting; 47.5 percent participation in national elections is a dismal record for a democracy.

The history of energy policy making as evidenced in nuclear energy is not illustrious. Secrecy, deception, and ineffectiveness in government agencies have not worked to reduce the public's skepticism about the government's ability to deal with technology-generated problems. Now increasing polarization within the scientific and technical community has diminished its credibility.

The temptation to believe that public education and participation are panaceas is strong but misleading. People tend to select information in accord with their own taste and bias; they also interpret the same information differently.[92] In a recent public education experiment about nuclear power in Sweden, eight thousand small study groups throughout the country each met with an energy expert to learn about nuclear energy. Those people who at the start were pronuclear, "heard" the information about energy needs; those who were antinuclear, "heard" the figures about risk. In both instances, information appeared not to change attitudes. Those who were antinuclear remained so; those who were skeptical had their position reinforced and, in many instances, became more skeptical; and those who were antinuclear remained so.[93] Psychological barriers to learning are intangible and formidable.[94] What appears to have defused the nuclear issue in Sweden was a national referendum, which recommended a gradual phase out of nuclear power plants, but more important, the educational experiment helped to create a national opinion that the entire debate had been conducted in public; there were no longer any nuclear secrets.

In the United States, participatory zeal has led to protracted law suits. For those eager to get on with technological solutions, these costly delays, which have slowed and, in some instances, paralyzed the introduction or further development of energy technologies, have been blamed often on public participation. Calculated in social rather than in strictly economic terms, these long delays could be considered to have been advantageous. As this chapter has indicated, the energy debate is a debate about values and a surrogate for many active tensions in the United States. Resolving the issues slowly and with increasing public awareness of the long-run implications of the end of cheap energy, can provide a constructive element in energy policy making. The crisis approach to problem solving has failed as the public reacts with cynical disbelief to news that alternates between shortages and glut. The social costs that can accrue from this anger might in time prove as "uneconomic" and destabilizing as the more readily measurable costs of delayed new technologies and inadequate power supplies.[95]

In the long run, it is the elected representatives who must formulate policy. Only by demonstrating willingness to consider public interests in decision making can government reduce the fears and tensions caused by its past indiscretions. If the scientists dominate policy decisions, technocracy may result; if public interest groups are intractable, the most promising policies cannnot be implemented. Public participation is a necessary but not sufficient condition for the formulation of energy policy. Resolving energy problems requires, then, a delicate balance among all three groups—government, experts, and the public.

NOTES

1. For a discussion of measuring the impact of public participation see Judy B. Rosener, "Citizen Participation: Can We Measure Its Effectiveness?" *Public Administration Review* (Sept.-Oct. 1978).
2. George W. Ball, former Under-Secretary of State quoted by John Newhouse, "Arms and Orthodoxy," *New Yorker* 58, (7 June 1982), 197.
3. The pronuclear argument is that had nuclear energy developed as rapidly as industry had intended, OPEC would have been unable to cripple the country by increasing oil prices, because nuclear power would have reduced the need for oil imports. This is disputed by those who believe that nuclear energy replaces only 10 percent of U.S. oil consumption. See Irvin C. Bupp and Rory O'Connor, "An Offer to Settle the Nuclear Debate," *Real Paper* (Boston, 13 Nov. 1981) for an exchange among pro, ambivalent, and antinuclear factions. For a different point of view regarding the failure of nuclear power, namely, its inadequacy as a product, see S. David Freeman (Director, Tennessee Valley Authority), unpublished remarks written for the Executive Session on Nuclear Power and Energy Availability, Kennedy School of Government, Harvard University, May 1982.
4. Dorothy Nelkin, ed., *The Technological Decisions and Democracy* (Beverly Hills & London: Sage Publications, 1979) p.95.
5. President Carter's Message to Congress, 12 Feb. 1980.
6. V.O. Key, *Public Opinion and American Democracy* (New York: Knopf, 1961).
7. Anthony Lewis, "The Mysteries of Mr. Lippmann," *New York Review of Books* (9 Oct. 1980), quotation of Walter Lippmann, *Public Opinion* (1922).
8. Ibid; quotation of Walter Lippmann, *Phantom Public* (1925).
9. Seymour Martin Lipset, "The Limits of Social Science," *Public Opinion* 4, no. 5 (Oct.-Nov. 1981), 5.
10. Representative of these were Robert Dahl, *Who Governs?* (New Haven: Yale University Press, 1961), a study of community decision making in one city; Samuel Stouffer, *Communism, Conformity, and Civil Liberties* (Garden City, NY: Doubleday, 1955), an analysis of the attitudes of citizens on basic questions of civil liberties; and Gabriel Almond and Sydney Verba, *The Civic Culture* (Boston: Little, Brown, 1965) a study of democratic political culture.
11. Norman Nie, John Petrocik, and Sydney Verba, *The Changing American Voter* (Cambridge, MA: Harvard University Press, 1979).
12. Herbert Hyman, John Shelton, and Charles R. Wright, *Education's Lasting Influence on Values* (Chicago: University of Chicago Press, 1975).
13. Nie, Petrocik, Verba, *The Changing American Voter,* n. 11, above.

14. Morris Janowitz, *The Last Half Century: Societal Change and Politics in America* (Chicago: University of Chicago Press, 1978).
15. Ibid.
16. Ibid.
17. Ibid.
18. CBS Morning News, 6 Aug. 1982.
19. Janowitz, *The Last Half Century,* n. 14, above.
20. United States Bureau of the Census, 1980
21. Nevitt Sanford, ed., *The American College: A Psychological and Sociological Interpretation of Higher Learning* (New York: John Wiley & Sons, 1962).
22. Evelyn Bromet, *Three Mile Island: Mental Health Findings* (Pittsburgh: Western Psychiatric Institute and Clinic, 1980).
23. ISR Newsletter: Institute for Social Research, "Public Support for Political Institutions," University of Michigan, 1979, p.4.
24. S. Martin Lipset, Personal Communication, July 1982.
25. Daniel Yankelovich, *Uncertain Power,* See chap. 2.
26. *New York Times Book Review,* 23 Sept. 1962, p.1.
27. Fred Hirsch, *Social Limits to Growth* (Cambridge, MA: Harvard University Press, 1976).
28. See "Limits of Scientific Inquiry" in special issue of *Daedalus,* 107, (Spring 1978).
29. E. F. Schumacher, *Small Is Beautiful* (London: Blond & Briggs, 1973).
30. Walter C. Patterson, *Nuclear Power* (New York: Penguin Books, 1976).
31. U. S. Court of Appeals, No. 81-113 1, (7 Jan. 1982).
32. For a discussion of U. S. Court of Appeals, District of Columbia see Eliot Marshall, "Fear as a Form of Pollution," *Science,* 215, (29 Jan. 1982) 481.
33. Stuart Langton, *Citizen Participation in America: Essays on the State of the Art* (Lexington, MA: Lexington Books, 1978).
34. Jeffrey Berry, *Lobbying for the People: The Political Behavior of Public Interest Groups* (Princeton: Princeton University Press, 1977).
35. Langton, *Citizen Participation,* n. 33, above.
36. Ibid.
37. Berry, *Lobbying for the People,* n. 34, above.
38. *Time* (21 June 1982) 39.
39. Dorothy Nelkin, "Anti-Nuclear Connections: Power and Weapons," *Bulletin of the Atomic Scientists* 37, (April 1981) 36-40.
40. *New York Times,* 12 June 1982, p.1.
41. Karl Mannheim, *Ideology and Utopia: An Introduction to the Sociology of Knowledge* (New York: Harcourt, Brace and World, 1946), 39ff.
42. Philip E. Converse, "The Nature of Belief Systems in Mass Publics," in *Ideology and Discontent,* ed. David E. Apter (New York: The Free Press and London: Collier-McMillan, 1964) pp. 206-61.
43. William L. Rankin, "Overview of National Attitudes Toward Nuclear Energy: A Longitudinal Analysis." Paper presented at annual meeting of the American Association for the Advancement of Science (Washington D.C., Jan. 3-8, 1982), in William Freudenberg, ed., *Nuclear Power and the Public: Are There Critical Masses?* (Boulder, CO: Westview Press, forthcoming).
44. See Introduction, *Uncerain Power.*
45. Ibid.
46. *Common Cause,* 8, (Feb. 1982), 23.
47. Paul Turner and H. J. Young, "Taking the Wrong View," report delivered at the Annual Conference of the Atomic Industrial Forum (San Francisco, CA, 2 Dec. 1981). Unpublished.

48. For further discussion of the potential and problems on polling public opinion see: Charles F. Turner, Elizabeth Martin, eds. *Surveys of Subjective Phenomena: Summary Report.* Panel on Survey Measurement of Subjective Phenomena, Committee on National Statistics; Assembly of Behavioral and Social Sciences, National Research Council (Washington D.C.: National Academy Press, 1981) p. 107; Daniel S. Greenberg, "The Plague of Polling," *Washington Post* (15 Sept. 1982); Charles W. Roll and Albert H. Cantril, *Polls: Their Use and Misuse in Politics* (Cabin John, MD: Seven Locks Press, 1972); Donald E. Warwick and Charles A. Lininger, *The Sample Survey: Theory and Practice* (New York: McGraw-Hill, 1975).

49. National Science Foundation "Public Attitudes Toward Science & Technology" *Science Indicators 1980* (Washington, DC: National Science Board, 1981) p.159.

50. Ibid., "NAS Survey."

51. Gabriel A. Almond, *The American People and Foreign Policy* (Westport, CT: Greenwood Press, 1977).

52. Ibid.

53. Ronald D. Brunner and Weston E. Vivian, "Citizens' Viewpoints on Energy Policy," *Policy Sciences,* 12, (Aug. 1980) 147-74.

54. Laura Nader, "The Politics of Energy: Toward a Bottom-Up Approach," *Radcliffe Quarterly* (Dec. 1981) 5-6.

55. Barry M. Casper and Paul David Wellstone, *Powerline: The First Battle of America's Energy War* (Amherst: University of Massachusetts Press, 1981).

56. Dorothy Nelkin, *Nuclear Power and Its Critics* (Ithaca: Cornell University Press, 1971).

57. For a discussion of public participation in nuclear-waste issues, see Dorothy S. Zinberg, "Public Participation: U.S. and European Perspectives" in *The Politics of Nuclear Waste,* ed. William Colglazier (New York: Pergamon Press, 1982) chap. 6.

58. "How Peterborough, N.H. Voted For Nuclear Freeze," *New York Times,* 26 March 1982, p.B5.

59. Nader, "The Politics of Energy," n. 54 above.

60. Brian Wynne, "Technology, Risk and Participation: On the Social Treatment of Uncertainty" in *Society, Technology, and Risk Assessments,* ed. J. Conrad, (New York and London: Academic Press, 1980) pp. 173-208, 281-287.

61. "Reagan Energy Program Called 'Power Failure,'" *The Energy Daily,* (Washington DC: Friday, 26 March 1982), p.3.

62. Burns Roper, Address to Atomic Industrial Forum, Annual Meeting, Washington DC, Nov. 1980.

63. Nelkin, *Nuclear Power and Its Critics,* no. 58, above.

64. *Science Indicators,* 1980, n. 49, above.

65. Daniel J. Kevles, *The Physicists* (New York: Knopf, 1978) p.375.

66. Cecil C. North and Paul K. Hatt, National Opinion Research (NORC) Study, March 1947, quoted in Joseph A. Kahl, *The American Class Structure* (New York: Rinehart & Co., 1953) p.72.

67. Spencer Klaw, *The New Brahmins: Scientific Life in America* (New York: William Morrow Co., 1968).

68. Allan Mazur, *The Dynamics of Technical Controversy* (Washington DC: Communications Press, 1981).

69. Ibid.

70. See Allison and Carnesale, *Uncertain Power,* chap. 7. Also see John Ahearne, "Nuclear Power: A Greek Tragedy?" *Progress in Nuclear Energy,* 7 (1981), 77-85.

71. Thomas Kuhn, *The Structure of Scientific Revolutions* (Chicago and London: University of Chicago Press, 1970).

72. For a history of the development of the H-bomb, see Herbert F. York, *The Advisors: Oppenheimer, Teller and the Superbomb* (San Francisco: Freeman Press, 1976).

73. Survey by Research and Forecasts, Inc. commissioned by Connecticut Mutual Life Insurance Co., *Connecticut Mutual Life Report on American Values in the 80s: The Impact of Belief,* Sept.-Dec. 1980, quoted in *Public Opinion,* (Oct.-Nov. 1981), 33.

74. "SE₂ Announces Survey Findings," *SE₂ Washington Report,* 1 (Winter 1982) 1.

75. Mazur, *The Dynamics of Technical Controversy,* n. 68, above.

76. J. Robert Oppenheimer, *The Open Mind* (New York: Simon and Schuster, 1955) p.115.

77. Allan Mazur, "Media Coverage and Public Opinion on Scientific Controversies," *Journal of Communication,* 31 (Spring 1981), 106-115.

78. Professors Kenneth Boulding, University of Colorado and John Edsall, Emeritus, Harvard University, had originally taken a public stand against nuclear power. Boulding's work with the CONAES group at the National Academy of Sciences led him to change his views "quite radically" to supporting nuclear power. Professor Edsall after studying the problems related to coal combustion became a "hesitant" supporter, although he is concerned that the recent construction errors of the nuclear industry demonstrate that it is not keeping its part of the "Faustian bargain." Personal communication with Edsall, May 1983.

79. Eugene Pokorny, *Cambridge Reports: Report to the Atomic Industrial Forum Meeting, April 6, 1982, New Orleans, LA.* Ironically, public opinion is not the limiting factor in building nuclear power plants; it has been superseded by construction costs. See Allison and Carnesale, *Uncertain Power,* chap. 7.

80. Rankin, Overview of National Attitudes Toward Nuclear Energy, n. 43, above.

81. Scott Fitz-Randolph, Winner/Wagner and Associates in address delivered to Atomic Industrial Forum Annual Meetings in Washington DC, 18 Nov. 1980.

82. Richard W. Riley, Governor of South Carolina, quoted in E. William Colglazier, ed., "Foreword," *The Politics of Nuclear Waste* (New York: Pergamon Press, 1982).

83. John G. Kemeny, "Saving American Democracy: The Lessons of Three Mile Island," *Technology Review* (June-July 1980).

84. Ibid.

85. Ibid.

86. Morris P. Fiorina, "Collective Responsibility in American Politics," *Daedalus* (Summer 1980) 42.

87. Lawrence C. Dodd, "Congress and the Quest for Power," in *Congress Reconsidered,* ed. Lawrence C. Dodd and Bruce I. Oppenheimer (New York: Praeger, 1977) pp. 209-307.

88. Bruce I. Oppenheimer, *Legislative Studies Quarterly,* 1 (Feb. 1980) 5-30.

89. Allan Mazur, "Disputes Between Experts," *Minerva,* 11 (April 1973) 243-62.

90. Dorothy Nelkin, "The Political Impact of Technical Expertise," *Social Studies of Science,* 5, no. 1 (Jan. 1975), 35-54.

91. Jon D. Miller, Kenneth Prewitt, and Robert Pearson, *The Attitudes of the U.S. Public Toward Science and Technology* (Chicago: National Opinion Research Center, University of Chicago, 1980) pp. 93,104,112; Jon D. Miller, unpublished data.

92. Paul Felix Lazarsfeld, Bernard Berelson, and Hazel Gaudet, *The People's Choice* (New York: Duell, Sloan and Pearce, 1944) p.86.

93. Dorothy S. Zinberg, "Public Participation in Nuclear Waste Management Policy: Brief History" in William Freudenberg, ed., *Nuclear Power and the Public: Are There Critical Masses?* (Boulder, CO: Westview Press, forthcoming).

94. For a discussion of research findings about barriers to learning see Herbert B. Hyman and Paul B. Sheatsky, "Some Reasons Why Information Campaigns Fail," *Public Opinion Quarterly,* 11 (1947), 413-423.

95. For a discussion of the social benefits of "delays and paralysis" see Brian Wynne, "Technology, Risk and Participation: On the Social Treatment of Uncertainty," in J. Conrad, ed., *Society, Technology, & Risk Assessment* (New York & London: Academic Press, 1980), p.197.

Chapter 2
THE FAILURE OF CONSENSUS ON ENERGY

Daniel Yankelovich

The vitality of a society, like that of a species, can be measured by its ability to adapt to change. The failure of the United States to change its orientation toward energy consumption quickly enough following the Arab oil embargo of 1973 represents one of the most serious failures of social adaptation in American history, for which the country shall be paying a price for years to come. The fact that between 1973 and 1979 the United States doubled its oil imports, that as late as 1978 we were still merely dabbling with the development of alternative sources of energy, that the American automobile industry was still planning to produce heavy, gas-guzzling cars—such mistakes will confound future historians. What source of resistance or refusal, they will ask, could have caused this intelligent, quick-moving country to persevere in such outmoded patterns of response?

In American democracy, one precondition of adaptation to new circumstances is the development of a national consensus. Not all issues on the public agenda require a wide base of public understanding and agreement to make adaptive headway, but energy use is an area where national progress will be slowed or stalled, despite technical breakthroughs, by the absence of a public consensus. For most issues, public consensus is not a prerequisite for policy change: a combination of active interest groups and a passive, uninterested public suffices to pass most legislation and regulation. But for a handful of issues (those that touch intimately on people's daily lives, behavior and values) the lack of public consensus proves an insuperable obstacle to successful adaptation. This is what happened with respect to energy in the 1970s.

If the country is to adapt to the new conditions that govern energy, how can national consensus be developed? Recent history provides documentation of two compelling examples of national consensus. They may be instructive. National consensus developed, swiftly and dramatically, on two crucial issues of our time: the need for a stronger national defense and the desirability of curbing the growth of the federal government. These two "case histories" stand in sharp contrast to the relative confusion in public attitudes on energy.

The swiftness with which a national consensus on defense developed is star-tling. Public opinion poll data could hardly be more clear-cut. Comparing attitudes in the early and mid-1970s with more recent opinion until 1982, one finds surprising shifts. In 1971, a paltry 11 percent of the public favored increasing our defense expenditures; less than a decade later, 74 percent favored such an increase.[1] In 1974 only 39 percent were willing to intervene in Western Europe in the event of a Soviet attack; in the aftermath of the invasion of Afghanistan, 67 percent said they would intervene. In 1975, only 32 percent wanted to strengthen the role of the CIA, compared with a majority that favored restraining the agency. In a perceived "more dangerous world," 79 percent now favor strengthening the CIA.[2] As recently as 1977 only 36 percent wanted the draft reinstated; now a majority favors some form of universal national service.

The specific numbers are less important than the magnitude and clarity of the shift: in less than a decade public attitudes in support of an assertive defense and national military posture grew from a handful of Americans to a more than two-thirds majority.

Public attitudes about the federal government began to change in the mid-1960s. Since that time, sentiment against the growth of government and a general mistrust of government have steadily increased, until today large major-ities of the public perceive the federal government as wasteful, inefficient, untrust-worthy, incompetent, and unresponsive. In 1964, by a two-to-one margin, the public believed that the federal government was run for the benefit of all the people. Now, over 60 percent of the public believe the government is run for the benefit of a few large interests, and only 24 percent believe it is run for all the people, an exact reversal of the 1964 data.[3] "The government wastes a lot of money that we pay in taxes" is an easy statement to agree with; but in 1958 only 42 percent did agree. By 1980, 80 percent of the public agreed.[4] Over the same period of time and in the same proportions, the public came to agree that "the government is getting too powerful for the good of the country." In the mid-1960s, the assertion that, "the people running the country don't really care what happens to me," was endorsed by only 25 percent. Today 65 percent agree with it. In the late 1950s three-quarters of the public agreed with the statement, "You can trust the govern-ment in Washington to do what is right most of the time;" today less than one-third agree.

Again, these are compelling reversals of *trends,* and not merely dramatic responses to "loaded" questions. Taken together, they portray a shift in public attitudes that, while subject to critical review and analysis, cannot be denied.

Public perceptions of bad faith, unresponsiveness, ineffectiveness, and ineffi-ciency have grown to the point where political efforts to reverse the past half-century of growth of government-centered programs receive widespread support from Democrats and Republicans alike.

Looking at these two examples of consensus, one in favor of national defense and one against growth of the federal government, I find three characteristics common to both. First, one sees a steady increase in public awareness of the issue over a period of years, accelerated and sharpened by events. Support for a stronger defense shot up after the failed rescue mission in Iran and particularly after the Soviet invasion of Afghanistan. The president's announcement that the latter was the greatest threat to world peace since World War II—coupled with our inability to respond with any action stronger than a boycott of the Moscow Olympic Games—communicated a feeling of impotence to the American public. In the same manner, opinion polls registered a swift rise in public frustration when the United States seemed unable to take action in response to the discovery of the Soviet combat brigade in Cuba. After each of these episodes, majority public support for increased defense spending rose measurably.

As the public watched massive cuts in social spending juxtaposed with rapid increases in defense expenditures during the first half of the Reagan administration, this majority, and the consensus it represented, began to unravel. Although in 1981 Gallup polls a 51 percent majority of the public said that the American government spent too little on defense, a year later only 19 percent held that view. The 32 percent decline represented the most precipitous one-year change on this issue since the Korean War. As a new awareness of the economic and social costs of rearming grew and was combined with growing fears of nuclear annihilation and of a government that was perhaps too willing to insert U.S. troops in precarious Third World situations, the consensus behind a "stronger America" remained, while the consensus in support of particular military policies began to erode.[5]

The change in public attitudes toward defense had been compressed into roughly an eight-year period (from 1972 to 1980), partly because so many events occurred to dramatize the questions. The revolt against growth in government has spanned a longer period, partly because, apart from Watergate, fewer specific events have occurred to galvanize opinion and fuel the trend.

A second characteristic of the processes by which consensus has emerged in these two examples is a "working through" by national leaders and elites, an awakening among them that the problem exists and must be addressed, and an agreement on the nature of the solution. University presidents, for example, who had long supported federal spending, found themselves taking positions, surprisingly, in line with the growing consensus against many aspects of government growth. When they confronted some of the contradictions and tensions that arise as the government involves itself more comprehensively with universities, they changed their views on the proper role of the federal government with astonishing readiness. Prominent Democratic politicians have admitted to feeling uneasy as they voted for spending bills. Their concern did not appear in public statements, and even in private conversations with colleagues they might say no more than "I wonder if we have the money to pay for this? Do we really know what we are doing?" But their private uneasiness gradually undermined the resolve with which these members of the national leadership asserted their accustomed points of view.

As the leadership worked through these issues privately, their public positions also changed.

The third important feature of these two examples of successful consensus building was the existence of a credible, easily articulated solution. In each case, the solution provided a core around which consensus could develop, and a program through which each consensus was translated into action.

In assessing the failure of any consensus to develop with respect to energy, it is instructive to notice that none of these three characteristic elements is present. First, the public never did become fully aware of the seriousness of the energy problem. Misleading and conflicting signals were directed at the American people for years. It is true that President Carter declared "the moral equivalent of war" on the energy crisis, but there was no concerted action by the government. There was no second act following his speech. Our national leadership misconstrued the public "learning curve" on the subject of energy; our leaders assumed that it would be sufficient to "inform" the public of the nature of the problem—give them the "facts" and allow logic, good sense, and patriotism to carry the day.

But the public construed the facts according to its own lights: the public inferred that the energy crisis was a sham. When petroleum products grew scarce, the public perceived that the oil companies and the government were conspiring to rig prices. That perception was abetted by contradictory and confused statements and policies from the national government and local agencies. The Department of Energy announced an imminent oil shortage; the Central Intelligence Agency took the opposite stance. Consumers who made good faith efforts to conserve electricity were rewarded with higher utility bills as rates were increased to compensate for lost revenues. As Hans Landsberg points out, federal government prods in 1977 and 1978, pushing electric utilities away from use of natural gas, looked quite confusing in 1979 when the word from Washington was, "Let's use natural gas."[6]

Cynically, the public predicted that as soon as there was a price increase there would be more oil at the pumps. And sure enough, after various price increases there was always more oil at the pumps. The reasons do not matter. What Washington says by way of explanation does not matter. The crucial question is, what signal is actually being *heard* by the public? People think for themselves. They may come up with the "wrong" conclusion, but in a democracy they do think for themselves. And in the present climate their thinking tends to be skeptical.

The development of consensus on the need for a new energy policy was also impeded by ideological divisions among leadership elites, to whom the public looked for guidance on a highly complex problem. Activists in the environmental field favored slow growth and the protection of the quality of life. Many opinion leaders, particularly in the universities and in the press, were unconcerned with problems of enlarging the supply of energy. Their concern was with fairness in the distribution of energy resources. Industrialists and conservatives, however, saw the energy question in terms of its impact on reindustrialization and growth. The public confronted this range of views with nonideological pragmatism. All of these views held some appeal, and the public tended to fashion an eclectic combination from all three. The national leadership remained divided and failed to utter a clear call.

Perhaps the key obstacle was the absence of any credible program of solution as a rallying point for agreement on energy. To be effective, such a program had to be simple to understand, ideologically appealing, and feasible. The programs around which consensus developed for national defense and against government growth displayed all three features. First, right or wrong, they were conceptually simple. To get more national security, increase the defense budget. To have less government, cut government programs and reduce regulation. These are easy to understand.

Second, the ideological appeals were equally striking. By increasing its defense budget, it was argued, America could regain respect worldwide and redeem its honor tarnished by events in Vietnam, Iran, Afghanistan, and Cuba. A larger defense budget would equip America to regain control of its destiny abroad. This appeal helped to win a presidential election.[7]

The appeal of the program to reduce government spending was equally compelling. The public's feeling of being pinched and constrained by inflation and the ever-bigger tax bite taken by government represents a loss of control by the individual. Cut back on government spending and, by implication, the citizen is made whole and autonomous again.

Third, the programs around which consensus has developed are eminently feasible. The Reagan administration has demonstrated that it is possible to get Congress to pass severe cuts in federal spending on most programs while preserving and strengthening national defense. That such a program seems able, on its face, to be carried out, adds intrinsically to its attractiveness. The manager of the Marin County (California) Water District observed correctly of citizen response to drastic curbs in the water supply and the sharp price increases during the 1976-77 drought, "When the community is convinced that the problem exists, and credible explanations of how to meet it are offered, people *will* cut back."[8]

The foregoing argues that on select issues consensus is a necessary condition for social adaptation, that consensus can be developed around specific concepts and programs, and that consensus on energy policy, for certain fundamental reasons, has not yet developed. But the state of public thinking about energy is not without hope. The country has learned much since 1973, and consensus on energy may well emerge in the future. Before summarizing the positive signs of a posible consensus, we should consider what still seem to be several important obstacles to its formation.

First, the largest obstacle remains the public's inadequate perception of the nature of the energy problem, at least insofar as an "informed" perception is vital to a useful public role in solving the problem. In part, the dilemma here, as cited earlier, is with leadership's definition of what constitutes an informed public. Despite the bombardment of raw information to which the public is exposed on the subject of energy (and other issues), the American people are generally unaware of *their own* choices and options to help address the problem. A flood of information does not automatically create a knowledge of feasible alternatives. Before average citizens are willing to change their minds or behavior, they must be provided with clear and credible signals that a problem exists. If, instead, they have reason to doubt the reality of the problem, or suspect that its nature is distorted by special interests, it will be difficult, if not impossible, to get people to confront the issues involved.

Second, people need an incentive to pay attention when information is conveyed. If, as has been the case on many energy issues, a blizzard of data and opinion discourages people from feeling that their own thinking and behavior make any difference, they will pay only superficial attention. Gas lines are such an incentive, as are unheated homes in winter, but by the time problems reach such a critical juncture, it is less a matter of pondering democratic participation than of grappling with mere survival and barely suppressed rage.

Third, if consensus building is to have a fighting chance, an "informed" public also needs *nontechnical* choices to consider. Soliciting public participation in the dispute between, say, coal-slurry transport systems and expanded coal-hauling capacity for the nation's railway grid, asks the public to grapple with complex technical (and political) nuances of land use, water rights, etc., and does not address the crucial value question on which public debate should be encouraged: to what extent do we want to mortgage the future for the sake of present consumption? Only such a debate, couched in terms that do not oversimplify issues, but that address genuine areas for public concern and action, is capable of generating a meaningful consensus. Even then consensus will develop only after a period of time has elapsed during which people are continually exposed to credible alternatives and allowed to "work through" the stages of comprehension, contemplation, and conclusion.

As evidence of a poorly guided debate on energy matters, we may consider the fact that the American public continues to see the energy "crisis" as a price problem; most people worry about spot shortages, while only 38 percent say they are worried about long-term shortages. Significantly, leadership groups no longer share this perception, and that alone is an important change over the past seveal years. A declining minority of government officials, business executives, and investors hold the view that shortages pose no threat in the long term, and that any problem of supply can be solved through pricing.

There is a difficulty, also, in the split that exists between the public and the leadership on the importance of conservation as a solution. More than 8 in 10 among leadership groups endorse conservation as part of the solution, while only 54 percent of the public, an inadequate basis for consensus, feels conservation is important.

The public still differs with leadership on the use of pricing to achieve conservation. A majority of the public believes that conservation can be achieved without higher prices. This majority is shrinking, however, suggesting that the public is moving towards a position similar to that of leadership, that the price mechanism must be used to enforce conservation.

The splits among leadership persist, though they are not so rigidly ideological as during the 1970s, and one finds more compromise between groups. Industrialists favor coal liquefaction, shale oil, and breeder reactors, while environmentalists put their emphasis on cogeneration, geothermal, and biomass. The two groups also differ on environmental protection, the former favoring a relaxation of laws and the latter urging more stringent environmental protection. (The public slightly favors the views of the business and industrial leadership.)

But the degree of agreement achieved since the mid-1970s is significant, and the views about which all segments have come to agree are more extensive than those held 8 or 10 years ago.

There is strong agreement by the public (68 percent) that the country is too dependent upon foreign oil, and the percentage of the public that blames the government for our failure to have a coherent energy policy has increased from plurality to majority status. Eighty percent of the public agree that the solution to the energy problem is one of developing alternative sources, and there is even stronger consensus on this point among leadership groups.

There is almost universal agreement among both the public and the leadership that solar energy must and will play an important role in the long-term future. In the short run, there is agreement, though less strong, that reduction of consumer waste is an important source of conservation, and that more efficient automobiles are a preferred mechanism of conservation. There is growing support among all groups for such conservation measures as improved home insulation and public education about the need for, and techniques of, conservation.

The change in American life that began in 1973 struck a country utterly unprepared. The sudden change in circumstances and expectations created by the energy crisis and the slowdown in the U.S. economy has made social adaptation both necessary and difficult. Social adaptation is an unfamiliar concept. In 1980, at a week-long Aspen Institute gathering of experts in the economics, regulation, and technology of energy, there emerged a series of policy recommendations on what would be, for the general public, arcane topics like import premiums, stationary oil-use backouts, and shortfall allocation systems. But the "final word" of the conference addressed the subject of *social* adaptation and consensus building. The conference report concluded,

> It may be that we simply cannot do the things suggested: gain long-term consumer acceptance for smaller and less powerful cars; develop a synthetic fuels industry that will change the environment and character of now-isolated regions; raise utility rates for current customers to save money for their children; or relieve our economy of decades of successive encrustations of regulation. . . .

It is not impossible to determine the economic and technical steps that are needed to deal with our energy problems. It is much harder to articulate these needs to the low-income pensioner struggling to pay fuel bills, to the worker who must commute long distances, or the rural Westerner whose way of life is threatened. But, if the energy problem cannot be explained to average Americans, it is unlikely they will support expert recommendations. Our ability to communicate, debate, and understand energy problems and the inherent clash of interests and values they precipitate may be at the heart of gaining consensus on what needs to be done. Resolution of these conflicts may be as critical to our energy future as economics and technology. It may, in fact, represent the ultimate challenge posed by the energy problem.[9]

It is about time that, as a society, we have gotten around to confronting this problem, and the challenge it contains.

NOTES

1. NBC/AP poll: Jan. 1980.
2. John E. Rielly, ed., *American Public Opinion and U.S. Foreign Policy* (Chicago: Chicago Council on Foreign Relations, 1979) p. 16.
3. General Election Studies, Institute for Social Research, University of Michigan, 1964-1978.
4. Ibid. Institute for Social Research, University of Michigan, 1958; and CBS/*New York Times* polls, 1980.
5. Gallup Poll Index, #199, 1982.
6. "Let's All Play Energy Policy," *Daedalus,* 109, (1980), 73.
7. See note 5 above concerning the erosion of defense-related attitudes. In March 1982, a 61 percent to 33 percent margin of the public agreed that "people like myself are bothered by how we are spending our defense dollar. . . . You don't get more national security by throwing money 'at the problem." (Yankelovich, Skelly & White Survey, *Time.*) Spring 1982.
8. *New York Times,* 14 Oct. 1980.
9. Aspen Institute for Humanistic Studies, "Options for Fueling America's Transportation," report of a workshop of the energy committee, (New York, 1980) pp. 44-45.

Chapter 3
ENERGY POLICY AND DEMOCRATIC THEORY

Richard E. Sclove

Energy policy is normally considered an economic issue, a matter of ensuring that safe and secure energy services are available at reasonable cost. But what if our energy policy choices were to undermine conditions necessary for a democratic society? Energy policy would then have to be reconceived as being of fundamental political concern.

This chapter represents an exploratory effort to interpret U.S. energy policy from the viewpoint of democratic theory. The conception of democracy I use has a number of attractive and compelling features, but is not usually regarded as bearing on technological practice. It is necessary, therefore, to show that democratic theory indeed erects constraints for the design and choice of technological systems, and then to apply the resulting general theory of democracy and technology to energy policy.[1]

The chapter has two principal parts. The first half is concerned with democratic procedure and concludes that the United States does not yet have an energy policy process that is consistent with a firm commitment to democracy. In the preceding decade some progress was made, but overall our national style of energy politics has shifted from being unduly technocratic in the 1970s to being unduly corporate-dominated today.

The chapter's second half moves beyond procedure to a discussion of the basic ideals and structure of a democracy, arguing that technological artifacts and systems can directly impair or strengthen the foundations of such a society. Regarding energy technology, this view predicts, in effect, that a more fully democratic process for determining energy policy would, in the interest of preserving democracy, reject nuclear power technologies. The grounds for this prediction can be analyzed and debated, but their ultimate test must await the creation of improved procedures for democratic discourse and choice.

DEMOCRATIC PROCEDURE

The first task is to establish a definition and standard of democracy in terms of which we can interpret the recent history of United States energy politics. Later I attempt to justify this conception of democracy and to extend it with respect to technology.

Fundamentally, a democracy is a society committed to the freedom and moral equality of its members. The institutions and laws—and, I shall argue, technologies—best suited to realizing these ideals vary from society to society and from era to era. Thus specific procedures, such as voting, that we normally associate with democracy, are indeed democratic only insofar as they do, in particular circumstances, advance democratic norms. If, for example, citizens elect a tyrant and ratify freedom-subverting laws, that outcome may properly be considered tragic rather than, on mere procedural grounds, democratic and therefore good.

In a democracy there will typically be legitimate roles for both direct participation and representative institutions, arranged in some complementary fashion. Representation is needed where limits on time, or other logistical difficulties, render universal participation impractical, or where direct participation promises less adequately to protect minorities' rights. But ideally, representative institutions should facilitate direct participation.

Direct citizen participation in political affairs helps to ensure that each person—s interests are taken into account in collective decisions. Participation can enable a person to feel free under law, because he or she has played a part in formulating, enacting, and interpreting the law. Moreover, through participation citizens can become aware of and develop their interests, while enhancing their self-esteem, knowledgeability, and political competence. Obviously, not everyone need participate in every decision that could conceivably affect him or her, but in a democracy the opportunity to do so ought to be available equally to all citizens.[2]

Policy analysts frequently imagine that there must be a trade-off between democracy and efficiency.[3] Is there not, for example, a risk that excessive meddling by politicians and citizens could jeopardize vital economic processes? This concern misconstrues both the meaning of efficiency and the nature of democracy.

An action is efficient if it accomplishes its end without unnecessary expenditure of scarce resources. But in a democracy social ends are not simply "given." They must be chosen through a legitimate democratic process, that is, through a process that effectively protects and advances the freedom and equality of all citizens. Thus rather than impairing efficiency, democracy is a precondition for legitimately specifying the ends with respect to which efficiency is defined.

The preceding considerations provide a rough standard with which we can review some of the highlights of U.S. energy policy as it developed during the 1970s: a democratic energy policy would be one resulting from a process that accords citizens an equal, and as extensive as possible, opportunity to participate knowledgeably and effectively in choosing policy ends and means, and that preserves these political conditions into the future.

A word about the structure of my argument. Since the ideal democratic society I postulate is unlikely ever to exist in its pure form, it may seem that my entire argument can be dismissed as irrelevant. Such dismissal is unwarranted. Analogous reasoning in 1850 might have found it futile to abolish slavery merely because the resulting society would still fall short of pure democracy. It is true that I establish a democratic ideal that is unlikely soon, if ever, to be fully realized, but my practical concern is with incremental steps toward the ideal, each resulting in a society preferable to its predecessor.

THE U.S. ENERGY POLICY PROCESS

One Step Forward

Throughout the 1960s and early 1970s the United States— *de facto* energy policy was to allow coal to be displaced by abundant, cheap oil and natural gas, while preparing to fuel ever-expanding economic growth via an ambitious, government-assisted nuclear energy program. Two developments (the emergence of an aggressive environmental movement in the late 1960s and the Organization of Petroleum Exporting Countries (OPEC) oil embargo of 1973-74) combined to thrust energy policy into political prominence , forcing traditional policy assumptions to be reexamined.

At the national level this process resulted in institutional reorganization that opened the energy policy process to many more political actors and groups. In two stages the government's unquestioned commitment to a predominantly nuclear energy future was broken.

In 1975 the Atomic Energy Commission was split into two independent agencies—the Nuclear Regulatory Commission (NRC) and the Energy Research and Development Administration (ERDA), which in turn was merged into the Department of Energy in 1978. ERDA was mandated to initiate a review of many long-neglected energy supply options. Then in 1977 the once omnipotent congressional Joint Committee on Atomic Energy was abolished, permitting new committees and more congressmen to play an active role in determining energy policy. The resulting legislative harvest from 1975 to 1980 included laws intended to promote energy conservation, solar energy and synthetic fuels development, cleaner combustion of coal, and gradual decontrol of oil and natural gas prices. An effort was also made to inhibit the international proliferation of nuclear weapons by placing restrictions on the export of certain dangerous nuclear power technologies.[4]

During this period increasing numbers of citizens began to educate themselves, and many tried to affect energy policy at both national and local levels. Some simply insulated their homes; others picketed proposed power plants or attempted to influence government and corporate decisions by working through environmental and consumer advocacy groups, as well as older, established organizations such as labor unions, the League of Women Voters, the National Association for the Advancement of Colored People, and the National Council of Churches. Citizen participation in energy policy was facilitated by procedural reforms embodied in legislation such as the Freedom of Information Act and the National Environmental Policy Act.[5]

In 1976 a young physicist named Amory Lovins achieved startling success in promoting the idea that the nation faced a critical choice between two mutually exclusive energy policy options. According to Lovins, a "hard energy path," relying on large-scale energy supply technologies such as coal- and nuclear-fired electric power plants, threatened unnecessarily to deplete nonrenewable resources, degrade the environment, jeopardize lives, eliminate jobs, squander capital, disrupt communities, and subject us all to rule by "elitist technocracy." In contrast, a "soft energy path" could be chosen that would use small-scale solar technologies, improvements in the efficiency of energy use, and limited quantities of fossil fuel to avoid each of these pitfalls, while promoting cultural diversity, thrift, self-reliance, and democracy. At first politely ignored by orthodox energy analysts and industry representatives, Lovins soon became an acknowledged political force, meeting with Canadian Prime Minister Pierre Trudeau, former Swedish Prime Minister Olof Palme, and U.S. President Jimmy Carter.[6]

Although one can take issue with various aspects of Lovins' argument, the ensuing public discussion was socially beneficial. While critics argued that he had presented an over-dichotomized choice between hard and soft energy paths, Lovins succeeded in articulating and legitimating a broader agenda for political discourse and decision about energy than had previously existed. Moreover, he brought to public attention the important idea that the design and selection of technological systems may embody critical social and political choices. For example, the choice between neighborhood-scale solar energy systems and a large-scale electric power plant involves more than deciding between competing sets of economic and environmental costs. It may also influence strongly the style and content of social interaction within neighborhoods. While the noneconomic values and social choices embedded in technological designs may not always be those that Lovins supposes, and the virtues of the values he espouses may be debated, heightened popular awareness of the idea that technological choices have political content is a precondition for informed democratic choice.[7]

In the 1970s energy decison making thus became more democratic. Legislative reform generated increased opportunities for citizen participation; the congressional committee structure was made more responsive to diverse social groups; and energy conservation and solar technologies were legitimated as potentially significant contributors to our energy future, permitting the articulation of a more extensive agenda for political debate.

There were also several less satisfactory dimensions to this history. First, while opportunities for citizen participation in the determination of policy increased, these opportunites were not available equally to all persons and groups. Those most active and influential appeared to be elite members of relatively privileged social groups.[8] This is easy to explain: there are great disparities among Americans in wealth, discretionary time, and information—resources needed for effective participation in politics.[9] Participation by a plurality of competing elites is preferable to participation restricted to members of a single monolithic elite, but neither form of participation is fully democratic.

Second, the sudden jump in petroleum prices in 1973-74 and again in 1978-79 created windfall profits for multinational oil companies, enabling them to diversify their investments into all types of energy supply systems. This concentration of political and economic power in the hands of a small number of corporations is troubling from the standpoint of democratic legitimacy.[10] Aside from permitting abuses of power that extend beyond the domain of energy policy, there is a risk that investment in energy technology research, development, and deployment will fail to match Americans' preferences.[11]

Third, continuing a trend prominent since World War II, expert technical advisors in the 1970s played an important role in shaping and legitimating government energy policy decisions. Because it is widespread and yet poorly understood, this practice warrants an extended analysis. I discuss two examples.

The first concerns the Nuclear Regulatory Commissions's use of a theoretical study of nuclear reactor safety, the so-called Rasmussen report (also known as the Reactor Safety Study, RSS, WASH-1400, and NUREG-75/014), to help secure congressional renewal of the Price-Anderson Act in 1975.[12] The Price-Anderson Act subsidizes nuclear power by setting an upper limit on electric utilities' financial liability to the public should a reactor suffer a catastrophic accident.[13]

As the act gradually worked its way through the congressional committee system in 1974-75, the Commission first briefed members of Congress on a draft of the Rasmussen report without disclosing substantive technical criticism by members of a Commission-appointed internal review team, rushed completion of the report to coincide with congressional schedules, and then presented the final report to the Congress without mentioning that copies had not been provided to independent scientists who had asked repeatedly to see them. Three years later the Commission felt compelled to withdraw its endorsement of the report, citing numerous technical shortcomings.[14]

A second example of the role of technical reports and experts in energy politics is provided by the 1977 report of an independent study group sponsored by the Ford Foundation: *Nuclear Power Issues and Choices* (also known as the Ford-MITRE report, the Report of the Nuclear Energy Policy Study Group, or NEPS).[15] Initiated at a time of intense national debate concerning nuclear energy, the report concluded that while commercial nuclear reactors of the type now in use (light water reactors) do not pose an unacceptable threat to the environment or to public health and safety, there were strong grounds for postponing any decision to introduce a "plutonium economy." A highly toxic radioactive by-product of the operation of nuclear reactors, plutonium can be recycled and used either as fuel in nuclear power reactors or in the manufacture of nuclear weapons. A plutonium economy would involve removing plutonium from the waste fuel rods discharged annually by reactors and reusing it in light water reactors or in a proposed advanced reactor, called a breeder reactor. The report opposed near-term commercial introduction of plutonium recycling or of breeder reactors, largely because of fears of clandestine diversion of plutonium by other nations or by terrorist groups for use in making atomic bombs.

The Ford-MITRE study's 21 authors were prominent scientists, economists, and political scientists who had not previously adopted strong public positions regarding the social acceptablity of commercial nuclear energy. Their report immediately became influential, in part because two of its authors had advised Jimmy Carter during his 1976 presidential campaign, while several others subsequently assumed important positions within the administration (including, for example, Secretary of Defense Harold Brown).

The day the panel's report was released, members gave a national press conference, talked with President Carter at a meeting arranged through his science advisor, and briefed congressional staff members at the Capitol. The *New York Times* reported that:

> Partly because the Ford Foundation panel included two top members of the Administration and partly because of previous comments of President Carter, the report's recommendations were widely seen as previewing what will probably be the Administration's own final position on nuclear power.[16]

The next day the President handed a copy of the report to visiting Japanese Prime Minister Takeo Fukuda, and within two weeks Carter announced a nuclear energy policy that reflected the report's principal recommendations.[17]

The Ford-MITRE study is clear, informative and relatively well reasoned. Nonetheless, it exhibits a number of arbitrary analytic and normative judgments. I give three examples.

First, the report's conclusion that, of the many risks associated with nuclear energy, the most serious are those concerning nuclear weapons proliferation and a plutonium economy is certainly defensible, but does not follow straightforwardly from uncontroversial premises. It does, however, reflect prior concerns of the study's authors. In seeking authoritative experts who had not previously established fixed positions concerning commercial nuclear power, the Ford Foundation had turned to the community of defense and arms control analysts. Nineteen of the report's 21 authors had prior professional experience in these areas. It can hardly be regarded as surprising that a group of experts, whose shared professional interest was in trying to prevent nuclear war, concluded that the single most troublesome feature of commercial nuclear reactors is that they produce material that can be used to manufacture nuclear weapons. In effect, the Ford Foundation had determined the report's general conclusions when it selected the study group's members.

Second, the report judged the risks of catastrophic nuclear power plant accidents (known as core meltdowns or China syndromes) to be socially acceptable by comparing an estimate of these risks with the deaths caused by coal-fired electric power plants and hurricanes. Because the actual risk of a core meltdown accident is not known, the argumentative strategy adopted was to use an extremely high upperbound estimate of nuclear power risks, and then show that this inflated figure was still within the bounds of known risks, from coal plants and hurricanes, that U.S. citizens routinely accept.

That was the *ostensible* strategy. However, in undertaking this comparison, the Ford Foundation report lapsed into inconsistencies and arbitrary judgments: (a) In selecting what it claimed was an "upper-limit" numerical estimate of the probability of occurrence of a core meltdown accident, the study arbitrarily omitted the possibility of sabotage as an accident initiating event—even though sabotage is discussed elsewhere in the report.[18] This omission biases the argument in favor of nuclear power, because coal plants are not vulnerable to sabotage-induced catastrophic failure. (b) The report failed to acknowledge that the uncertainty in its estimate of the other terms used in its calculation is so great that the numerical values chosen are, contrary to claim, not plausible upper bounds.[19] (c) The report was unable to establish a consistent, qualitative standard of comparison of nuclear energy risks with other risks. Specifically, in comparing nuclear- with coal-induced fatalities, the study did not explicitly mention that, in general, people are more concerned when many deaths occur at once (as would happen following a major nuclear accident) than when the same number of deaths occur one-by-one over many years (as is the case with most coal-induced fatalities). The study did implicitly indicate an awareness of this issue in choosing also to compare nuclear risks with the deaths caused by hurricanes. However, that comparison is problematic insofar as people are generally more concerned when deaths are caused through human agency (e.g., a technology-related catastrophe) than through what is perceived as a natural occurrence (hurricanes).

It is not surprising that the report had trouble developing a consistent basis for risk comparisons. In fact, no simple quantitative comparison of nuclear power risks with others can be justified, because nuclear power risks are *qualitatively* unique, and, therefore, *quantitatively* incommensurate with others. In making these criticisms I do not intend to express any personal judgment concerning the magnitude or acceptability of nuclear power risks; I wish merely to observe that the Ford-MITRE study's arguments are not unimpeachable.

Finally, a third arbitrary element in the report is its adoption of a purely instrumental perspective toward technology, a limitation shared by most policy analyses. Recently scholars from many disciplines outside the natural sciences and economics have noted that technological artifacts—and styles of technological design and performance—constitute complex systems of personal and shared meaning.[20] As such, technologies play an essential role in the maintenance and production of culture. To nuclear opponents, for example, nuclear power plants have come variously to symbolize annihilation, the rape of nature, technology out of control, big business/big government conspiracy, oppression, and even fascism. Nuclear advocates associate nuclear power with such themes as progress, economic growth, affluence, rationality, mastery over nature, and international cooperation, peace, and justice. These symbolic attributions are as prevalent among scientists and policy anaylsts as among laypeople.[21] Thus among the real human consequences that will attend any political decision are the loss or affirmation of meaning, purpose, and value. A fundamental inability to take account of these symbolic and semantic dimensions of sociotechnological dispute subverts the aspiration of rational policy analysis to consider comprehensively all impacts of proposed actions.

I have not criticized the Ford-MITRE study because I think it is a poor piece of work. On the contrary, overall it provides a model of clear and cogent reasoning. My point is that rational policy analysis—whether it goes by the name policy study, decision analysis, operations research, cost-benefit analysis, technology assessment, risk assessment, planning, or systems analysis—unavoidably reflects subjective judgments. These occur, for example, in choosing which issues to address; in the precise manner in which the issues chosen are defined, bounded, and formulated; in selecting and justifying evaluative criteria; in choosing and interpreting factual evidence; in the manner of rendering judgments where evidence is absent or uncertain; and in deciding how to interpret the symbolic (as opposed to purely instrumental) dimensions of sociotechnological practice.[22]

Subjective judgments need not be regarded as arbitrary if they are identified, if reasons are advanced in their favor, and if they have withstood strong counterarguments.[23] Whether arbitrary or not, the existence of these subjective dimensions means that expert policy advice must always be regarded as knowledge that is socially contingent rather than simply reality determined.[24] Objectivity remains important as an ideal toward which to aspire, but it can never fully be realized in practice. Because expert counsel unavoidably embodies subjective elements, both the content and process of expert advising must be interpreted and evaluated critically. Political decisions should reflect the objective and (legitimate) subjective judgments of all types of citizens and of their legitimate representatives, and not, merely or disproportionately, the subjective judgments of experts.

How then are we to interpret the significance of the privileged political role in policy formulation that is played by technical experts such as the authors of the Rasmussen report and the Ford-MITRE study?

From Plato's philosopher-kings to Thorsten Veblen's faith in the rationality of the engineers has emerged the idea of benign technocracy—rule by an efficient, politically neutral, technically trained elite.[25] Some would say that technocrats already rule in the United States. That is not the case. Rather, technical experts share power with other elites, but in so doing they occupy a distinctive niche within the political division of labor. By participating in politics *as* experts, technocrats contribute to the propagation of a false idea that the issues at stake in sociotechnological controversy are predominantly or exclusively technical and objectively decidable rather than political. The consequences of this misrepresentation are several: (a) citizens and their representatives are misled about their interests in such disputes; (b) the need for public, reasoned normative discourse in conjunction with sociotechnological disputes tends to go unrecognized and unfulfilled; (c) technical discourse becomes distorted as it becomes a medium for the tacit negotiation of social objectives, meanings, and power relationships; and (d) illegitimate financial, and knowledge- and credential-based barriers to participation in political discourse are erected as experts (or those persons and institutions that can afford to hire experts to represent them) become able to exert disproportionate influence on sociotechnological decisions.[26]

It is not even correct to argue that democratic discourse should establish ends, whereas experts may neutrally determine means to those ends. Means are not value neutral. They embody subordinate, unintended, and "unrecognized" ends, and, thus, have a habit of subverting the ends with respect to which they were (ostensibly) chosen.[27]

Nor can it be argued that because technocrats are not a monolithic group, but rather exhibit diverse, pluralistic, and conflicting personal values, they can as a group legitimately represent citizens. Experts' similar social backgrounds, self-selection in career choices, socialization as they become experts, and tendency to acquire specialized competence at the expense of integrative knowledge and experience, render them statistically unrepresentative, in values and outlook, of the larger citizenry.[28]

Moreover, technical advisors function imperfectly as representatives because their accountability to citizens is so attenuated that it is practically nonexistent. For example, in the United States formal accountability—if it can be called that—of the technical advisor to a mid-level government administrator occurs only through that administrator, and then only if (a) the administrator violates a procedural law that is subject to judicial review with public participation or (b) the administrator is called to account by a superior, who is in turn accountable to a congressional committee, whose members periodically stand for reelection.

Finally, as noted above, the public participation of technical experts in politics tends to mask political issues as technical ones, consequently to restrict citizens' and their representatives' ability to form an accurate conception of their own and others' interests, and to erect other obstacles to fair and effective citizen participation and representation. These ill effects could be lessened or eliminated if the ways in which expert advice reflects subjective judgments were universally acknowledged. But the myth of objective technical advice is not easily dispelled, because experts who enjoy political power, politicians and businesspersons who enjoy using experts to legitimate policy, and corporations and other powerful actors whose power would be diluted were there broader citizen participation, all share an interest in this myth and a substantial ability to maintain and propagate it.

Thus while some progress was made in the 1970s toward establishing a more democratic energy policy process, that progress was marred by the fact that the new opportunities to participate in energy politics were not available equally to all citizens; by the large and expanding political and economic power of multinational energy corporations; and by the distortion of democratic discourse resulting from the over-extended and misrepresented participation of technical experts in the formulation and legitimation of policy.

A Step Backwards

Recently, some of the salutary trends toward democratization in energy politics that evolved during the 1970s have been halted or even reversed. The proximate cause was the 1980 election, but its historical roots include the changing nature of international political-economic relations. The perceived decline in American economic productivity, the flight of U.S. capital to other nations, and the adverse trend in the U.S. balance of trade have all contributed to an attack on "big government"—and particularly on government regulation of business—that has been translated into diminished opportunities for egalitarian public participation in politics.[29]

With respect to energy policy the Reagan style was partially foreshadowed by President Carter's proposal in 1979 to create an Energy Mobilization Board. Responding to, or perhaps attempting to capitalize on, the Iranian revolution and the subsequent decline in world oil production, Carter sought to create a three-member board with the authority to expedite the issuance of national, state, and local permits required for the construction of new energy production facilities.[30] In effect, the board would have been authorized to hasten or even bypass government hearings that provide a forum for citizen participation in energy decision making. Congress responded favorably, but the proposal foundered when the House and Senate were unable to reach a compromise on legislative wording.

President Reagan has taken a number of steps that directly and indirectly affect opportunities for citizen participation in energy policy formulation. By adopting changes in income tax and regulatory policy that are more favorable to the rich than the poor, while contracting social welfare programs, the administration and Congress have exacerbated the disparity in the social distribution of those resources that are needed for fair and effective participation in politics.[31] The president has furthermore diminished opportunities for citizens to monitor government activities, and, therefore, to hold their elected and appointed representatives accountable, by weakening the Freedom of Information Act and by tightening the rules governing the classification of secret government information.[32] These changed rules are probably most threatening with respect to the possibility of assessing domestic and international "intelligence" activities and military policy, but energy policy, too, is affected. For example, only through the Freedom of Information Act was it possible to learn that the Atomic Energy Commission (the Nuclear

Regulatory Commission's predecessor) was aware of technical defects in the Rasmussen report at the time that it published a draft of the study and used its results for political purposes.[33]

Regarding energy policy, the Reagan administration has behaved in a manner that might at first seem an improvement: the administration has made relatively little use of technical experts in either the legitimation or formulation of its energy policies. But instead of replacing technocratic advisors with institutions designed to facilitate reasoned political discourse, democratic citizen participation, and fair representation, the president has appealed to the "genius" of decentralized decision making through the free market.

Unfortunately, the administration's free-market ideology has no reasonable bearing on the energy industry, where innumerable and (for the most part) unremovable market imperfections together constitute a gross deviation from the necessary conditions for a genuine competitive free market.[34] Among these imperfections are pervasive health, safety, environmental, political, and social externalities[35] associated with each form of energy supply; OPEC's ability to manipulate petroleum supplies and prices; oligopoly in many energy industries and in regional energy markets; natural monopolies in the electric utility and natural gas industries; unequal and imperfect information on the part of residential energy consumers and suppliers; and the well-known tendency of private firms to underinvest in technological research and development for fear that other firms will duplicate and capture most of the economic benefits resulting from any innovation.[36] In effect, uncritical reliance on the decentralized "genius" of the market assures suboptimal social results, while tending to shift economic and political decision making power into the hands of large corporations and wealthy individuals, at the expense of other citizens.[37]

Moreover, in its actual policy the administration has deviated from its professed adherence to a free-market philosophy in a manner that further concentrates power in the hands of large corporations. Specifically, while gutting government support for solar energy and energy conservation, the administration has continued heavy subsidization of the commercialization of nuclear power and synthetic fuels technology.[38] Such subsidization favors two technologies that (owing to barriers to market entry and economies of scale in production) are most likely to be produced by large corporations, while it disadvantages solar and energy conservation technologies that could be produced on a competitive basis by smaller firms.

I have not argued that democracy entails the abolition of markets. Markets are social contrivances and institutions.[39] Through the use of tax or price incentives, markets may sometimes be preferable as policy instruments to direct, continuous regulation of individual and corporate behavior,[40] but only if their performance is evaluated and guided by a democratic political process. That evaluation cannot be solely in terms of aggregate macroeconomic indicators such as inflation, unemployment, or gross national product, for statistical indicators do not adequately reflect the complex concerns and rich texture of our private and collective lives.

Democratic political monitoring of the economy must extend to holistic interpretation and evaluation of the concrete collective consequences of individual, group,
firm, and state behavior. In other words, to an interpretation of the extent to which
the individual choices we make are in the aggregate consistent with the shared ends
for the protection and advancement of which we live in a democratic society.[41]

We can now complete the interpretation of the interrelated social roles of
technocrats and markets in the U.S. energy policy process. Benign technocracy—
the myth of planning, macroeconomic steering, or policy analysis and implementation, by a value neutral technical elite—subverts democracy in diverse ways.
Self-regulating competitive markets neither do nor can exist,[42] and in practice
President Reagan's "free-market" philosophy merely enhances the political and
economic power of large corporations and wealthy individuals. Together, the
competing myths (and allied social practices, structures, and constituencies) of
benign technocracy and of self-regulating markets constitute a powerful, self-
perpetuating ideological system that diverts public attention and political energy
from the possiblity of establishing a nonideological system of belief, social
organization, and sovereignty.[43] The alternative, a more fully developed democracy, would be politically legitimate in virtue of being able to win our informed,
reasoned, and rational allegiance.

To this point I have not treated energy policy as though it were much different
from other types of public policy. If anything, one might think, energy policy is
distinctive only in being highly technical and inextricably linked to health, safety,
environmental, macroeconomic, industrial, military, and foreign policies—and
for these reasons unusually complex. If democracy needs revitalization, would it
not be better to start with simpler and, with respect to democratization, perhaps
more important problems?

No. For reasons discussed below, democratization is especially important with
respect to complex sociotechnological policy areas such as energy.

DEMOCRACY AND TECHNOLOGY

Technology as Law

What is a technological system? There is no definitive answer, but one general
property of technological artifacts and systems is that they are polyvalent in
function. That is, each tends to perform an indefinitely large number of social
functions beyond its designed intent. For example, light water reactors are routinely associated with the production of warm rivers, population exclusion zones,
radioactive waste, weapons-useable plutonium, fear of catastrophic accidents,
reduced emission of fossil fuel combustion products, well-paid construction jobs,
export earnings, the need for a centralized federal regulatory apparatus, presidential investigatory commissions, international negotiations, grassroots political
activism, mistrust of authority, and so on. They also produce electricity. Reactors
are thus polyvalent in function.

Technological systems, especially once a group of people has become dependent on them, may prevent or promote certain forms of social relations and activities. Hence it is not unusual to discover that technologies ostensibly designed for such mundane tasks as transportation, primary production, or manufacturing also constitute social systems of cooperation, isolation, or domination.[44] For this reason, scholars of sociotechnological practice have come to regard technological artifacts and systems as being, among other things, analogous in their social function to political laws.[45] That is, both laws and technological systems are social artifices that restructure and redistribute social opportunties and constraints. As do laws, technological systems condition the forms of social relations that can exist now and in the future. Thus both laws and technologies have the potential to condition the possibility of democracy itself.

A brief detour through normative political theory can help us interpret the significance of this functional analogy between technology and law, in the process clarifying and attempting to justify the conception of democracy on which I have been relying. I have tended to use the terms *freedom, equality, respect,* and *dignity* loosely, as though their meaning and appeal were self-evident and independent of one another. It might also appear that I think *democracy* is good merely because by tradition we think it is. But each of the preceding italicized concepts can be shown to relate logically to the others. The central concept is freedom, and there are sound reasons, apart from tradition, to think that we ought to live in a democracy. Here I can give only a quick paraphrase of an argument that is rooted in the philosophy of Rousseau and Kant.[46] (I do not cite these philosophers as authorities—that is, persons to be believed because they are famous or dead. Rather, I refer to specific arguments they made that seem plausible.)

Kant believed that freedom is a supreme good, that is, good for its own sake and not merely because it is instrumentally useful in securing other goods. Kant argued that in order to be free (that is, to be autonomous, self-determining with respect to ends, and self-actualizing with respect to talents and capacities), it is necessary to act on the basis of something, he called it a principle of pure reason, other than mere psychological inclination. A necessary condition for freedom is to obey a moral rule that we prescribe to ourselves. To do otherwise is to be a mere instrument of our own passions or of someone else's will. Acting morally thus expresses and realizes our freedom in ways that cannot be expressed when we do not behave morally, even when we choose among our own competing psychological inclinations and passions. Only as free beings do we become more than mere instruments. We become ends-in-ourselves: beings endowed with dignity.

What are the principles of reason (the principles that we obey for their own sake because they are correct) that we should prescribe to ourselves? Kant argued that there is only one such principle, and it is the same for all beings with a capacity to reason. He called it the categorical imperative—essentially an extension and formal restatement of the Golden Rule. In Kant's reformulation: "Act only according to that maxim by which you can at the same time will that it should become a universal law."[47]

Loosely translated: do unto others as you would have them do unto you. Among other things, treat others with the equal respect that you wish they would accord you and your interests, including your highest order interest in freedom.[48] In short, in the Kantian system morality, freedom, equality, respect, and dignity are all logically related.

Rousseau recognized that to fully develop and realize our freedom—to live the extended and formalized Golden Rule—we must live socially. And a necessary condition for living socially, without sacrificing our freedom, is to live according to principles of social cooperation, laws, that collectively we prescribe to ourselves and that reflect our common interests, particularly our highest order interest in preserving our freedom and equality.[49] For laws that compromise our shared interests or that are imposed on us without our consent or participation constrain rather than realize our freedom. That is the essence of Rousseau's argument for direct democracy. In short, it is only through living together socially in a democracy that we realize our capacity as free beings.

If we accept the argument of Kant and Rousseau, then we have sound reasons, apart from tradition, for aspiring to live in a democratic society. Democracy (meaning a society of autonomous, morally and politically equal, self-legislating, and self-governing persons) is the political form that can best realize human freedom.[50]

Freedom consists in prescribing laws to ourselves. Technology functions socially in a manner analogous to law. It follows that we are unfree unless we "prescribe" technology to ourselves. We must democratize technological policy processes not merely because in a democracy all policy processes should be democratized, but also because technological artifacts and systems that we design and deploy today condition the possibility of democratic practice in the future— just as the technological systems that we have inherited from the past are conditioning the possibility of democratic practice today.

Technology as Symbol and as Ideology

There are further reasons to democratize technology policy processes. As noted above, one general property of technological systems is that they are polyvalent *in function*. A second general property is that they are polyvalent *in meaning*. That is, technological artifacts unavoidably acquire and bear a host of private and social meanings. Similarly, styles of technological design and performance constitute elaborate systems of nonverbal communication.[51] In short, technologies play a constitutive role in the maintenance and production of culture.

Americans, for example, tend to have deep seated feeling about automobiles. We understand that cars are variously symbols of personal autonomy, control, social status, sexual drive, progress—and more recently of suburban sprawl, urban alienation, and economic decline.[52] Not without reason has the automobile often been used as the governing metaphor to describe American life.

For democratic practice, recognition of the cultural dimensions of technology has important implications: First, a democratic society must, in order to respect the equal worth of its citizens, strive within reason to ensure that the opportunity to participate effectively in the maintenance and production of culture—to discover and create shared meaning, purpose, and value—is available equally to all. Insofar as technological choices have direct and decisive cultural consequences, they should be made democratically.

Second, elaborating on the preceding point, technologies sometimes embody ideals or threaten objects that people hold sacred. For example, in industrialized nations the nuclear power controversy has for committed activists on all sides assumed the status of a Holy War. Similarly, in many siting disputes that plague large-scale energy projects the opponents of the proposed facility (be they conservative farmers fighting a powerline in Minnesota or Native Americans opposing uranium mining in the Black Hills) are protecting land they regard as sacred from technological violation.[53]

In a democracy when noninstrumental values and meanings conflict, conflict resolution procedures must accord equal weight to each person's beliefs, at least until a legitimate democratic process establishes that one or another group's beliefs and practices jeopardize the ends and means of democracy itself. This is essential because we are dealing here with what Kant called the realm of ends, what anthropologists call the sacred sphere of exchange. As Kant observed:

> In the realm of ends everything has either a *price* or *dignity*. Whatever has a price can be replaced by something else as its equivalent; on the other hand, whatever is above all price, and therefore admits of no equivalent, has a dignity.[54]

It is a realm in which persons and things are regarded as ends-in-themselves, beyond the instrumental purposes they may also serve. Procedures that treat persons or sacred objects as "things" to which a price can be imputed jeopardize or annihilate their supreme value, their dignity.[55] This is perhaps what is most wrong with (a) power plant siting and safety hearings that require participants to justify their claims exclusively in terms of instrumental reasons and values, (b) with insensitive monetary compensation schemes for lost life or limb, (c) with state-sanctioned appropriation of land and resources, and (d) with attempts to measure environmental (and other external) costs and benefits based on consumers' willingness to pay.[56] In each case the procedure fails to respect the dignity of persons and their rational interest in striving to preserve that which is sacred to them.

The symbolic dimensions of technological practice provide a third reason for democratization. Democracy is possible only if citizens can acquire evidence and theory needed to make informed judgments. A severe threat to the possibility of democracy is ideology, by which I mean the prevalence of distorted, interest-serving beliefs that systematically misrepresent social reality, particularly by concealing injustice.

Considered as systems or modes of nonverbal communication, technologies have the potential to propagate ideological beliefs. For instance, the technical organization of work in industrial societies, especially the maintenance of sharp separation between those engaged in innovative research and design and those employed in routine production, seems subconsciously to convey to all concerned a notion that the particular technologies we have are technically necessary. That is, contemporary technological practice is so organized that we tend unquestioningly to believe (roughly) that: (a) science is true; (b) technology is a natural by-product of science; and (c) therefore the technological designs and systems we have at present are natural, inevitable, and could not rationally have been otherwise. In a democracy each of these ideas, communicated in part through our very style of technological practice, would have to be subjected to critical, reasoned democratic appraisal, for together they help curtail a collective search for technologies that might better facilitate the realization of democratic ideals.

Democratizing technological design and policy processes would not entail that each time we wished, for example, to buy a fork or sell a pencil sharpener, we would first have to appear before a citizen tribunal or committee of Congress. Not all technological artifacts and systems significantly legislate, embody, or threaten sacred value, help to propagate ideological beliefs, or otherwise condition the possibility of democratic practice. But in a democratic society anyone who believes that a particular technology, set of technologies, or technological system does activate one of the preceding threshold criteria, must have a fair and effective opportunity to make that case in an appropriate political forum.

Technological Somnambulism[57]

There is a final reason to democratize technological design and policy processes: the preceding reasons are not widely understood. We tend to think of technology as know-how or instrumental reason, as what engineers do, as an economic factor of production, or as machinery. Nothing in our upbringing, education, or working lives encourages us to see that technologies (aside from everything else they do and are) function as legislation and are constitutive of culture.

Our habit of technological somnambulism is constituted and reinforced by a system of competing and contradictory ideologies: "technological neutrality" and "autonomous technology"[58] (which correspond rather closely to, respectively, the myths of neutral expertise and of self-regulating markets that help block democracy throughout the society). These are ideological beliefs *about* technology; they are not necessarily communicated primarily *through* technical practice. As with the ideological system of free markets and benign technocracy, in attacking each other the competing ideologies (and allied social structures) of technological neutrality and technological autonomy preserve each other by distracting attention from the possibility of adopting a more realistic, discerning, and self-aware conception of technology.

Autonomous technology is the view that technological change is a self-governing and inexorable process. It is as though something called The Machine or Technology had acquired a life and momentum of its own that is beyond human ken or control.[59] In reality technological change has no life, no purpose or direction, of its own; it merely appears that it does because societal myths, such as that of the Invisible Hand, have led us to assume that technological change would automatically serve the public interest.[60] As a result, until recently there has been almost no public attention paid to the technological design process, or to the cumulative social effects associated with the introduction of new technologies. In short, if technological change is in any sense out of control, it is not because it is genuinely an autonomous or inevitable process. Rather, we have allowed arbitrary market forces, private firms, and quasiautonomous government bureaucracies to determine our choices for us.

Technological neutrality, in contradistinction to autonomous technology, is the dogmatic belief that technological artifacts and systems are neither intrinsically good nor evil; they are morally, politically, and socially neutral.[61] Each can be used either for good or evil.

This idea, reasonable at first glance, is ultimately inadequate because it attempts to collapse the unbounded polyvalency[62] of technological phenomena onto a single, homogeneous linear metric with something called Good at one end, Evil at the other, and Neutrality at the zero point between. If we recall the analogy between technology and law, the inadequacy becomes obvious: no one claims that laws are neutral. The qualitative richness of technological phenomena cannot be reduced to a linear metric—much less to an absolute, propertyless neutral point.[63]

In the past 15 years sociotechnological controversies,[64] and an emergent interest in "alternative" and "appropriate" technologies,[65] have constituted a slight antidote to our technological narcolepsy. Still, public discourse and decisions regarding technology are cast largely in the restrictive concepts of economics, engineering, and the natural sciences. In the technological realm we have hardly begun to cultivate or institutionalize the necessary art of political, cultural, and moral discourse. Thus a final reason for placing the democratization of technological design and policy processes high on any general agenda for democratizing society is that we tend to be less aware here than in other policy areas of what is at stake.

ENERGY TECHNOLOGY FOR A FREE SOCIETY

The preceding arguments concern technological systems in general. It remains to be seen how these concerns apply to energy technology . As a starting point I shall consider Amory Lovins' claim that:

Soft technologies are not intended to solve all the political problems that have plagued our nascent democracies for millenia. Their aim, and mine, is rather more modest. They do enable us to avoid the high political costs (centrism, autarchy, technocracy, vulnerability) of a hard energy path—if we let them work by pluralistic personal choices, through ordinary market and social processes, rather than mistakenly imposing on them the coercive central-management style that hard technologies require. Thus soft technologies permit, but do not entail, a free and equitable society. The choice is ours.[66]

My discussion will be selective and not fully conclusive, for such issues are not logically separable from criticism, choice, and evaluation in terms of particular social norms. Legitimate answers can ultimately only be determined through democratic discourse and action. My basic concern is to consider whether certain energy technologies are strictly inconsistent with, or in some sense conducive to, democracy. I will not directly ask whether these technologies are economically competitive, unacceptably hazardous to human health and safety, environmentally destructive, or aesthetically pleasing. The latter questions have been much discussed elsewhere,[67] and the former question—which I believe reflects our highest-order shared interest—has been least discussed.

To begin the discussion of Lovins' claim, I do not believe that "personal choices, through ordinary market and social processes" will result in an acceptable or legitimate political outcome, because existing "ordinary market and social processes" are not sufficiently democratic. If our present decision processes are relied upon, it will be purely fortuitous if the resulting technologies do not reflect in their design a contingent constraint against the possibility of democratic practice in the future.

While Lovins opposes all so-called hard technologies, he is most opposed to nuclear power. A central question, then, is whether nuclear power constitutes a necessary or contingent constraint, or neither, on the possibility of realizing a democratic society. Among many possible subquestions, I consider the potential threats to democracy associated with: (1) the introduction of a plutonium economy, (2) the risk of nuclear reactor sabotage, (3) the complexity of nuclear energy technology, (4) the symbolic dimensions of the nuclear controversy, and (5) the centralized management and regulation, and the large scale, of nuclear energy systems.

(1) Introduction of plutonium recycling in existing (light water) reactors, and the use of breeder reactors, would provide an opportunity for criminals, terrorists, or agents of foreign governments to attempt to steal plutonium for use in the fabrication of nuclear weapons. If theft of plutonium were detected or suspected, the need to retrieve it would be so great that there would be tremendous temptation to violate the civil liberties of U.S. citizens. This threat has been carefully discussed elsewhere.[68]

President Carter deferred the decision on whether to introduce a plutonium economy. President Reagan and the Congress favor licensing a commercial plutonium reprocessing plant and a demonstration commercial breeder reactor. In my view the potential irreversible threat to civil liberties is so grave that every possible step, consistent with democratic practice, should be taken to prevent the commercial use of plutonium worldwide. At a minimum, it seems unconscionable and short-sighted to proceed until citizens have had ample opportunity thoroughly to discuss and understand the significance of the issue.[69]

(2) It is impossible for me, or for any other citizen who does not have the appropriate security clearance, to assess the adequacy of the procedures in force at reactors to protect them against terrorist attack or internal plant sabotage. "Successful" sabotage could kill thousands or (including delayed cancer fatalities) tens of thousands of persons, while seriously injuring hundreds of thousands.[70] The adequacy of the design and implementation of sabotage prevention measures *must* be kept secret to help prevent potential saboteurs and terrorists from determining the "best" way to try to overcome those procedures. Yet keeping them secret means that citizens can neither develop an informed opinion of their own and others' interests vis-à-vis nuclear energy nor competently monitor the performance of their representatives, which directly contradicts a necessary condition for democracy. Therefore, it is my belief that nuclear plants are contingently undemocratic. (They are only contingently, and not necessarily, undemocratic because they could conceivably be democratic if they were deployed in a world in which there were not, and never could be, any terrorists or saboteurs.)

Moreover, imagine, as could certainly occur, that I or another citizen were to think of reasons why nuclear plants are more vulnerable to sabotage than is commonly supposed. Publicizing those reasons could increase the risk of sabotage and would, therefore, probably be immoral. Yet not publicizing them would deprive citizens of information needed to decide whether building and operating nuclear energy systems is in our communities' interest. That this situation could arise—perhaps, in fact, it has already arisen—means that nuclear power has the potential to restrict ordinary citizens' freedom of communication, further impairing a necessary condition for democracy.

(3) It is sometimes argued that nuclear energy systems are so complex that ordinary citizens cannot understand them and, therefore, cannot rationally decide whether or not it is in their interest to permit the use of nuclear power. This has been advanced as another reason for judging nuclear energy systems to be undemocratic.

I do not find this a persuasive reason. "Complexity" is largely in the eye of the beholder. I am not persuaded that nuclear energy systems are intrinsically more "complex" than are the day-to-day problems that confront many citizens (although admittedly a mistaken judgment with respect to nuclear energy could have unusually large adverse social consequences).

More importantly, I have no reason to believe that "ordinary" persons are intrinsically less capable of making sound political judgments than are the persons who make such arguments or other experts who dominate the public nuclear debate. Nuclear power does not seem at fault for being too complex to understand; rather our political system is seriously defective for not facilitating reasoned public discourse and collective citizen self-education on energy and other "complex" political issues.

(4) To many nuclear advocates, civilian nuclear power technology symbolizes and embodies values that they hold sacred. To many nuclear opponents the same technology symbolizes the annihilation of values that they likewise hold sacred. As I think that we each have a right to find meaning, purpose, dignity, and sacred value where we can, I believe that the conflicting symbolizations of nuclear advocates and opponents should be respected, and respected equally, at least until a legitimate democratic process determines that progress toward the ultimate shared end of that democracy, the realization of universal human freedom, is jeopardized by the beliefs and practices of one group or another. Pending the creation of such a process, we confront a logically irreconcilable conflict in the symbolic dimension. On this basis we can say nothing determinate about the social acceptability of nuclear energy. We can, however, say something important about the manner in which decisions regarding nuclear power must be made.

As observed earlier, those decisions must occur within an institutional context that clearly respects the dignity of each person for whom nuclear technology symbolizes the affirmation or destruction of sacred value. Pending the establishment of a fully democratic society, that can probably only occur if the setting for social discourse and decision making about nuclear energy is one that is demarcated ritually from the economic and day-to-day political realm. The setting must be one in which to the greatest extent possible each person is the moral and political equal of every other person.

The attainment of consensus is not assured in such settings (although it does become more probable). Even if consensus is not achieved, and decisions must, consequently, be made by compromise, bargaining, or vote, only in such settings can all parties have rational grounds for feeling respected *by* the process, and, therefore, be rationally warranted in *respecting* the process and its outcome.[71]

(5) Finally, are nuclear energy systems—which I have already argued are undemocratic because of the risks they pose to civil liberties, and the need to shroud their activities in secrecy—also undemocratic because of their large-scale and centralized regulatory and management structures?

Scale and centralization can be confusing concepts. A democratic society might have a mixture of large and small scale technologies. From the viewpoint of democratic theory, the scale of technological systems is not directly relevant. What matters is whether the social relations expressed through, and constituted in part by, technological practice are authoritarian and repressive, on the one hand, or cooperative, egalitarian, and freedom realizing on the other. These freedom-related attributes correlate only partially with the scale of institutions and of technological systems.[72]

Moreover, although it might be expensive and run counter to recent historical trends, future nuclear power plants could be relatively small. Consider, for instance, the research reactors on university campuses and the relatively small reactors that power nuclear submarines. In fact, a number of prominent scientists who worked on the U.S. atomic bomb project during World War II believed that nuclear energy would be deployed on a decentralized, small-scale basis:

Nuclear power plants would make feasible a greater decentralization of industry, a desirable factor in the world economy. . . .

It is the belief of many scientists and engineers connected with this work that a comparatively small standardized nuclear power plant will be developed. If this reasonable prediction comes to pass, such power plants can be placed at strategic points on all established utility company systems. This would greatly reduce power transmission costs and insure partial operation of the system even if the standard [oil, coal and hydro] superpower stations of the system were inoperative.[73]

Centralization, too, is an ambiguous and confusing concept. Do we mean centralization in design, choice, management, or regulation? Are autos decentralized because they are personally owned or centralized because they are produced in large factories?

The centralized, undemocratic management and regulation of nuclear plants could to some extent be reformed. Large nuclear plants have several hundred employees. It is difficult to design a reactor, but for years many of the people who have built and operated them have had relatively little formal education. Reactor operation requires some closely coordinated activity, so a hierarchical work structure is probably needed. But a reasonable level of internal democratization could occur through upgraded training coupled with routine rotation of workers and managers.[74]

Centralized national regulation is needed to oversee the plethora of dangerous activities associated with the nuclear fuel cycle. If that regulatory apparatus were democratized, nuclear energy systems would probably be safer, because there would be no secrets, and we could all hold the representative regulators strictly accountable. But here we encounter the social constraint noted earlier: we cannot risk fully democratizing nuclear energy systems because we do not live in an ideal global democracy. If we did, there would by definition be no terrorists, saboteurs, or dangerous, contending governments.

There are, thus, firm limits on the extent to which nuclear energy systems can be redesigned or reformed to be consistent with democratic ideals. Moreover, having nuclear power now in our imperfect democracies conditions against the possibility of moving toward greater democratization. Why should my community or neighbors decide to build soft energy technologies— technologies that do not restrict, and that in some cases facilitate, the transition toward democracy—when we are surrounded by a nuclear fuel cycle that subjects us to its economic, environmental, health and safety, social and (especially) political effects regardless of what we do? (I stress the word "political" because moving toward democracy is, I have argued, our highest-order shared interest.) While surrounded by the nuclear fuel cycle, we cannot make a choice between (a) soft energy technologies and their various locally concentrated, self-imposed and (therefore) legitimate and acceptable political effects and (b) nuclear power and its various regionally and globally distributed, antidemocratic and (therefore) illegitmate and unacceptable political effects. Whether or not we choose soft energy technologies, nuclear power and its adverse political effects are still imposed on us. Thus by reducing (or even eliminating) incentives to behave in ways that would otherwise permit us to protect and advance our freedom, nuclear power, in effect, helps coerce us into acting in a way that preserves undemocratic technological and social structures.

Moreover, as Lovins has argued,[75] if much of our society's limited capital is tied up in building nuclear plants, which cost billions of dollars apiece, finding capital with which to build soft technologies is going to be more expensive than it need be—perhaps prohibitively so.

Finally, the adverse political effects associated with nuclear power are unlike those associated with many other technologies, in that many of them are extremely persistent and irreversible.[76] For instance, plutonium that "escapes" from the controlled plutonium economy will remain toxic and useable in nuclear bombs, and, therefore, a potential threat to civil liberties, for tens of thousand of years. Radioactive waste produced by reactors will remain toxic for hundreds of thousands of years.[77] And widespread deployment of nuclear reactors and their attendant supporting infrastructure entails so much commitment of capital that dependence on a large, nationwide nuclear power system cannot (at any time or for any reason, by us or our children) quickly be phased out without causing serious economic loss and disruption. Knowledge of these long-range and irreversible external effects has a demoralizing and crippling effect on our ability to commit ourselves to serious political activity, of any sort, for we are not sure that there will *be* a future. Or if there is, that it will be one worth working for. The uncertainty we experience as to the possible existence of a future in which our projects will endure deprives us of the symbolic sense of immortality that we need in order to find meaning and purpose in our lives today.[78]

This, I think, is what Amory Lovins has meant by arguing—repeatedly and not fully persuasively—that hard and soft energy paths are mutually exclusive. I believe that Lovins' conclusion is correct, but his arguments are imperfect. Nuclear power systems are not inalterably undemocratic because of their scale, complexity, and centralized management. Rather, they are undemocratic because, through regionally and globally distributed threats to our civil liberties, freedom of information and communication, ability to project a meaningful future, and other adverse external effects, they reduce the degree of democracy now possible, while conditioning against the possibility of progressing toward greater democratization.

NOTES

1. I wish to thank Joshua Cohen, Hayward Alker, Dorothy Zinberg, Woodward Wickham, Lawrence Lidsky, Peter J. Lipton, William W. Hogan, Robert H. Williams, and David Kirsh for criticism of preliminary drafts of this essay. Naturally, I assume full responsibility for all flaws that remain.
2. Carole Pateman, *Participation and Democratic Theory* (Cambridge: Cambridge University Press, 1970); Dennis F. Thompson, *The Democratic Citizen: Social Science and Democratic Theory in the Twentieth Century* (Cambridge: Cambridge University Press, 1970); Jane J. Mansbridge,*Beyond Adversary Democracy* (New York: Basic, 1980).
3. See, for example, Michel J. Crozier, Samuel P. Huntington, and Joji Watanuki, *The Crisis of Democracy: Report on the Governability of Democracies to the Trilateral Commission* (New York: New York University Press, 1975).
4. The history of U.S. energy policy is discussed in Charles O. Jones, "American Politics and the Organization of Energy Decision Making," *Annual Review of Energy,* 4 (1979), 99-121; Walter A. Rosenbaum, *Energy Politics and Public Policy* (Washington, DC: Congressional Quarterly Press, 1981); Otis Dudley Duncan, "Sociologists Should Reconsider Nuclear Energy," *Social Forces,* 57 (Sept. 1978), 1-22.
5. Dorothy Nelkin and Susan Fallows, "The Evolution of the Nuclear Debate: The Role of Public Participation," *Annual Review of Energy,* 3 (1978), 275-312; Robert Cameron Mitchell, "From Elite Quarrel to Mass Movement," *Society,* 18 (July-Aug. 1981), 76-84.
6. Amory Lovins' most influential writings on energy are "Energy Strategy: The Road Not Taken," *Foreign Affairs,* 55 (Oct. 1976), 65-96; and *Soft Energy Paths: Toward a Durable Peace* (Cambridge, MA : Ballinger, 1977). Many criticisms of Lovins' argument, and hisresponse, appear in U.S. Select Committee on Small Business and the Committee on Interior and Insular Affairs, *Alternative Long Range Energy Strategies,* 2 vols. (Washington, DC: GPO, 1976 and 1977). These reports are published in abridgement as Hugh Nash, ed., *The Energy Controversy: Soft Path Questions and Answers* (San Francisco: Friends of the Earth, 1979).
7. On Lovins' claim that soft and hard energy paths are mutually exclusive see Nash, ed., *The Energy Controversy.* On Lovins' claim that energy technologies embody social and political choices see Denton E. Morrison and Dora G. Lodwick, "The Social Impacts of Soft and Hard Energy Systems: The Lovins' Claims as a Social Science Challenge," *Annual Review of Energy,* 6 (1981), 357-78. On the general significance of agenda building and scheduling within the political process, see Roger W. Cobb and Charles D. Elder, *Participation in American Politics: The Dynamics of Agenda-Building* (Baltimore: Johns Hopkins University Press, 1972).
8. This judgment is based on a decade's experience as a participant-observer in various capacities in the politics of U.S. energy policy. Pertinent evidence and argument may be found in F. Clemente et al., *Public Participation in Energy Related Decision Making: Six Case Studies* (McLean, Va.: MITRE Corp., Dec. 1977); K. Guild Nichols, *Technology on Trial: Public Particiaption in Decision Making Related to Science and Technology* (Paris: OECD, 1979); Allan Mazur, *The Dynamics of Technical Controversy* (Washington, DC: Communications Press, 1981), esp. chaps. 4 and 9; Dorothy Nelkin and Michael Pollak, "Public Participation in Technological Decisions: Reality or Grand Illusion," *Technology Review,* 81 (Aug.-Sept. 1979), 54-64.

9. See, for example, Lester C. Thurow, *The Zero Sum Society: Distribution and the Possibilities for Economic Change* (New York: Basic, 1980), esp. chap. 7; Kenneth J. Arrow, "A Cautious Case for Socialism," in *Beyond the Welfare State*, ed. Irving Howe (New York: Schocken, 1982), pp. 261-76. The structural advantage in politics of producer groups (e.g., private corporations) over labor and consumer groups is analyzed in Charles E. Lindblom, *Politics and Markets: The World's Political Economic Systems* (New York: Basic, 1977); Mancur Olson, *The Logic of Collective Action: Public Goods and the Theory of Groups* (Cambridge, MA: Harvard University, 1971); Edward S. Herman, *Corporate Control, Corporate Power* (Cambridge: Cambridge University Press, 1981).

10. Regarding the power of multinational energy companies, see Dudley J. Burton, *The Governance of Energy: Problems, Prospects and Underlying Issues* (New York: Praeger, 1980); John J. McCloy et al., *The Great Oil Spill: The Inside Report, Gulf Oil's Bribery and Political Chicanery* (New York: Chelsea House, 1976); Thomas D. Duchesnau, *Competition in the U.S. Energy Industry* (Cambridge, MA: Ballinger, 1975), esp. pp. 170-76 and Appendix H.

11. Regarding research and development, see Hans H. Landsberg et al., *Energy: The Next Twenty Years* (Cambridge, MA: Ballinger, 1979), chap. 15; John E. Tilton, *U.S. Energy R & D Policy: The Role of Economics* (Washington, DC: Resources for the Future, Sept. 1974), p. 134.

12. *Reactor Safety Study: An Assessment of Accident Risks in U.S. Commercial Nuclear Power Plants* (Washington, DC: U.S. Nuclear Regultory Commission, Oct. 1975).

13. K.S. Shrader-Frechette, "Technology, Public Policy, and the Price-Anderson Act," in *Research in Philosophy and Technology,* 3 (1980), 313-42.

14. *N.R.C. Statement on Risk Assessment and the Reactor Safety Study Report (WASH 1400)* (Washington, DC: U.S. Nuclear Regulatory Commission, 18 Jan. 1979); H.W. Lewis et al., *Risk Assessment Review Group Report to the U.S. Nuclear Regulatory Commission* (Washington, DC: U.S. Nuclear Regulatory Commission, Sept. 1978); Daniel F. Ford, *A History of Federal Nuclear Safety Assessments: From WASH 740 Through the Reactor Safety Study* (Cambridge, MA: Union of Concerned Scientists, 1977).

15. Nuclear Energy Policy Study Group, *Nuclear Power Issues and Choices* (Cambridge, MA: Ballinger, 1977). Cited hereinafter as NEPS.

16. *New York Times,* 22 March 1971, p. 51. The precise influence of the Ford-MITRE study on the president's nuclear energy policy, and on the Congress, is hard to establish insofar as Carter had previously indicated publicly that he was deeply concerned about the relationship between nuclear weapons proliferation and commercial nuclear power.

17. *Energy Daily,* 8 April 1977, pp. 1 and 3; and 22 April 1977, pp. 1 and 9-10.

18. Compare NEPS pp. 229-30 with pp. 306-08.

19. The Ford-MITRE (NEPS) study estimates the upper-bound risk of a nuclear meltdown accident as the product of three terms:
(Probability per reactor-year of 5×10^{-3} for meltdown)
X (Probability of 2×10^{-1} for breach of containment, given meltdown)
X (10,000 average prompt and delayed fatalities per breach)
= 10 expected fatalities per reactor-year.

The first term (5×10^{-3}) is not a plausible upper-bound, because it fails to reflect the (unknown, unknowable, and, therefore, incalculable) probability of sabotage as an accident initiating event (see NEPS, pp. 306-08). The second term (2×10^{-1}) doubles the Rasmussen value, but since the point of the exercise was to compute an upper-bound— on the assumption that the Rasmussen report's probability calculus is unreliable—the probability of breach could plausibly have been set equal to 1 (because, for example, there is no actuarial experience with meltdown and very little is known about the probability of water/molten metal steam-explosion, given a meltdown). The 10,000-fatalities term borders on the meaningless, partly because it implicitly incorporates the radioactive inventory release fractions that are given in the Rasmussen report (Appendix VII, sect. 1), contrary to the spirit of an upper-bound estimate, and because it fails to grapple effectively with the enormous range of expected fatalities deriving from site-specific variation in population and weather conditions. Moreover (as NEPS acknowledges on p. 308), if sabotage were included as an initiating event, the number of expected prompt and delayed fatalities would be higher.

20. D.O. Edge, "Technological Metaphor," in *Meaning and Control: Essays in Social Aspects of Science and Technology*, eds. D.O. Edge and J.N. Wolfe (London: Tavistock, 1973); Mary Douglas and Baron Isherwood, *The World of Goods* (New York: Basic, 1979); Heather Lechtman and Robert Merrill, eds., *Material Culture: Styles, Organization and Dynamics of Technology* (St. Paul,MN: West, 1977); Don Ihde, "Technology and Human Self-Conception," *Southwestern Journal of Philosophy*, 10 (1979), 23-34; Richard Sclove, "Decision-Making in a Democracy," *Bulletin of the Atomic Scientists*, 38 (May 1982), 44-49 (cited hereinafter as Sclove, "Decision-Making").

21. Richard E. Sclove, *Scientists in the U.S. Nuclear Debate*, S.M. Thesis, Dept. of Nuclear Engineering, MIT Press , Jan. 1978; Dorothy Nelkin and Michael Pollak, *The Atom Besieged: Antinuclear Movements in France and Germany* (Cambridge: MIT, 1981).

22. Robert Lekachman, *Economists at Bay; Why the Experts Will Never Solve Your Problems* (New York: McGraw-Hill, 1976); Charles E. Lindblom and David K. Cohen, *Useable Knowledge: Social Science and Social Problem Solving* (New Haven: Yale University Press, 1979); Sclove,"Decison-Making," esp. the works cited in n. 9.

23. See Fred R. Dallmayr, "Critical Theory and Public Policy," *Policy Studies Journal*, 9 (1980-81), 522-34; Jurgen Habermas, *Toward a Rational Society: Student Protest, Science and Politics*, trans. Jeremy J. Shapiro (Boston: Beacon, 1970), chaps. 4-6.

24. Michael Mulkay, *Science and the Sociology of Knowledge* (London: George Allen and Unwin, 1979).

25. Langdon Winner, *Autonomous Technology: Technics-out-of-Control as a Theme in Political Thought* (Cambridge: MIT Press, 1977), chaps. 4 and 6.

26. See Habermas, *Toward a Rational Society;* David Dickson and David Noble, "By Force of Reason: The Politics of Science and Technology Policy," in *The Hidden Election: Politics and Economics in the 1980 Presidential Campaign*, ed. Thomas Ferguson and Joel Rogers (New York: Pantheon, 1981), pp. 260-312.

27. Laurence H. Tribe, "Technology Assessment and the Fourth Discontinuity: The Limits of Instrumental Rationality," *Southern California Law Review*, 46 (June 1973), 617-60; Winner, *Autonomous Technology*, n. 25, above, pp. 29-30, 233-34, and 238-52.

28. Robert K. Merton, *The Sociology of Science: Theoretical and Empirical Investigations* (Chicago: University of Chicago, 1973), chaps. 12 and 13; Lekachman, *Economists at Bay*, esp. chap. 3; Ina Spiegel-Rosing and Derek de Solla Price, eds., *Science, Technology and Society: A Cross Disciplinary Perspective* (Beverly Hills: Sage, 1977), esp. chaps. 4, 8, and 10.

29. Ferguson and Rogers, eds., *The Hidden Election*, n. 26, above.

30. Christopher Madison, "New Board to Cut Red Tape May Cause Some Problems of Its Own," *National Journal*, 12 (10 May 1980), 760-64.

31. Robert Lekachman, *Greed is Not Enough: Reagonomics* (New York: Pantheon, 1982); Frances Fox Piven and Richard A. Cloward, *The New Class War: Reagan's Attack on the Welfare State and Its Consequences* (New York: Pantheon, 1982).

32. Howell Raines, "Reagan Order Tightens the Rules on Disclosing Secret Information," *New York Times*, 3 April 1982, pp. 1 and 9; Christopher Paine, "Secrets," *Bulletin of the Atomic Scientists*, 38 (April 1982), 11-16.

33. Ford, *A History of Federal Nuclear Safety Assessments*, n. 14, above.

34. Actually, there are unremovable market imperfections present in all, not merely energy, markets. See, for example, Walter Nicholson, *Microeconomic Theory: Basic Principles and Extensions* (Hinsdale: Dryden Press, 1972), chaps. 21 and 22; Francis M. Bator, "The Anatomy of Market Failure," *Quarterly Journal of Economics*, 72 (Aug. 1958), 351-79.

35. In economic theory an "externality" is an impact or effect that is imposed on someone without the mediation of markets, prices, or cash transfer. Thus external impacts occur without any opportunity for (positive or negative) economic feedback to their producers. See E.J. Mishan, *Introduction to Normative Economics* (New York: Oxford University Press, 1981), chap. 8.

36. See Tilton, *U.S. Energy R&D Policy;* Landsberg et al., *Energy*, n. 11, above.

37. Producer groups (e.g., energy corporations) have a structural political-economic advantage over consumers within unregulated—or undemocratically regulated—markets (see the pertinent cites in n. 9, above); large corporations particularly are able to translate their economic strength into political power, and *vice versa* (see the works cited in n. 10, above).

38. John Tirman, "Investing in the Energy Transition: From Oil to What?" *Technology Review*, 85 (April 1982), 64-72; *F.A.S. Public Interest Report*, 34 (Nov. 1981), 1-7.

39. Karl Polanyi, *The Great Transformation: The Political and Economic Origins of Our Time* (1944; rpt. Boston: Beacon Press, 1957); Albert O. Hirschman, *The Passions and the Interests: Political Arguments for Capitalism Before Its Triumph* (Princeton: Princeton University Press, 1977).

40. Charles L. Schultze, *The Public Use of Private Interest* (Washington, DC: Brookings Institution, 1977).

41. Democratic interpretation would require some redistribution of private resources (to help equalize opportunities for self-education and political activity) and experimentation with new political institutions to supplement existing ones. Steps toward describing or creating such institutions are discussed in Nelkin and Pollak, "Public Participation in Technological Decisions"; Nichols, *Technology on Trial;* Sclove, "Decision-Making," pp. 47-48; James D. Carroll, "Participatory Technology," in *Technology and Man's Future*, ed. Albert H. Teich, 2nd ed. (New York: St. Martin's Press, 1977), pp. 336-54.

42. See n.34, above; and Polanyi, *The Great Transformation*, n.39 above.

43. I use the term "ideology" to designate a distorted representation of reality that is generated by and helps preserve an unjust social system. By "ideological system" I mean two or more competing ideologies—and their allied social structures—which, by battling with one another, seem to observers and participants to constitute the entire realm of possible belief and social systems.

44. Langdon Winner, "Do Artifacts Have Politics?" *Daedalus*, 109 (Winter 1980), 121-36; David Dickson, *The Politics of Alternative Technology* (New York: Universe Books, 1974); Lewis Mumford, "Authoritarian and Democratic Technics," *Technology and Culture*, 5 (Winter 1964), 1-8; Andy Zimbalist, ed., *Case Studies in the Labor Process* (New York: Monthly Review Press, 1979); Murray Bookchin, "Self-Management and the New Technology," *Telos*, no. 41 (Fall 1979), 5-16.

45. J.D. Carroll, "Participatory Technology," pp. 337-38; Winner, *Autonomous Technology*, pp. 317-25; Winner, "Do Artifacts Have Politics?" pp. 127-28.

46. See especially Immanuel Kant, *Foundations of the Metaphysics of Morals*, trans. Lewis White Beck (1785; rpt. Indianapolis: Bobbs-Merrill, 1959); Jean Jacques Rousseau,

The Social Contract, trans. Maurice Cranston (1762; rpt. Harmondsworth: Penguin, 1968); Ernst Cassirer, *The Question of Jean Jacques Rousseau,* trans. Peter Gay (Bloomington: Indiana University Press, 1963). Any merit in the reconstruction given here of Kant's and Rousseau's thought is owed to Professor Joshua Cohen, and particularly to his lectures in democratic theory at MIT, Spring 1982. Professor Cohen is not, however, responsible for any errors or weaknesses or for the application and extension of the theory with respect to technology.

47. Kant, *Foundations,* p. 39. On p. 48, n. 14, Kant explains ways in which the categorical imperative extends beyond the Golden Rule.

48. On freedom as our highest-order good, see ibid., esp. pp. 9-17 and 68; and Rousseau, *Social Contract,* Bk. I, chap. 4, p. 55.

49. There are at least two reasonable ways in which to interpret Rousseau's argument for the sociality of freedom: (a) Following *The Social Contract,* Bk. I, chap. 6, we can regard human interdependence as a simple, evolutionary existential fact. The objective of the social pact is then simply to make the best of a given condition of human experience. That is, by direct, collective self-legislation we maximize our liberty subject to the constraint that we *do* live socially. (b) Following *The Social Contract,* Bk. I, chap. 8, we can regard culture and democratic community as necessary conditions for fully realizing our capacities as moral and free beings: "And although in civil society man surrenders some of the advantages that belong to the state of nature, he gains in return far greater ones. . . . [M]an acquires with civil society . . . moral freedom, which alone makes man the master of himself; for to be governed by appetite alone is slavery, while obedience to a law one prescribes to oneself is freedom."—*Social Contract,* p. 65

50. Rousseau actually argues for direct democracy in legislation (which is largely sufficient for the argument I make in the text), not direct democracy in all social practice. However it can, I believe, persuasively be argued from Rousseau's premises that democracy ought to be extended to other spheres and social practices. Rousseau's argument against self-governance, for example, rests upon an over-dichotomized distinction between *general* laws and *particular* policies and executive acts (see *Social Contract,* Bk. II, chaps. 4 and 6; and Bk. III, chap. 1). In any given instance of governance there are normally many competing possible interpretations of the law, as well as many actions that would each formally (or at least arguably) be consistent with each of these interpretations. As a possible constraint on freedom, execution is, thus, in practice functionally fully analogous to legislation, and, therefore, if there is good reason for citizens to participate in the ratification of laws, there is equal reason for them to participate in the formulation of particular policies and in the application and implementation of laws.

51. See n. 20, above.

52. James J. Flink, "Three Stages of American Automobile Consciousness," *American Quarterly* (Oct. 1972), 451-73.

53. Barry M. Casper and Paul David Wellstone, *Powerline: The First Battle of America's Energy War* (Amherst: University of Massachusetts Press, 1981); "Black Hills Gathering: People Unite for Survival," *Science for the People,* 12 (Nov.-Dec. 1980), 17-26.

54. Kant, *Foundations,* n. 46, above, p. 53.

55. See also Steven Kelman, "Cost-Benefit Analysis: An Ethical Critique," *Regulation,* 5 (Jan.-Feb. 1981), 33-40; Peter Marris, *Loss and Change* (Garden City, N.Y.: Anchor, 1975), chap. 8.

56. Power plant hearings are criticized in Clemente et al., *Public Participation in Energy Related Decision Making;* Casper and Wellstone, *Powerline.* Monetary compensation is discussed in E.J. Mishan, *Cost Benefit Analysis,* 2nd ed. (New York: Praeger, 1976), Part 5. Willingness-to-pay is discussed in A. Myrick Freeman, III, *The Benefits of*

Environmental Improvement: Theory and Practice (Baltimore: Johns Hopkins University Press, 1979).

57. This term is borrowed from Langdon Winner, *Technologies as Forms of Life*, TS, Delivered to the Boston Colloquium for the Philosophy of Science, 7 March 1978, 19p.

58. Both ideologies have been brilliantly described by Winner in *Autonomous Technology*, n. 25, above, although he does not fully explain their dynamic, dialectical relationship.

59. This view has been expressed most forcefully by Jacques Ellul, *The Technological Society*, trans. John Wilkinson (New York: Vintage, 1964).

60. For criticism of the myth of autonomous technology see Winner, *Autonomous Technology*, n. 25, above, Dickson, *Politics of Alternative Technology*, n. 44, above.

61. The claim that technological artifacts and systems are neutral is advanced in, for example, Alvin M. Weinberg, "Technological Optimism," *Society*, 17 (March-April 1980), 17-18.

62. Sclove, "Decision-Making," n. 20, above, pp. 44-46.

63. For criticism of technological neutrality see Dickson, *Politics of Alternative Technology*, chap. 1; Winner, *Autonomous Technology*, esp. pp. 191-208 and 238-51. On the irreducibility of quality to quantity see Nicholas Georgescu-Roegen, *The Entropy Law and the Economic Process* (Cambridge, MA: Harvard University Press, 1971), chaps. 2-5.

64. On the recent history of sociotechnological controversies see Mazur, *Dynamics of Technical Controversy;* Spiegel-Rosing and de Solla Price, eds., *Science, Technology and Society*, esp. chaps. 10 and 11.

65. For guidance to the literature on appropriate technology, see Ken Darrow and Rick Pam, *Appropriate Technology Sourcebook*, Vol. 1, revised, June 1978; and Ken Darrow, Kent Keller, and Rick Pam, *Appropriate Technology Sourcebook*, Vol. 2, Jan. 1981. Both are available from Appropriate Technology Project, Volunteers in Asia, Box 4543, Stanford, CA 94305.

66. Select Committee on Small Business, *Alternative Long Range Energy Strategies*, p. 767.

67. See, for example, Landsberg et al., *Energy;* Robert Stobaugh and Daniel Yergin, eds., *Energy Future: Report of the Energy Project at the Harvard Business School* (New York: Random House, 1979); Committee on Nuclear and Alternative Energy Systems, *Energy in Transition 1985-2010* (Washington, DC: National Academy of Sciences, 1979); Henry W. Kendall and Steven J. Nadis, eds., *Energy Strategies: Toward a Solar Future* (Cambridge, MA: Ballinger, 1980).

68. Russell W. Ayres, "Policing Plutonium: The Civil Liberties Fallout," *Harvard Civil Rights Civil Liberties Law Review*, 10 (Spring 1975), 369-443.

69. This is only "at a minimum" because my argument neglects obligations we may have or feel to future generations. See n. 76, below.

70. See NEPS, chaps. 7 and 10.

71. For one illustrative example of such a setting, see the community hearings described in Nichols, *Technology on Trial*, pp. 68-77. On the relationship between consensus and compromise, bargaining, and voting, see Mansbridge, *Beyond Adversary Democracy*.

72. Regarding authoritarian versus cooperative technologies see Mumford, "Authoritarian and Democratic Technics"; Bookchin, "Self-Management and the New Technology." Scale certainly has something to do with the quality of social relationships, but the causal link is probably not as tight as technological determinists and some soft technology enthusiasts suppose. See H. Paul Friesma et al., *Centralized Power: An Examination of the Effects of Centralized and Decentralized Electric Generating Systems on the Political Authorities of Local Governments* (Washington, DC: Environmental Policy

Insitute, 1979); Robert A. Dahl and Edward R. Tufte, *Size and Democracy* (Stanford: Stanford University Press, 1973).

73. *The International Control of Atomic Energy: Scientific Information Transmitted to the United Nations Atomic Energy Commission,* June 14-Oct. 14, 1946, Prepared in the Office of Bernard Baruch (Washington, DC: GPO, 1946), pp. 121-7.

74. Joseph R. Egan, "To Err is Human Factors," *Technology Review,* 85 (Feb.-March 1982), 23-29.

75. *Soft Energy Paths,* pp. 49 and 59-60.

76. On irreversibility and intertemporal equity see William Ramsay and Milton Russell, "Time-Adjusted Health Impacts From Electricity Generation," *Public Policy,* 26 (Summer 1978), 387-403; Douglas MacLean, "Benefit-Cost Analysis, Future Generations and Energy Policy: A Survey of the Moral Issues," *Science, Technology, and Human Values,* 5 (Spring 1980), 3-10.

77. It is sometimes claimed that the risks associated with radioactive waste disposal are relatively small and can easily be managed (see, for example, Bernard L. Cohen, "The Disposal of Radioactive Wastes from Fission Reactors," *Scientific American,* 236 [June 1977], 21-31). Such judgments overlook: (a) the possibility that unforeseen modes of waste release from a depository exist; (b) the risk that waste will not in practice be emplaced and managed in accordance with design; (c) the uncertain state of knowledge regarding geology and waste behavior *in situ;* and (d) the risk of subsequent illicit recovery of waste in order to extract fissionable isotopes for use in nuclear bombs.

78. Robert Jay Lifton, "Protean Man," in *The Psychoanalytic Interpretation of History,* ed. Benjamin B. Wolman (New York: Harper Torchbooks, 1973), pp. 33-49; Robert J. Lifton, *The Broken Connection: On Death and the Continuity of Life* (New York: Touchstone, 1979), chaps. 22 and 23.

PART II

ENERGY AND THE EVALUATION OF RISK

In the preceding chapters, the authors examined the significance of consensus in national energy policy planning. They analyzed the role of the president in providing the leadership necessary to convince the public that energy policy planning should receive high priority. In addition, they asked if consensus, except at a high level of generalization (e.g., there should be an energy policy), could be achieved. For some, it was an unrealistic expectation, while for others, it was not even desirable because of the inflexibility that would result from comprehensiveness. In this section, the authors extend the investigation of this underlying theme by analyzing the role of risk and risk assessment in energy policy. What are the risks and by what criteria are they assessed? Who bears them? At whose cost? And—are they ethically defensible?

Each of the authors examines a different dimension of the questions. Roger Kasperson in *The Neglect of Social Risk Assessment* demonstrates how the "hard core drive out the soft" . . . that is the quantification of controversial issues even when imprecise often takes precedence over more qualitative variables and obscures the unfairness of the distribution of risk on the society. Douglas MacLean in *Valuing Human Life* illuminates the complexity of making decisions about risk by examining the philosophical questions that arise when an attempt is made to convert quantity to quality when the value of a human life is at stake. Is it possible to subject a society's sacred values to traditional methods of cost accounting? Both authors explore these questions in the context of nuclear power policy planning which demands balancing technical, social, and political decisions, in order to achieve the measure of public consensus needed to implement acceptable policies. In both cases they offer a framework within which to analyze and resolve these constraints.

In *Media Coverage of Complex Technological Issues,* the authors William Colglazier, Jr. and Michael Rice present two high-risk situations, a nuclear power accident (Three Mile Island) and the proliferation of nuclear weapons (The Nuclear Weapons Freeze Proposal) and analyze both in the light of public anxiety, the role of nonelected experts (i.e., public interest scientists), and the behavior of the media that by emphasis or avoidance bears much of the responsibility for educating the public about the risks inherent in technology-related issues, particularly in nuclear-related technologies that are dominated by fear of catastrophe.

The discussions of risk in social-political studies most often cover the spectrum of risk from individual (i.e., the likelihood of injury or death resulting from working with a specific energy-related resource such as a coal-mining accident or radon-induced cancer from uranium ore mining) to global risk (i.e., the likely effect on the ecosphere of accumulating concentrations of acid rain, or inadvertant climate changes induced by the increased generation of heat). In the last chapter in this section, *The Utility Director's Dilemma: The Governance of Nuclear Power,* the authors, Graham Allison and Albert Carnesale, raise the question of risk in the form most familiar to industry—the risk of capital in building nuclear power plants. They argue that in order to preserve the nuclear power option, nothing less than fundamental changes in their governance will be required, from plant management to the reform of the licensing process and the reorganization of nuclear regulatory institutions.

These chapters demonstrate that risks ranging from threats to health and human lives to financial investments benefit from being assessed in the context of the society's values and institutions. The authors argue that not only must these risks be identified, but they must be evaluated by many different groups (e.g., scientists, ethicists, private sector managers, government officials, the media, and the public) so that the severity of the risks and the choice of risk each energy decision entails is part of the public debate.

Chapter 4
THE NEGLECT OF
SOCIAL RISK ASSESSMENT

Roger Kasperson

THE NEGLECT OF SOCIAL RISK ASSESSMENT IN ENERGY POLICY MAKING

As the United States lurches toward a *de facto* energy policy, issues of risk have become curiously central in scientific and public debate. A new breed of professional, the risk assessor, populates the halls of government, consulting firms, and electricity utilities. Woe to the fresh graduate seeking employment who cannot bandy about such terms as "fault-tree and event-tree analysis," the "quadratic linear" curve, "risk acceptability," and "WASH-1400."

In June 1981 the Society for Risk Analysis held its first annual meetings in Washington, D.C., with the intriguing title "The Analysis of Actual vs. Perceived Risks." Such topics as passive restraints in automobiles, cigarette smoking, and the health impacts of toxic wastes were discussed. The program included several nuggets, such as Norman Rasmussen's speaking on "perceived risk." The emphasis on social issues in risk management suggests an emerging recognition in this rather inchoate field that the quantitative assessment of public health risks has outstripped our ability to learn the meaning of such numbers or to generate similar numbers for the other, more elusive risks that worry people.

This chapter refers to "social risks." By this term I intend two separate meanings, which confront the guardians of safety in the United States. First, there are categories of risks that do not fall comfortably into our ongoing efforts to prevent the maiming of life and limb. The continuing concerns over civil liberties and the concentration of political power in certain energy systems suggest the types of risk involved. For convenience, we may think of these as risks to society, to community, to the institutions through which society operates, and to the values upon which the institutions rest.

Second, after a particular physical risk has been estimated, its social significance must be inferred. Problems of both types pose formidable difficulties for risk managers, who by legislative mandate, capability, and indeed inclination are often poorly equipped to solve them. The record of institutional responses to this nexus of risk problems shows certain recurring failures.

This chapter considers four such recurring problems:

1. the sustained poor quality of assessments of social risks in large-scale energy efforts,
2. the failure to address and provide suitable institutional mechanisms for overcoming problems of inequity in the distribution of risks,
3. ambiguity as to the appropriate functions and roles of formal risk assessment in fashioning safety policy and regulations, and
4. continuing confusion as to appropriate means for determining risk acceptability in standard setting.

The intent here is to inquire into the nature of these problems and to suggest why they are so resistant to solution. Each problem is illustrated by an example currently the subject of social controversy.

PROBLEM 1: THE FAILURE TO ASSESS SOCIAL RISKS

Over the next several decades, the United States will plan and begin the implementation of a complex system of nuclear waste handling, movement, and storage. First, to relieve pressure upon the three commercial facilities currently still accepting waste, storage capacity for low-level waste will have to be increased. Also imminent is the development of interim storage either at reactor sites or in away-from-reactor (AFR) facilities. Meanwhile, planning is under way for geological mine repositories for the long-term storage of both spent fuel and high-level defense wastes. These repositories are slated to begin operation toward the end of the century.

Since remoteness from population centers is a prime safety consideration in site selection, this network of facilities will be located chiefly in rural America where small communities are least prepared to act as hosts and most vulnerable to potential adverse impacts. Deploying a mature waste-handling system for, say, 250 GWe of nuclear electricity, plus the weapons-producing reactors, is likely to prove a difficult undertaking, particularly given the volatile nature of the nuclear issue. Waste management will require approximately a 100-year hands-on institutional commitment (from waste generation to decommissioning and postclosure monitoring); a complex network of generating, storage, and disposal facilities; and an extensive system of waste transportation probably involving most of the 48 conterminous states. The likely social and institutional issues raised by waste management will include trade-off decisions between this and future generations, and the imposition of risk upon politically vulnerable people.

After a decade of institutional failure to fashion an effective waste-management system, Washington has absorbed the message that significant social issues pervade radioactive waste decisions:

- a U.S. Nuclear Regulatory Commission (NRC) task force concluded in 1978 that "past failures of proposed radioactive waste management systems have stemmed in large part from neglect of nontechnological necessities in the implementation of systems."[1]
- the 1978 Deutch Report was predicated on the assumption that "policy and programs must be credible to and accepted by the American public."[2]
- the 1979 Interagency Review Group on Nuclear Waste Management argued in its *Report to the President* that "the resolution of institutional issues . . . is equally as important as the resolution of outstanding technical issues and problems," and that such resolution "may well be more difficult than finding solutions to remaining technical problems"[3]
- President Carter observed in his 1980 message that past governmental efforts "have failed to involve successfully the States, local governments, and the public in policy or program decisions," and noted the evident complexities and difficulties "from a technical and, *more importantly,* from an institutional and political perspective." (italics added)[4]

Although every major report on nuclear waste has called social and institutional issues the paramount obstacle, there is today remarkably little understanding of the likely social impacts of the network of facilities and waste movement that will be required. Neither the Department of Energy (DOE) nor the Nuclear Regulatory Commission (NRC) has an adequate program to assess such issues. In fact, the responsible government agencies possess very little capability to determine whether reports that trickle in from their contractees are useful or not.

The failure to assess social impacts and to fashion appropriate institutional responses probably ensures continuing debacles in the waste program. The failure is not unique to radioactive waste management. The Three Mile Island accident found the NRC lacking expertise in human factors and unable to deal with mental distress, the main environmental impact of the accident upon the region. The MX missile system has been put forth with scant attention to its social impacts. The poor quality of analysis in the social and economic sections of environmental impact statements is well documented. Even the language we use is suggestive of the state of affairs. "Nontechnological issues" tells us only what an impact is not; "institutional" concerns usually cover issues that are not institutional at all.

The Social Impacts of a Nuclear Waste Repository

The failure to assess social impacts adequately is unmistakable in governmental efforts to site a high-level nuclear waste repository. There are good reasons to expect that the implementation of a waste repository will create novel problems.

First, as the turbulent search, both here and abroad, for sites for a high-level waste repository amply indicates, substantial political conflict is almost certain to occur. The siting of a nuclear waste facility cannot be dissociated from the nuclear controversy as a whole; the sites, and their inhabitants, will become testing points for those committed to and those opposed to the nuclear enterprise.

Second, these facilities, and especially the high-level waste repositories, are first-of-a kind ventures: they have never before been implemented in the same form within the same social context. No previous experience will alert us to miscalculations and adverse impacts, or suggest the workability of prospective designs and processes for overcoming such problems. Instead, it is necessary to depend upon knowledge accumulated with other remote, large-scale industrial projects whose relevance and applicability are uncertain.

Third, unlike most nuclear power reactors, the facilities will only slightly benefit the host communities. What they will bring to these communities are risks, which, though judged small by most technical experts, are still not well understood. These risks are particularly feared by the public. The acceptance by communities of uncertain risks with few compensating benefits will require a high degree of trust and confidence at a time when their absence has plagued the orderly development of nuclear power in the United States.

Evaluating these thorny problems is made more difficult by the underdeveloped state of theory and methodology in social impact analysis. To understand the variety of harms that a particular change may precipitate in a small community, it is necessary first to understand the structure and dynamics of that community. Even with this knowledge, one must trace the causal chain of social perturbations that lead to certain associated consequences. The tendency in most social impact studies, however, has been to treat the affected communities as largely inert objects, assumed to be similar in population size, upon which outside forces act. A simple model keyed to the size and timing of in-migration has been used to distribute a series of expected outcomes, usually restricted to those problems for which quantitative data and indicators are readily available rather than to those problems of greatest concern or potential impact. Rarely have the long-term social changes associated with a project been included as a part of the assessment. The preparers of such analyses have often found it unnecessary to set foot in the communities under study. It is not surprising, then, that such analyses have earned the social impact sections of environmental impact statements the near universal disdain of both the academic and practitioner communities. Conventional social impact studies, in short, are unlikely to identify and evaluate the range of social and economic harms which small communities may experience as a result of the construction of a nuclear waste storage facility and will not, in the view of this researcher, provide an adequate basis for fashioning appropriate impact management and compensation programs.

The work conducted to date by the DOE does not meet even the standard of the rather dreary conventional social impact analysis. To cite an example of the social science work that runs through the radioactive waste program, the Board on Radioactive Waste Management of the National Research Council recently informed DOE that the socioeconomic assessment in its Generic Environmental Impact Statement (Draft) suffered seriously from

1. failure to estimate systemic impacts of changes in scale, especially the socioeconomic and institutional impacts of a stable 400-GWe nuclear economy;
2. lack of sensitivity of estimates of effects to choice of reference site;
3. inappropriate application of the analysis across various disposal options;
4. overly simplistic indicators for assessing complex social and economic impacts; and
5. incomplete analysis of impacts associated with repository decommissioning.[5]

These problems were not resolved in the final statement, and it is doubtful, in fact, that it is now within the capability of DOE to conduct quality work in this area. Much the same can be said for the National Plan for radioactive waste management. Finally, although the Office of Nuclear Waste Isolation alludes to a Social and Economic Program Plan that will be developed to guide "societal issues management and resolution" and to support "development of national consensus by identifying, managing, and resolving societal concerns about nuclear waste isolation," as part of its *Technical Program Plan,* no such plan or coordinated set of supporting research in fact exists.

What may be the reasons for the recurring failure in social impact assessment? Part of the problem lies in the traditional missions of the atomic energy agencies, which have emphasized the technical and engineering aspects of nuclear power, particularly radioactive wastes. They have been reluctant to venture into social issues because of both their lack of capability and their rejection of the legitimacy of such issues. (Psychological stress is presently an excellent example.)

Incentive is lacking, too. So the regulatory agencies continue to be clobbered by the social scientists who review their work. So what? Except for the larger societal controversy, nothing encourages the nuclear agencies to improve the scope and quality of this work.

PROBLEM 2: EQUITY AND RISK MANAGEMENT

Difficult value issues pervade energy policy questions. In fact, the social problems with radioactive wastes referred to in the previous discussions stem largely from difficult value trade-offs that underlie management choices. Among these value problems, equity issues are common, yet central to judgments about the safety of technologies. Equity issues arise from a variety of situations—the uneven geographical distribution of risks, disagreement between those who assume risks and those who reap benefits, the differential rewards resulting when control measures are introduced, and the intergenerational impacts of technology. How to determine and ensure equity in public policies and regulatory decisions is one of the fundamental ongoing questions of our society. Existing institutions obviously have great difficulty in confronting such problems: the Congress is often vague as to how such issues should be resolved, and the regulatory agencies tend to regard the normative problems as outside their spheres of competence. As a result, equity issues are often the underlying conflict, but they are never brought to the surface for explicit treatment. Equity trade-offs often remain shrouded by the technical options or economic considerations presented in impact or planning documents. Explicit equity battles often rage outside established institutional processes.

The central equity question in energy policy deliberations is: how do we distribute fairly the positive and negative impacts associated with energy production and use? An equity analysis to answer this question would consist of two parts:

1. A statement of the distribution of impacts, beneficial and harmful, over a given population resulting from some decision, process, or policy. This entails an empirical analysis which includes
   a. specification of those "things," such as social goods, opportunities, and outcomes experienced, to be distributed;
   b. a specification of the relevant categories of the population to be used as the framework of distribution, indicating whether or not past and future populations are to be included;
   c. combining (a) and (b), a statement of impact distributions resulting from alternative solutions.
2. A standard, or principle, by which the "fairness" of a particular distribution may be judged and the preferability of one distribution over others determined. The principle provides a standard of comparison to which a moral imperative is attached.

Both parts of the equity analysis present problems. In regard to the empirical distributions, the lack of competent social impact analysis has already been noted. But even better understood impacts may be difficult to project far into the future or for distant societies. Similarly, there is no consensus as to what moral imperatives should guide decisions as to "fairness," and regulatory agencies are probably not the appropriate locus for such judgments.

Differential Protection of Workers and Publics

As an illustration of recurring failures arising from inadequate response to equity problems, consider the differential protection of workers and the public from technological hazards—an issue, only now emerging, which could become a powerful social issue for the 1980s.

Whereas workers were protected historically in limited ways at the expense of the public surrounding the workplace, the burden seems to have shifted dramatically, if perhaps unintentionally, to worker exposure to benefit the public. Existing public health standards suggest that society tolerates, indeed approves, a differential exposure of workers and the public to technological hazards. In the case of nuclear power, for example, the *occupational* standard until very recently was 12 rems in a given year, and an average annual exposure of 5 rems, as opposed to a *public* permissible exposure of .5 rems to the individual member of the public, a factor-of-ten difference. Our plotting of the evolution of general standards for ionizing radiation (figure 4.1) illustrates the magnitude of differential risk recognized for workers and the public, although the workers were the first to be protected. Differential exposure also occurs, of course, by types of workers; maintenance workers receive much higher radiation doses than those conducting routine work in nuclear power plants.

A comparison of ionizing radiation dose-limit standards for radiation workers and the general population illustrates two common patterns in risk management:

1. concern for worker safety generally precedes concern for public safety—in this case, by about 25 years.
2. workers' acceptable risk levels are set considerably higher than the public's—in this case, by a factor of 10.

(Standards are based on NCRP recommendations generally adopted in the U. S. for occupational release of ionizing radiation, and are in addition to exposure from medical and natural background sources. The 1925 First Congress on Radiation recommendation, "1/10 dose required to burn skin," is expressed as an estimate of *actual* worker exposure for that period—about 100 rems/person/year.)

Recently, a research group at Clark University surveyed the public and occupational health standards for some 10 technological hazards—CO, NOx, O_3, SO_2, HC, Pb, Be, Rn, noise, and ionizing radiation—and found that allowable exposures for workers tend to be several orders of magnitude higher than those for the public; that public exposure tends to be set below the medically hazardous level; that occupational exposure tends to be set above the medically hazardous level; and that the relationship between occupational and environmental health standards tends to be nonuniform.[6] The group has also examined occupational and environmental standards of advanced industrial societies. Occupational standards, in particular, appear to vary significantly, exhibiting an east-west trend in which the Soviet Union has the most protective standards, and the United States the least. This is probably not surprising, given the different underlying values of a socialist and a capitalist society. Yet when U.S. and U.S.S.R. occupational and environmental standards are compared directly (table 4.1), differential protection of workers and the public is tolerated no less in the Soviet Union than in the United States. Data for other countries bear out this general pattern; a double standard of protection is apparent across economies, political systems, and ideologies.

Four different moral justifications have been presented for this double standard:

1. *Utility:* A greater exposure of workers is justified because the resulting benefits to society outweigh the harms to the individual. Reducing workplace risk would

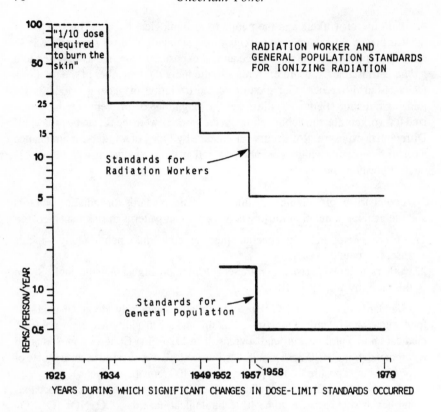

Fig. 4.1 A comparison of ionizing radiation dose-limit standards for radiation workers and the general population illustrates two common patterns in risk management: (1) concern for worker safety generally precedes concern for public safety—in this case, by about 25 years; and (2) workers' acceptable risk levels are set considerably higher than the public's—in this case, by a factor of 10. (Standards are based on NCRP recommendations generally adopted in the U.S. for occupational release of ionizing radiation, and are in addition to exposure from medical and natural background sources. The 1924 First Congress on Radiation recommendation, "1/10 dose required to burn skin," is expressed as an estimate of *actual* worker exposure for that period—about 100 rems/person/year.)

involve higher production costs, reduced employment opportunities, and possibly new or substitute hazards. "Becoming richer is becoming safer," it is argued; increased wealth across society improves nutrition, medical care, and recreation.

2. *Ability:* The worker, it may be argued, is better able to bear risk than the general public. The weak, the ill, and the aged tend to be underrepresented in the worker population. In addition, the workers have greater knowledge and experience of the hazard and are better able to defend themselves.

Table 4.1 A COMPARISON OF U.S. AND U.S.S.R. WORKPLACE AND ENVIRONMENTAL STANDARDS (Mg/M³)

		BENZENE	CARBON MONOXIDE	LEAD	MERCURY	NITROGEN OXIDES	OZONE	SULFUR DIOXIDE	HYDRO-CARBONS	PART-ICULATES
U.S.	WORKPLACE	30	55	0.05	0.05	9	0.2	13	500 or 1000 ppm	—
	ENVIRONMENT	—[1]	10[3]	0.0015	—	0.1[4]	0.235[5]	0.08[6]	0.016[7]	0.0075[8]
USSR	WORKPLACE	5	20	0.01	0.01	5	0.1	10	300	
	ENVIRONMENT	0.8[2]	1.0	0.0007	0.0003	0.085	no standard	0.05		0.05

[1]emission standards only
[2]averaged over 2 hours
[3]averaged over 8 hours
[4]averaged over 1 hour

[5]averaged over 1 hour
[6]mean for 1 year
[7]averaged over 3 hours
[8]annual geometric mean

Sources: D. R. Greenwood, G. L. Kingsbury, and J. G. Cleland, *A Handbook of Key Federal Regulations and Criteria for Multimedia Environmental Control*, EPA-600/7-79-175 (Washington: EPA, 1979); International Labour Office, *Occupational Exposure Limits for Airborne Toxic Substances* Occupational Safety and Health Series No. 37 (Geneva: ILO, 1977).

3. *Compensation:* The worker is, in the view of many, paid to assume risks. Economists argue, for example, that wages include a "risk premium," an increment to the basic wage which compensates the worker for riskier jobs. The market thus neatly resolves the equity problem by allowing risk-tolerant workers to seek riskier and higher-paying jobs, whereas risk-averse workers can seek safer, if lower-paying, jobs.

4. *Consent:* The worker knew what the risks were upon entering the job and consented to accept them. Work is often hazardous and generally regarded as such. Risk is part of the reasonable price workers accept for the benefits of employment.

Each of these moral justifications is suspect. The empirical evidence to support the claim of utility is often lacking. Workers often possess little or no information about a hazard and usually cannot migrate to other jobs if they wish. The wage compensation of risk-bearing remains an untested hypothesis. In a series of articles in *Environment* (1981-1983), the Clark group has confronted the empirical questions and moral arguments.

Report,e suggests a number of reasons why this and the countless other equity problems embedded in technology policy prove so difficult for institutional response. First, the empirical details of the equity issues are rarely made explicit in the scientific information that supports impact analysis or policy choices. The empirical distributions will prove difficult to derive in many cases. This is certainly true of the differential protection example presented above, where one searches in vain for explicit treatment of trade-offs. Second, the values to guide the standard of fairness are rarely undisputed, and different conceptions of equity lead to very different policy preferences. Third, of course equity is only one, and usually not the most important, policy goal. Although current controversies over the deployment of technologies customarily appear to be driven as much by questions of risk distribution as total risk, decision processes do not reflect this. Proponents of equity have to fight their way into the decision arena. Finally, for many issues we simply lack adequate institutional mechanisms for achieving equity. If it were accepted that protection from technological hazards should be apportioned more fairly, what means would we use? Do we have adequate institutional devices to resolve the potential inequities to future generations from toxic chemicals?

PROBLEM 3: THE ROLE OF FORMAL RISK ASSESSMENT

Perhaps no area of risk management has received greater attention over the past decade than the energy sector. As critics pinpoint new risk issues, voluminous formal risk assessments mushroom (e.g., WASH-1400 in the United States, Canvey Island in the United Kingdom, the German Reactor Study, and KBS 1 and 2 in Sweden). Nuclear power has been at the forefront, of course, but increasingly our attention is expanding to embrace other energy sources—coal, solar power, and even energy conservation (radon and indoor pollutants). Despite these laudable efforts, social controversies continue, indeed thrive! A societal consensus on energy risks continues to elude us, and the public appears as confused as before, and perhaps even more risk averse.

We have rushed to formal risk assessment without first understanding the contributions of such assessments to risk clarification, safety policy making, and the deescalation of scientific debate and social controversy. What exactly do they do? The experience of WASH-1400, designed in part to settle the reactor-safety debate, served only to enlarge it.[7] The Inhaber Report provoked acrimonious scientific debate over the relative safety of different energy sources.[8] Even the Lewis Report, by a blue-ribbon panel of experts, probably provoked more controversy, due to the reaction of the NRC and the press, than it removed.[9] It is unclear whether this thriving new industry of risk assessment is the result of genuine need or simply a fad. What should be our expectations of this curious new mode of scientific expression?

The Kemeny Commission: A Post Mortem

The accident at Three Mile Island nuclear power plant on March 28, 1979, was by common consensus the worst in the history of commercial nuclear power generation in the United States. It is not surprising that the accident provoked a series of assessments of its significance for the safety of nuclear power. Prominent among these was the report of the President's Commission on the Accident at Three Mile Island (1979), popularly known as the Kemeny Commission.[10]

The report issued by the commission is of a genre of formal risk assessments. Unlike WASH-1400 and the Lewis Report, which relied heavily upon expert assessment dealing with the quantitative problablistic assessment of risk, the Kemeny Commission inquired into the larger issues of nuclear safety as indicated by a particular accident. Because of the significance of the crisis and the direct responsibility of the commission to the president, the report had a unique opportunity to contribute to the shaping of nuclear safety policy in the United States. It is in a number of respects a "best case" analysis of what such major assessments might accomplish.

What has this commission accomplished? Table 4.2 presents a summary of the response to key commission recommendations and is discussed at length elsewhere.[11]

First, it is apparent that the major elements of societal response were set in motion within several months after the accident, well in advance of the appearance of the Kemeny Report in October 1979. As a presidential commission, the Kemeny Commission had considerable symbolic value and undoubtedly contributed to the mandate for change, but it identified few issues not treated previously or in other post mortems of the TMI accidents.

Table 4.2

SOCIETAL RESPONSE TO KEY KEMENY COMMISSION RECOMMENDATIONS
(as of February 1982)

RECOMMENDATION	RESPONSE
RESTRUCTURE/IMPROVE NRC (A1)	President does not accept Kemeny reorganization recommendations. Congress retains collegial structure with strengthened powers of chairman. Chairman designated as spokesman in emergencies.
	Assessment: basic problems of the Commission referred to in Report remains unresolved, restructuring is not achieved but substantial improvement in emergency response and some improvement regulating operating reactor capabilities. In Sept. 1980, however, the Nuclear Safety Oversight Committee finds evidence of a "business as usual mindset in NRC."
IMPROVE ACRS (A3)	NRC opposes any mandatory response to ACRS recommendations. On Feb. 11, 1980, ACRS charges NRC "largely ignores" its input on Kemeny Commission responses.
	Assessment: no substantial action undertaken to improve ACRS. It is unlikely that the ACRS can and/or will influence major changes within the NRC.
ESTABLISH NEW OVERSIGHT COMMITTEE (A2)	Exec. Order establishes Nuclear Safety Oversight Committee on March 18, 1980. Committee issues three letter reports to the president on NRC action plan, radiological consequences of nuclear accidents, and emergency response planning, but its mandate is not renewed by the Reagan Administration.
	Assessment: Committee has provided limited but useful function. Failure to renew its mandate weakens overall safety assurance.
UPGRADE REACTOR OPERATOR & SUPERVISOR TRAINING (A4, C1, C4)	Nuclear Safety Analysis Center establishes computerized communication system connected to all utilities on operating incidents. NRC proposes upgrading in formal education: senior reactor operators, 60 college credits in engineering; shift supervisors, a BS degree in engineering. Utilities improve training in emergency events. No change proposed in formal education of reactor operators. Memphis State University inaugurates new training program in cooperation with utilities. Severity of licensing exams increased; failure rate rises from 5 to 30 percent. NRC declines to accredit training programs.
	Assessment: upgrading becoming evident though requirements still lag behind those in Europe.

Table 4.2 (continued)

SOCIETAL RESPONSE TO KEY KEMENY COMMISSION RECOMMENDATIONS
(as of February 1982)

RECOMMENDATION	RESPONSE
INCREASE SAFETY EMPHASIS IN LICENSING (A10)	NRC reorganizes licensing staff to correct weaknesses in licensing process. Increased attention to operator training, utility management, emergency planning, reactor design features, and evaluation of plant operating experience; NRC decides against Office of Hearing Counsel. 1981 licensing plan reduces role of intervenors.
	Assessment: actions to date fill a number of gaps in safety coverage, but the degree of substantial improvement unclear. NRC licensing of Sequoyah plant questions commitment to safety. Reduced role of intervenors weakens safety focus.
IMPROVE SAFETY INSPECTION AND ENFORCEMENT (A11)	NRC establishes resident inspectors at power plants, requires annual evaluation of licensees, improves reporting requirements. A new NRC Office for Analysis and Evaluation of Operational Data established (prior to Kemeny Report) in July, 1979. Fines for utilities increased. Bingham Amendment calls for "systematic evaluation" of all operating nuclear power plants, a possible 5-8 year effort which has evoked opposition.
	Assessment: Although too early to tell, indications are of substantial improvement in inspection and regulation of operating reactors. But position of top leadership of NRC during Reagan Administration will be important. Bingham Amendment will require significant new NRC resources.
IMPROVE TECHNICAL ASSESSMENT AND EQUIPMENT (D1-D3)	Utilities initiate improvements in control room design and instrumentation.
	Assessment: substantial improvements implemented or ongoing in improved instrumentation, equipment, and monitoring.

Table 4.2   (continued)
SOCIETAL RESPONSE TO KEY KEMENY COMMISSION RECOMMENDATIONS
(as of February 1982)

RECOMMENDATION	RESPONSE
INITIATE NEW REACTOR RISK ASSESSMENTS (D4-5, D7, E1)	NRC reorients risk assessment research program with new attention to higher probability events, accident mitigation, and human factors. Retrospective iodine release study of TMI accident suggest possible past overestimate of consequences by factor of 10. Utilities establish improved monitoring and dissemination system of operating incidents. NRC establishes Division of Human Factors and initiates effort to define level of acceptable risk. Epidemiological studies of effects of low level radiation initiated. EPA recommends against 10-fold reduction in occupational standard. Probabilistic risk assessments initiated by utilities at 8 power plants. Radiation Policy Council established in Executive Branch.
	Assessment: significant changes instituted to give new priority to TMI-like events, to human factors, and accident mitigation. Individual plant risk assessments should improve safety performance and enlarge accident response capability.
IMPROVE INDUSTRY ATTITUDES AND PERFORMANCE (B1-B3, B5)	Industry establishes two new institutions: Institute for Nuclear Power Operations (INPO) with power plant evaluation and training as primary functions and Nuclear Safety Analysis Center (NSAC) with analysis of operating experience and other technical assessment its primary activities. International cooperation with NSAC makes world experience data base a possibility.
	Assessment: substantial industry response: new institutoins and important safety vehicles. Still unresolved are prevailing attitudes and assurance of high level of overall technical competence in individual utility management structure.
MORE REMOTE SITING OF NUCLEAR POWER PLANTS (A6)	NRC proposes (NUREG 0625) upper limits on population densities around plants and making siting criteria distinct from engineered safeguards. Estimates suggest 49 of 84 currently operating plants would fail to meet criteria. Strong industry opposition.
	Assessment: proposal currently mired in controversy; no change to date, but new plants not presently being ordered in any event. Since no retrospective application of criteria, limited safety impact on 100-150 GWE nuclear system.

Table 4.2   (continued)
SOCIETAL RESPONSE TO KEY KEMENY COMMISSION RECOMMENDATIONS
(as of February 1982)

RECOMMENDATION	RESPONSE
IMPROVE EMERGENCY RESPONSE AND MITIGATION (A7-A8, E3-E5, F1-F3, G1-G4)	NRC issues new rule on emergency response plans, extending 5-mile zone to 10-mile and 50-mile radii. All operating reactors required to have emergency plans approved by April, 1981. NRC installs a crisis management communications link of all power plants to NRC headquarters. New rule mandates that state be able to notify every person within 10 miles of a nuclear power plant of accident within 15 minutes and evacuate population. Proposal to distribute potassium iodide pills mired in controversy. *Nucleonics Week* survey finds confused and uncertain response by states. No notable improvement in mass media capabilities, despite an NRC pilot program.
	Assessment: although utilities and the NRC have improved their emergency response capabilities, the overall capacity of society to respond to a major accident remains in doubt.
EDUCATE THE PUBLIC (F4, G5)	NRC plans to investigate need for literature. No program instituted to date.
	Assessment: no substantive response despite widespread scientific belief as to need.

Second, the response by industry has been timely and effective. In comparison, the regulatory responses have been delayed and uneven, and the mass media have generally failed to respond to recommendations for change. The overall regulatory response has also been heavily dependent upon the role of industry. Ironically, the long-term effect of the accident may be to further self-regulation in nuclear power.

Third, the changes instituted by industry and government have tended to address only obvious gaps and specific problems apparent in the accident. The more fundamental and integrative problems of capability and attitudes, which formed the primary concern of the Kemeny Commission, and the need for new initiatives and ideas remain essentially unaddressed. One Kemeny Commission pronuclear member noted that "industry's concern with meeting the formalism of NRC regulations is still inhibiting and throttling new ideas and technical innovations more directly related to safety."[12]

Fourth, although the record since the Kemeny report reveals an unprecedented imposition of new requirements on operating reactors, a comprehensive rationale for "backfitting" requirements is yet to be instituted. In fact, various new rules and regulations were implemented in advance of the definition of the acceptable level of risk desired (a safety goal), upon which such changes logically were based.

Fifth, the rash of post-mortem assessments appears to have had few long-term impacts on the overall nuclear debate or on public attitudes. A survey of the response of pro- and antinuclear journals indicates, not surprisingly, a tendency to find what one wants to find in the results (table 4.3). A content analysis of issues treated in these journals before the accident and since the Kemeny Report indicates no substantial restructuring of the agenda of debate. The Kemeny Report experience suggests that formal risk assessments add new issues to the agenda but resolve few existing points of contention.

Finally, although there was a discernible "blip" in the trend lines of public attitudes following the accident, polls since that time have shown opinions tending to stabilize at or near preaccident levels (with perhaps some movement from "no opinion" to opposition).[13]

PROBLEM 4: RISK ACCEPTABILITY IN STANDARD SETTING

Over the past decade, new legislation to control technological hazards, the birth of the "new" regulatory agencies such as EPA, OSHA, and the CPSC, and a series of well-publicized technological "scares" have centered attention upon the degree of safety to which environmental and workplace regulation should aspire. Although the regulatory agencies are customarily faulted for their desultory progress in standard setting, opponents have not been slow in challenging decisions, once made, concerning the level of risk appropriate for certain hazards. The OSHA standard on vinyl chloride, though upheld in court, has produced spirited and extensive opposition from the manufacturers over the validity of the assumptions and evidence underlying the regulation. The saccharin decision, though clearly mandated by law, provoked Congress to prevent implementation of a regulatory ban. The Supreme Court decision on the OSHA regulation to control the exposure of workers to benzene required a determination of the presence of significant risks that could be reduced by the new standard, but not that the work environment be made risk free. The Reagan administration's proposal to relax or eliminate 35 air quality and safety regulations has raised anew the conflicts between an ailing economy and lifesaving measures. The Three Mile Island accident of 1979 has provoked increased calls for a safety goal to which all nuclear regulation and licensing should aspire.

Regulators are loath to make normative judgments; Congress sets objectives only in a very general and vague manner; and a benefit-oriented Office of Management and Budget will have regulators looking over its shoulder. This is a social-risk issue of considerable magnitude. The term "risk acceptability," conveys the impression that society purposely accepts risks as the reasonable price for some beneficial technology or activity. For some special cases this may approach reality. Hang gliding, race-car driving, and mountain climbing are all high-risk activities in which the benefits are intrinsically entwined with the risks. These activities are exhilarating partly because they are dangerous. But most risks of

Table 4.3 CONCLUSIONS DRAWN FROM THE KEMENY COMMISSION REPORT

Group or Journal	CONCLUSION REACHED		
	Vindication of Industry	Balanced Judgement	Indictment of Industry
Nuclear News	No conclusion that nuclear power too dangerous. Accident caused by operating error. Apart from control room, NRC primary cause of accident.		
Nuclear Industry	Plants are safe; it is people who are not. Nuclear power safe if managed well.		
Public Utilities Fortnightly		Mechanical malfunctions were exacerbated by human error. Deficiencies in equipment, training, and attitudes pervaded the industry and NRC changes required if nuclear power not to be eliminated by public opinion.	
Critical Mass Energy Project			A serious indictment of the nuclear industry and a clear vindication for the nuclear critics. Nuclear power is shown to be unsafe.
Union of Concerned Scientists' *Nucleus*			A far-reaching indictment of practices of NRC and industry. Report fails to address problems of safety deficiencies.
Friends of the Earth, *Not Man Apart*			Commission did not go far enough in implicating the risks of nuclear power.

concern are the undesired and often unforeseen by-products of otherwise beneficial activities or technologies.

Acceptability is the concept that underlies judgments of safety. W.W. Lowrance, for example, argues that "a thing is safe if its attendant risks are judged acceptable."[14] Setting aside for the moment the important questions of how and by whom such judgments are made, probably no risk is acceptable if it can be readily reduced still further. To suggest otherwise is to invoke moral justification for trading practical constraints against human lives, a position that most risk guardians will wisely evade. The marketplace, then, is a poor guide to what risks are acceptable, as attested to by the century-long struggle by workers to reduce workplace risks. The occurrence of a risk suggests more about the balance of political forces at that time than about its acceptability to those who bore the risk.

What does it mean to accept a risk? Does the commuter who disdains seat belts accept the risks of automobile driving? Do workers in textile plants accept the risk of cotton dust exposure? Do teenage girls with cigarettes dangling from their fingers accept the risk of smoking? At this individual level, guidance can be found in the practice of informed consent formulated to protect subjects in human experiments. Here risk acceptance involves several important ingredients: the provision of full information concerning potential risks, evidence that the subject understands the information, genuine freedom of choice for entering into the experiment, and the option to terminate one's participation at any time.

On the basis of the informational criterion alone, few risks meet the test of acceptance. Whereas some classes of risk (e.g., those of high probability and acute consequences) are undoubtedly better understood than others (e.g., those of low probability and chronic consequences), it is only for a minority of risks that the public approaches full information and understanding. Nor is this irrational. Given the relentless barrage of risks that confront us, limitation of information is undoubtedly a prerequisite for warding off hypochondria if not despair. There are also large classes of risks, including many of those most feared by the public, that are involuntary in nature. In short, most technological risks are not accepted; they are imposed, often without warning, information, or means of redress.

Since most risks are imposed on a less than fully informed risk bearer, the response is more properly thought of as tolerance or acquiescence rather than acceptance. With limited choice and imperfect knowledge, the individual does not resist the imposition of the risk. As knowledge of the risk and range of choice grow, the individual will usually become more risk averse, and the degree of risk acceptance will increase. The area between the tolerated and the accepted risk is the latitude available to the risk guardian for standard setting (figure 4.2). This structure of risk response is, of course, specific to a particular point in time and may be expected to change.

Judgments of appropriate risk levels are inherently problems of ethics and politics. Debates over risk are often at root debates over the adequacy and credibility of the institutions which manage the risk and not debates over the actual level of risk. Within the latitude available for risk setting, the risk manager must weigh and trade off multiple objectives and conflicting values. In such decision situations, the preferred choices will not always be those with the lowest risk. Above all, the public wants to be assured that these decisions are made fairly and with a strong commitment to the safety and well-being of the public.

Fig. 4.2 Schematic diagram of individual response to risk.

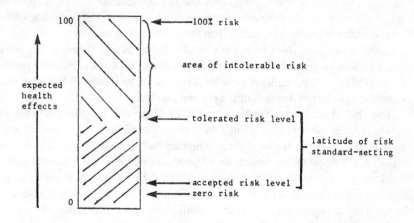

The level of safety to which nuclear power should aspire provides an excellent example of this recurring problem. It has been for some time a question of concern to both regulator and industry alike and was accorded high priority as a policy need by both the Rogovin Report and the NRC Lessons Learned Report.[15,16] In the absence of a safety goal agreed upon by society, the adequacy of the NRC response to the Three Mile Island accident is impossible to assess and creates a large uncertainty in the licensing process. Congress also pressed for such a determination: the Bingham Amendment, for example, required a proposed safety goal for nuclear reactor regulation by June 30, 1981. By February 11, 1982, the NRC released a draft safety goal which immediately set off widespread debate.[17]

Can the determination so eagerly sought be made in a defensible manner? If so, how should this and other such judgments be made? First, it should be noted that it is difficult to imagine a more difficult test case. Nuclear power has a number of characteristics which make the public extraordinarily risk averse:

• There is substantial linkage in public response between nuclear power and nuclear weapons, a connection that contributes to deep-seated fear over the technology. This concern is particularly apparent in women, who are substantially more opposed to nuclear energy than men.

• Its hazards have attributes beyond the quantitative level of risk, as measured by probabilities multiplied by consequences, particularly dreaded by the public, including particularly its catastrophic potential, its means of exposure (radiation), and the particular mode of consequence (cancer).

• Difficult value issues pervade the deployment of the technology, involving on the one hand, the need for adequate energy supplies versus issues of human survival, future generations, and democratic process on the other hand.

• Widespread distrust of the institutions that manage nuclear energy is apparent, while a committed opposition exists to amplify whatever errors or mishaps occur in management and to link peaceful and military uses of nuclear technology.

In such a situation, there is very strong likelihood that a judgment by experts as to an adequate safety goal will prove unacceptable to at least a substantial portion of the public, will be defined as self-serving or as misleading, and will itself become the subject of a new controversy and conflict.

How should such determinations be made? There will be great temptation to include this and other judgments in a more general campaign to tidy up this mish-mash of risk decision through some common and consistent standard for risk imposition. Several means have been proposed: some see in the historical pattern of risk occurrence, evidence that society has arrived at a balance between risk and benefit.[18] Others see the need for a consistent quantitative level of risk to serve as the basis for all regulation.[19] Still others would have cost effectiveness serve as the guiding principle in responding to risk across technologies.[20]

This search for an analytic fix for the risk-acceptability problem is misguided. Worse still, it reveals a profound misunderstanding of the nature of the problem. First, it wrongly assumes that one risk is like any other, whereas it is patently clear that risks are multidimensional phenomena that fall into complex groupings. Death by cancer is not the same as death by accident, catastrophic risks are more feared and exact a greater social toll than smaller fatality risks, and imposed risks are unlike voluntary risks. Research at Clark University over the past five years has identified some 12 hazard attributes that, when factor analyzed for some 93 technological hazards, fall into six major factors which differentiate such hazards (table 4.4).[21] When compared with studies of public response to the same hazards, conducted by Paul Slovic and colleagues at Decision Research, Inc., a remarkably close correspondence emerges between the structure of technological hazards and the nature of public response, providing hope that an overall taxonomy of such hazards is possible which will have strong public policy relevance.[22] But it makes clear that regulatory approaches to risk will need to be plural, taking account of major important differences among risks.

Second, decisions on risk levels do not occur in isolation from other social objectives and constraints. Each risk decision, then, tends to be technology, or even situation, specific.[23] The particular set of values, scientific information, cost considerations, and safety opportunities differ from one risk to another, and from one time to another, for the same risk. Moreover, different regulatory agencies have different legislative mandates and program priorities for the same risks. Sound decisions on risk levels and distribution, therefore, will *and should* show substantial variation even among similar risks. This does not mean, of course, making decisions case by case, but rather by classes. However untidy this variation

Table 4.4 Proposed Taxonomy

CLASSES	EXAMPLES
1. Multiple Extremes	Nuclear war, Recombinant DNA, Deforestation
2. Intentional Biocides	Pesticides, Nerve gas, Antibiotics
3. Persistent Teratogens	Uranium mining, Radioactive Waste, Mercury
4. Rare Catastrophes	Recombinant DNA, LNG, Satellites
5. Common Killers	Automobiles, Handguns, Medical x-rays
6. Diffuse Global Threats	Fossil fuel (CO_2), SST (NO_x), Coal Burning

may appear to some, it is an inescapable reality of responsible and rational risk management (a conclusion shared, by the way, by two recent appraisals of the risk acceptability issue[24,25]).

If we reject an analytic fix, how can such decisions be made? The answer may lie in the domain of process and not in particular modes of analysis. Viable decisions on risk levels and distribution require a process consistent with Western democratic theory and directive to the risk guardian. Since the public cannot hope to inform itself and participate in the innumerable decisions on risk, it delegates authority to the legislators, who pass laws, and to the regulators, who implement them. Doubts as to the credibility of these institutions and processes have provoked much of the current debate over risk decision making. If and when that credibility is recovered, "How safe is safe enough" will cease to be the subject of societal debate. In the meantime, extraordinary efforts will be required for the recovery of trust and for socially acceptable decisions on risks.

A viable process for risk decisions is one that recognizes the requirements of procedural justice and democratic responsibility. The details of such a process are the subject for a lengthier discussion; suffice it to note here six major considerations for such a process:

1. Appropriate considerations and information to support judgments on tolerable risk are essential and should include, at minimum, the systematic treatment of contextual considerations, equity analysis, and public preference analysis (figure 4.3).
2. Decisions on risk are rarely made in isolation but are part of broader societal choices on the use and expansion of particular technologies and activities. "Best solutions" involve choices that take account of competing social values and multiple goals. The appropriate role of the scientist lies in the estimation and measurement of risk and the creation of information needed to assess its meaning, but not in determining its preferred level or distribution.
3. Attempts to find an analytic fix for the risk-tolerability problem are misguided. Risk standard setting should begin with the recognition that such standards should be plural in nature, varying in level and distribution with magnitudes of

benefits, equity consideration, opportunities for risk reduction, availability of less risky alternatives, public preferences for risk reduction, and other considerations.

4. Risks cannot be made fully voluntary if society is to realize the potential good associated with existing and new technologies. But the emphasis in risk management should be on avoiding rather than mitigating risk, in making unavoidable risks as voluntary as is feasible, and on compensating the bearers of unavoidable risks from beneficiaries where possible.

5. Since risks tend to be imposed rather than accepted, the burden of proof should be on the risk creator to demonstrate the need for the technology and the absence of the risk.

6. Fairness in risk imposition is best achieved by the active participation of risk bearers in their own behalf in decisions on the tolerability of particular risk levels and allocations. Risk bearers should not be dependencies in the decision process, but require their own technical capability, right to negotiation, and legitimacy in the process. They also have the right to full information as to the risks to be imposed upon them.

CONCLUSION

From the preceding discussion, several suggestions may be offered to explain the continuing failure in institutional responses to this particular set of social risk problems.

1. It must be appreciated that these are, in fact, very difficult problems. Ionizing radiation is one of the best understood of chronic hazards, yet consider the recent history of BEIR-III in trying to reach a scientific consensus. By compari-

Fig. 4.3 Expert assessment for judging risk intolerability.

CONTEXTUAL ANALYSIS	EQUITY ANALYSIS	PUBLIC PREFERENCE ANALYSIS
Risks in the context of:	*The distribution of risks, benefits, and control costs over:*	*Public risk reduction preferences as indicated by:*
—natural background levels —other extant risks —magnitude of benefits —costs of control —risks of available substitutes	—workers and publics —generations —backyards —social groups	—incurred risk inference —legal legacy inference —expressed values

son our understanding of the "causal path" of exposure leading to consequences in social risks is rudimentary indeed. Given the paucity of theory to guide a defensible social risk assessment or an explicit setting of "acceptable" risk, a risk guardian would be making himself and his agency highly vulnerable to outside criticism and attack.

2. Social risk issues are remote from the traditional mandates, accumulated experience, and expertise of the energy agencies. Engaging such issues is difficult, perhaps impossible, without the development of new capabilities and perhaps new organizational structures. For agencies accustomed to technology development, public health questions, and engineering approaches, social risk issues pose an ill-defined collection of frighteningly "soft" assessment issues.

3. Social risk questions are pervaded by value issues for which there are, in many technological disputes, discordant positions. Although it is exactly for such decisions that society elects and employs public officials, current institutional means for specifying and trading off conflicting values remain underdeveloped, and public officials eschew visible choices.

4. There are few incentives for risk guardians to broaden risk assessments to include social risk or to make explicit how the social meaning of risk is inferred. But there are strong reasons to avoid such issues: to avoid conferring legitimacy on such problems, to prevent a dramatic increase in decision complexity, and to preclude the opening of new battlegrounds for the technological wars.

It would be unreasonable to expect, then, that these problems of social risk will quickly disappear from the agenda of conferences such as this one. Unhappily, it is also probably true that existing institutions will continue to buffer themselves from such problems and that their resolution will continue to be fought outside established processes.

NOTES

1. U.S. Nuclear Regulatory Commission, *Proposed Goals for Radioactive Waste Management* (Washington, D.C.: The Commission, 1978).
2. U.S. Task Force for Review of Nuclear Waste Management, *Report of Task Force,* DOE/ER-004/D (Washington, D.C.; U.S. Department of Energy, 1978).
3. U.S. Interagency Review Group on Nuclear Waste Management, *Report to the President,* TID-29442 (Washington, D.C.: U.S. Department of Energy, 1979).
4. U.S. Office of the President, *Message from the President of the United States Transmitting a Report on his Proposals for a Comprehensive Radioactive Waste Management Program,* 96th Congress, 2nd Session, House Document 96-266 (Washington, D.C., 1980).
5. National Research Council, Committee on Radioactive Waste Management, Letter to Dr. Colin A. Heath, U.S. Department of Energy, 18 April 1980.
6. Patrick Derr, Robert Goble, Roger E. Kasperson, and Robert W. Kates, "Worker/Public Protection: The Double Standard," *Environment,* 23 (Sept. 1981), 6-15, 31-36.
7. U.S. Nuclear Regulatory Commission, *Reactor Safety Study—An Assessment of Accident Risks in U.S. Commercial Nuclear Power Plants,* WASH-1400, NUREG-75/014 (Washington,D.C.: The Commission, 1975).

8. H. Inhaber, "Risk with Energy from Conventional and Nonconventional Sources," *Science,* 203 (1979), 718-723.
9. Risk Assessment Review Group, *Report to the U.S. Nuclear Regulatory Commission,* NUREG/CR-0400, (Washington,D.C.: The Commisssion, 1978).
10. The President's Commission on the Accident at Three Mile Island, *The Need for Change: The Legacy of TMI* (Washington, D.C.: The Commission).
11. Roger E. Kasperson and Arnold L. Gray, *Risk Assessment Following Crisis: A Retrospective Assessment of The Kemeny Commission Report* (Worcester, MA: Clark University, Center for Technology, Environment, and Development, 1982).
12. Thomas H. Pigford, "The Management of Nuclear Safety: A Review of TMI after Two Years," *Nuclear News,* 24 (March 1981), 41-48.
13. Robert Cameron Mitchell, "Polling on Nuclear Power: A Critique of the Polls after Three Mile Island," in Albert H. Cantril,ed., *Polling on the Issues* (Washington, D.C.: Seven Locks Press, 1980) pp.67-98.
14. W.W. Lowrance, *Of Acceptable Risk: Science and the Determination of Safety,* (Los Altos, CA: W. Kaufman, 1976).
15. U.S. Nuclear Regulatory Commission, Special Inquiry Group, *Three Mile Island: A Report to the Commission and to the Public,* NUREG/CR-1250, 2 vols. (Washington, D.C.: The Commission, 1980).
16. U.S. Nuclear Regulatory Commission, Special Review Group, *Lessons Learned from Three Mile Island,* NUREG-0616 (Washington, D.C.: The Commission, 1979).
17. *New York Times,* 12 Feb. 1982, p.B-8.
18. C. Starr, "Social Benefit Versus Technological Risk," *Science,* 165 (1965), 1232-1238.
19. J. Reissland and V. Harries, "A Scale for Measuring Risks," *New Scientist,* 83 (1979), 809-811.
20. R. Wilson, "The Costs of Safety," *New Scientist,* (1975) 274-275.
21. C. Hohenemser, R.E. Kasperson, and R.W. Kates, "Causal Structure: A Framework for Policy Formulation," in C. Hohenemser and J. X. Kasperson, eds., *Risk in the Technological Society,* AAAS Symposium Series (Boulder, CO: Westview Press, 1982).
22. Ibid, P. Slovic, B. Fischhoff, and S. Lichtenstein, "Rating the Risks: The Structure of Expert and Lay Perceptions."
23. B. Fischhoff, et al., *Approaches to Acceptable Risk: A Critical Guide,* NUREG/ CR-1614; ORNL/sub-7656/1 (Oak Ridge, TN: Oak Ridge National Laboratory, 1980).
24. Ibid.
25. S.L. Salem, K.A. Solomon, and M.S. Yesley, *Issues and Problems in Inferring a Level of Acceptable Risk,* RAND/R-2561-DOE (Santa Monica, CA: Rand Corp., 1980).

Chapter 5
VALUING HUMAN LIFE

Douglas MacLean**

I.

The nuclear power controversy only occasionally rises to the level of a debate about scientific issues. More often it is a political or ideological conflict that has somehow come to focus on such matters as the safety of light water reactors, the risks of radioactive wastes, and the proliferation of nuclear weapons. New scientific analyses never seem to make these debates go away, or even to change them very much, and one suspects that the deeply divided community of scientific and engineering experts may not be entirely detached from political and ideological convictions.

Like other political controversies, this one is rhetorically charged. The proponents of nuclear power, for example, often describe the debate as expressing a fundamental division between technological optimists and technological pessimists.[1] Of course, this description is meant to derogate the pessimistic nay-sayers, who are charged with wanting a risk-free society. These Luddites, extraordinarily fearful of any new-found risk, persist in misunderstanding and exaggerating the dangers of nuclear power. Worse, they stubbornly refuse to compare nuclear risks to others, especially to the risks of alternative technologies for producing electricity. The nuclear critics see their opponents not merely as optimists but as blind lovers of new technologies, especially big, expensive, and complicated technologies. The self-described optimists seem, to the pessimists, more like kindred souls to Marinetti and his socially irresponsible band of futurists.

As we might expect, the real world is not so simple. The optimist versus pessimist dichotomy is a red herring, an absurd description of the nuclear power debate. When Barry Commoner, a leading nuclear critic, rhapsodizes about the commercial feasibility of photovoltaic cells or sophisticated systems for producing

*The views in this paper have been shaped by discussions with many people. I am particularly indebted to Geoffrey Brennan, Steven Kelman, Mark Sagoff, James Vaupel, and Susan Wolf. My research has been supported by the National Science Foundation, grant number PRA-80-20019.

methanol from biomass, he exemplifies a paradigm of technological optimism.[2] And the gloomy projections of nuclear engineers that discount solar and conservation technologies, calling them unrealistic or fantastic, are pure expressions of technological pessimism.

The motivation to oppose nuclear power is more complex. This selective pessimism focuses on a particular technology, and it often has little to do with empirically based doubts about the tolerance of containment vessels in pressurized water reactors or the reliability of their backup feedwater pumps. Some of the fears are not tied to a concern for safety at all. The same person who protests against a reactor siting proposal one day may go rock climbing or hang gliding the next, and she will probably use the most technologically sophisticated equipment she can afford, because she is keenly aware of the risks she accepts. Nuclear power is symbolic, and it invites opposition that ranges from an expression of distrust of technical expertise,[3] to vague associations with bombs and destruction,[4] doubts about our social management capabilities for achieving technically possible safety standards,[5] collective social guilt,[6] and anxieties about the threats posed by this particular technology to the future health of democratic social institutions.[7]

None of this is to deny that there are important health and safety risks associated with nuclear power (and with its alternatives), risks that are debated and enveloped in uncertainty and ignorance. My claim is only that political and social issues are also central to this debate and perhaps dominate it. It is important to point out, of course, that not every social, moral, or ideological anxiety deserves to be weighed in our decisions. Some concerns may simply be irrational, but in order to determine which ones ought to be taken seriously and which dismissed, we have to consider each one directly and on its merits. This is, broadly speaking, a function of the political process. Just as it is important that our assessment of the risks be comprehensive and based on the best science and most sophisticated techniques available, so it is important that these other issues be treated in the best and most appropriate manner. In this way, we balance our concern for physical safety with our concern for our other social values. In short, this is how we attempt to make the best decisions and policies we can, all things considered.

The relationship between these two concerns—assessing risks and evaluating them in the broader context of forming public policies—is the topic of this chapter. Various methods of quantified risk assessment (QRA) have been developed to help us with the former task. The question is to what extent these techniques might also help us with the latter task. That is to say, in what ways should our decisions and policies be analytically determined? This is the broad question I want to raise, but I will focus my discussion on one much debated issue: the social value of human life.

I will begin by describing a few of the general features of QRAs that will show how values are implicitly or explicitly assigned to human lives. Then, I will consider the objections to this manner of valuing human life. My purpose is to show how an indiscriminate use of analytic or scientific approaches to decision making distorts social values and is, therefore, to be opposed. QRAs are indispensable for making wise decisions and policies. They give us useful information especially about technological risks. But in order to realize the benefits of these techniques, we must also be aware of their limitations. In some contexts, it may be possible to apply a QRA as a decision procedure, but wrong to do so nevertheless. The implications of this argument, though critical, are not all negative. In the final section of this chapter, I will mention why I think we can benefit by acknowledging that the nuclear power controversy is fundamentally political, not scientific or technical.

II.

Quantified risk assessment stands for many different techniques, which share the goal of finding some scale for comparing risks. A risk assessment is concerned with three things: discovering and measuring the risk in some area or associated with some technology, comparing the risk to other risks, and measuring and comparing the costs and benefits linked to different levels of risk and safety. Leaving aside the problems of identifying all the risks, costs, and benefits and assigning them noncontroversial and nonarbitrary values—the measurement problems—QRAs can be a powerful aid to making rational decisions. They enable us to put an issue like the nuclear power controversy in a broader context and to make more general comparisons. They help us discover our myopia and, perhaps, our inconsistent attitudes.

This generality brings with it a certain detachment from the details of a particular controversy. What happens to these details? If they cannot be quantified and made part of the risk, benefit, and cost trade-off, then we may wish simply to dismiss them as irrational, or we can try to measure and include them as costs. Thus, it is often suggested that nuclear power must be made safer than other technologies because it evokes such extraordinary fears. Perhaps we should spend more for greater safety in this area in order to mollify or compensate the pessimists for their fear. It is easy to see why people would object to seeing their concerns simply ignored (which, to repeat, is not to say that some concerns should not be ignored). It is more important, however, to understand why someone might object to more all-encompassing applications of QRAs or risk-cost-benefit analyses. This will help us identify their limitations.

The central question in the QRA literature—How safe is safe enough?—may not be the most basic question if, as in the nuclear power controversy, the oppostiion is focused as much on the technology *per se* as on its risks. The opposition to other economically attractive technologies (such as those that may add carcinogens to food, or fertilize plants with nondegradable toxic chemicals, or add pollutants to our air and water, or endanger workers) are similarly motivated by a variety of reasons. Some of these reasons have little to do with levels of risk or with the balance of costs and benefits but are very much concerned with the way that certain things and certain values are being regarded in the decision making process. These values may resist inclusion in any QRA.

Knowing the amount of risk and the cost of containing it further, however, can convince us that some of these reasons for opposing a technology are elitist, narrow-minded, or too expensive to take seriously. Conflicts can arise between those values that can be measured and those that cannot.

Consider the charge that QRAs assign a monetary value to life. The objection is not that the assigned value is typically too low, but that this is an inappropriate or unacceptable way to show our concern for human life or to express this social value in our laws and policies. The rationalization for assigning a value to human life is usually based on the following truth.

> Modern technologies, we are reminded, are mixed blessings. Citizens of modern industrial societies are learning a harsh and discomforting lesson: the benefits from technology must be paid for not only with money, but with environmental degradation, anxiety, illness, injury, and premature loss of life.[8]

In order to reduce the risk of early death (say, death before age 65) that these technologies impose, we must give them up, along with their benefits, or else we must invest other resources to control them, thereby giving up benefits elsewhere. But an unconstrained attempt to eliminate the risk of early death would consume all our resources long before these risks were squeezed to zero. Obviously, we need to make trade-offs, and finding a social value of human life is merely an attempt to help us do this in a rational and systematic way, one that allows us to make across-the-board comparisons.

There is a mild irony in this reasoning, for another way of putting the argument is to point out that we must trade lifesaving and risk reduction for other benefits, because maximizing life expectancy is not our only valued goal. That is, we are willing to trade some *quantity* of life for a better *quality* of life. Because QRAs help us see risk reduction in terms of costs and foregone benefits, they help to defend and promote these other values that comprise the quality of life. Proponents of QRA quantify the value of human life in order to protect life's quality.[9] This is precisely what their critics take them to task for doing.

Risk reduction is seen as an economic problem, and it is typical in textbooks on the subject to see the value of a human life viewed in economic terms. "In economics, in "normative" or allocative economics at least, the worth or value of a thing to a person is determined simply by what a person is willing to pay for it."[10] The critics of QRA object to seeing the values that give life its meaning or cherished quality, perhaps especially the value to society of human life itself, reduced to commerce and willingness to pay. But can this objection be justified? How else are we to compare and measure all these different values, costs, and benefits?

The social value of human life is a standard against which we can compare proposals to alter the risk of early death in exchange for costs and benefits. We can use it to evaluate new but risky technologies or expensive programs aimed at reducing some risk. In its least controversial form this value should not be thought of as putting a dollar tag on human lives. It is meant, instead, to apply where the lives are not identifiable humans but only statistical figures. A small per capita change in risk is accompanied by some expected economic change. Then, by scaling these numbers—that is, multiplying them by enough people (perhaps adding a factor for large numbers)—we arrive at what can be described statistically as the number of lives saved or lost in exchange for some level of economic costs or benefits.[11] The standard or normative value can be used to tell us whether a program spends too much or too little to save lives, whether we could save more lives for the same resources somewhere else, or whether the benefits of a new technology are worth its risks. Using a social value of human life as a norm in this way can lead us to policies that are efficient or cost-effective in reducing risks.

This method can also be adjusted to serve other social values. If we want to target our risk reduction efforts to pay more attention to *early* deaths, rather than maladies that afflict primarily the elderly, for which expensive cures may yield relatively smaller benefits, then we can measure the cost of saving a unit of average life expectancy, rather than the cost of an average life saving.[12]

A social value of human life can also help us promote goals of justice and social equality, by breaking down life-expectancy estimates for different social groups and aiming risk-reduction efforts at correcting significant differences. I suspect we could save more lives and improve life expectancy, all at less cost, by diverting some of the money we currently spend on airline safety to prenatal and infant health care among the poor. A QRA could be employed to measure these improvements. If this were feasible, it would give us data to support arguments for redistributing resources in order to achieve greater equality in life prospects. Commercial air travel carries risks to life that, when measured, are relatively low. They are kept this low at a high price. That is to say, the value of the lives of air passengers is high when compared to the value of lives in other areas of risk, as shown by the amount spent for safety attained. Does the public demand this expensive safety, or is it demanded only by that influential minority who fly frequently? However the facts turn out, the questions of equality or justice we raise here can only be answered by quantitative data, which risk assessments provide.

Efficiency can conflict with equality, of course, and when it does we have reasons to constrain our efficiency-directed behavior. Analytic approaches to decision making cannot replace distributive principles, but must be combined with them. I will not pursue this point further, however, because scarcely anybody would deny it or advocate an unrestricted obedience to maximizing some value in a QRA. In the rest of this chapter, I will leave aside the issues of justice and equity, and focus, instead, on other social values.

III.

I have argued that a social value of human life, once it is noncontroversially established, can be put to many good uses as a standard or norm against which to compare and evaluate social programs and policies. The obvious next question is to ask how we can establish this general value. One early attempt was rather crudely economic.

Using this method, the value of preventing early death was determined by estimating a person's expected lost income.[13] Strictly speaking, the value of life *to society* with this calculation would be lost income less personal consumption. This view enjoys support today from a dwindling minority of risk assessors. Its fall from favor is due to the fact that this measure turns out to be embarrassingly discriminatory. It judges certain lives (such as lives of the poor, the old, women, poets and blacks) to be less valuable than others, a judgment seriously at odds with strongly held moral convictions.

A different approach, indeed one that is very popular, values life by determining our willingness to pay (corrected, perhaps, for income effects) for risk reduction.[14] Insurance markets provide the best and most general example of how people express a value for risk reduction through their willingness to pay. Almost everyone seeks some kind of insurance. The price of the premium and the extent of the coverage indicate what people will pay to reduce a risk of enduring a much more serious loss.[15]

Where life and health are involved, we can look for data in insurance markets, but we can also look at other insurance products. A willingness to pay to reduce the risk of early death is revealed in the purchase of smoke detectors in homes, safety devices in automobiles, and yearly medical check-ups, to name a few. Wage differentials for hazardous work provide another well-researched area of revealed preference for risk-benefit trade-offs.

The crucial fact in using a willingness to pay criterion for determining the social value of human life is that not everything is reduced to dollars. It is, rather, that risks, costs, and benefits are all put on a single scale or common metric, which can be applied across all contexts. Dollars are just a convenient shorthand for determining a general preference ordering. We need to know what a person will give up for something he values more. It is the uniform ranking that is important here—the universal comparability and exchangeability, independent of context—not the numbers that are used to express it.

Decision analysis, one of many QRA techniques, begins simply by determining how individuals rank and order their different preferences. When decision analysts speak in terms of willingness to pay, this is because most preferences have economic ties to the use of some resource. So it is convenient to ask under what conditions a person would give up what she wants or switch preferences. The individual can decide however she likes. If the preference is *absolute,* if it is something a person would never give up, then we can assign it an infinite price. If it is like most preferences, however, we can imagine alternatives so wonderful or sacrifices so great that some trade-off or switch point can be determined. This reasoning applies as well to preferences for saving lives and reducing risks. We could do away with monetizing all values, if that seems too gross, without attacking anything essential to the valuing of lives through QRAs.

Any ordering that corresponds to strength of preference will serve the purpose. The proponents of QRA defend these methods as neutral and uncontroversial processes of decision making. "Analytic approaches to decide risk-benefit issues," say two of its defenders, "ideally come closer to maximizing net social benefits than any other approach."[16] They continue:

> The attraction of analytic methods (cost-benefit analysis, decision analysis) is their capacity to make explicit the assumptions, value judgments, and criteria used for making a decision. The analytic approaches are considered logically sound and sufficiently flexible to accept any value system. Given a sufficient set of values and criteria, a cost-benefit analysis could ideally indicate the decisions that would best balance technological risk and benefit (assuming that both tangible and intangible costs and benefits are included).[17]

The social value of human life is part of this neutral balancing act.

IV.

In order for QRA methods to be "sufficiently flexible to accept any value system" our "set of values" must have a uniformity of structure that would allow broad-based comparisons on a single scale without distortions. But values are not like that, and so distortions occur when we abstract from the context and causes that reveal our preferences. We value some objects for what they are, others simply for the experiences they cause or the happiness they produce, and these different kinds of values spell out different requirements—different relationships to valued objects and different ways of expressing values. We might say that values differ in their nature and quality, and that this diversity is an important aspect of the quality of life. If QRAs cannot account for this fact, then there are limits to their applicability, and if we ignore these limits we are not being neutral.

I have no general theory of value to present here, but I will describe some complexities that demonstrate limits to what QRAs can measure and compare. These complexities are relevant to how we value human life through our public policies. I will begin, at some distance from the subject of risk, with an example.

There sits in my dining room a late-eighteenth-century Russian samovar. It is one of the few antiques I own. I assume its history would be reflected in its economic value. A modern reproduction might sell for $100; mine, for all I know, might go for thousands. People value genuine ones more and, consequently, are willing to pay more for them.

My samovar, however, is not for sale. It is a family heirloom that goes back several generations on my mother's side. Her parents, fleeing persecution, came to this country with the few family treasures they could transport, and they gave these to my mother, their only child. She recently passed them on, one to each of her children, and I got the samovar. I doubt that it works; I doubt that I will ever have occasion to make tea for thirty; but the samovar is the only family heirloom I possess.

Now, this bit of personal history affects the samovar's value for me, but it would distort the truth to the point of absurdity to say that it *increases* the value. Rather, it changes the value, by giving me a special relation to that object. When I say it is not for sale, I mean that I would not sell it for any price. I would not trade it for a ranch on Maui or an original Velazquez oil, which fetch prices about as close to infinite as anything I could truly crave. If a guest at my house, upon admiring my samovar, were gauche enough to ask me what I would sell it for, the correct response is "It's not for sale;" not, "You couldn't afford it." To sell it would be to sever a family link, and that is, literally, to give up something that is priceless.

It is worth emphasizing, however, that in saying the samovar is not for sale I am not, of course, claiming that I could not conceive of any circumstances where I would give it up. (Suppose my daughter needed an operation and . . . .) Were such circumstances to befall me, moreover, my selling price would be considerably less than the market value of a Velazquez. I would not even claim, right now, that the samovar is worth more than a Velazquez; only that it is not for sale.

Suppose, instead, that my mother gave the samovar to my brother, and he died with instructions in his will to sell all his possessions at auction and give the money to charity. How much would I be willing to bid for it? Suppose I am forced to bid against a dealer trying to corner the market on samovars, and she is willing to bid very high for it. Because of its history, I would be willing to bid more for this samovar than for one identical to it in all other respects, but not too much more. I can easily imagine losing out to the dealer, but this only emphasizes my point. The value of the same object is different in the two situations, not different *quantities*, but different values. They defy comparison on a single scale.

Surely any attempt to account for the quality of human life must allow for the different kinds of valuings that give life its characteristic richness. This is why it is so ironic that decision analysts insist on weighing the quality of life against its quantity and then proceed to measure quality as a simple map of consumer preferences. The quality of life includes more than what can be measured in terms of quantities of benefits or the degree to which preferences are satisfied. It must also include a richness of experience that allows for different kinds of relationships to the things we value, even to the same object in different contexts. The values that give life its quality are themselves qualitatively different. They command our allegiance in different ways, and they give rise to different kinds of duties and commitments.

Some of our values, no doubt, can be reduced without remainder to the satisfaction they provide us. They can be measured by the strength of our preferences for them. But I do not get much satisfaction from my samovar; I do not measure its value much more highly than other, comparable antiques. I am simply bound to it. My commitment determines how I think and decide and choose.

To be bound to, or to opt for, certain kinds of relationships, especially personal relationships, may involve a commitment explicitly not to treat the benefits of the relationships as exchangeable and not to allow the benefits to determine our decisions. This is not to deny that there are costs and benefits involved, as every lover or parent knows. To value a reputation, to value something aesthetically, or to value a cultural tradition is not to register benefits that are fungible for consumer goods. We may be aware of their costs, and we may choose to give them up, but the contexts where this becomes acceptable or necessary are likely to be too specific and unique to establish any general trade-off or switch point.

V.

As individuals, we value some objects, activities, and features of our lives and environment in ways that cannot adequately be taken into account by assigning them a quantity of importance; they cannot independent of circumstance, be balanced against or exchanged for other things of more, less, or equal importance. Likewise, as members of a community, we value some objects, practices, and features of our institutions and environment in an analogously complex and varied range of ways. The value of human life is such a communitarian value, one that is socially acknowledged and reinforced. This shows itself most dramatically, perhaps, with outpourings of attention, and money, when some identifiable person's life is in peril. It shows itself too in the care we lavish on the old and the incurably ill, whose lives are of little worth to society. We refer to this value when we say that human life is sacred.

This value is not the same as the social value of human life that is a statistical concept in QRA. It would seem to be pointless, therefore, to criticize one because it does not happen to be the other, to oppose QRA because its social value of human life does not approach risk reduction with the idea that human life is sacred. The objection is frequently made;[18] so is the reply that QRA only values risk reduction, and that its "social value of human life" is merely a statistical construct.[19]

This reply is too dismissive, for even if these two social values of human life refer to different entities or practices, they may be incompatible nevertheless. Whether they are will turn on what the sacredness of human life means and on how QRA is applied.

We can all agree that human life is special. Moral rules, in large part, direct our behavior in ways that pay homage to this specialness. We sacrifice welfare and take on enormous inefficiencies in order to treat persons fairly or to accord them respect. Likewise, we go to lengths and pay considerably to save identifiable lives. We do these things, as it were, in spite of the facts. We are not an endangered species; no individual is inexpendable. We do all this simply because we are committed to treating human life specially, that is to say, as sacred.

In characterizing the sacredness of human life, we again confront the difficulties of the appropriate manner of valuing, the relationship between us and the object of value. It is easy to confuse the specialness of the relationship with the specialness of the object. This mistake can lead to analyses of the value of life that are implausible, such as the following:

> Human lives have characteristics that differentiate them significantly from the vast array of valued outputs that are derived from public programs. They cannot be produced by traditional industrial processes; property rights for them cannot be secure; and they cannot be legally transferred. For these reasons, among others, they are considered a sacred commodity.[20]

Property rights and laws of transfer, of course, refer to social practices. But this analyst also claims that human life is sacred because of the unique way it is produced. Apart from the technological pessimism of this claim (which appears increasingly to be unwarranted) this view is mistaken for analyzing the sacredness of human life as a special feature of a commodity. The sacredness of life, one might think, leads us to regard human life as not a commodity at all.

More commonly, in the QRA literature anyway, sacredness is given a purely subjective reading: to regard something as sacred is to express a never yielding preference for it. This results from interpreting sacred, correctly, as priceless, defining "priceless" to mean "of infinite value," and then dismissing it. Human behavior, we can all agree, shows unequivocally that our preferences for protecting and prolonging human life are not infinite, in the sense that we would never choose to stop spending to reduce risks. We are not willing to spend *any* amount to protect human life. If that is what sacredness means, then human life is not sacred. This interpretation, unfortunately, is fostered as much by the critics of QRA as by its defenders; it is, nevertheless, a caricature. It is tantamount to interpreting "what does it profit a man if he gains the world but loses his soul?" as meaning one human soul has value greater than the international aggregate of GNPs. The sacredness of life deserves a better reading than this.

A more subtle interpretation of what we mean in calling human life sacred is suggested in Kant's argument that human beings, as rational agents capable of morality, have a *dignity*. Whatever has dignity, according to Kant, "is above all price and therefore admits of no equivalent."[21] But dignity is not simply a property of animals with our genetic structure.

According to Kant, human beings have dignity in virtue of their ability to act freely and on the basis of their reason according to self-given and rational law. Each human being's reason, the very property in virtue of which he has dignity, compels him to recognize the dignity of others, a recognition that is expressed by his giving himself the law always to treat each person as an end-in-himself, and never merely as a means. The fact in virtue of which each human being has dignity is the same fact that compels him to recognize the dignity of all human beings. It is thus both the source of the claim each person makes on every other person and the basis for each person's recognition of the claim every other person makes on him.[22] What is important is the *nature* of this property, which demands expression in actions of a certain type. It compels each person to treat every other person as an end and never merely as a means, not even as a means to the greatest social good.

In saying that human life has a dignity, and not a price, Kant does not at all mean to say that human life has an infinite price or worth. This misses the point entirely. Whatever has a price has a different kind of value—typically, as a means for some end, say happiness. But Kant thought that the human capacity to reason, not the capacity for happiness, was the source of moral obligation; thus, Kantians are critical of moralities aimed primarily at maximizing happiness. Putting happinesss in the place of autonomous reason is incompatible with a conception of human beings as having dignity. Kantianism is rather starkly opposed to the kind of utilitarianism that forms the theoretical basis of most of the decision sciences.

I shall approach this idea in another way, one which also demands a more subtle analysis of value than those just criticized (but which may be inconsistent with Kantianism in other ways that we will not pursue). Stuart Hampshire has described utilitarianism as an optimistic morality spawned by a vision that clear, scientific thinking on ethical issues can reduce moral inefficiencies in the world and guide people to happier lives.[23] Hampshire makes clear that this school of thought underlies the decision making techniques of the kind designed to help determine when a human life is worth saving for n dollars, but not for more than that. Then he describes, with sympathy, a certain revulsion to the perception that these techniques are being implemented in sweeping ways. He says:

> [To some], it seems now obvious that the large-scale computations in modern politics and social planning bring with them a coarseness and grossness of moral feeling, a blunting of sensibility, and a suppression of individual discrimination and gentleness, which is a price that they will not pay for the benefits of clear calculation.[24]

It may appear that Hampshire is sympathizing with people who would simply and sentimentally reject clear thinking about unpleasant topics. Instead, Hampshire is objecting to a tendency to use these techniques for valuing life in ways that trample and distort our values, values that we know by intuition and which are sustained primarily by the force of custom, tradition, and ritual. QRA is an example of the kind of "computational morality" Hampshire is opposing, the analytical techniques aimed at rationalizing the process of decision making.

One damaging effect of these analytic techniques can be to discourage consideration of objections to a decision, and instead to register only the disaffection a person feels as a result of his objecting to what is being done. But Hampshire's focus is different. He thinks much of our moral life is governed by ritual.

> Moral prohibitions in general, and particularly those that govern the taking of life, the celebration of the dead, and that govern sexual relations and family relations, are artifices that give human lives some distinctive, peculiar, even arbitrary human shape and pattern. They humanize the natural phases of experience, and lend them a distinguishing sense and direction, one among many possible ones.[25]

These artifices are essential to express the value of human life. The error of computational moralities, which would include some uses of QRA, is in their carrying "the deritualization of transactions between men to a point at which men not only can, but ought to, use and exploit each other as they use and exploit any other natural objects, . . . "[26] In other words, they give human life only the value of price.

Hampshire's view of morality is strongly historical, conservative, and ritualistic. Whatever else we might say about it, his account of the way we value human life undeniably echoes Durkheim, whose definition of sacredness is by now standard in the sciences that study culture. A value is sacred if it is acknowledged in special, different ways. It can demand ritualized behavior, because such behavior easily invites symbolic interpretations. Thus, attention is publicly drawn to beliefs and feelings the members of society hold to be of special significance. These rituals and values, moreover, are social. Regarding some values as sacred, according to Durkheim, is to perform a socially integrative function. It fills "the need of upholding and reaffirming at regular intervals the collective sentiments and collective ideas which make [a society's] unity and its personality."[27] Or, as two followers of Durkheim put it: "A society is held together by its internal agreement about the sacredness of certain fundamental moral standards."[28]

In a recent critique of cost-benefit analysis, Steven Kelman implicitly makes the same point. The word "priceless," he notes, is "pregnant with meaning."[29] Had President Kennedy announced in his inaugural address that "we were willing to 'pay a high price' or 'bear a large burden' for liberty, the statement would have rung hollow."[30] It would also have changed the meaning, by suggesting a budget priority instead of a steadfast moral commitment.

This Durkheimian interpretation gives us a more adequate idea of what it means to treat something as sacred. It helps us explain how we can both determine something's worth or price and insist that it is priceless. Something may be marketed in one context and treated as sacred in another. Is this irrational? It does mark a refusal to generalize behavior in consistent ways, according to some conceptions of consistency. But sacredness demands a break in behavior. In a broader sense of rationality, one that is supposed to make our lives intelligible to us, the question is more difficult to answer. A proof of irrationality demands that sacred or ritual behavior, publicly acknowledged, is somehow shown to be incompatible with our goals and interests. The proof must judge the quality of our valuings.

VI.

How compelling is the idea that human life is sacred? And how does sacredness bear on QRA recommendations for valuing life? Lacking a simple, definitive answer to these difficult questions, I will create two examples that force us to think about them.

Imagine a collection of miners attending a union meeting. They are gathered to vote on a general approach to safety in the mines, and all the money to be spent reducing risks will be allocated according to the miners' decision. Their primary interest, we may suppose, is to minimize their risk of being the victim in an accident. The safety experts have presented a convincing case at the meeting that the way to minimize risks is to put the entire safety budget into accident prevention, and to give none at all to the purchase of rescue equipment. Rescue attempts are costly and inefficient. Except for very rare cases where they require no special effort or equipment, rescues would no longer be attempted under the proposed plan. Existing rescue equipment would be sold, and that money too would go to prevention. Without rescue operations, the miners can expect their risks to be reduced somewhat; but they know that when the next accident occurs, it will trigger no rescue action.

Does it make sense for the miners to oppose a proposal to forego future rescue operations? Imagine someone at the meeting rising to speak out against this proposal. He might argue that he would not like to work in this kind of risky business, knowing the implications of this policy. He finds it too chilling to think that if he were trapped, official policy would dictate that nothing be done; and he finds it just as awful when he thinks that the person trapped might be someone else, one of his fellow workers. (This kind of purposeful neglect in the intelligence business is exploited in spy novels to help create a ruthless, creepy atmosphere.) This miner concludes that the higher risks of a policy with rescue attempts is better, because it is more humane. Is this a reasonable objection? How should a rational miner vote? How would *you* vote?

If you find yourself at all moved by this objection, even if you are not entirely convinced by it, then it supports several points. One is that minimizing the risks is not our only interest in designing a risk policy. More importantly, however, since most QRA techniques enable us to balance risk reduction against other benefits, it is important to ask how this issue should be decided. QRA would attempt to find some way to measure the miners' sympathies with this objection—their anxieties about the proposed policy. It treats these feelings as added costs, to be balanced against the added risk reduction. It is not the anxieties, the increased fear or a measurable decline in morale, that provokes this opposition, however; rather, it is their cause. This policy, in the view of the objector, fails to show a proper *concern* for the people who must daily confront dangers. Rescue operations have a symbolic aspect to them, which, according to this objection, must be weighed against efficiency.

Other miners, we may suppose, might disagree. They would prefer simply to minimize the risks. But then a commitment to certain principles is at stake, which can only be resolved in some broadly political way. It cannot be settled by analytic measuring-and-comparing techniques that bury the reasons for different positions beneath the strength with which they are held.

The dangerous attempts to locate and retrieve downed military pilots and other wounded or lost personnel, often behind enemy lines, provide an example of rescue operations that defy economic and even risk-reduction justifications. The cost of training pilots may be offered as an economic reason for rescue, but, according to naval officers with whom I have spoken, it is not seriously believed. I am told the reason has something to do with morale, which can be interpreted as a bit of ritualized behavior aimed at showing that the military cares about the lives of the people they send out to be shot at. In the introduction to his fine account of the Vietnam War, Philip Caputo says, "I have also attempted to describe the intimacy of life in infantry battalions . . . Two friends of mine died trying to save the corpses of their men from the battlefield. Such devotion, simple and selfless, the sentiment of belonging to each other, was the one decent thing in a conflict noted for its monstrosities."[31]

Let us try a second thought experiment, about which I would expect more general agreement. Suppose it were possible to implement an organ transplant scheme that would select healthy people in some fair and random way, who would be killed and whose organs would be given to save some larger number of lives. Let us imagine that at least four lives would be saved for every person killed. Now suppose further that it could be determined that, within such a scheme, a person's risk of dying either from organ failure or from bad luck in the donor lottery would be less than the risk of dying from organ failure in the absence of such a scheme. The costs of administering the scheme are not great, and it would free additional resources currently expended less efficiently (and less effectively) to maintain patients for whom transplantable organs are unavailable. These resources could be used to save lives elsewhere. Thus, if we imposed the scheme on the whole society (in a fair and equitable manner), we would reduce everybody's risk of dying from organ failure, and could reduce other risks with the extra resources. This scheme will only work if adopted everywhere—it must be imposed universally or we should abandon the idea. It is efficient; it is fair. People are willing to pay to reduce risks. Should we impose such a scheme?

Perhaps general public anxiety would increase under this scheme, as people worry about the chance that their number will be called and they will be rounded up off the street and strapped to a table. The scheme's defenders might find this anxiety puzzling and irrational. Why don't healthy people now fear sudden organ failure? Why should anxiety about dying increase when measures are imposed that *reduce* everyone's risks of premature death? If someone were to press a defense of the scheme, he could argue further for measures to reduce the anxiety. Education might help and, failing that, we could administer drugs to eliminate the fear.

Probably the objection that first comes to mind is that this scheme is immoral because it requires us to kill innocent people. It is like the philosopher's example of the sheriff and the extortionist. The extortionist commits a capital offense, and then kidnaps four innocent people and threatens to kill them unless the sheriff finds another innocent person (whom the extortionist dislikes) guilty of the crime and hangs him. One innocent person is killed in order to save four innocent people.

There is an important difference in the examples, however. The organ transplant scheme is implemented beforehand, and everyone's risk is, *ex ante,* the same. Assuming we do not know how our organs will hold up over time, it might seem like a good bet. We can imagine that people might band together in voluntary associations of this kind. So why would it be wrong to adopt it universally, as public policy? In other words, it is an insufficient reply to dismiss this suggestion because it involves wrongful killing. We need to know why this, and not many other cases similar in certain respects, is wrongful killing.

Why, that is, do we not think of this scheme, when it is adopted, as simply imposing a technological risk on the entire population, one that is a necessary concomitant of the benefit of overall risk reduction? Why are the cancers attributable to environmental or workplace hazards, caused by industrial decisions, not considered wrongful killings? Is it because in the organ transplant scheme the *identities* of the victims are known (but only *after* implementing the policy) where in environmental cases only the numbers are known (although sometimes *prior* to the decision)? We need to know why this is a relevant difference in determining what is a wrongful killing. Remembering that the transplant scheme *reduces* our overall risk of early death, why should we consider it so horrible if a government agency calls our number in a donor lottery, and not so bad when mother nature calls it in the distribution of weak organs? After all, we can identify the victims of kidney failure, too.

Perhaps we see the issue not as hinging on the concept of wrongful killing, but as involving an unfair redistribution of risks. The transplant scheme brings healthy people into a risk pool they would otherwise avoid. The risks that nature imposes are unfortunate, but the risks we impose take on moral overtones. If this is the case, however, then why is it not thought to be unfair to have a policy to site hazardous technologies (e.g., electric power plants, toxic waste dumps) in rural areas as a way of reducing total risks? That too seems to involve redistributing the risks, for the sake of the whole, to the few whose only fault is to live in sparsely populated areas.

These questions, I think, may have answers. I am confident that the organ transplant scheme, anyway, can be shown to be wrong because it involves wrongful killings. The explanation, however, relies ultimately on singling out this particular way of treating people and showing it to be unacceptable. People do not want simply to reduce their risks, and they certainly do expect public policies to express and respect the value of human life. We have a long tradition of maintaining moral distinctions between killing and allowing to die, one that prohibits us from sacrificing people as a means to some end, even good ends like risk reduction. This proposal ignores that moral distinction.

VII.

Let me summarize the claims I have been defending. The many different methods of risk assessment are attempts to help us design rational policies to control technological (and other) risks. Their goal is to find methods for making broad comparisons possible, which will enable us to determine trade-offs between risk reduction and the benefits that further risk reduction would force us to give up. This is sometimes explained as the attempt to balance quantity of life and quality of life. In order to compare the different values, QRAs seek neutral ways of measuring them. This involves assigning them quantitative weights, or, at the very least, ranking them on a single scale according to how individuals, in various contexts, reveal their preferences.

I have explored several areas where converting quality to quantity forces distortions in our values. The reason for this is that values themselves differ in quality, here interpreted as the different kinds of duties they impose and the different kinds of behavior that constitute the appropriate expressions of different values. The different ways of valuing are an essential aspect of the quality of human life. The first example (the samovar) was meant to show that the value of an object in one context may not accurately express its value in all contexts.

The discussion then turned to the value of life itself, to the quality of sacredness. This led us to interpret sacredness as referring to the manner of valuing, rather than referring either to special objects or to special preferences that indicate an infinite price or unwillingness to trade. The examples that followed were attempts to illustrate how the sacredness of human life might lead to objections to the QRA value of life.

Now, none of this is meant to suggest that QRA is objectionable *in toto* and should be abandoned. That would be silly. It always helps to know the costs, even the costs of keeping some values sacred; moreover, sometimes these costs are the overriding concern, so that QRA should be applied to make our decisions. We want to be efficient, and we want to be fair. QRA (and the decision sciences generally) are invaluable tools for achieving each of these ends.

Nevertheless, our values may sometimes call on us to act inefficiently according to any measure of efficiency that is not empty or trivial, and in these cases QRA will be unable to tell us what we want. Furthermore, decision sciences cannot be applied to tell us when we are dealing with one of these cases. This information must be uncovered in other ways, through the political process.

Defenders of QRA often characterize the basic social question they are address-ing to be: How safe is safe enough? Wherever our technological risk issues are politically sensitive and arouse public interest, I suggest that it is seriously misleading to become preoccupied with this question. If the public is wildly inconsistent about the safety it demands from different technologies, this is probably because the technologies or the risks in question are symbolic of other issues, which pertain to the quality of life and the important public expression of certain values. Any general measure of the amount of safety we are or should be willing to pay for is a piece of technical information that may have very little relevance to more fundamental decisions about social ideals. When policy makers pay excessive attention to the technical question, they ignore the more basic issues within which the technical questions arise.

It is no wonder, then, that many of the regulatory agencies dealing with risk, and the experts who advise them, have become nearly paralyzed. They have been looking to analytic techniques to answer political questions. They try to convince and reassure a wary public, but they often fail to address, and thus they reinforce, its basic concerns. They are caught in a nasty spiral of distrust. We can begin to extricate ourselves from this situation only by paying closer attention to the kinds of issues we are confronting.

Nowhere is this problem and the potential for doing better more apparent than in designing an energy policy and, in particular, a policy for nuclear power. We should attempt to separate the nuclear power issues in the United States into those that involve only technical risk questions and those that center on other questions. In the process of identifying the technical issues, we can discover where we have a social consensus or shared commitments. We should hope to find such a consensus about safety issues involved in licensing and operating existing or ordered light water reactors and in disposing of nuclear wastes. Since no nuclear experts are perceived as neutral (and this, too, is partly for symbolic reasons, having little to do with their past record), standards should be set by panels deemed by all parties to be fairly representative. They would surely debate different experts' assess-ments, but they would also ultimately agree on standards that the public would likely accept. QRAs would play a significant role in setting these standards.

The other kinds of issues in the nuclear power debates cannot be treated as easily; we should therefore treat them differently and, wherever possible, sepa-rately. Examples include policies for encouraging expansion of nuclear power in the United States, establishing liability for accidents, reprocessing spent fuels, and developing a breeder reactor program (the latter two, in part, because of their perceived relation to weapons proliferation risks). Neither the estimated safety risks nor economic considerations are all that divide the public on these issues. The real points of dispute over such matters seem to be more about the impact of different policies on the future shape of society, and whether these aspects of nuclear technologies are compatible with our social values and democratic institu-tions. Although I do not foresee how these issues can be easily resolved, it seems useless to cast them in terms that can be processed by QRAs, cost-benefit analysis, or any other decision science. Political problems demand political solutions.

NOTES

1. See Alvin M. Weinberg and R. Philip Hammond, "Limits to the Use of Energy," *American Scientist,* 58 (1970), 412-418; also Weinberg, "Some Views of the Energy Crisis," *American Scientist,* 61 (1973), 59-60; also Gerald Feinberg, "Material Needs and Technological Innovation: Some Hopes—and Some Doubts," in *International Resource Flows,* eds. Garvey and Garvey (Lexington, MA: Lexington Books, 1977), pp. 149-172.
2. Barry Commoner, *The Politics of Energy* (New York: Alfred Knopf, 1979), pp. 49-65.
3. Evidence of, and reasons for, the distrust of experts are demonstrated in discussions of the accident at Three Mile Island. See Daniel Ford, *Three Mile Island: Thirty Minutes to Meltdown* (New York: Penguin, 1982); Mark Stephens, *Three Mile Island* (New York: Random House, 1980); *Report to the President's Commission on the Accident at Three Mile Island,* John G. Kemeny, Chairman (Washington, DC: U.S. Government Printing Office, October 1979); and *Three Mile Island: A Report to the Commissioners and to the Public,* NUREG/CR-1250, Mitchell Rogovin, Director, Vol. I, (Washington, DC: U.S. Nuclear Regulatory Commission, 1980).
4. World Health Organization "Mental Health Aspects of the Peaceful Use of Atomic Energy: Report of a Study Group," *World Health Organization Technical Report Series* no. 151 (Geneva: World Health Organization, 1958). Summary in "Mental Health and Atomic Energy," *Science* 127 (1958), 140-141. See also Spencer Weart, *Scientists in Power* (Cambridge: Harvard University Press, 1979), chaps. 4-10.
   These associations run so deep that it would seem exceptionally naive merely to dismiss them, as if they were based on some simple misunderstanding about the worst possible acident in a standard nuclear reactor. Bombs are associated with radioactivity, an association that predates the discovery of fission in 1939. These associations were widespread enough that in 1930 Robert Millikan, an American physicist, felt called upon to deride the "advocates of a return to the 'glories' of a pre-scientific age," who "pictured the diabolical scientist tinkering heedlessly, like a bad small boy, with these enormous stores of sub-atomic energy, and some sad day touching off the fuse and blowing our comfortable little globe to smithereens." *Science and the New Civilization* (New York: Scribners, 1930). The term "atom bomb" was first made popular in H.G. Wells, *The World Set Free: A Story of Mankind,* first published in the *English Review* (1913-1914), 16-17. For these references I am indebted to Spencer Weart, "Nuclear Fear: A History and An Experiment," unpublished, May 1980.
5. R.J. Lifton, *Death in Life: Survivors of Hiroshima* (New York: Random House, 1968).
6. Todd LaPorte, "Nuclear Wastes and the Rigors of Nearly Error-Free Operations: Problems for Social Analysis," *Society/Transactions* (1981); also *Report of the President's Commission on the Accident at Three Mile Island,* no. 3, above.
7. Amory Lovins, *Soft Energy Paths* (New York: Harper and Row, 1979), chap. 2; also Barry Commoner, *The Politics of Energy,* no. 2, above. For a general discussion and further references, see Langdon Winner, "Do Artifacts Have Politics?" *Daedalus* 109 (Winter 1980), 121-136.
8. Paul Slovic and Baruch Fischhoff, "How Safe is Safe Enough?" in *Risk and Chance,* ed. J. Dowie and P. Lefrere (Milton Keynes: The Open University Press, 1980), p. 121.
9. See, for example, Philip Cook and James Vaupel, Foreword, *Law and Contemporary Problems,* 40, Issue on Valuing Lives (1976), 1.

10. E. J. Mishan, *Cost Benefit Analysis* (New York: Praeger, 1976), p. 24.
11. Thomas Schelling, "The Life You Save May Be Your Own," in *Problems in Public Expenditure Analysis* ed. S.B. Chase (Washington: Brookings Institution, 1968), pp. 127-162.
12. James Vaupel, "Early Death: An American Tragedy," *Law and Contemporary Problems* 40 (1976), 73-121.
13. Allen Kneese, "Research Goals and Progress Toward Them," in *Environmental Quality in a Growing Economy* ed. H. Jarrett (Baltimore MD: Johns Hopkins Press, 1966); also R.G. Ridker, *The Economic Costs of Air Pollution* (New York: Praeger 1967); also R.F.F. Dawson, *Current Costs of Road Accidents in Great Britain*, Road Research Laboratory Report LR 396 (London: Department of the Environment, 1971). For criticism, see Joanne Linnerooth, "The Value of Human Life: A Review of the Models" *Economic Inquiry* 17 (1979), 52-74.
14. Linnerooth, no. 13, above; also E.J. Mishan, "Evaluation of Life and Limb: A Theoretical Approach," *Journal of Political Economy* 79 (1970), 687-705.
15. G. Fromm, "Civil Aviation Expenditures," in *Measuring Benefits of Government Investment* ed. R. Dorfman (Washington: Brookings Institution, 1965).
16. Chauncey Starr and Chris Whipple, "Risks of Risk Decisions," *Science* 208 (6 June 1980), 1119.
17. Ibid., p. 1115.
18. For example, Michael S. Baram, *Regulation of Health, Safety and Environmental Quality and the Use of Cost Benefit Analysis*, Final report to the Administrative Conference of the United States (March 1979), p. 27.
19. For example, Thomas Schelling, "The Life You Save May Be Your Own," no. 11, above.
20. Richard Zeckhauser, "Procedures for Valuing Lives," *Public Policy* 23 (1975), 425.
21. Immanuel Kant, *Foundations of the Metaphysics of Morals,* trans. L.W. Beck. (Indianapolis: The Bobbs-Merrill Co., The Library of Liberal Arts, 1959) p. 53.
22. For a fuller interpretation of Kant along these lines, see John Rawls, "Kantian Constructivism in Moral Theory: The Dewey Lectures 1980," *Journal of Philosophy* 77 (1980), 515-572, especially 543-547.
23. "Morality and Pessimism," in *Public & Private Morality* ed. Stuart Hampshire (Cambridge: Cambridge University Press, 1978) pp. 1-22, at p. 4.
24. Ibid., pp. 5-6.
25. Ibid., p. 16.
26. Ibid., p. 18.
27. Emile Durkheim, *The Elementary Forms of the Religious Life,* trans. J.W. Swain. (London: George Allen and Unwin, 1915), p. 427.
28. Edward Shils and Michael Young, "The Meaning of the Coronation," *Sociological Review* 1 (1953), 63-81, at p. 80. For an excellent general account of these issues, see Steven Lukes, "Political Ritual and Social Integration," *Sociology* 9 (1975), 289-308.
29. Steven Kelman, "Cost-Benefit Analysis: An Ethical Critique," *Regulation* (Jan.-Feb. 1981), 33-40.
30. Ibid., p. 40.
31. Philip Caputo, *A Rumor of War* (New York: Holt, Rinehart & Winston, 1977).

Chapter 6
MEDIA COVERAGE OF COMPLEX TECHNOLOGICAL ISSUES

William Colglazier, Jr. and Michael Rice

Experts invariably complain about newspaper and television coverage of complex scientific and technological issues. They criticize the media for being too simplistic, getting the details wrong, creating misleading impressions, and sensationalizing stories. The experts are concerned about perceived journalistic distortions because they see the media as the main conduit of information to the general public. And public opinion is seen as having considerable influence on societal decision making. Therefore, in the opinion of many scientists and engineers, misleading coverage can adversely prejudice the formulation of sound public policy.

Ironically, some experts argue both for greater public understanding of science through better media coverage and for severely restricting the public's role in scientific and technological decision making. In this chapter, we distinguish between these two concerns regarding the public and controversial policy issues of science and technology, that is, between the adequacy of the media in informing and educating the public and the most appropriate role for the general public in decision making. The two areas are certainly intertwined, but not easily dissected.

We first examine media coverage and public participation in three areas dealing with nuclear energy: the Three Mile Island accident, the nuclear weapons freeze proposal, and radioactive waste disposal. We assess the relevance of some criticisms of the media by the "so-called" experts, the degree to which the media have met information needs important to the public, and the degree to which the nonelected public has participated in and influenced national policy. We attempt by these case studies to illustrate ways in which the public's involvement in decision making relates to the adequacy of reporting. Assuming that the media can always do a better job, suggestions are then made for improving media treatment through innovative approaches and increased sensitivity by journalists regarding the format, sources, and frequency of their stories.

COMPLAINTS AND SUGGESTIONS FROM THE EXPERTS

A typical response of scientists and technologists to doing something specific about "poor" media coverage is to form a committee to challenge erroneous reporting whenever it occurs. Several such groups have been formed in the wake of the Three Mile Island accident.[1]

The recommendations for doing something more substantial usually go unfulfilled. Some proposals are well intentioned, such as the frequent ones on how to improve the scientific literacy of the public, but they are often too vague or poorly focused to stimulate remedial action. Some of the studies on science literacy have recognized the need for beginning at the grade school level, which shows the magnitude of the task.[2]

Some proposals by experts are no more than thinly veiled attempts to repeal the First Amendment, which probably says more about the sophistication of some scientists (even very eminent ones) in dealing with the media and the public than about any antidemocratic sentiments on their part. An example of this category is a proposal by one physicist to combat a type of media distortion that he believes is prevalent.[3] For him, the media rely too frequently on quotations from scientists whose views are considered not to be in the mainstream or from well-known scientists who speak publicly on issues outside their professional expertise. His proposal is for the scientific societies to administer tests certifying those scientists technically competent to speak to reporters on certain issues. It suggests the frustrations and naivete of some of the scientific community in seeking to improve journalistic accuracy and general science literacy.

Many scientists feel that the media have overemphasized certain hazards, such as those from low-level radiation. One sample of this type of criticism was the din heard and reported at a convention of radiation control experts:[4]

"Experts on Radiation Control Share Critiques of Journalism"
Cancer-causing and chromosome-changing effects of nuclear radiation have been overstated and misstated by journalists, state radiation experts were told this week.

Nearly 300 delegates at the 14th annual National Conference on Radiation Control here heard speakers say that coal plants emitted as much radiation as nuclear plants and were a far greater threat to public health through mine accidents and respiratory disease.

Margaret A. Reilly, chief of environmental radiation, Pennsylvania Department of Environmental Resources, said that "to a great extent" journalists "overplayed" the nuclear power accident at Three Mile Island near Harrisburg, Pa., in 1979.

Another scientist checked the *New York Times* index to see how many entries there were for accidents involving radiation, as compared with other types of accidents. Over a five-year period prior to the Three Mile Island accident, he found 200 entries per year about accidents involving radiation; 120 on motor vehicle accidents; 50 on industrial accidents; and 25 on asphyxiation. Auto accidents, for example, kill over 50,000 people per year; industrial accidents kill, on the average, 12,000 people; and asphyxiation, roughly 5,000 people. His concern is that the press does not emphasize sufficiently the relative hazards, where risk is defined as the probability times the consequence of an accident. The public seems to fear things that have catastrophic potential even when the probabilities are small.

Opinions of scientists on the role of the public in decision making on controversial technological issues also cover a wide spectrum. At one extreme is the position represented by one very well known scientist, Dr. Rosalyn Yalow, a Nobel Prize winner, concerning genetic engineering experimentation. Recombinant DNA research became visible to the public beginning in 1974 when a group of prominent scientists wrote an open letter to *Science* magazine. The letter recommended that researchers hold a conference to discuss the possible risks of certain types of experiments and to postpone those experiments until the hazards could be ascertained. With science writers invited to observe, the conference was held at Asilomar in 1975. Dr. Yalow's retrospective position is described in an illuminating letter from a newspaper science writer:[5]

Yesterday I had a most fascinating discussion with Rosalyn Yalow. I had intended to interview her about low-level radiation for a story, but we soon got involved in a long argument over the role of the public in decision-making on issues emerging from science and technology.

Her position was the strongest I'd ever heard from a scientist: namely, that the public should play no role at all, and that the scientific community should consider all the technical facts available and then render the ultimate decision. I said I thought Asilomar represented just the opposite position: it opened the Recombinant DNA problem to public scrutiny. It showed that scientists could be highly responsible. And despite the fact that a very few years of public concern and even some hysteria followed during which all kinds of laws and regulations were debated while some experimental work was held in abeyance, ultimately both the public and science were well-served because the public's confidence in the responsibility of scientists was heightened and controls were minimized.

Yalow responded with the argument that the original letter in *Science* from Maxine Singer was a great mistake, that the Berg committee and the publicly-announced "moratorium" was an even bigger mistake, and that the Asilomar meeting itself was the biggest mistake of all because the press was there and all the discussions became public knowledge. What should have happened, Yalow said was this: when it became apparent that there might be potential hazards in some aspects of recombinant DNA experiments, all the scientists involved should have met privately; decided what research needed to be done to establish the nature of the hazards if any; agreed privately to publish *nothing* until all the problems were resolved, and then secretly agreed on what types of experiments should be barred for a while and what kinds of containment facilities (if any) should be required for various levels of experiments. All this, she insisted, should have been done in secret!

Our conversation was interesting, too, because I had brought a Chronicle photographer with me and he asked me in some puzzlement later whether Yalow wasn't being terribly inconsistent in arguing on the one hand for greater public understanding of science and greater coverage of science by the press, while at the same time arguing that the public should be kept in the dark about the most serious and potentially hazardous consequences of scientific applications.

At the other extreme from Dr. Yalow's position is the view that there should be considerable participation by the nonelected public, even at the grassroots level, in societal decision making on controversial technological issues. One proposal recommends throwing the experts out to "keep technocratic elites from subverting the traditional political function of ordinary citizens and their representatives."[6] More often the call for greater democratization of the policy debate and decision process comes not from a desire to exclude the experts, but from a belief that public acceptability is central to the resolution of some controversial problem, such as energy-facility siting.

The fundamental objectives for increased public participation are: (a) to improve the quality of decision making through the solicitation of broad public input and review, (b) to enhance the legitimacy of and build support for a decision, and (c) to inform and educate the interested public.[7] If the disclosure of information is the keystone of an open society, the free flow of information should be impeded only for substantial reasons. Of course, the limits on what should be disclosed have been drawn differently by some scientists and journalists, such as whether the details of thermonuclear weapons design should have been published in the magazine *The Progressive*. (Some scientists sympathetic to public participation felt that nuclear design details have little to do with the public's ability to comprehend the fundamental issues of the weapons debate, and this disclosure could potentially harm national security by accelerating proliferation.) Nevertheless, the more democratic view in the scientific community generally holds that the decisions themselves cannot be left to the experts alone even though public involvement may slow down and complicate decision making.

Whatever one's position on the desirability of increased public involvement in science policy decision making (the scientific community has no monolithic view) the dominant view on media coverage among scientists is that it leaves much to be desired. We address next specific criticisms by the experts in three areas dealing with nuclear energy and assess the degree to which information needs important to the public have been met.

THE THREE MILE ISLAND ACCIDENT

Many scientists were quite critical of the coverage of the Three Mile Island accident.[8] President Carter who was trained as a naval nuclear engineer also "thought the news accounts were outrageous, exaggerated and irresponsible."[9]

The technologists showed little sympathy for the plight of journalists, who were trying to obtain hard facts from cautious experts during those first few days.

The scientists and engineers at an Aspen Institute roundtable discussion in June 1979 on the Three Mile Island accident generally felt that the media frightened the public with the worst possible case analysis, emphasizing a potential China Syndrome (dispersal of intense radioactivity from a breach of containment by melted nuclear fuel) and creating possible panic and unnecessary evacuations.[10] They felt that the media gave wide coverage to those at the ends of the spectrum in the nuclear power debate and not to the scientists in the middle, and that the media exaggerated the hazards of the very low levels of radiation actually received by the surrounding population. They also felt the media failed to give wide enough publicity afterwards to the fact that no one was hurt and that the fears about a hydrogen bubble explosion were incorrect. And they felt that the media did not put the risks and benefits of nuclear power to health and national security in perspective, did not properly compare them, with the risks and benefits of other energy sources.

A case can be made, however, that the media produced the qualitative information for answering questions of confidence uppermost in the public consciousness, that is, how much should the public trust the experts and how competent are the experts. One message conveyed to the public was the impression that they had been deceived about the potential dangers of a nuclear accident, the so-called "credibility meltdown." Before the accident, many experts effectively told the public not to worry. For example, the Reactor Safety Study of the Nuclear Regulatory Commission had emphasized that the risk of death from a reactor accident was about as likely as dying from a meteor impact.[11] Actually many scientists felt that although nuclear power was safe compared to alternatives, the tremendous amount of radioactivity contained within reactors made it something that counseled extreme caution.[12] During the accident even the NRC was the source of some of the alarming statements reported by the press; being confronted with the possibility of a serious accident at TMI was a sobering experience for them, too.[13] Another message conveyed by the media was the existence of confusion and uncertainty among the experts, fueled by quotes such as that by the Chairman of the Commission, who said that he and the Pennsylvania governor felt as if they were "blind men staggering around making decisions."

The public's reaction to that confusion resulted in a considerable loss of confidence in experts and in nuclear power following Three Mile Island.[14] One physics professor at Harvard said, "Let me, just for the sake of being ornery, propose that it is just possible that the public has now a very good measure of the experts' credibility. The public perception, right or wrong, is now that this nuclear power is a very difficult art, [and that] it is by no means mastered. Engineers and scientists [are] unmasked once more [as] remarkable optimists, whereas the public must, as part of its effort to survive, be skeptics."[15] Being skeptical of the pronouncements of the experts is certainly also true for the press.[16]

The current stagnation of the nuclear industry probably has more to do with the financial risks, as perceived by utility directors and financiers, than with the technological risks as perceived by the public.[17] Nonetheless, regaining public confidence in nuclear power is important to many experts, and at a minimum it seems to require convincing the public that the experts have learned the lessons of Three Mile Island.[18] This leverage has enabled public opinion to affect government and industry policy.[19]

THE NUCLEAR WEAPONS FREEZE PROPOSAL

The peaceful uses of nuclear energy have always had difficulty shaking the indirect connection to nuclear weapons, and opponents of nuclear energy have been quite willing to capitalize on a weapons link in making their case to the public. The civil nuclear power industry has been critical of those, including at times the public and the media, who do not distinguish clearly and precisely between the two aspects. They even became upset with the Reagan administration, nominally a supporter of the industry, for suggesting that military plutonium needs could be met by reprocessing civilian spent reactor fuel. The industry seeks to separate as much as possible nuclear power technology from bombs in the public consciousness. Yet the connection has always existed, not only symbolically but substantively, since civilian reactor fuel could possibly be utilized by countries or terrorists to make weapons. The experts themselves have heatedly debated how easy or practical it would be for civilian nuclear power to be the route to a nuclear weapons capability. Therefore, it is perhaps not surprising that the public may, at times, have been confused by the distinction.

Besides the scientists and engineers knowledgeable about nuclear technology, there are other experts who deal with nuclear energy for military purposes. They are the scholars and insiders who debate strategic nuclear weapons and deterrence policy. The experts were taken by surprise in early 1982 with the growing public sentiment for a freeze on nuclear weapons production and deployment. The Reagan administration was confounded by the bipartisan clamor because it had interpreted the 1980 election as a societal consensus for a military build-up. The liberal "arms control" community was also astonished by the domestic public reaction because two years earlier the SALT II Treaty, which was a much less drastic proposal, did not have sufficient public support to be ratified in the Senate. Therefore, whether an expert had favored or opposed SALT II, there was a degree of universal frustration with the public's attitude being both volatile and simplistic. The arms control community could generally support the freeze as a movement because it placed pressure on the Reagan administration to negotiate with the Soviets—but many of these same pragmatists could not support the freeze as a serious arms control initiative. Speaking for the more conservative administration, the then Secretary of State Alexander M. Haig said that a nuclear freeze was "bad defense policy, bad arms control and bad for the NATO alliance."

The media were not blamed as a cause of the public outcry, but some experts clearly felt that the media exacerbated the situation by not educating the public to the complexities of nuclear weapons policy. Some of the numerous problems cited by the experts when a freeze proposal is examined in detail are:

1. How to define it precisely?
2. How to verify it?
3. Would it freeze current imbalances and instabilities and prevent the deployment of more stable systems?
4. Would it freeze Soviet superiority in medium range theatre nuclear weapons in Europe?
5. Would it be negotiable?

Because of these and other questions, many experts, including many supporters of SALT II, do not consider the freeze as the right or best approach to strategic arms contol.

The Reagan administration, which called SALT II "fatally flawed," felt that the media also unduly aroused public nervousness by exaggerating some of the president's and his advisors' statements on nuclear war, such as the winnability and survivability of a protracted nuclear exchange, the use of a demonstration explosion at the onset of a European conflict, the superiority of Soviet strategic systems, the inevitability of a conflict with the Soviets, and the need for a large U.S. civil defense program. Secretary of Defense Weinberger demonstrated the administration's heightened sensitivity to press coverage on these issues when he stated, "Our entire strategic program, including the development of a protracted response capability that has been so maligned in the press recently, has been developed with the express intention of assuring that nuclear war will never be fought" and nowhere "do we mean to imply that nuclear war is winnable."[20] But the establishment media were as annoyed as the experts over the perceived flaws in the simplistic freeze proposal. Quoting the *New York Times* editorial in March 1982:[21]

> The freeze is a simplistic diplomatic formula. . . . But it is neither simple nor innocent. . . . The proper antidote to an unworkable freeze is the completed but ignored SALT II treaty, which the Reagan Administration foolishly dismissed as "fatally flawed."
>
> Why then do so many members of Congress and prominent Americans agitate for a freeze instead of the treaty? Because the Reagan Administration has failed to demonstrate that it will arm wisely and negotiate effectively. The Administration is being subjected to public pressures that it brought on itself.

The *New York Times* urged a vote against the various ballot referendums in November 1982 on the freeze even though it felt "the popular movement from which it springs deserves encouragement."[22]

A case can be made that the public was not interested in the esoteric debate on strategic doctrine, but did want to deliver a message to the experts and the politicians. In effect, the public used the media both to build a grassroots movement and to communicate with the decision makers. The freeze proposal was attractive to ordinary citizens not only because it was simple and easy to understand, but also because it took the initiative away from the experts.[23] The public had become disillusioned with traditional approaches of both the "arms controllers" and the "defense strategists."

The popular freeze movement obviously finds its roots in the public's schizophrenia concerning the Soviet Union and nuclear war, both of which cause anxiety. Although the Reagan supporters capitalized on the public's mistrust of the Soviet Union in helping to defeat SALT II, their rhetoric following the election was sufficiently bombastic to frighten the public concerning the likelihood of nuclear war. Thus, the public's concern about Soviet intentions and military power contributed to the Reagan consensus for an across-the-board U.S. defense build-up; but the fear of nuclear war led to the freeze movement only one year later. This public schizophrenia was documented in a private opinion poll by Richard Wirthlin for the White House in 1982 and reported in the *New York Times*:[24]

> The most striking finding he (Wirthlin) reported was that Americans were less divided over the issue than they were confused. First, in a poll taken in early April, Mr. Wirthlin found that 58 percent of the public agree with this one-sided proposition:
> "A freeze in nuclear weapons should be opposed because it would do nothing to reduce the danger of the thousands of nuclear warheads already in place and would leave the Soviet Union in a position of nuclear superiority."
> But an equally unbalanced statement, made several minutes later in the polling interview, produced a statistically equivalent majority of 56 percent on the pro-freeze side:
> "A freeze in nuclear weapons should be favored because it would begin a much-needed process to stop everyone in the world from building nuclear weapons now and reduce the possibility of nuclear war in the future."
> And 27 percent of the sample agreed with both propositions for what Mr. Wirthlin calls "the most singular inconsistency on any question we've ever asked."

Later polls substantiated this dichotomy in finding that most Americans "support the concept of a freeze, but they turn against the proposal if it means that the Soviet Union would gain a military advantage."[25]

In seeking to maintain their control over this issue, the experts and politicans could plausibly claim that these polls were consistent with the view that "leadership will be a critical factor in determining how Americans come to view the freeze."[26] The experts would be deluding themselves if they do not recognize that the freeze movement was primarily a campaign to affect presidential policy, and it worked. The Reagan administration was effectively forced by public sentiment into accelerating its preparations for and entering into negotiations with the Soviets on both theatre nuclear weapons (where the United States proposed the "zero" option seeking to dismantle existing Soviet systems in Europe) and on strategic nuclear weapons (where in the Strategic Arms Limitation Talks —START— the United States proposed significant reductions). Arms control proponents were at least relieved that the Reagan proposals, while one-sided, were crafted in a way that could possibly lead to serious negotiations.

Thus, as with the previous example of the Three Mile Island accident, the public became disenchanted with the experts and used the media to convey its sentiments. The media, with the polls and stories about the freeze, were more a conduit of information than a shaper of public opinion. In both the TMI and freeze cases, the public was not interested in the details and complexities of the issues. Instead, it wanted to tell the experts and politicans that it no longer had faith in the traditional approaches and was unwilling to leave the issue to the experts alone.

RADIOACTIVE WASTE DISPOSAL

Many experts see radioactive waste disposal as a solvable technical problem— one that is not overwhelmingly challenging or even particularly interesting scientifically. They feel disposal would not be unusually or exceptionally hazardous if done with reasonable care.[27] But the public's perception is quite different. The public thinks that the experts have not yet been able to find a solution, that the government has not competently managed existing nuclear wastes, that the hazards may not be sufficiently understood, and that the government has not kept its promises to citizens living near candidates for a disposal site.[28]

Consequently, gaining access to states, even to characterize potential sites, has encountered difficulties. Many states and local communities have declared outright bans on waste disposal or its transport within their borders, adopting a "not in my backyard attitude." Even with the legal supremacy of the federal government, the persistence of the states and the public in raising these roadblocks might, some scientists feel, result in political considerations dominating technical judgment. The importance of these political problems has now been recognized to such an extent that, as expressed in an interagency study during the Carter administration, "the resolution of institutional issues . . . is equally as important as the resolution of outstanding technical issues" in nuclear waste management, and that such resolution "may well be more difficult than finding solutions to remaining technical problems."[29]

The media have again been blamed for exacerbating the problem with the public. The media are criticized for exaggerating past problems, such as the leaks that occurred in the tanks storing military high-level waste at the Hanford reservation, the poor technical judgment demonstrated in the attempt to site a repository in Kansas, the water management problems with several of the closed commercial low-level waste disposal sites, and the problems with cleaning up the high-level wastes stored at the closed West Valley reprocessing facility. The media have also been criticized for not properly putting the risks, which the experts perceive to be quite small, in perspective for the public and for overemphasizing the so-called unique aspects of radioactive waste, that is, its being highly toxic, lasting for centuries, and potentially causing cancer and birth defects. And some experts have felt that the media have not educated the public about the detailed safeguards of the disposal technology, which has been conservatively designed with multiple barriers for containing the waste and guarding against unforeseen problems.

Again, however, the dominant message grasped by ordinary citizens about radioactive waste disposal is that the public should be careful about what the experts say and promise. The major reason for this disenchantment is the perceived mismanagement and the broken commitments by the government rather than any inaccurate, distorted or slanted coverage on the part of the media. The public is not particularly interested in the details of radioactive waste management, but wants to have confidence in the institutional process and in political representatives monitoring the experts. Consequently, the lack of confidence in the experts has resulted in the intrusion of the political process into nuclear waste decision making. The consequences are well expressed by Richard Riley, the governor of South Carolina:[30]

Heretofore, such decisions were the sole purview of those trained in the mystical sciences that produced new elements of nature, and our faith in them was absolute. Such absolute faith has, however, been shaken and our attitudes toward such decision making have been drastically transformed.

Because of this transformation, we have gone beyond the question of "what will we do with this waste?" There are some who still say that public officials, like governors and state legislators, do not understand, much less know how to resolve, issues involving complex questions of nuclear physics and that the keystone to our democracy, the voter, simply cannot grasp many of the facts having a bearing on this question. Therefore, they contend that the decision on "what to do" should remain solely in the community of those who do understand.

This simply cannot be. The public is aware and is concerned. It may be that, on occasion, their reactions are not equal to the risks. But the public's concerns are real nonetheless. And without a serious effort to rebuild public confidence, our ability to manage these wastes will be seriously threatened.

Therefore, if the questions are truly "Who will decide what will be done?" and "How will they decide?", those of us who are involved in these decisions must ensure that the demands of the political process are balanced with and informed by the appropriate scientific expertise. Within such a scientific/political debate, all parties must be prepared to substantiate the basis for their recommendations. It will be this substantiation, presented in a spirit of openness, available for scrutiny and criticism, and this kind of substantiation alone, that will provide the confidence so necessary to nuclear waste management decisions.

Of highest importance, today, is not only what is to be done, but also how we decide it is to be done. A process of decision making must be established that will allow us to have confidence in the results of that process. There will be remaining uncertainties no matter what the decisions are. Only confidence in the process which leads to those decisions will enable us, as a society, to live with those remaining uncertainties.

EXPANDING THE MASS MEDIA'S TREATMENT OF COMPLEX ISSUES

Even though the criticisms of the media by the experts may be somewhat self-serving, let us assume that mass media could do a better job of treating the difficult, debatable issues involving science, technology, and society for the public. Energy issues, like those of national security, nuclear arms, and biomedical ethics and practice, display two characteristics that are hard to resolve: (1) they turn on trade-offs of risk, cost, and benefit and involve uncertainties that typically require a highly trained specialist to fully understand; and (2) their effects on society as a whole are too fundamental to be left (in a democracy) to the experts alone to decide. So even if, unlike many experts, one thinks that the media are already doing a pretty good job of presenting these issues, there is still reason to wish that they would do better. They are the primary means by which a free society is able to narrow the knowledge gap between the expert few and the inexpert many.

Improving Format

Format is the way information is organized to attract and satisfy the viewer, listener, or reader. Behind any choice of standard format is the journalist's assumption that presenting information in the right way will, more or less automatically, help present the right information—that is, it will get the attention of the people who want it or are presumed to need it, and it will be for them both reliable and useful.

The right format is no guarantee, of course. A journalist can take all the proper steps and make everything easy to understand, and still get it wrong. But many of the reasons heard for faulty reporting actually have had to do with "how" rather than "what"—reasons given by media professionals and outside critics alike:

- There's not enough time or space to deal with complex issues.
- A visual medium just can't handle abstract relations that have to be expressed in words or, worse, mathematical equations.
- Complexity isn't easy, but today no one wants to have to work at understanding anything.
- Issues aren't events, but the news media are event-oriented, so while people are fed an endless diet of disasters, crises, and personality conflicts, either the issues are ignored or they are distorted in the light of the latest alarming event.

In short, format is not the sole determinant of media excellence or effectiveness, but it does set the outer limits of what media practitioners can present, and of what their consumers can consider.

Some formats are so familiar, readers and viewers tend not even to recognize them as such. They are accustomed to using them as given, and they would have to break habits to imagine them otherwise. The standard newspaper article, for example, contains a set of factual ingredients that every reporter knows must go into it and every reader expects to get out of it. Reporters are at pains to avoid giving any overt sign of their own judgment on the merits of the people, actions, or proposals they report. The defining format of the news story becomes all the clearer when compared with the editorial. Not only is the editorial laid out in a way plainly distinct from the news pages, but also, unlike the news article, it is supposed to present the opinion of its author, in this case, the ownership or management, and readers understand that this is its purpose.

A more recently established newspaper format is the "op-ed" piece, named for its appearing opposite the editorial page. In character, it shares much with the traditional "Letter to the Editor," as well as with the signed column, usually syndicated, that appears at regular intervals. In fact, most op-ed pages still feature regular columnists, but the comparative novelty to be found on the op-ed page is the *ad hoc* signed column solicited from, or submitted by, a nonjournalist. The author is often writing about an area that is his or her professional speciality and, therefore, is an expert attempting to communicate with the public. Readers understand every piece on an op-ed page, whether by a journalist or a nonjournalist, to be the opinion of its writer, not necessarily that of the newspaper, and are not surprised when it goes beyond analysis to advocacy—the format not only permits, but invites that.

Successful formats have the effect of creating standing expectations. Once exposed to the variety of personal viewpoints presented on an op-ed page, for instance (if readers find it stimulating or satisfying) they look for more in the same vein the next time they pick up that newspaper, and the format makes it so easy to find the right page that they hardly think about it. This habit of mind, once formed, is just as influential with writers and editors, too, whose knowledge of the requirements of the format becomes almost instinctual. The format exists as an implicit pact between writer and reader: they share the sense not just of what will fit the physical space provided on the page, but of what is "fitting" in the larger sense.

It is this power to organize the expectations and patterns for giving and getting information through the mass media that makes the choice of format, or the creation of a format, potentially so important to the achievement or failure of public understanding over the long term.

In choosing or creating formats, it helps to remember (if only later to try to defy) the apparent limits to what the mass media can do and accomplish. One set of limits is marked by the trade-off between time and audience, that is, between the time an article or program or series asks a reader or viewer to give to absorbing it, and the number of people who will in fact give that time. Generally, the more time asked, the fewer people will be held. Like all sound rules, this one can be stretched. Dramatization helps to overcome the short spans people allow for news and information in their leisure time. So does an on-camera personality whose charisma promises more than an analytical adventure. But exceptions aside, if one wants to reach millions, do it in a minute or two. If one is content to reach fewer, take more time.

Another set of limits is the trade-off between effort and audience. The harder readers or viewers have to work at understanding what is presented, the fewer will choose to do so. One can regret that this is so, and can join the chorus of concern about the public's apparently increasing expectation of instant, effortless media gratification, but beseeching the media is not the way to change the trend. Perhaps strengthing early education would be.

In any case, the high-minded calls for better, more thorough media coverage of complex issues can, if not careful, take on a dreamy quality. For most people the consumption of news and other current information about society is a leisure-time activity; it is not something done "on the job." For the person who has finished a hard day's work or had to attend to household or family cares, it is not easy to spend an hour on the impact of genetic engineering on agriculture, or an evening weighing the risks of piling up nuclear wastes against the risks of retarding nuclear energy development.

Even if a good citizen does spend time in that way—a quality program like *Nova* on public television does reach such an audience—then what is he or she to do? Write a letter to somebody? Wait to be picked for a public opinion survey? Join a single issue interest group and try to hold an elected public official hostage to his or her own view? One must ask what can reasonably be expected of an informed, active citizen in an age when the issues of energy and other fundamentals of modern life are not only dauntingly numerous but excruciatingly complicated. Without an answer to that, it becomes pointless to ask how the media can do a better job.

Confronted by so much information, so many appeals, dealing with social complexities that seem far beyond individual control, all but a handful of people finally look, whether they realize it or not, for someone or some institution they can trust, not for more information. If one could be sure that a lobbying group, a powerful official, or an eloquent public figure would devote hard thinking and sympathetic values to the issues, then one would not have to master the competing considerations oneself. He or she could pledge trust and support to the chosen representative, be it Exxon, the Sierra Club, the Secretary of the Interior, the senior senator from Massachusetts, or whoever.

That sort of pledge of trust to a political figure, party, or cause was not so unusual in former days when most citizens thoroughly accepted the idea of representative democracy, in which the ordinary person's public duty was largely fulfilled by going to the polls. It was enough to elect trustworthy officials; they, in turn, would deal with the issues.

Trusting leaders to make the right choices is still the predisposition of many, but not most, Americans. Most neither trust anyone to represent them on every issue, nor do they labor to research and formulate their own positions. Instead, trust is offered and withdrawn selectively, and it is more likely offered to someone or some authority who appears to have no vested interest in the outcome of an issue than to someone who has a stake in the power or profit to be gained.

Enter the journalist in the context of a recognizable format. Besides its power to organgize information in ways that readers or viewers come as much to expect as accept, the format appeals to a sense of trust. Every format is essentially a kind of promise that someone—usually, in fact, a whole set of people operating in a professionally organized way—has done most of the work. Someone has searched the libraries; someone else has conducted field interviews; still other people have taken the photographs or shot the film, designed the diagrams, and finally reduced all the material they have gathered to a well-ordered piece, one that is easy and maybe even fun to follow. All these media people have saved time and effort for the audience. To the extent readers and viewers value that contribution for a given subject, they choose, at the least, to pay attention. To the extent they believe the media have done the work without prejudice and with respect for their ability to make up their own minds, they may take the findings as if their own.

Given a fair, and not too boring or demanding, presentation, readers and viewers are ready to give the journalist or format their provisional trust. They may think that they have no greater part in the political process than to read, watch, and listen, and their threshold of interest may not exceed wondering how badly they are now being used and by whom, but by trusting the journalist, program, or column, they feel that someone may be representing them in a influential way after all. More than to the president, our congressmen, or other elected officials, the public may delegate, depending on the issue, to John Chancellor, to the op-ed page of the *New York Times,* or to *Nova* or *60 Minutes,* the role of standing up for their interests in the realm of political and corporate power. The media have not seized this role: the public has conferred it on them.

If a member of the public is uncomfortable, however, with relying on the mass media, as they are, to represent him or her, he or she can try to do two things: (1) to reinvigorate the more traditional seats of representative power—the political parties, the ranks of elected officials, the unions, the citizens groups; and (2) while accepting the media's larger *de facto* role, to urge them to address, more directly and visibly, the concerns and values held by large segments of the public. The latter possibility is obviously the more relevant to an exercise of proposing new media formats. How the media might present more explicitly the public's key concerns could be answered by new formats for the purpose. But would this constitute what is meant by the media's "doing a better job?" What would be the measures for judging whether a new media format met enhanced expectations?

Rather than presume we would know a better format when it appears, we should lay out the different possible criteria for judging its success or failure. Here are some criteria—not all compatible—that have occurred to various people who have tried this exercise. The successful format should . . .

- observe the rules of accuracy and fairness that we generally expect of most journalism;
- make people feel they have a part to play in the large decisions affecting the whole society;
- give people not just the feeling they have a part to play, but a real part to play;
- inform the general public of what people in leadership positions are doing or proposing to do;
- inform people in leadership positions of what people in the rest of society expect of them and what they think, fear, want, and value generally;
- attract and hold viewers (or readers or listeners) in competition with other formats and the many other uses people make of their leisure time;
- foster public confidence in the experts, officials, and other leaders who bear the greatest responsibilities;
- concentrate on policy choices that are simple to understand, that appeal to fundamental values, and that are possible to implement;
- factor in the larger social impact of any issue that may otherwise appear to concern only the directly interested parties;
- deal frankly with ambiguity—to combat the illusion that there are simple answers to complex problems.

That list is offered neither as a recommendation nor as a comprehensive account of the criteria by which one might identify a successful format. It is offered to illustrate that what one thinks works depends on what one wants it to do or achieve, and this, when it comes to new formats, is by no means an expectation that is held uniformly by everyone who wants the media to do a better job. A media professional is likely to be offended, in fact, by more than one of these proposed criteria. "Fostering public confidence in experts, officials, and leaders" is not the job of the media, it will be argued, except as that happens as the natural result of accurate coverage of whatever they do that might earn such confidence. Similarly, the media have no business leading people to feel they have a part to play in the larger social decisions if in fact they are excluded or barely considered in the decision process. The media executive or practioner will say that criteria such as these are not the proper tests of good journalism, but the hallmarks of effective, perhaps even deceptive, public relations by those who have an interest in protecting or polishing their reputations.

The interesting challenge is to propose criteria for a successful format that would be congenial both to the media professional and to the interest group (say, scientists and technologists) who want the media to do better.

In any case, if we are serious about this exercise, we cannot stop at simply exhorting the media to do better at explaining to the broad public what those who are expert and responsible already know. Even if that advice were not dismissed as self-interested, it would at best produce an improvement by degree in one of the jobs that media people believe they are already conscientiously trying to do.

Instead, the challenge to the media might be to expand on another job they already do, but, at present, in limited ways—by reports of opinion polls, by publishing letters from readers, and so forth. That job is to report to those in leadership positions what the many other people think and feel about the actions being taken and the choices being made purportedly on their behalf. If the customary job of the media has been to report on the top to those below, this comparable job would be to report from the bottom up. If the media could do this more regularly and more conspicuously than they do now, two distinctive benefits might be achieved: (1) people would sense they have a new, acknowledged, and readily accessible route to being heeded; and (2) those who bear governing responsibilities would be better attuned to what is expected of them by the public they serve. In considering new media formats, then one should think particularly of those that might work "from the bottom up."

Producing innovations in format is an open-ended exercise. The suggestions below are meant just as starters. Producers and editors may be jealous, by the way, of their craft or professional prerogatives, how they supervise the work of reporters in given instances, or what they judge to be worth covering. But, typically, they are not all closed to format ideas from whatever source they come. Formats quickly become everyone's property anyway; the appearance of a successful one, unless it contains uniquely unduplicable talent or other ingredients, is soon followed by imitators. To begin, consider these.

The Science Columnist.

The U.S. news media have apparently never set out to establish science columnists or commentators whose pieces would appear with the same regularity and prominence as their regular political columnists. One exception is Ira Flatow, whose science news reports for National Public Radio's "All Things Considered" obviously go beyond straight reporting to a candid and considered analysis of social significance. Certain leading newspapers do have their own science reporters and feature writers, but where is the syndicated science columnists whose name and values would be as readily known as William Buckley's or David Broder's? (Daniel Greenberg who appears in the *Washington Post* is one exception.) The science editors and writers for the major newspapers and weekly newsmagazines do not qualify because, given the formats within which they work, individual attribution and viewpoint are subordinated to the identity of the editorial product as a whole.

The Adversaries' Forum.

The format in which two (or four or more) exponents of opposing views on an issue are given equal opportunities to persuade the reader or viewer is not unknown, but is not widely used either. It is found in the public television series, *The Advocates,* which has often debated public policy choices involving technological considerations. It is occasionally found in "The News of the Week in Review" section of the *Sunday New York Times* (one edition, for example, featured a full page of opposing views on the question of when a human life begins). But rarely is it found elsewhere. Some have criticized formats like *The Advocates* for forcing complex issues into an "either-or" framework that exacerbates antagonisms and inhibits subtler and more accommodating approaches to reaching broadly acceptable decisions. In defense, others have noted that, given society's established use of the advocacy system and adversarial debate in the courts and legislative settings, it is inevitable that difficult issues will be reduced to a point of choice, and at that point being counted "for" or "against" the proposed choice is how one plays a part in a democracy. In any case, such formats display the indisputable virtue of "built-in" fairness: the even-handed presentation of opposing views is required by the very structure.

The Science Serial.

When scientists complain about the media's treatment of science, they often charge that it fails to convey the systematically organized knowledge necessary not only to doing but even simply to understanding modern science. Individual stories and programs come and go, but nowhere in the media are their subjects shown to cohere as parts of a larger, encompassing body of theory and work. Bronowski's *The Ascent of Man* is sometimes pointed to as a first step toward remedying that failure. Newspapers and magazines might also take the serial approach (*Life* did in the '50s) as a way of revealing, step by step, the "figure-to-ground" relationships of science. It seems ironic that television, which is usually accused more than the print media of giving complex issues the once-over-lightly treatment, has taken the lead in devising popularly attractive ways (*Cosmos* being the most recent example) to engage the lay public in a continuing investigation of science from a particular point of view over a sustained period of weeks. Now print might do well to be the imitator, just as the appearance of new popular science magazines was prompted, at least in part, by the success of the public television series, *Nova.* Even these new magazines, like *Omni,* might redeem their promise to be more than speculative fiction and feature journalism if they were to launch the occasional serial in which, through monthly installments, the rudiments and most important developments of a given field would unfold from basics to present knowledge. (The word, "serial," rather than "series," means an extended exposition, like *The Ascent of Man,* that proceeds from beginning to end over the span of its several chapters or episodes. Its conceptual framework depends on all its parts to make the whole. This is in contrast to the regular "series"—like *Universe* with Walter Cronkite or the weekly

"Science Times" section of the *New York Times*—where the substance of each edition stands on its own though it appears in a regularly recurring format.)

These suggested format innovations obviously do not exhaust all the possibilities that should be tried. Nor should any of the successful formats now in use be immune to attempted improvements. Some of the highest quality efforts have been refined and improved over the years. It had often been the premier newspapers and public television that have led the way. Some of the best recent efforts using formats that they pioneered include: the *Nova* segment looking in depth at genetic engineering; the PBS serial on Oppenheimer; the *New York Times* "Science Section" with its core of expert science writers like Walter Sullivan; and the *New York Times*-CBS News polls, which have shown the evolution and rationale of public thinking on strategic arms control. The continued diffusion and imitation of these proven formats will continue to upgrade media coverage of controversial technological issues.

Increasing Sources

> . . . A truck carrying nuclear waste has just overturned and one of its cannisters has cracked and may be leaking radioactive material . . . A major breakthrough in energy technology has been announced by a company which claims it will now be possible for factories to convert to coal cheaply and burn it cleanly . . . A new controversy has arisen over the announcement by a group of scientists who claim to have developed a new "gene-spliced" agent that is effective aginst many cancers . . .
>
> On any given day in the next year, the Managing Editor of any daily newspaper in the country might well get a call advising him that one or more of the above stories has just "broken." He has four hours (if he's lucky) until deadline. Where does he go? Whom does he or his reporter call?

The above quote[31] comes from the introduction to the Media Resource Service (MRS) of the nonprofit Scientists' Institute for Public Information (SIPI). The MRS has proven to be an innovative and singularly useful contribution for providing journalists with ready access to representative scientific expertise on fast breaking news events. It began as an informal program whereby Fred Jerome, information director of SIPI and a former journalist, would put reporters in touch with scientists and engineers who held a variety of positions on controversial technical issues. After a deluge of requests during the Three Mile Island accident, the service was formalized into the MRS and now provides a data base containing information on 7000 selected scientists who have agreed to answer questions from the media on issues in their respective fields of expertise. The scientists are categorized by discipline, area of expertise, position on controversial issues, and geographic location.

Any representative of the media can call SIPI's toll free number and describe the information or speciality sought. The SIPI staff searches its computer data base and provides within hours the names and phone numbers of three to five scientists representing a range of views. Thus, reporters, editors, and publishers across the country can be referred rapidly to a cross-section of responsible scientists on a wide variety of issues. The service has proven to be useful to both the large media outlets and small newspapers and broadcasters. As one journalists said, "It adds a science consultant even to the smallest newsroom." It also frees journalists from having to depend exclusively on the well-known star performers and media personalities in the scientific community.

The MRS, which has responded to over 1500 queries since its inception, has been periodically evaluated by SIPI by contacting journalists a few days after they have used the service. A recent survey of 50 users found that almost without exception they felt: the response time was fast enough for their needs, they were given the names of enough scientists, and they were able to reach the scientists who provided appropriate information and represented differing views. All 50 said that they would use the service again.

SIPI has also instituted Media Roundtables, which involve small groups of journalists and scientists in off-the-record discussions of science policy issues. These have also proven to be very popular and useful to journalists.

Being Sensitive to Frequency

Deciding on what is newsworthy is the prerogative of the journalist. But as Allan Mazur of Syracuse University observed:[32]

Science and technology are rife with controversial and newsworthy events, only a few of which are reported in the media. . . . When media coverage of a controversy increases, public opposition to the technology in question (as measured by opinion polls) increases, when media coverage wanes, public opposition falls off.

Mazur traced fluctuations over a multiyear period in the quantity of media coverage and in public opinion as determined by polls for two controversial issues: fluoridation and nuclear power. Although the data were crude and incomplete, the variations in the quantity of media coverage appeared to correlate with the ebb and flow of public opposition to these technologies. In addition, detailed polling following the TMI accident also showed the same phenomenon. Within two months after the accident, public opposition to nuclear power decreased as media coverge tapered off. The release of the Kemeny report six months later caused a brief resurgence of opposition, which again fell off two months later. Mazur concludes:[33]

It appears that the public has an inherently conservative bias. If doubt is raised about safety issues, many in the public prefer to err on the side of safety, as if saying, "When in doubt, reject the technology—better safe than sorry." Thus, the appearance of dispute works to the benefit of the opponents of the technology.

Because of the public's tendency toward conservatism or skepticism when media coverage increases, journalists should at least be sensitive to how their choice of which controversial issues to cover might bias public opinion. If even raising the possible dangers of a given technology creates fear and opposition to it, the responsible journalist, in order to be scrupulously fair, may have to be more than fair to the defenders of that technology. The potential conflict occurs, of course, with the journalist's need to be somewhat skeptical of pronouncements from the establishment.

Optimism About the Future

The attention paid to science in the mass media has grown markedly over recent years, often because of the parallel growth of complex social and technological issues that require, in part, a scientific understanding to resolve. This is a situation much to be preferred over a time not so long ago when U.S. television offered no regularly scheduled weekly treatment of technical or scientific subjects in any format, when the general reader interested in such issues faced a gap where nothing existed between *Scientific American* on the one hand and *Popular Mechanics* on the other, when the common perception was that the scientifically trained person had little to say or contribute except when it came to atomic bombs. Now the energy crisis, together with space exploration, the arms race, and the advances in biomedicine, have changed all that. The media (partly leading, partly responding to, public tastes and interests) are trying to do an effective and attractive job. But they can properly be pressed to do better. In particular, they should be encouraged to try new formats (like the adversaries' forum) and to build new linkages with the scientific community (like the Media Resource Service). Both types of innovations can serve to improve public understanding not once, but time after time, until they become a defining part of what we mean by the mass media.

NOTES

1. One example is the Committee on Energy Awareness, Washington, DC, which was set up by the utility industry in the wake of Three Mile Island.
2. The National Academy recently established a Commission on Precollege Education in Mathematics, Science, and Technology because, as stated by the Academy's president, Frank Press, the country is in danger of "raising a new generation of Americans that is scientifically illiterate." See "Reagan Warns Schools Are Failing to Meet Science and Math Needs," *New York Times*, 13 May 1982.
3. A proposal submitted to the Panel on Public Affairs of the American Physical Society.
4. *New York Times*, 30 May 1982.
5. Letter from David Perlman, Science Editor of the *San Francisco Chronicle*, to Marcel La Follette, Editor of *Science, Technology and Human Values*, on 6 Nov. 1981. Published in *Science, Technology and Human Values*, 7 (Winter 1982), 103-104 (reprinted with permission).
6. Richard Sclove, "Decision Making in a Democracy," *Bulletin of the Atomic Scientists*, 38 (May 1982).
7. *Evaluating Public Participation in Low Level Radioactive Waste Management*, Report to the Department of Energy, The Keystone Center, Keystone, Colo. (March 1982).

8. For example, see "Public Attitudes to Technological Progress," *Science*, 205 (20 July 1979), 281-285, and remarks by E. William Colglazier, Jr., "Mass Media Coverage of Scientific and Technological Controversy," *Science, Technology and Human Values*, (Summer 1981).

9. "Three Mile Island: Where TV Scored, Where It Struck Out," *TV Guide* (4 Aug. 1979).

10. Conference cosponsored by the Center for Science and International Affairs at Harvard University and the Scientists'' Institute for Public Information with support from the Aspen Institute for Humanistic Studies, 12 June 1979. Reported in *Science*, 205 (20 July 1979), 281-285.

11. Executive Summary, Reactor Safety Study, Nuclear Regulatory Commission, WASH-1400 (Oct. 1975).

12. See, for example, Alvin Weinberg, "Can We Fix Nuclear Energy," (1979). Scientists' support of nuclear power is supported by surveys conducted in 1980 by Stanley Rothman, Smith College, and S. Robert Lichter, George Washington University, unpublished.

13. David M. Rubin, "What the President's Commission Learned about the Media," *The Three Mile Island Accident: Lessons and Implications*, (New York: Annals of the New York Academy of Sciences, 1981) Vol. 365.

14. Allan Mazur, "Media Coverage and Public Opinion on Scientific Controversies," *Journal of Communication*, 31 (Spring 1981). See also David Burnham, "The Press and Nuclear Energy," *The Three Mile Island Accident: Lessons and Implications*, n. 13, above.

15. Participant at the Aspen Institute Conference, n. 10, above.

16. The need for reporters to maintain a healthy skepticism of establishment views has been argued vociferously in the case of nuclear weapons strategy and military affairs. See: Roger Morris, "Reporting for Duty: The Pentagon and the Press," *Columbia Journalism Review* (July-Aug. 1980); Alan Wolfe, "Defense Crisis at "The Times'," *The Nation* (15 Nov. 1980); and Fred Kaplan, "Going Native Without a Field Map," *Columbia Journalism Review* (Jan.-Feb. 1981).

17. See the chapter by Carnesale and Allison in this volume for an analysis of "The Director's Dilemma." Also discussed in the draft report of the "Executive Session on Nuclear Power and Energy Availability," John F. Kennedy School of Government, May 17-18, 1982, unpublished.

18. The need for regaining public acceptability is stressed in the draft report of the "Executive Session on Nuclear Power and Energy Availability" n. 11, above, and by A. Weinberg, n. 12, above.

19. Part of the reason that the utility industry created the Institute for Nuclear Power Operations and the Nuclear Safety Analysis Center following the Three Mile Island Accident was to demonstrate its commitment on safety to the public. See the full page advertisement by the Edison Electric Institute in the *Washington Post*, 19 Dec. 1979, p. A25.

20. "Weinberger Confirms New Strategy on Atom War," *New York Times*, 4 June 1982.

21. "The Answer to Freeze is SALT," *New York Times*, 21 March 1982.

22. "Against the Freeze Referendums," *New York Times*, 24 Oct. 1982.

23. A point of view emphasized by Professor J. Kenneth Galbraith at a seminar at Harvard University, May 1982.

24. "Nuclear Issue Yields Run on Pollsters," *New York Times*, 6 May 1982.

25. "Poll Shows Nuclear Freeze Backed if Soviet Doesn't Gain," *New York Times*, 30 May 1982.

26. Ibid

27. Policy statement of the American Nuclear Society on High-Level Waste, American Nuclear Society, 1979.
28. E. W. Colglazier, Jr., ed., *The Politics of Nuclear Waste* (Elmsford, NY: Pergamon Press, 1982). See also Fred C. Shapiro, *Radwaste: A Reporter's Investigation of a Growing Nuclear Menace* (New York: Random House, 1981).
29. Interagency Review Group on Nuclear Waste Management, *Report to the President* TID-29442 (March 1979), p. 87.
30. Richard W. Riley, "Foreword," *The Politics of Nuclear Waste*, ed. E. W. Colglazier, Jr., (Elmsford, NY: Pergamon Press, 1982), p. xi.
31. Information booklet on the Media Resource Service, Scientists' Institute for Public Information, 355 Lexington Avenue, New York, NY 10017, 1981.
32. Allan Mazur, "Media Coverage and Public Opinion on Scientific Controversies," *Journal of Communication* 31 (Spring 1981).
33. Mazur, n. 14, above.

Chapter 7
THE UTILITY DIRECTOR'S DILEMMA: THE GOVERNANCE OF NUCLEAR POWER

Graham Allison and Albert Carnesale

If you were a member of the board of directors of an American electric utility company, would you vote today in favor of a new commitment to a nuclear power plant?

Assume, for purposes of this hypothetical question, that the management of the company, in whom you have utmost confidence, has demonstrated to the board's satisfaction that:

1. Meeting minimum projections of growth in demand for electricity in the area served by the utility will require an additional 1200 megawatts (MWe) of electric generating capacity by the early-to-mid-1990s;
2. The realistic alternatives are a nuclear plant and a coal-fired plant;
3. Financing for the project can be secured at the prevailing interest rates, which, though high, can nevertheless be covered by either of the proposed projects and in a manner consistent with the financial health of the utility; and
4. Careful analysis of the costs of construction, capital, fuel, and operations, and of the changes in the rate base, rate charged users, and return of the two alternatives yields the following best estimate: at the same rate of return to the utility, the price of electricity from the nuclear plant would be substantially lower than from the coal plant (perhaps as much as 30 percent lower).

Under these circumstances, would a prudent director vote for the nuclear plant?

Probably not. In fact, no new nuclear plants have been ordered in the United States for five years, a period in which dozens of coal plants have been ordered. The absence of new orders for nuclear plants is generally attributed to two factors: a decline in the growth of demand for electricity in response to sharp increases in electricity prices, and high interest rates and heavy competition for capital in financial markets. Both factors are clearly important. Our hypothetical question, however, assumes favorable resolution of both: the utility needs to add new electric generating capacity to meet projected demand, and it has access to capital at serviceable, though high, rates. After incorporating uncertainties about costs of construction, fuel, and operations of both projects, the analysis estimates that this particular nuclear plant will produce electricity for almost one-third less than the coal-fired plant. And yet the director hesitates. Why?

The underlying problem comes into focus as one confronts a question that has not been articulated, but that must be the emerging nightmare of many prudent utility directors. What is the risk to the company that after it invests $2-3 billion in a 12- to 14-year process of constructing a new nuclear power plant, the plant will not be able to operate? What is the risk to the utility that the return on the $2-3 billion invested will be zero? What is the risk that events *beyond the control of the company,* and beyond its analysts' best forecasts, will delay by several years the date on which the plant comes on line, will double the cost, or will otherwise affect its operation in a manner that could destroy the stockholders' equity and the utility?

If the decision to order the new nuclear power plant were made today, the plant could begin producing power between 1995 and 1997. What could happen in the interim? Could some future president or Congress, governor or state legislature, Nuclear Regulatory Commission (NRC) or public utilities commission (PUC) be antinuclear? In fact this period is likely to include two or three presidents, three or four governors, and six or seven Congresses, state legislatures, NRCs, and PUCs. Is there reasonable likelihood of an accident of Three Mile Island (TMI) proportions or worse during the ensuing 12–14 years at one or more of the 200 nuclear power plants operating in the world? How could that affect public opinion, political referenda, and, thus, the prospects for the utility's new nuclear plant? (TMI-1, an operable plant, has not been permitted to restart after the TMI-2 accident.) These "political" uncertainties cannot be quantified in the more precise terms preferred by the analysts who compare costs of alternative projects. But can the prudent director ignore these risks in the investment decision?

Obviously there is also some risk that the coal-fired plant might be subjected to crippling delay. One cannot exclude the possibility of a new wave of environmentalism that would highlight the health effects of burning coal that persist even after the company has abated air pollution by modifying its plant and its operations. (The best current scientific studies indicate that the mortalities and morbidities from coal are likely to exceed those from nuclear power generation.) But these risks appear of a markedly lower order than those posed by the new nuclear power plant.

If this simplification of the Director's Dilemma is roughly right, and if it is no less favorable to the nuclear option than is the real world (and we believe both conditions are satisfied), then commercial nuclear power in the United States has reached a dead end. The absence of orders for new nuclear power plants for the past five years, the cancellation or postponement of 80 earlier orders, and the abandonment of more than 10 partially constructed plants on which several billions of dollars had been spent may not be just a prolonged hiatus in the stop-and-go history of American nuclear power. It may signal the end of new orders for nuclear power in the United States under the current system for the decade ahead and perhaps beyond.

If so, the nation will have two options. The present goal of national policy—which is to preserve safe, cost-competitive nuclear power as one of several sources for meeting the nation's energy needs—could be abandoned. Alternatively, the system that governs nuclear power could undergo major surgery, change profound enough to affect the calculus of a prudent director. Yet neither the program advocated by President Reagan, nor any of the recommendations of recent commissions and committees, nor even the wish-list of the most strident nuclear advocates identifies proposals that solve the Director's Dilemma.

Our objective here is to develop a realistic diagnosis of the problem of nuclear power in the United States today. Accurate diagnosis should stimulate more realistic thought about remedies.

FOUR PERSPECTIVES ON NUCLEAR POWER

In examining the subject of nuclear power, what one sees depends very much upon one's point of view. Images differ starkly. From one perspective irresistible forces compel any responsible nation to maintain nuclear power as one important source for meeting energy demands. From a second perspective the obstacles blocking the path of nuclear power in the United States appear insuperable. Viewed from a third angle the capability of the American nuclear enterprise to preserve the nuclear option has been compromised by a series of seemingly irreversible choices.* A final perspective sees the present impasse for nuclear power in the United States as inevitable.

Irresistible Forces?

Nuclear power can be used to produce electricity, a commodity consumed by our nation in ever-increasing quantities. Before the oil shock of 1973, demand for electricity grew at about seven percent per year. Since the shock, growth has been reduced by more than half, but it remains substantial. How will the needed expansion in generating capacity be accomplished? "Unconventional" sources, such as solar cells, windmills, and geothermal energy, will make some contribution. But for the economical generation of electricity on a large scale over at least the remainder of this century, the United States must rely upon the "conventional" sources: hydro, fossil fuels (oil, natural gas, and coal), and nuclear. The range of realistic choices is even narrower.

America's hydroelectric potential has been exploited rather fully. The price of oil has increased about fifteenfold in less than a decade. Moreover, whatever the price, the supply is insecure. More than one-third of the oil consumed in the United

---

*We use the term "nuclear enterprise" to encompass those individuals and organizations with a clear stake in the successful continuing use of nuclear power, including research scientists and engineers, designers, equipment vendors, architect-engineering firms, utilities, and regulatory agencies.

States is imported and for some of our most important allies, such as West Germany and Japan, the fraction imported is close to 99 percent. The fate of the Western economies is in the hands of a small number of oil-exporting nations whose vital interests and objectives often differ from our own and whose stability is uncertain.

Natural gas, the fuel most readily substituted for oil, is also imported by virtually all of the industrialized Western nations, including the United States. Few would argue that we should expand our use of expensive, vulnerable oil or natural gas to produce electricity, if cheaper, more abundant and secure domestic sources of energy were available. And they are, in the forms of coal and uranium. The bulk of any expansion of our electric generating capacity over the next two decades must be based on one or both of these two sources.

Neither coal nor nuclear power alone can be counted upon to meet our needs. There are practical limits to the rate at which the nation can expand its capacity to mine and transport coal, and there are situations (for example, small power plants) in which nuclear is uneconomical or otherwise inappropriate. Moreover, both coal and nuclear power have important adverse effects upon public health and safety and upon the environment. Uncertainties abound in the estimates of the severity of these problems, but the most authoritative recent scientific estimates find that the threat to public health, safety, and the environment from coal exceeds that from nuclear power:

> . . . Even when the possibility of reactor accidents is included, the adverse health effects of nuclear power are less than or within the range of health effects from coal.[1]

> The maximum estimates of nuclear power risks are within the range of risks for the coal cycle.[2]

> Some [energy-related] activities involve environmental effects that are of such potential magnitude and are so difficult to control as a technical matter that they may ultimately constrain the use of some energy sources; the aforementioned possibility of an adverse climatic effect of carbon dioxide from fossil fuel burning is the principal example in this category, to which other analysts might add radioactive waste disposal.[3]

Given these uncertainties, the current U.S. policy appears compelling: to preserve the nuclear power option, rather than rely solely upon coal, to meet our future needs for electricity.

Insuperable Obstacles?

Obstacles to preservation of the nuclear option include a concentration of negative symbols, a schizophrenic attitude toward safety, uncertainties of enormous proportions and importance, and a history of incredible actions by nuclear proponents.

Concentration of Negative Symbols.

The dominant symbol associated with nuclear technology is "the bomb" or, more vividly, the image of a mushroom cloud. The "wonder of atomic energy" first entered public consciousness as an explosion of sufficient force to level an entire city and kill hundreds of thousands of its inhabitants. The association between nuclear weapons and civilian nuclear power is not merely one of historical origin. On the contrary, in recent years this connection has been central to the nonproliferation policies of the United States and a number of other countries. Despite strenuous efforts over decades to convince the public that "nuclear power reactors cannot explode like bombs," nuclear power proponents have been unable completely to rid their product of its psychological ties to the images of evil and the potential catastrophe associated with nuclear explosions.

Nuclear explosions release energy not only in the familiar forms of blast and heat, but also in the form of nuclear radiation. Even under ideal operating conditions, some radiation escapes from nuclear power plants. Such radiation is viewed at best as mysterious, and more commonly as insidious. To make matters worse, the result of exposure to the invisible rays can be cancer, a most feared disease, or, possibly even more troubling, a legacy of birth defects in future generations. Some of the nuclear wastes produced today will remain radioactive for tens of thousands of years, with the attendant risk that generations far in the future will be exposed to cancer and birth defect-inducing radiation directly attributable to the current generation's use of nuclear power.

Bombs, explosions, radiation, cancer, birth defects, and eternal risk—a concentration of more powerfully negative symbols for a technology could hardly be conceived.

Safety Schizophrenia.

How safe is safe enough? Our society is plagued by this unanswered and perhaps unanswerable question. We have no agreed objective criteria for judging the acceptability of a given risk. Individuals differ in their assessments of the benefits of driving, drinking, artificial sweeteners, nuclear power, and of the costs of abstaining. The risks could be reduced to zero by absolute abstention, but what would be the newly acquired risks of traveling on horseback, smoking pot, consuming more sugar, or mining and burning coal? Risks can almost always be reduced, but at some cost.

The problem is aggravated when, as in the case of nuclear power, the "downside risk" appears high, that is, when there appears to exist some possibility, even if remote, of catastrophic loss. How is one to assess the risk of nuclear power? How valuable is the benefit, that is, how badly do we need the electricity? How do the expected values of the costs—in dollars, lives, illnesses, damage to the environment, etc.—compare with those attributable to alternative methods for producing the needed electricity? How do the downside risks compare? How much money should be spent to make nuclear power safer than it is now (for example, by putting all nuclear plants underground)? At what point does it no longer make sense to spend money further to reduce the risk? How safe is safe enough?

Prolonged pondering of these questions can lead to withdrawn, bizarre, and sometimes delusional behavior, and to intellectual and emotional deterioration. These are the symptoms of a psychosis properly labeled "safety schizophrenia." Unfortunately, the incidence of the disease in the United States has reached epidemic proportions.

Conflicting Evidence.

Reaching an informed and independent judgment on the desirability of nuclear power is a challenging task. To become fully informed one must have access to all of the available information. But, because there is a long history of secrecy associated with nuclear matters (beginning in the United States with the Manhattan Project of World War II), few feel confident that they have such access, and most are certain that they do not.

Many believe further that the available information, even if accessible, is insufficient to permit formation of a truly informed judgment on nuclear power. They point to the lack of meaningful scientific data bases on the health effects of low doses of radiation, on the likelihoods and consequences of severe nuclear reactor accidents, on the difficulty of isolating nuclear waste from the biosphere, etc. The sophistication and complexity of nuclear science and technology appear to most of the public to defy comprehension, let alone predictability. And the so-called experts are of little help, for they rarely seem able to reach unanimous agreement on anything of importance. Even some of their basic theories appear to be in contradiction. Is there a threshold dose for radiation damage? Is there such a thing as a "hot particle" that is almost sure to cause cancer? Would radioactive iodine be released in large quantities in the event of a nuclear accident? Is there danger of a hydrogen explosion in case of a loss of flow of reactor coolant?

Yet, in the midst of these uncertainties, one piece of incontrovertible evidence stands out: the civilian nuclear power industry has a safety record unsurpassed, indeed, not even approached, by any other major energy industry. This may or may not be true in the future, but it is today.

Incredible Actions.

In light of the negative symbols, the safety schizophrenia, and the uncertainties associated with nuclear power, one can appreciate the enormity of the task of gaining its acceptance by the public. The history of the nuclear enterprise is marked by events that raised rather than lowered the levels of public concern and suspicion (e.g., the partial meltdown of the Fermi reactor case; the abortion of the radioactive waste disposal project at Lyons, Kansas; and the lack of emergency management capabilities demonstrated in the Three Mile Island affair).

Irreversible Choices?

A cursory examination of the history of nuclear power in the United States reveals a number of clearly important choices made along the way, some explicitly and others implicitly, some by action and others by inaction. Among the most critical of these decisions: to place nuclear energy under civilian control; to charge the federal government with the development and promotion of nuclear power; to make traditional utilities the operators, and private vendors the suppliers, of nuclear power plants; and to regulate nuclear energy through an agency dealing exclusively with nuclear energy.

Civilian Control.

The decision to place nuclear energy under civilian rather than military control was taken with the signing of the Atomic Energy Act of 1946. It was a conscious decision, having been the focus of the first open debate over a nuclear issue.

What if the other fork in this road had been taken and nuclear energy in the United States had been placed under military control? How would the nuclear enterprise be different today? Would the military have been strong advocates of the rapid development and deployment of nuclear power plants to produce electricity for use by civilians, or would other potential uses of nuclear energy have occupied much higher places on the list of priorities? What if Admiral Rickover had been in charge of all of America's reactor programs? After all, there are stark contrasts between the naval reactor program run by the admiral and the civilian reactor programs "run" by the five-member NRC, along with the Department of Energy, the Environmental Protection Agency, state PUCs, private vendors, and public and investor-owned utilities. Today DOE operates more than 35 nuclear reactors for research or military purposes. Somehow these reactors have been constructed and operated without the controversy that surrounds civilian nuclear power.

Government Development and Promotion.

The choice of government control over *all* aspects of nuclear energy also was made with the passage of the Atomic Energy Act of 1946. The act established a framework for maintaining the government monopoly in the nuclear field; gave the government exclusive ownership of fissionable materials and facilities for their production and use; specified that studies of nuclear power could be conducted only under contracts with the AEC; and stated as one of its purposes "to insure the broadest possible exploitation of the [nuclear] fields." While subsequent legislation, especially the Atomic Energy Act of 1954, ended the government monopoly and loosened the bonds of secrecy, the governmental commitment to development and promotion of civilian nuclear power remained unchanged.

Another die cast with the passage of the 1954 act was the establishment of a licensing process administered by the AEC. The agency responsible for development and promotion of nuclear energy was also to be its regulator. This arrangement persisted for 20 years, fully covering the formative years in the development of the nuclear power enterprise. Not until the Energy Reorganization Act of 1974 were these functions separated, with the Energy Research and Development Administration (ERDA) (later DOE) responsible for coordinating research and development on all sources of energy, and with NRC responsible for regulating nuclear energy.

Might the course of nuclear power in the United States have been different if government had not assumed responsibility for development and promotion of the technology? Would commercialization have proceeded nearly so rapidly without the infusion of government funds? Would the distinctions between bombs and power plants have been easier to make? Would the regulators have acted differently if the government—indeed, the agency—of which they were a part had not been promoting nuclear energy? Would they not have been seen by the public as more credible? In light of this background, can the regulators be expected ever to gain the public's confidence?

Private Vendors and Traditional Utilities.

The departures from the free enterprise system embodied in the 1946 act had not gone unnoticed. Even supporters of the legislation characterized it at times as "socialistic" and "totalitarian," but they felt that the aberration had to be tolerated for some period of time in order to protect the secret of the bomb. Nor did the issue die with the passage of the 1946 act. The 1946 confirmation hearings for David Lilienthal's appointment as first chairman of the AEC focused more on forms of government than on forms of energy.

In the midst of congressional hearings to consider modifying the 1946 act to break the government monopoly, the AEC decided in late 1953 to support the construction of a demonstration pressurized water reactor (PWR) power plant. After soliciting proposals, the AEC selected Westinghouse Electric Company to build for Duquesne Light Company a 60-MWe PWR power plant at Shippingport, Pennsylvania. In less than four years, the reactor was operating. Supporters of private nuclear power completed their victory with the signing of the Atomic Energy Act of 1954. The act allowed private industry to build and operate nuclear plants on its own initiative, liberalized patent restrictions applying to nuclear technology, and established the framework for regulation of privately owned reactors by the AEC.

Embodied in all of these events were two critical decisions: nuclear power plants were to be supplied by private vendors and owned and operated by traditional utilities. The former decision appears to have been made far more consciously than the latter.

What were the alternatives? Government could have retained its nuclear monopoly and constructed and operated all nuclear power plants, civilian and military. Government could have served as the supplier of reactors to private utilities, much as it now provides fuel-enrichment services. Perhaps the government could have restricted itself to operations and permitted private vendors to design and construct the power plants, much in the manner that private vendors provide tanks, ships, and planes for operation by the army, navy, and air force. Select private vendors could have operated the plants that they themselves constructed, with the electricity sold to traditional utilities for distribution.

How might the selection of each of these alternatives have altered the evolution of the nuclear enterprise?

Nuclear Regulation.

Should the agencies and processes by which nuclear power plants are regulated differ from those for electricity-generating plants using other kinds of fuel? This question was never raised, explicitly or implicitly, in the debates leading to the 1954 act's assignment to the AEC of responsibility for the regulation of nuclear plants. The hearings were conducted by the Joint Committee on Atomic Energy, which had jurisdiction over *atomic* energy and not over other forms of electricity production. Moreover, this was the period when the military aspects of nuclear energy and political and economic ideology concerned legislators much more than safety and environmental regulations.

Though not recognized at the time, the assignment of nuclear regulatory responsibility to the AEC in 1954 represented two critical "choices": to house in a single agency (the AEC) potentially conflicting interests of development and regulation; and to separate regulation of nuclear power plants from the regulation of other ways of producing electricty. The first of these was redressed in some measure by the establishment in 1974 of the Nuclear Regulatory Commission. The second choice, isolation of nuclear regulation, is no less important.

How might the evolution of nuclear power in the United States have been different if a single agency had been responsible for the regulation of all power plants, whether nuclear, fossil-fueled, or other? If the AEC had not been responsible for developing and promoting nuclear power, would it have been more credible as a guarantor of safety? If the regulatory process focused attention on the issue of costs and benefits of a nuclear plant compared to a coal-fired (or other) plant for supplying electricity, how might the debate have evolved?

Inevitable Impasse?

Any useful assessment of the status of the nuclear enterprise must include both static and dynamic indicators and both objective and subjective elements. All of these influence the future course of events.

Objective Status: Hiatus or Impasse?

The more important objective elements are these:

• More than 70 nuclear power plants operating in the United States;
• Approximately 80 plants at various stages of construction;

• More than 10 plants under construction, with combined sunk costs exceeding $4 billion dollars, canceled in the past two years;
• More than 80 previously planned plants deferred or cancelled in the past five years;
• Five orders for new plants placed in the past eight years (compared with over 100 orders in the preceding eight years); and
• No orders for new plants placed in the past five years.

It is clear that nuclear power has reached a hiatus, and perhaps an impasse. This situation can be attributed in part to a reduction in the rate of growth of demand for electricity, to high interest rates, and to keen competition for capital in financial markets. But there are other factors operating as well, as evidenced by the fact that there have been orders for 125,000 MWe of coal-fired capacity in the past seven years, of which 24,000 MWe were ordered in the past three years. (A typical nuclear power plant of contemporary design produces approximately 1000-1200 MWe.)

Is Anybody Happy?

Is anybody happy with the current nuclear enterprise? Apparently not. Nuclear advocates bemoan the unreasonably high and ever-changing standards imposed upon the industry, the absence of a visible commitment by the government to the future of nuclear power, the delays imposed by a labyrinthine regulatory process, the capriciousness of the regulators, and the unwillingness of public utility commissions to set rates that cover the real costs of supplying electricity. Nuclear opponents deplore the enormous risks associated with nuclear technology, the subsidies provided by the government, the labyrinthine formalism of the regulatory process, the kinship between the regulators and the regulated, the capriciousness of the regulators, and the high cost of nuclear electricity. Potential investors, like other analysts, lament most of all the uncertainties shrouding the future of the nuclear enterprise.

Does It Matter?

Does it matter whether nuclear power has reached an impassse? Yes. If no (or only a very few) orders for new plants are placed in the coming years, the United States probably will be unable to maintain the option of having nuclear power serve as a major component of its mix of energy sources. If the nuclear power field were perceived widely to be at a dead end, the best of its highly trained scientists, engineers, and technicians would be the first to leave it. And the best of the new generation of students would be the last to enter the declining field of study. The perception of a dead end for nuclear power could well be a self-fulfilling prophecy.

What would this mean for oil imports? For each nuclear power plant (of 1200 MWe capacity) that is *not* operated, and for which oil ultimately must be substituted for uranium, America's demand for imported oil increases by about

30,000 barrels per day, adding (at current prices) about a third of a billion dollars annually to our trade deficit with the oil-exporting countries and making us all the more vulnerable to disruptions in oil supply.

With few nuclear plants coming on line, would the hazards of nuclear power decline? Not necessarily, at least not for some time. If vendors were to leave the nuclear business, intimate knowledge of existing power plants and of their design would degrade rapidly. If the enterprise were to be perceived as a "loser," personnel in the reactor control rooms and at the regulatory agencies would be less able, heightening the risks at the 75–150 plants now operating and under construction.

It *does* matter if nuclear power has reached a dead end. Whether the event is to be applauded or lamented is a matter of personal judgment, but it cannot be viewed as inconsequential.

Was It Inevitable?

Was the impasse inevitable? Was it naive to expect any enterprise, no matter how gifted and fortunate, to surmount the obstacles in the path of nuclear power?

Recall some of the alternative paths that might have been followed. All nuclear energy activities might have been placed under military control, and power reactors constructed and operated with the degree of secrecy associated with nuclear-weapons production facilities and storage sites. Development and promotion of nuclear power might have been relegated to the private sector, so that commercialization would have begun much later and proceeded at a much slower pace. The government might have assumed responsibility for design, construction, and operation of all nuclear power plants. These would have been quite different nuclear worlds. It is conceivable that in one or more of these worlds the nuclear impasse would have been avoided.

Could there exist a technology with all of the negative attributes of nuclear power that could meet the test of public acceptance? Evidently so. Nuclear weapons have all of these negative attributes, plus one: they are designed to explode! Yet thousands of these weapons are located throughout the United States—some on airplanes, some on intercontinental ballistic missiles filled with explosive chemical propellants, and some on smaller missiles in nuclear-reactor-powered submarines—and all this with little public concern about accidents. In addition, DOE operates more than 35 reactors around the country, and the navy has well over 100 on submarines and surface ships, all with remarkably little public controversy with regard to safety.

Was the commercial nuclear impasse inevitable? Possibly so, but probably not.

THE SHAPE OF THE GOVERNANCE PROBLEM

What is the Objective of National Policy?

The Atomic Energy Act of 1954 (as amended) declares it "to be the policy of the United States that . . . the development, use, and control of atomic energy shall be directed so as to make the maximum contribution to the general welfare . . . ," and it seeks "to encourage widespread participation in the development and utilization of atomic energy for peaceful purposes to the maximum extent consistent with the common defense and security and with the health and safety of the public."

The language of the act is, of course, subject to interpretation. In our view, however, the minimum objective of nuclear governance consistent with national policy is to maintain the option of nuclear power as one of the mix of sources for meeting America's energy needs. (The question of whether the national policy should be changed, either to be more positive toward the use of nuclear energy or more negative, is not addressed here.) To maintain the nuclear option means to preserve the ability rapidly to expand the role of nuclear power in America's energy mix. This requires that the nation maintain capabilities for design and manufacture of nuclear equipment, and for construction and operation of nuclear power plants and the facilities (e.g., for uranium enrichment and fuel fabrication) associated with them. In short, if the United States is to preserve the nuclear option, it must maintain an active nuclear enterprise. This, in turn, can be accomplished only if a way out of the current nuclear impasse is found.

What Conditions Are Necessary To Achieve The Objective?

Three conditions must be met by the nuclear enterprise if commercial nuclear power is to have a future in the United States: it must be (1) economic, (2) safe, and (3) acceptable to the public.

To be "economic," nuclear power must be competitive with the realistic near-term alternative for the production of electricity on a large scale—under current circumstances, coal-fired plants. This requires that the expected cost of electricity from a nuclear plant be less than (or comparable to) the expected cost of electricity from a coal-fired plant, and that the return on investment from a nuclear plant be higher than (or comparable to) the return from a coal-fired plant. Because a prudent potential investor takes into account not only the expected values of cost per kilowatt hour and return on investment, but also the uncertainties associated with these estimates, nuclear power can be "economic" only if the downside risks associated with investment in a nuclear plant can reasonably be assumed by a utility.

To be "safe," nuclear power must be competitive with coal with regard to the hazards presented to public health and the environment. This requires that the expected adverse effects on public health and the environment arising from the use of nuclear power, including normal operations and accidents throughout the fuel cycle, be evaluated. The uncertainties in these estimates are large for both nuclear and coal, and nuclear power can be "safe" only if the downside risks to public health and the environment are not unreasonable compared to those of coal.

"Acceptable to the public"—the third necessary condition for a nuclear future—is more difficult to specify precisely. No matter how economic or safe nuclear power might be in fact, it has no future in a democratic society such as ours unless it meets the test of public acceptability.

Unless nuclear power meets a threshold test in each of these three dimensions, namely, economy, safety, and public acceptance, the objective of preserving the nuclear option will not be realized. Failure to attend to all three dimensions is ultimately self-defeating.

What Factors Affect The Necessary Conditions?

A host of factors affect the ability of the nuclear enterprise to meet the threshold tests. Among the factors that seem to us to be important are nuclear technology; siting; financing; government subsidies; regulation; plant design, construction and operation; the safety record; waste management; and communications.

Government can influence every one of these factors. The extent of that influence varies from one factor to another, and in no case is its control complete. The potential for influence by the overall nuclear enterprise, of which government is but a part, is much greater, though still far from absolute. But all of the factors can be affected by the enterprise in ways that enhance (or undermine) the ability of nuclear power to meet the threshold tests of economy, safety, and public acceptance.

REGULATING NUCLEAR POWER

Is the U.S. Nuclear Regulatory Commission well designed to accomplish its mission? This question is addressed by a number of the studies performed in the wake of the accident at Three Mile Island, but it deserves further examination.

A Much Maligned Agency That Has Much To Be Maligned For

The President's Commission on the Accident at Three Mile Island (the Kemeny Commission), the NRC Special Inquiry (the Rogovin Study), the General Accounting Office (GAO) Evaluation of the NRC's Performance in Its First Five Years, and other related studies offer strikingly similar diagnoses and prescriptions.[4] The consensus finds:

• Preoccupation with equipment and design to the neglect of operators and training and management and enforcement.
• Complacency stemming from a fixation with making reactors as safe as possible, reinforced by 400 reactor-years of operations without a major accident, leading to the view that "accidents can't happen," to insufficient attention to "what if?" and to lack of preparation for the unexpected.
• An aimless NRC: confused, mismanaged, unmanaged, bureaucratic—failing on virtually every item on GAO's checklist of good administrative practice.

We have little quarrel with this consensus, as far as it goes. But when reviewed at a greater distance from TMI, we are struck by the extent to which these studies reflect a tunnel vision not unlike that for which they criticize the NRC. On the basis

of analyses dominated by a single nuclear incident, they recommend more attention to links in the chain of vulnerability insufficiently attended in the TMI case. In
effect, they concentrate on the question: Given this accident, how could the
nuclear regulatory process be changed to avoid future accidents of this kind? How
could additional regulatory activity better prepare to fight the most recent war?
(One is reminded of Mark Twain's cat, which sat once on a hot stove and learned
never again to sit on any stove.)

With a single exception (NRC Special Inquiry), these studies fail to recognize
that they are recommending reallocation of the scarce resources that determine the
capacity of the NRC. Lists of reforms are advocated with more attention to
worthiness of intent than to likely result. Recommendations are presented with
little indication of basic considerations, such as the following: Which recommendations will be hard to implement and which easy? Which recommendations are
feasible given realistic estimates of the capacity of NRC? Which deserve relatively
greater attention and effort (and, conversely, what other activities deserve less)?
Should the total resources devoted to these tasks be increased, and, if so, by how
much? Which recommendations, if implemented, might have a substantial effect
on safety, public acceptability, and cost?

It is instructive to imagine what the consensus findings and recommendations of
these studies would have been if, instead of TMI, the most recent incident had been
a terrorist takeover of a nuclear power plant. Would the recommendations have
focused on the training of armed guards, perhaps at the expense of training reactor
operators?

Net Assessment: What Are The Key Questions?

Assessment of the nuclear regulatory process must ask three key questions:

- What is the impact of the NRC—net—on public health and safety?
- What is the impact of the NRC—net—on the cost of electricity produced by
  nuclear power?
- What is the impact of the NRC—net—on public acceptance of nuclear power?

In none of the studies we have reviewed can we find these questions asked, and
they are certainly not answered. Evidence and analysis in studies throws some light
on these issues. But their failure to put these questions squarely led us to think hard
about whether these are indeed the key questions. We are persuaded they are. They
are complex and elusive. The unwieldiness of a question, however, does not
diminish its importance.

Assessment requires a judgment about results rather than intent. Net assessment requires judgment, not just about direct consequences (even if unintended),
but also about the reactions of other factors in the system, and ultimately about the
effect—net—on the variable of value. Thus, the NRC regulatory process could
impose obstacles that would deter a utility, or its supplier, from taking the initiative
in proposing a measure for improved safety. Similarly, the "goldfish bowl" quality

of the regulatory process might deter NRC staff members from raising, even to their colleagues, questions related to safety, for fear that such questions, when made public, would be interpreted by some as evidence of inadequate safety. Indeed, those who value safety (whether they be proponents or opponents of nuclear power) must worry whether abandonment of the nuclear option might lead to such an exodus of talent and capacity from the current industry that the increased risk of accidents at the more than 70 current operating reactors would exceed, at least over the next decade, any risk posed by new reactors.

The GAO report observes that "the five year period [following the creation of the NRC] has been one of continuing nuclear power plant cancellations in parallel with dramatically increasing concern over nuclear power plant safety." GAO rightly resists attributing to the NRC the decline in orders for nuclear plants and the increase in public concern about safety. But whether NRC has contributed more to the solution than to the problem remains an open question.

No Strategy

All the studies we have reviewed malign the NRC for lack of leadership, competence, imagination, and energy. In its technical review, GAO finds NRC failing on virtually every item on the checklist of good administrative practice.

None of these criticisms reaches, however, to what we believe is the largest failing: *NRC has no strategy.*

• No *overview* of the complex array of factors from which safety costs and public acceptability emerge.
• No *deliberate priorities* in allocating its efforts.
• No *operational plan.*

In response to criticism of recent years, NRC has adopted the names of some of these elements, for example, "the action plan." But neither in the NRC's annual report, nor in the commissioners' replies to criticism of recent years, nor in conversation with members of the commission and staff have we been able to find an agency strategy. Indeed, we believe that individual commissioners would largely agree with this charge.

NRC: Is the Current NRC Well Designed to Achieve Its Mission?

The poor performance of the NRC stems substantially from its design. The agency's lack of strategy is but the largest of its many failings.

These incapacities were predictable. Indeed, they were predicted. Based on his 1974 study, *Regulatory Agency Chairman and the Regulatory Process,* David M. Welborn offered the Administrative Conference of the United States his views on "potential problems in the organizational planning for the new Nuclear Regulatory Commission." He identified "the major problems that will be confronted: the relationships among the chairman, the other commission members, and agency staff in management matters," and he forecast problems in the appointment and supervision of personnel, the distribution of business among personnel and organizational units, and the use and expenditure of funds.

An even more succinct summary of the disadvantage of the commission design was compiled by the President's Council on Executive Organization, which issued the "Ash Report" in 1971. The council concluded that:

- Collegial bodies are inefficient mechanisms for formulating and implementing policy in a timely matter;
- They tend to disagree on major policy issues and therefore wait for individual cases in which to decide issues;
- They fail to coordinate policy with other agencies;
- They tend to concentrate on details and create backlogs in dealing with important issues;
- They do not adapt easily to new technology and industry innovation;
- They create a legalistic environment that contributes to a passive, overly judicial approach to regulation;
- They allocate resources poorly within their own agencies; and
- They tend to defeat the political accountability required for public responsibility.

We find it difficult to improve on Commissioner Bradford's summary: "The current situation at the NRC is analogous to the results that one would expect from hitching five horses to different points around a sled."[5] As another commissioner has asked: If a member of the commission had a strategy, what would he do with it?

Given the NRC's record of nonperformance, a strong case can be made for abolishing the commission, if for no other reason than to make it an example for other nonfunctioning agencies. But NRC's limitations reflect its statutory, congressional, and legal setting. It is difficult to judge whether the single-headed executive agency recommended by both the presidential commission and the NRC Special Inquiry would be able, at this stage in the game, to make much difference in coping with the fundamental problems.

Debate over the reorganization of 1980, which considered not only the administration's proposal to strengthen the NRC Chairman and Executive Director for Operations, but the proposals of the NRC Special Inquiry and the presidential commission as well, generated a host of arguments. Our examination of the organizational issues leads us to conclude that the key considerations are three. First, while sufficiently able leadership can make virtually any organizational form work, the NRC's reputation as a loser and the tight relationship between failure and form suggest that a new organization would much improve prospects for developing an ambitious new strategy. Second, if the objective is to develop a strategy that can substantially affect the likelihood that nuclear power meets the threshold test on the three critical dimensions, the current NRC is the wrong mechanism. The prospect that a multiheaded commission, even with a strong chairman, could develop an overview, establish deliberate priorities, and develop operational plans seems unlikely. Third, one of the tests to be met is that of credibility, and the NRC does not have it and is unlikely to gain it. Nothing undermined NRC's credibility more than its inability to act with authority during TMI. The 1980 reorganization did little to help the NRC to be competent or to appear competent.

The strongest arguments against these proposals for a single-headed executive agency (along the lines of the Environmental Protection Agency) are (1) that the administrator of such an agency, appointed and subject to removal by the president, could be subject to undue influence from the president, especially during a political season; and (2) that since the agency might actually have a capacity to act, there would be greater risk of precipitous change in the direction of action, especially with a change in leadership. Two further considerations are frequently adduced in this debate, but seem to us of less merit: the proposition that the commission form assures a "diversity of views" in policy making that would be stifled by a single-headed administrator, and the assertion that the commission form and processes allow the public more effective participation than the alternative. Given the diversity of public opinion, the reflections of that opinion in the congressional committees to which the NRC reports, the opportunities for intervenors throughout the nuclear regulatory process, and the vigilance of the courts, the case for enshrining conflicting views in what should serve as the executive of the agency seems to us to guarantee nothing more than paralysis. Such diversity in the agency's leadership is hard to distinguish from cacophony.

After these and other arguments have been raised, one's conclusion depends on the weight one attaches to the competing objectives. Government affords few "dream organizations"—organizational schemes whose merits dominate all other alternatives in the minds of all individuals, no matter how much their views might differ on central goals to be served. At this point, preferences for replacing the NRC with an executive-branch regulatory agency, and seeking analogous congressional consolidation of committee jurisdiction, should depend on judgments about the importance of preserving the nuclear option and on the prospects for achieving success by this route rather than by other possible courses of action.

ACTION

The first step toward sound policy is realistic diagnosis of the problem. We offer the Director's Dilemma and our analysis of it as a means to focus attention on the right problem. It is not our objective here to prescribe what could or should be done. Nevertheless, if correct, our diagnosis has important implications for the current debate about remedies.

The current menu of proposed cures includes: reorganizing the nuclear regulatory institutions, reforming the licensing process, planning for emergencies, preparing for a long-term nuclear future, managing nuclear wastes and improving plant construction, maintenance, and operations. President Reagan's announced program to revive nuclear power selects three from this list: streamlining the licensing process, permitting commercial reprocessing of reactor fuel, and resolving the issue of radioactive waste. The relevant question is: if the president's package were adopted and fully implemented, what effect would it have upon the director's calculus? Indeed, if the entire menu of proposals currently on the table were fully implemented, what effect would that have upon our hypothetical director?

The entire package, fully adopted, would not be likely to give nuclear power any more of an advantage than the 30 percent cost advantage hypothesized in the Director's Dilemma. While some of the proposals could also favorably affect safety and public acceptability in ways important to the director, could not too much still go wrong in too many ways beyond the control of the company? The antinuclear initiative, the moratorium-producing accident, the safe-energy president or governor—none would be precluded or rendered significantly less likely by the adoption and implementation of the full menu of proposals currently under debate. The downside risk in the $2–3 billion venture remains intimidating.

At this point, given the history of failure to meet simultaneously the threshold tests on safety, cost, and public acceptability, the nuclear enterprise may have reached a dead end. If so, and if nuclear energy is to survive as a viable component in America's energy mix, it will be necessary to look beyond the confines of the current debate to more fundamental changes in the governance of nuclear power.

Such a search has been neither the purpose nor the focus of this study. But we offer below two illustrations of the kinds of changes that conceivably could be made, and that would in principle affect in important ways the director's calculus and the prospects for nuclear power.

First, government could limit, share, or assume the downside risk now paralyzing the utility director. The utility industry in the wake of TMI has moved to organize an insurance scheme for covering the costs of replacement power when a nuclear power plant is not in operation. (In the case of TMI, these costs have now run over $750 million.) And the Price-Anderson Act already limits the extent of a utility's financial responsibility for off-site damage from a nuclear accident. Federal legislation could provide for the government to share, or perhaps even assume fully, the costs of specified kinds of undue delays in the operation of a nuclear plant. Formulating a plan that did not provide perverse incentives would be difficult, as it is in all kinds of disaster-related insurance, since the actions of the insured party may affect the probability of the disaster. But such legislation could be crafted, and some forms of sharing of the downside risks could importantly affect the director's choice about his company's commitment to a multi-billion-dollar investment.

Some pessimists would observe that what Congress can give, Congress can take away. Legislation establishing federal responsibility for enough of the downside risk to make an investment in a nuclear power plant attractive to a director could, in the future, be repealed or changed. Thus even the option of federal sharing or guarantees may not be sufficient.

There remains at least one further option: nationalization. The U.S. government could create a national nuclear power agency that owned and operated all nuclear plants, selling electricity to utilities for distribution. Such a program could include a national security/terrorism/secrecy dimension as part of its rationale. Alternatively, government ownership and operation of nuclear power plants could be done on a regional basis, or the nationalization could be extended even beyond nuclear power to all electricity production, and even to distribution. Obviously, nationalization is an extreme remedy, well beyond any current discussion, and probably well beyond the feasible political set. And even if nationalized, a nuclear power agency would still be forced to meet threshold tests of economy, safety, and public acceptability, as demonstrated by the successful, but now politically controversial, French nuclear power program.

Our purpose in identifying two radical alternatives is not to argue their feasibility or their desirability. It is to suggest the kinds of changes that might preserve the American nuclear power option, and thus to suggest how far beyond the realm of proposals now on the table realistic thinking must begin to stretch.

NOTES

1. Nuclear Energy Policy Study Group, *Nuclear Power Issues and Choices* (Cambridge: Ballinger, 1977), p. 19.
2. National Research Council, Committee on Nuclear and Alternative Energy Systems, *Energy in Transition, 1985–2010: A Final Report* (San Francisco: W.H. Freeman, 1980), p. 221.
3. Hans Landsberg, et al., *Energy, the Next Twenty Years* (Cambridge: Ballinger, 1979), p. 26.
4. See, for example: U.S. Senate, Committee on Environment and Public Works, *Nuclear Accident and Recovery at Three Mile Island*, 1980; U.S. General Accounting Office, *Three Mile Island: The Most Studied Accident in History* (EMD-80-109), 1980; U.S. Nuclear Regulatory Commission, Advisory Committee on Reactor Safeguards, *A Review of NRC Regulatory Processes and Functions* (NUREG-0642); U.S. Nuclear Regulatory Commission, TMI-2 Lessons Learned Task Force, *Final Report* (NUREG-0585), 1979.
5. *Congressional Quarterly*, November 24, 1979, p. 2667.

ADDITIONAL READINGS

Ahearne, John. "Nuclear Power: A Greek Tragedy?", in *Progress in Nuclear Energy*, Vol. 7 (Oxford: Pergamon Press, 1981).

Bupp, Irvin C. and Derian, Jean-Claude. *Light Water: How the Nuclear Dream Dissolved* (New York: Basic Books, 1978).

Lilienthal, David. *Atomic Energy: A New Start* (New York: Harper and Row, 1980).

Pigford, Thomas. "The Management of Nuclear Safety: A Review of Three Mile Island After Two Years," in *Nuclear News,* (March 1981).

Roberts, Marc and Bluhm, Jeremy S. *The Choices of Power: Utilities Face the Environmental Challenge* (Cambridge, MA: Harvard University Press, 1981).

Rolph, Elizabeth S. *Nuclear Power and the Public Safety: A Study in Regulation* (Lexington, MA: Lexington Books, 1979).

United States Congress, Congressional Budget Office. *Delays in Nuclear Reactor Licensing and Construction: The Possibilities for Reform* (Washington, DC: Congressional Budget Office, 1979).

PART III

ENERGY AND GOVERNMENT

Market forces in the guise of higher prices have affected consumer behavior; conservation and efficient use of energy have increased and overall energy consumption has dropped. Nevertheless, as the authors of the following chapters argue, market forces by themselves are insufficient as a substitute for the governance of energy policies. Because of the inherent instability of oil supplies and the need to provide for national security through energy security, the necessity for government planning at local, state, and federal levels remains. Henry Lee in *National Energy Policy from State and Local Perspectives* traces the 1970s history of state and local governments' attempted partnership with the federal government in response to "the energy problem." He identifies the factors that allowed for "aggressive response" by state and local governments and argues that as energy prices fall and the federal government withdraws incentive, energy will disappear as a separate policy issue and be integrated into state and local policy making.

In *Selling Saved Energy: Three Case Studies,* Peter V. Davis examines the conservation programs initiated by three states and analyzes the political, social, and psychological barriers that existed at the grassroots level. He demonstrates how different policy design and implementation led to failure or success in overcoming these barriers.

On the federal level, Alvin L. Alm, in *Energy Security: Act Two* examines the dangers inherent in a lack of policy consistency in regards to U.S. development of a coherent response to oil supply interruptions. By examining macroeconomic management during a crisis, the management of strategic supply stockpiling, and modes of international cooperation, he identifies the troubling failures that have resulted in the absence of the development of political consensus needed to translate desirable policies into action, and the opportunities available for diminishing risks to national security.

Chapter 8
NATIONAL ENERGY POLICY FROM STATE AND LOCAL PERSPECTIVES

Henry Lee

On a steamy evening in July 1977, the governors of the 50 states arrived at the White House for a two-day meeting to discuss the energy problem. President Carter had convened the meeting ostensibly to solicit support for his energy program, which was encountering opposition on Capitol Hill. At the first official event, dinner in the East Wing, the governors were seated in groups corresponding to six energy issues. Energy conservation and renewables was one of the issues, and several governors, including Michael Dukakis of Massachusetts and Rudy Perpich of Minnesota, were joined by a handful of officials from the White House and the Federal Energy Administration to discuss possible new directions for a federal-state partnership, a partnership that had begun four years earlier with the Arab oil embargo, when the federal government had sought state assistance in implementing federal oil allocation programs. Energy offices were set up in most states for this purpose, and for several years after 1973, emergency planning remained their dominant concern.

In the mid-1970s, Congress made three policy decisions that had a significant effect on the states.[1] First, it decided that energy conservation was to be a major part of any federal energy program and that reliance on price alone to achieve conservation was neither sufficient nor politically tenable. Second, the de-centralized nature of the decision process for energy efficiency investments made it impractical to implement and deliver such programs from Washington. Third, since the federal government had already developed a relationship with the states through the federal oil allocation programs, it made sense to continue that relationship. Congress saw the states as valuable delivery mechanisms to achieve federal energy goals.

The passage of the Energy Policy and Conservation Act of 1975 (EPCA) and the Energy Conservation and Production Act of 1976 (ECPA) resulted in the establishment of two categorical grants to fund state programs. Emphasis was placed on energy conservation, and states were required to meet several mandatory provisions in order to obtain a share of the approximately $65 million authorized by

Congress.[2] These two programs significantly changed the scope and direction of state energy offices, which over a three-year period transformed themselves from allocation and contingency offices into offices whose primary functions were the development and implementation of programs to promote conservation and renewables.

What Governors Dukakis and Perpich suggested on that July evening was that the federal-state partnership, established by EPCA and ECPA, be placed on a permanent foundation, and, to attract broader support, be expanded to include energy production and the development of a state capability to handle energy emergencies. Determining how this was to be accomplished and what constituted a "permanent foundation" was left to a proposed federal-state task force. Although no one could know at the time, the July meeting marked the zenith of the federal-state partnership in the area of energy. Ironically, the effort to place the partnership on a permanent footing eventually led to proposals for its elimination.

The process of developing relevant legislation took a twelve-month period. Budgetary concerns and continued disputes between the Department of Energy and the federal Office of Management and Budget resulted in substantial amendments to the plan envisioned by Governors Dukakis and Perpich, but the bill sent to Congress in the late spring of 1978 was a significant step towards meeting the original goals. The bill would have (a) consolidated all the existing federal-state energy programs except the low-income weatherization program into a single categorical grant; (b) given the states more flexibility by removing most of the existing mandatory requirements and broadening the scope of the program to include energy production and renewables; (c) required the development of a formal plan outlining actions to be taken to establish emergency contingency plans and the commercialization of renewable energy resources; and (d) increased the monies flowing to the states.[3] Having succeeded in convincing the Executive branch, the states now looked to Congress for passage of this program; but here they ran into opposition — primarily from local governments.

Until the spring of 1978, federal legislation on energy had largely ignored local government. In the ensuing months, three factors came together to propel local governments into what had heretofore been an exclusively federal-state arrangement. First, success stories from such localities as Davis, California, and, later, Portland, Oregon and Seattle, Washington, were perceived as being more impressive than the success stories that could be culled from two years of state implementation of EPCA and ECPA. Further, Congress noted with approval that these successes were achieved with minimal outside financial assistance.

Second, the lobbying arms of local government, including the National League of Cities and the U.S. Conference of Mayors, saw the administration preparing to commit a relatively large amount of money to the states to undertake projects that local governments felt they could handle better. These groups pressed for a program that would either obtain for local governments a separate but equal energy partnership with the federal government, or make local government a joint partner with the states.

Third, support in Congress for categorical state programs began to diminish. There was an underlying sentiment that such programs, especially those funded by EPCA and ECPA, were of marginal value and that perhaps it was time to give locals a chance to see what they could do.

Furthermore, by insisting on more flexibility and fewer mandatory requirements, the states also evidenced a dissatisfaction with the status quo. They were no longer satisfied with being a delivery vehicle for federal programs. With the introduction of this new legislation, the states were seeking more federal dollars with less federal direction. This position did not generate much enthusiasm for their cause in the halls of Congress.

The result was that many congressmen seemed to favor the idea of establishing a federal-local relationship. Senator Charles Percy of Illinois and Senator Paul Tsongas of Massachusetts introduced legislation such as the Local Energy Management Act of 1978 and the Community Energy Act of 1980. Simultaneously, the Carter administratation's legislation reconstructing the federal-state relationship received a lukewarm reception, especially in the House Subcommittee on Energy and Power.

The ensuing debate between state and local governments was bitter. Both sides ended up losing. Neither the federal-state legislation nor bills favoring local government received sufficient support to reach the floor of the House during the 1978, 1979, and 1980 sessions.

Though admittedly oversimplified, the arguments in the congressional debate can be summarized as follows: the states contended that they were more efficient and experienced than locals, while possessing a better understanding of local needs than the federal government did. To give increased responsibility to local governments, the states claimed, would only result in duplication of effort and wasted monies.

The locals argued that states had excluded them from participation in the development and implementation of the EPCA and the ECPA plans. Further, locals felt they possessed far more legal authority to implement programs in the residential and commercial sectors, were more sensitive to the needs of the people served by these programs, and were in a better position to build coalitions and consensus in support of specific programs. As Harvey Ruvin, representing the National Association of Counties, pointed out at the Senate hearings: "The average citizen has little or no contact with state governments. The state capital is physically and psychologically remote to him, whereas his city and county governments are continually visible."[4]

In retrospect, strategies adopted by both local and state officials undermined much of the potential support for either the existing federal-state partnership or its expansion. The states sought to move away from their role as delivery agents of federal energy programs. By doing so, they cast doubts on the legitimacy of that role and their ability to fill it. The locals, by concentrating on stopping an expansion of the federal-state partnership, lost an opportunity to justify federal support for local governments by developing an agenda that would have locals complement rather than compete with the states. Neither states nor locals developed even a modicum of consensus about (a) what the role of each ought to be, (b) how energy responsibilities should be divided, and (c) why Congress should appropriate federal monies to support state and local programs. Their failure undermined any attempt to establish a more permanent federal-state-local relationship and fostered doubts about the effectiveness of existing programs and the need to continue them.

These doubts were to set the stage for policies of the Reagan administration. As this chapter is written, the future form of the relationship between the federal government and state and local governments is uncertain. The new administration has proposed several new directions that are in many ways a result of the questions and doubts raised in the earlier debate. They argue that the price of energy is the most effective inducement for private investment in energy efficiency improvements and that many of the government programs designed to either complement or supplement those price signals are no longer needed.[5] If this be the case, a state system to deliver these programs is no longer required. This new policy was proposed to nail shut the coffin on the concept of the states as a delivery arm for federal energy programs, yet, the lid had been placed on the coffin by the states themselves in the preceding years.

The administration, through the Department of Energy (DOE), argued that the decision to establish energy programs and the format of those programs should be left to state and local officials.[6] Since earmarking federal funds for such projects limited choice, block grants giving states substantial flexibility were proposed to replace the existing cornucopia of federal-state energy programs.[7]

Inherent in the Department of Energy's argument was the assumption that the societal externalities at the national level, such as national security and protection from future oil price shocks, were inconsequential, and, thus, the need for specific federal government involvement was reduced, if not eliminated. Whether or not these societal externalities existed at the state or local level was a question each state and local government had to answer for itself. Therefore, according to DOE, existing levels of federal energy monies flowing to the states could no longer be justified and should be reduced. Interestingly, the states objected to the department's posture on the funding figures much more than its philosophical arguments about the viability of the federal-state relationship. Many members of Congress, though, thought the state's position inconsistent. They found it hard to justify additional monies if states were unwilling to meet a minimal agenda of congressionally mandated programs.[8]

Does this new direction mean that existing state programs will wither and die? Does it mean that we will see no new local energy efforts? I believe not. However, an estimation of the social benefit of this new direction depends on whether one is in favor of the new Reagan energy policy or the policies voiced in the previous administration. To an advocate of the former, there is no longer a need for federal intervention in the energy market; programs at the state and local levels should now be evaluated purely on their potential to meet state or local goals. If, as a result of this policy, states and locals choose not to continue existing programs or to change them significantly, society benefits, since limited societal resources are being reallocated to more beneficial uses. States and locals have a choice according to this argument, and if they attach a low priority to energy conservation, why should the federal government force them to continue such programs? If state and local governments wish to continue them, they will now have the ability to target their efforts toward areas with a high local priority. Further, once states and locals have both flexibility and accountability, they may be more willing to address some of the basic structural issues that have prevented an effective relationship between these two levels of government. Finally, if states and locals are to be given the freedom to shape energy programs so as to maximize the state and local benefits, then it follows that they would be prepared to shoulder more of the costs inherent in obtaining these benefits.

The counter argument is that the price of imported oil does not reflect its social cost. The price this country pays in terms of balance of payments deficits, inflation, and continued vulnerability to supply cutoffs justifies government intervention to accelerate the response to the market. Proponents of this view also point out that even if one deregulates gas, removes windfall profits taxes, and raises electricity rates to their replacement value, it will not be until the late 1980s that one will finish this task, and during the interim the "market-signals" will be badly distorted. They further argue that because individual state governments do not completely appropriate the benefits from decreased vulnerability or improved balance of trade, they will not continue to support a strong state energy presence.

Improved targeting, cited as a benefit by the proponents of the Reagan administration policy, is perceived by opponents as an invitation to the states and locals to get out of the energy business. Increasing flexibility without continued funding is seen as encouraging the states and locals to improve their programs, on the one hand, while withholding the capacity to realize those improvements, on the other.

The struggle between the administration and the congressional advocates of a more interventionist federal energy role remains to be decided. Barring a major energy crisis, however, the trend will continue toward less federal funding for state and local energy programs.[9] How state and local governments will respond to these changes and their implications is the subject of the remainder of this chapter.

Post Arab Embargo

During the 1973-74 cut-off of Arab oil and the subsequent price increases, states established or designated allocation offices to work in concert with the federal government. Although officials from the (then) Federal Energy Office promised to reimburse the states for these efforts (and later fulfilled this promise), there was no guarantee at the time that this money would be forthcoming. The crisis atmosphere of the first three months of 1974 was a sufficient incentive for many states to establish such offices.[10]

In the two years following the embargo, the state and local concerns began to shift from emergency planning to a concern about high energy prices. If one compares the energy agenda of state legislatures in major energy consuming states in 1974 with the same agenda in 1976 and 1977, one finds a distinct move away from contingency planning toward programs aimed at mitigating the effects of higher oil costs. Issues such as the utility fuel adjustment clause, the veracity of the oil industry, the commercialization of renewable alternatives, and energy conservation dominated legislative energy agendas.

The problem of higher oil prices was more pronounced in the Northeast which was heavily dependent on oil. Only 16 states use oil as a dominant fuel for heating, commercial, industrial, or utility purposes (table 8.1). The remaining 34 states depend either on natural gas, which continues to be regulated at a price far lower than that of oil, or on electricity, which is also regulated significantly below its replacement cost. Therefore, the effects of energy price increases during the mid-1970s was focused on only 16 states.

Four Categories of State Response

The response of the states to the energy problem can be divided into four major categories. (1) Those 16 states highly dependent on oil, which were under political pressure to establish aggressive energy programs; (2) states that relied heavily on natural gas and electricity and thus placed a greater emphasis on regulatory programs focused toward these two sources of energy; (3) energy producing states, which already possessed a sophisticated government infrastructure to regulate and promote production; and (4) large agricultural or rural states in which allocation of supply remained an important issue, but energy programs aimed at policy issues were of less importance.

States such as Oregon, Washington, and Minnesota adopted energy programs even though they were less impacted by the oil price shocks of 1973-74. State-specific supply problems combined with political pressure account in large part for these three exceptions, and for this reason we have added them to our 16 oil dependent states to create a grouping of 19 states.

In examining state responses to the energy problem, several conclusions emerge. First, the characteristics of the energy problem differed from one region to the next. If the problem of gasoline availability is ignored, the brunt of the burden of higher oil prices fell disproportionately on 16 states, or approximately 30 percent of the nation. The remaining 70 percent retained access throughout the 1970s to regulated natural gas and average-price electricity to heat and cool their homes and power their factories.

TABLE 8.1 States in which Oil is Dominant Fuel

1975	OIL AS % of INDUSTRIAL ENERGY USE	OIL AS % of COMMERCIAL ENERGY USE	OIL AS % of RESIDENTIAL ENERGY USE	OIL AS % of INPUT TO ELECTRIC UTIL.
California	7.3	11.7	1.8	38
Connecticut	25	41.6	40	60
Delaware	27	42	34	64
Florida	18	2.4	4	55
Hawaii	21	22	6	99.3
Maine	31	59	63	18
Maryland	10	32.7	26	40
Massachusetts	20	55	51	79
New Hampshire	21	49	57	29
New Jersey	21	42	40	62
New York	8	42	37	48
North Carolina	13	19	22	0.4
Pennsylvania	8	30	26	8
Rhode Island	22	54	50	99
Vermont	44	42	55	0.8
Virginia	18	15	22	45
U.S. AVERAGE	7	26	19	16

Note 1. Energy used in industrial and residential sectors includes energy losses in generating and distributing electricity. This inclusion accounts for low percentages in the industrial sector.

Note 2. In addition to distillate and residual oil, petroleum use in the industrial sector normally includes LPG, motor gasoline and jet fuel—none of which is included in this table.

Source: *State Data Report*, Department of Energy; September 1981.

Second, the later crises that this 70 percent of the nation did confront were more crises of supply than of price; the natural gas crisis in 1977 and the threats of coal shortages due to UMW strikes focused on availability more than price.

Third, because each of these regions faced different energy problems, the solutions that they sought also had to be different. Too often, analysts overlook these differences. For example, in comparing the energy program of an agricultural state dependent on natural gas with that of a northeastern industrial state dependent on oil, one should not expect identical allocations of state resources or the same programmatic emphasis. Rather, one would expect the agricultural state to emphasize allocation programs, and the industrial state to address the problem of higher energy prices. Or, compare a large industrial state, such as New York or New Jersey, with a midwestern industrial state, such as Wisconsin or Michigan. In the former, multimillion dollar energy bureaucracies developed to implement a multitude of programs aimed at promoting energy conservation, renewables, and coal. Wisconsin and Michigan, however, had smaller energy agencies, but developed sophisticated public utility commissions.

For each of these states to adopt the same type of energy program or to allocate the same level of resources would have been very poor public policy since the importance and dimensions of the problem differed from one state to the next.

Finally, energy is a means to meet an end. In some cases, this end is the production of goods. In others, it is the ability to cool and heat homes. In others, it is the transportation of people and goods. Energy availability and price affect each of these ends.

FACTORS SHAPING THE RESPONSE

State response to the oil price shocks of 1973-74 was most pronounced in the 16 oil-intensive states (the New England states, the Mid-Atlantic states, Pennsylvania, Virginia, North Carolina, Florida, California, and Hawaii) plus Minnesota, Oregon, and Washington.

Five factors played a major role in shaping the response of these states: (1) the perception of the relative seriousness of the energy problem;(2) the availability of federal monies; (3) the presence of a legislatively established energy program and the time frame in which it was established; (4) the importance of the environmental and consumer movements; and (5) the fiscal capability of the states.

Two additional factors played significant roles, but neither is easily evaluated or measured. The first is political tradition. Minnesota and Wisconsin, for example, have had activist-oriented political leadership. Men such as Robert LaFollette and Hubert Humphrey were representative of that tradition; and although tradition by itself will not determine actions, it does establish expectations in the mind of the public.

In other states without such a tradition, the leadership of key individuals moved their political systems to act aggressively. Governor Jerry Brown and state Senator

Charles Warren of California and Governor Tom McCall of Oregon, though only one of several factors, were catalysts in the process that produced aggressive energy programs.

Perceptions of The Seriousness of The Problem

Decisions on the structure and substance of a state's response to a major problem are made by top elected officials. Issues given priority by these officials have an advantage in the allocation of limited state resources. Public expectations play a major role in the designation of priorities. For example, if there is a fire in a town, one does not expect the governor of the state to put it out, but rather expects local officials to make sure the fire department does its job. However, issues such as the economic health of the state and public safety statewide are the responsibility of state officials.

Therefore, if an issue is perceived as having a direct impact on the state's economy or on its public safety, governors and legislators will feel pressure to respond in proportion to the extent of that perceived impact. All issues are in competition with one another for attention in the political system. Senior elected officials have limited political capital to expend. They must spend it as judiciously as their limited fiscal capital. Priorities have to be set through a process that weighs the importance of each issue in comparison to others, one that considers the importance of energy as compared with another, such as unemployment, housing, community development, and environmental protection.

In the mid-1970s, states that perceived the energy problem as a major contributor to their economic problems tended to act most aggressively. It was the change in the degree of importance of energy as a contributor to the state's economic problems, rather than its absolute contribution, that focused the attention of the political establishment. Obviously, states that experienced the greatest change in the cost of energy tended to be the states in which the greatest pressure was placed upon elected officials to act. Rapid increases in price have the potential to create political shock waves, which in turn, create a demand for a visible government response.

When elected officials respond to public policy contingencies, especially of the shock variety, there is a strong political incentive to make their response visible. Visibility is best obtained by establishing an agency or other institution with an exclusive focus on that particular issue. If this does not make good management sense, it makes good political sense, and any management problem can be rectified later when the public's attention is diverted.

This type of response is muted by a reluctance to transfer powers away from existing agencies, even powers necessary for the newly created agency to fullfil its mandate. The result is newly created agencies with scant authority and highly dependent on the willingness of other agencies to cooperate with them. These older agencies are only "willing" to the extent that they perceive a commitment by the elected political leadership to the new agency.

Finally, when an issue attracts significant public attention, elected officials have a strong incentive to control the substance and timing of the response. Officials hesitate to transfer control not only to other agencies, but also to governmental subdivisions such as cities and towns. Thus, it is no accident that initially both funding and responsibility (but not legal authority) for meeting the state energy problem were highly centralized, and these centralized agencies were given unusual flexibility to circumvent administrative regulations, such as Civil Service codes.

As the relative importance of energy diminished, some state energy agencies began to lose this flexibility. For example, Connecticut, which established a strong, independent energy agency in 1974, integrated the agency into the State Budget and Planning Agency by 1977. Energy agencies in other states began to look towards sister agencies and, in some cases, local communities to shoulder some of their responsibilities. The tendency to decentralize, though it made pragmatic sense, often was inversely proportional to the priority placed on energy by the governor and other state leaders.

Impact of Federal Aid

Of all the influences that shaped the structure and substance of state programs in the 1970s, none was greater than the availability of federal grant monies. These monies significantly altered not only the scope of the state response, but the process by which that response evolved.

There is no doubt that without federal grants, the states would not have appropriated funds sufficient to establish and implement the number of projects and programs that they undertook in the period 1976-1981. For example, New York received almost $7 million annually in federal funds in the late 1970s, most of it earmarked for energy conservation. New York's General Assembly most likely would not have appropriated a similar amount for that purpose. Massachusetts, North Carolina, Rhode Island, New Hampshire, and several other states depended almost entirely on federal grants to fund their programs.

By giving the states a large amount of money earmarked for energy, the federal government reinforced the states' tendency to establish autonomous energy operations, and did little to persuade the states to give those operations significant legal authority. In many states, well funded but relatively powerless energy offices existed side by side with less well funded, but powerful public utility commissions. This paradox underlay a short-lived movement during the Carter administration to transfer federal monies from state energy offices to the PUCs.[11]

The transfer of federal monies directly to the governors gave them unusual leverage vis-a-vis the state legislatures. Even in states where the receipt and expenditure of federal funds were subject to legislative review, governors retained enormous bargaining power. Legislatures were inclined to acquiesce to governors able to bring several million dollars of federal monies into the state and were likely to limit demands for special concessions for their districts.[12] In the absence of federal funds, governors would have had to share more control of the energy agency and its programs with the legislatures. Because federal monies were available, states with active and imaginative officials were able to experiment with programs that would have been impossible to implement if the arduous state legislative process had had to be honored.

The result was the establishment of energy offices with ample funding, high public visibility, but with a limited amount of legal authority and a set of programs that in many states had not been forced to go through the normal legislative process.

As a result of federal budget cutbacks, these programs must now go through the state legislative process, and in many states they must go through it without the legislative constituencies built up over time on behalf of other programs, such as health, social welfare, and housing. In some states, energy programs will be able to compete, but there will be an adjustment process, one that will result in a greater sharing of control among institutions within government—specifically, the legislature, other state agencies, and local governments. As the flow of federal dollars dries up and energy is seen as a lower priority, there will be increased retrenchment and in some cases program elimination.

Timing of the Establishment of the Energy Agency

People's perception of any one problem is continually evolving not only because the problem changes, but also because changes are constantly taking place in the composition of other problems that compete for society's attention. Because of the dynamic nature of the public policy agenda, the time at which the legislative process acts on an issue affects the form and substance of a state's long-term response to that issue. Once the drawn-out legislative process has developed a program, it can be changed and amended only with difficulty. A legislature's action on a measure in one year is rarely the same as the action it would take in another year. The actors, the events, and the dynamics are constantly changing.

In most states, the legislation establishing the state energy agency included specific programmatic provisions. These reflected the state legislature's perception of the energy problem in one particular year. Subsequent changes in that perception could not be quickly incorporated into those programs, since the amendment process is slow and depends on intense political stimuli. The budget process does provide a vehicle for some change, but it focuses authority in either a budget or ways and means committee, neither of which originated the enabling legislation.

States that passed legislation in 1974 and early 1975 placed a strong emphasis on emergency preparedness. An example of such a state is Connecticut, which enacted legislation in 1974 to establish a well-funded independent energy department. By 1977, the public concern over energy emergencies had declined. The de-emphasis of the issue led directly to a de-emphasis of the agency, which was rapidly subsumed by the state Office of Policy and Management.[13] Further, the prominence of such issues as utility rates and coal conversion induced Connecticut officials to pay more attention to their Public Utility Commission. As a result, more resources were allocated to the commission and less to the energy agency.

By contrast, states that waited several years to pass legislation found themselves in a very different position. The New York Energy Department was established in 1977 and given significantly different powers than those granted to its Connecticut counterpart. The New York statute emphasizes specific energy conservation programs and provides the agency with far-reaching powers in the case of an energy emergency. Included are provisions for research and development in renewables, as well as a mandate to develop policies and programs to lessen New York's dependence on imported oil. This statute clearly reflected the public perception of the energy issue in 1976-77, while the Connecticut statute clearly reflected the perception in 1974. Ironically, by delaying formal action on the establishment of a state agency, New York placed itself in a much better position than Connecticut to develop programs and policies relevant for the latter part of the 1970s. States that enacted energy programs in 1976-77 captured the benefits of a still-heightened public concern for the issue of energy together with a greater legislative understanding of the problem.

After 1977, public concern began to decline, only to increase during the Iranian crisis of 1979. But this new crisis was accompanied by a strong disillusionment about government energy programs. Energy departments established after 1977 were not given the far-reaching authority or the broad agenda of those constituted earlier.

Environmentalism and Consumerism

In the late 1960s and early 1970s the environmental and consumer movements came of age. Where these movements were strong, they significantly influenced public policy priorities.

Although they are often lumped together, the environmental movement was substantively different from its consumer counterpart. The environmental movement has as its basic premise the recognition that we must pay a cost today in order to preserve our natural resources for tomorrow, while the consumer movement places a higher value on the immediate health and welfare of people. Higher resource prices reduce the rate at which resources are exploited and are thus favored by many environmentalists. These same price increases place an incremental burden on the ability of the consumer to afford the resources and they are opposed by consumer advocates. This fundamental philosophical difference between the two movements inevitably affected the composition of their constituencies and the goals of their organizers.

Environmentalism.

Environmentalism was a dominant factor in shaping American politics in the late 1960s and early 1970s. One has only to look at the number of public policy initiatives, at both the federal and state levels, dealing with environmental issues during this period to realize its significance. Both of the major federal agencies, the Council on Environmental Quality and the Environmental Protection Agency, were established in the early 1970s. Legislation dealing with clean air and water, toxic hazardous substances, pesticides, and general environmental protection, was enacted during this period.

In those states in which the environmental movement was especially strong, there was pressure to support energy solutions perceived as environmentally benign. Alternatives such as energy conservation and the commercialization of renewables were more acceptable politically than such conventional alternatives as coal, nuclear, and off-shore oil development.

Almost every one of the 19 oil dependent states examined in this report demonstrated a strong commitment to environmental protection. For example, even before the oil embargo, Connecticut, Maryland, New York, Oregon, and Washington had adopted power plant siting laws.[14] California, Maryland, Minnesota, Connecticut, Massachusetts, North Carolina, Virginia, and Washington were among the first states to adopt rigorous environmental protection acts, patterned after the National Environmental Policy Act.[15]

Although it is difficult to single out any one set of environmental regulations as an indicator of the level of state concern for the environment, land-use regulation probably comes the closest to being a barometer. Unlike air, water, and solid waste regulation, there was minimal pressure from the federal government on states to adopt land-use controls.[16] Furthermore, in many areas of the nation, these controls were perceived as a gross infringement by government upon individual rights.

In 1976, the Council on Environmental Quality conducted a survey of state land-use programs.[17] They cited 11 different program elements, including coastal zone management, wetlands management, land-use permitting systems, power plant siting, surface mining controls, and flood plain management. Although many states, due to geological or geographic factors, were logistically prevented from adopting some of the elements, it is useful to examine our 19 states in light of the survey's findings.

With the exception of Massachusetts and New Hampshire, the 19 states were the national leaders in land-use regulations. On the average, they adopted 6.3 of the 11 program elements, compared to a 4.3 average for all 50 states. In fact, the other 31 barely averaged over 3.1.

It is significant to note that those states that adopted aggressive energy programs were in almost every case the same states that had adopted aggressive environmental programs. Further, in most of these states, the commitment to environmental protection significantly influences the shape and substance of their energy programs. A commitment to energy conservation, commercialization of renewables, and an environmentally sensitive siting procedure for energy procedures were major elements in all of their programs. Several of the intensive oil-consuming states acted to curtail the use of, or access to, specific alternatives to oil such as coal and nuclear because they considered the potential damage to the environment from them to outweigh the energy benefits. Massachusetts, New York, and California all supported court suits to delay offshore oil exploration. California voted to place a moratorium on the construction of nuclear power plants, and Connecticut aggressively opposed the conversion of their oil-fired electrical generating capacity to coal.

Consumerism.

One of the difficulties in discussing consumerism is to define it. At the very least, its definition could include three fundamental elements. The first is the belief that the burden of liability in the areas of health and safety should be moved from the shoulders of the consumer to those of the producer. Examples of this form of consumerism were commonplace in the early 1970s (the years in which both the Occupational Safety and Health Administration and the Consumer Products Safety Commission were established).[18]

The second element also deals with liability, but focuses on fraud and deceptive practices rather than health and safety. The premise is that, in the marketplace, the consumer is entitled to "perfect information," and if that information is either unavailable or manipulated for the purposes of fraud, then government has a responsibility to intervene. The Federal Trade Commission (FTC) was established to protect the consumer's right to accurate information, and almost every state has within its enforcement apparatus consumer protection mechanisms similar in some way to the FTC.[19]

The third element affects the distribution of wealth between consumers and producers.[20] Price and allocation controls are examples of this element of consumerism.

In the area of health and safety liability, the states seem to feel that responsibility for regulation lies primarily with the federal government. They fear that unless the federal government is involved, the states will relax health and safety standards for the purpose of gaining a competitive economic advantage over their neighbors.

Though scant in comparison to the activities of the federal government, there has been some state consumer action. For example, many states have had boards of registration and safety inspectors for large boilers, utility plants, and autos, as well as health agencies that focused on traditional public health problems including drinking water and food sanitation.

But in general, regarding the area of consumer liabilities, there is little data to support conclusions that would differentiate our 19 states from the reaction of states in general, since the major impetus for action lay not with the states, but in Washington, D.C.

Unlike health and safety liabilty, the prevention of fraud and the dissemination of consumer information are responsibilities that many states have chosen to assume. Fraudulent practices and misrepresentations, such as short-measuring gasoline, offering outrageous land deals, mislabeling products, advertising falsely, and racial and sexual discrimination are all targets of state consumer programs.

Several states, including New York, New Jersey, Ohio, Illinois, Florida, and California, established a vast network of consumer protection agencies at the state, county, and, in some cases, local levels. These agencies not only supply information, but are usually empowered to seek legal redress to protect consumers.[21] In the early and mid-1970s some states moved aggressively to expand their consumer programs by adopting legislation to regulate certain practices.

In 1978, the Council of State Governments produced a summary of state consumers laws enacted prior to 1977.[22] One finds that the northeastern states, all of which are included in our oil-intensive category, had enacted a large percentage of these laws. Only California, Oregon, and Washington had demonstrated equal legislative enthusiasm for consumer protection. Further, consumer protection departments were more commonly found in the Northeast and Midwest than in other regions of the country.

As a rule, states with a tradition of activist state government tended to have a commitment to consumer-related issues. This tradition is compatible with a philosophy that government should assume an aggressive role in policing the marketplace. Many of the 19 oil dependent states were sensitive to consumer-protection issues, and this sensitivity undoubtedly influenced the substance of their energy programs.

The third premise of consumerism deals with distribution, or the allocation of costs and benefits between the producer of a commodity and the consumer. In the case of energy, the distribution was affected significantly by price controls, which transferred billions of dollars from producers to consumers.[23] States with large producer populations would be expected to oppose price controls, and those with a small or negligible production capacity to support those controls. Harvard University Professor Joseph Kalt has studied this tendency using 36 votes between 1973-77 in the U.S. Senate on issues relating to crude oil prices.[24] With the exception of one senator each from New York, Maryland, Virginia, and North Carolina and the two senators from Oregon, all of the senators from our 19 states demonstrated a preference for shifting benefits from producers to consumers.

Most of the exceptions can be explained on the basis of conservative ideologies. The votes cast by Oregon Senators Hatfield and Packwood, however, reflect factors beyond energy—including political philosophy and the strength of the environment movement in that state. In fact, the votes of the senators from Oregon were a harbinger of the inevitable conflict between consumerism and environmentalism.

These findings are not surprising. They indicate a dominant view held in the 1970s by the oil consuming states, which argued that consumers should be protected from oil price increases and that the redistribution of billions of dollars from producers to consumers was a necessity to realize this goal. Oil price controls were the most visible manifestations of this distribution debate, but there was also intense pressure in all of these states to keep the price of other forms of energy, such as electricity and natural gas, low. In fact, in many states the key index in the mid-1970s by which the public judged the success or failure of an energy program was its ability to prevent or minimize energy price increases. Energy prices were the problem, and any solution to the problem had to involve controlling them. In the same way that intervention in the marketplace was justified to protect the public against deception, fraud, and health hazards, intervention could be justified to protect consumers against higher energy prices. Again, those states with a greater tradition of intervention were more likely to pursue such a strategy.

It was not until the latter part of the 1970s, and in some states not until after the Iranian crisis of 1979-80, that concern with price began to be replaced by a concern with costs. The difference between these two terms may be subtle, but it is significant. Concern with cost led states to stress conservation and low-cost alternatives to oil, rather than to emphasize the controlling of price. Concern with price did not disappear, but its relative importance declined as the importance of cost containment increased. This transition was probably the most significant change in the perceptions of the energy problem in the oil consuming states during the 1970s.

The environmental and consumer movements still have influence today, but not to the degree evidenced in the early and mid-1970s. In the area of the environment, some of the opposition to offshore oil exploration has lessened, and the conversion of electric utility plants from oil to coal has gained strength. Renewables, which were perceived as new exciting energy technologies in need of paternal protection by government, have now entered an adolescence and the public expects them to compete in the market with less government support.

The consumer movement has split between those who emphasize distributional effects and those who emphasize containing energy costs. Although the strength of the former may be less than in the 1970s, it is a sleeping giant, waiting to be woken by the shock of yet another major shift in the distribution of income between producers and consumers. Natural gas price increases or electric rate reform could provide such a shock; another oil disruption and its subsequent impact on oil prices would almost certainly revitalize the movement.

Fiscal Capability

During the mid-1970s, many states enjoyed significant fiscal surpluses, while a small minority of states confronted significant budget deficits. The surpluses were cited by members of Congress as evidence that states should pick up a much greater share of the cost of certain programs. For example, during the debate over the Energy Management Partnership Act, both the executive and legislative branches insisted that any such action include requirements that states provide some matching monies as a condition for receiving federal funds. The reaction by the states to this proposal was divided. Fiscally healthy states that had appropriated funds to support a portion of their energy program found this requirement reasonable (California, Oregon, and Minnesota). States that either depended entirely on federal monies or lacked the revenue surpluses objected strenuously to supplying matching monies (Massachusetts).

This absence of state monies for energy was not entirely related to the fiscal solvency of the state. In many cases it also reflected the perception of the importance of energy within that state. However, states with significant budgetary surpluses found it much easier to make choices between competing programmatic priorities than did states without surpluses.

Today, there is extensive public pressure upon every state to tighten its fiscal belt. The surpluses of the 1970s are absent. The competition between priorities will be more intense. Energy programs established and funded during earlier years will undergo rigorous scrutiny by legislative budget committees, and the level of activity for these programs will decline more rapidly than it would if states were richer.

SUMMATION

We have identified seven variables which affect the composition and structure of state energy programs in the 1970s. Five of these have been evaluated in some depth: (1) the composition and seriousness of the energy problem; (2) the availability of federal funds; (3) the presence of a legislative-established energy program and the time frame in which it was established; (4) the importance of the consumer and environmental movements; and (5) the fiscal capability of the state.

Although each of these factors has changed over the last five years, the relative magnitude of their significance has not changed appreciably. California and Oregon are still more environmentally oriented than Arkansas and Alabama. The one exception to this generalization is in fiscal capability. The oil-producing states have enjoyed an appreciable advantage over the consuming states in revenues and, thus, have more flexibility in dealing with the reduction in federal energy funding. This fact could result in the ironic situation in which the most comprehensive energy conservation programs may be in the most intensive energy producing states.

LOCAL GOVERNMENTS

Thus far, this chapter has dealt almost exclusively with factors that shaped state energy programs. Local governments are also actors on the stage of subfederal energy policy, and it is useful to explore their response to the energy issue.

In recent years, it has become increasingly apparent that local governments have the potential to play an important role in the development and delivery of energy programs. As local officials like to point out, they, rather than the states, possess the authority to tax property, regulate the way buildings are built and operated, control the spatial development of construction through zoning, and deliver most of the nation's housing programs. The recognition of this reality was a contributor to the emerging interest in Congress in 1979 and 1980 in a separate energy grant program for local governments.

Unfortunately, when one examines the accomplishments of local governments during this era, one finds that the potential far outstrips achievements. There were significant success stories—cities whose programs were more effective and more imaginative than most state programs. Yet even in these cities, innovative programs had difficulty sustaining momentum. The low-cost energy efficiency improvement program put together in Fitchburg, Massachusetts was very successful in its inital winter. It not only reached an amazingly large proportion of the homes in the city of Fitchburg, but it also generated enormous media coverage.[25] Yet, that success seemingly has not been transferable to other cities.[26]

Few localities have been willing, even for a short period of time, to make energy a high priority. In the same way that states must continually balance various demands for money and other resources, so too must localities balance many priorities, all in competition for a limited supply of political and budgetary capital. City officials are elected to handle an array of traditional responsibilities, ranging from police and fire protection to local economic development and the delivery of educational and recreational services. Although the amount of federal and state monies flowing to cities to meet these responsibilities increased dramatically in the 1970s, it did not keep up with demand for these services. Cities and towns often found themselves financially squeezed. This situation was especially apparent in the Northeast, which happened, also, to be the part of the country hardest hit by the increase in oil prices.

The expanding demand for city services in a time of financial constraint made it difficult for many city governments to turn their attention to issues such as energy, which was not considered part of local government's traditional agenda. For a local official, it was hard to justify expending political capital on a subject for which there were few, if any, public expectations, especially if such an expenditure required diverting resources away from functions for which such an expectation did exist. City governments have difficulty in directly capturing the benefits of energy programs, since such programs do not visibly affect their fiscal accounting, but rather a hypothetical societal balance sheet.[27]

Still, local governments were not without their successes. During the Arab embargo of 1973-74, the most impressive single program developed at any level of government was the Los Angeles energy conservation program, which was able to effectively reduce electrical consumption by 20 percent.[28] Portland, Oregon; Seattle, Washington; Wichita, Kansas; Davis, California; and St. Paul, Minnesota adopted imaginative energy-efficiency initiatives. Mayors and city councils in these cities were willing to commit significant resources to the development and delivery of these programs.

In almost all of these cases, four factors converged to one degree or another to create an environment conducive to local governments' dealing with issues such as energy: (1) the presence of vigorous leadership by senior elected officials who were willing to assume a degree of political risk in altering the traditional agenda; (2) a relatively greater tradition of open government and local resource managment; (3) a pervasive belief that improving the energy efficiency of the city would improve the long-run economic health of the city; and (4) an extensive participatory process that served to legitimize the issue of energy in the eyes of the electorate.[29]

The integration of these four factors required an exogenous catalyst to focus public attention on the issue of energy, and the embargo of 1973 and the events which followed served that purpose. Today, however, the political environment has changed dramatically. If it was difficult to integrate these factors in the mid-1970s, it will be even more difficult to do so in an year in which energy has been relegated to a lower priority at the federal and state levels.

In the 19 states examined, a consistent pattern emerged in which senior elected officials perceived themselves to be under strong public pressure to respond to the energy problem. Among local officials, this expectation was absent or weak. Although there were prominent exceptions, in most cities the public expectation was that energy issues would be handled by the federal or state government. Energy was simply too broad an issue to be addressed by any single city or town. Further, in many of the oil-intensive states, energy was considered to be, in part, a consumer or an environmental issue, and the responsibility for these issues was thought to rest with the federal and state governments. In cities such as St. Paul and Portland, the mayor and members of the city council had to make a significant effort to develop the constituencies necessary to alter public perceptions. For without this contituency, there was no way in which elected officials could access the political benefits necessary to justify an enormous investment of their political capital.

Despite the absence of visible energy initiatives by city officials, many cities are today in a better position to address energy issues than they would have been if they had attempted to develop large energy bureaucracies. First, the public's demand for visible, independent energy initiatives at the federal or state levels is disappearing, thus necessitating a painful transition period for those programs. Most local governments will not have to experience such a transition. Second, the potential for local governments to affect energy use emanates from their authority to regulate the construction and operation of buildings, control local transportation patterns, and deliver a wide variety of services relating to housing. In each of these areas, higher energy prices are a major constraint. For example, in most of our 16 oil-intensive states, the cost of fuel is the most significant contributor to the cost of operating a housing unit, and ranks second to capital in terms of total costs.

If local housing officials must be concerned with energy prices, so too must social welfare planners. Low-income families unable to afford heat turn for help to the most accessible officials. More often than not, those officials are representative of the local government. The responsibility for social programs may be fragmented between various levels of government, yet, by virtue of their accessibility, responsibility for individual social welfare problems usually falls upon local officials. If one further considers that a high proportion of the nation's elderly and poor live in cities, and that higher energy prices have demanded an increasingly larger share of their limited income, it is evident that local officials cannot escape the implications of higher energy prices for their existing social welfare programs.

Finally, there is a link between energy and economic development. Such development attracts investments in newer buildings, which are usually more energy efficient. Further, increases in economic activity provide an investment climate conducive to further development. Energy costs are not the only variable in location decisions by business and industry, but they are a consideration. They are also a consideration in determining the economic viability of many marginal businesses housed in older, less efficient facilities.

This perception of a link between energy and economic development has been the driving force behind many of the more visible local energy programs emerging from the 1970s. Although it is doubtful that many cities will follow the lead of St. Paul, it is also clear that local policy makers creating economic development strategies for the 1980s will have to consider energy as a major factor.

Extrapolating from the last seven years, we reach several conclusions about the shape of local energy initiatives in the 1980s. First, unless there is a dramatic change in the level of public concern regarding energy issues, few local governments will be induced to deal with energy issues in isolation from other responsibilities. Highly visible, independent programs such as those proposed in Portland and Davis will be replicated only where energy issues are given a higher priority than other issues in the competition for local resources. At the moment, public perception does not place energy on the list of priorities for local governments.

Second, as long as energy prices are a resource constraint in the delivery of traditional local services and programs, local governments will have to integrate energy considerations into their existing programs. Although local governments were, for the most part, bypassed by federal energy grant programs, these grants resulted in the implementation of state programs that supplemented or substituted for city efforts. For example, if the federal and state governments had done nothing in the areas of energy use in buildings, city governments would have been under public pressure to intervene. Whether this pressure would have been sufficient is another matter.

The reduction of federal energy funding will have an indirect effect on local governments. If the federal government does not address certain energy problems, pressure will increase on state and local governments to do so. The significance of this indirect effect and the influence of energy as a local resource constraint will be directly proportional to the future increase in the price of energy. If energy prices continue to increase slower than the rate of inflation, public concern about energy will decline. This decline will translate into less consideration by local governments of energy issues, thus more than offsetting the indirect pressure to do more as the federal government withdraws. If, however, energy prices increase more rapidly than inflation, more public pressure will be brought to bear on local officials to act. If there is no federal or state presence, local governments may feel the pressure to act far greater in the 1980s than in the 1970s.

Finally, in thinking about the future role of local government, it is essential to remember that energy prices will not remain constant. Price fluctuations, up and down, will probably be commonplace throughout the next two decades. Therefore the prominence of energy as both a state and local priority will also change.

True, in the early years of the 1980s, it seems that both real energy prices and the scope of goverment energy programs are decreasing. Yet, even if the nation escapes cut-offs of foreign oil supplies, natural gas prices will increase, and electricity prices will rise as new, expensive generating capacity is brought on line. The effect of these price increases will vary by region. States and localities where oil price increases are greatest may be less affected both because they use less of these other fuels, and because they have already begun the adjustment process to higher energy prices. Cities in the Midwest and the Southeast may not be so fortunate.

Energy as a resource constraint will affect programs such as housing, and social welfare, now being implemented by local government. Local officials, in turn, will have to expend fiscal and political capital for energy-related programs in direct proportion to the magnitude of the constraint.

The State-Local Partnership

To the extent that energy remains or becomes a priority issue, state and local governments will be under greater pressure to fill the vacuum left by the withdrawal of the federal government. If this argument is correct, state and local governments will no longer be able to ignore each other in the development and implementation of energy programs.

The lack of a working relationship between state and local governments led to bitter debate over the proposed Energy Management Policy Act. This act would have established a broad federal-state energy partnership and was torpedoed by a well-orchestrated campaign of organizations representing local governments who felt that the act would have legitimized the tendency of state energy officials to ignore their local counterparts.

If the federal government withdraws and the financial resources of the states are thus dramatically curtailed, states will have to find more effective means of developing and delivering energy-related services. As state and local officials come to see energy prices as a resource constraint rather than a resource crisis, they too will be inclined to address energy within the context of existing programs such as transportation, housing, and community development—programs, which have already developed working relationships with local governments.

If either of these eventualities comes to pass, state and local governments will have to recognize that each possesses characteristics conducive to the effective development and implementation of energy programs and that often these characteristics are complementary rather than redundant. For example, state government is better situated to enforce equity considerations in the formulation of public policy. Equity often refers to fiscal disparities, in which poorer communities cannot deliver the same level of services as can wealthy communities. State governments, through their power of taxation and disbursements, can correct these disparities by taxing the wealthy communities and dispersing the revenues equitably to all communities. State government is also better positioned to set and implement subsidies for conservation and renewables or for low-income energy assistance.

Equity can also refer to the spillover problem, in which benefits or costs created in one jurisdiction spill over into another. The classic example of this problem is pollution, which spews forth from a factory in one locality but is breathed by people living in another. A second form of the spillover problem is the free-rider syndrome, in which actions by one community benefit neighboring jurisdictions. States, again, can even out these inequities through their regulatory powers. For example, if energy efficiency provisions should be mandated through building codes, it makes sense to have one code promulgated by the state, since the benefits of such a code would be shared by more than one city or town.

Local communities have a better understanding of the concerns of their citizens and are ideally placed to integrate those concerns into programs and policies. Local officials are more accessible to the public and thereby can be held more accountable for their actions. States are, for the most part, heterogeneous, made up of numerous communities, each with distinctive constituencies. Recognition of these constituencies and their needs is essential. For example, in the delivery of energy information programs or certain targeted subsidies, knowledge of the specific needs of the recipients is critical if these programs are to be of value.

There are numerous examples of programs for which state governments could provide funds, information, guidance, and in some cases, regulatory directives to local communities, who could provide the means to deliver, enforce, or implement the programs in a sensitive and responsive manner. The argument put forth during the debate in Congress over the Energy Managment Policy Act by both state and local officials (that each was the only level of government capable of developing and delivering energy programs) simply does not hold up under scrutiny.

SUMMARY

From the assessment of the evolution of state and local energy programs, we can reach four major conclusions.

First, as energy prices change, so too will the inclination of state and local governments to intervene in the energy marketplace. If prices continue to decline in real terms, so too will the readiness of governments at both levels to intervene. The opposite will be true if prices increase.

Second, the beginning of the 1980s represents a transition period. States and localities which responded aggressively to the oil price increases of the 1970s or to significant regional energy problems will reduce the scope of their involvement as the incentives to respond decline. The rate of this reduction will be affected by the same factors that affected the scope and shape of the original involvement.

Third, barring a major disruption in oil supplies, state and local governments will perceive energy as a resource constraint rather than a crisis, and this perception will strongly encourage the integration of energy concerns into economic development, transportation, and social welfare policies and programs.

Fourth, to the degree that natural gas and electricity prices are the major contributors to higher energy prices in the first half of the 1980s, many of the states and localities that have not paid as much attention to energy issues as their oil consuming counterparts may feel public pressure to do so. But it is the rate of change in *relative* prices that catalyzes public reaction, not the absolute change.

Finally, it is clear that no matter what the current political situation might suggest, under certain circumstances, government will continue to involve itself with the issue of energy. As long as energy is a resource constraint, state and local governments must deal with it. The pendulum of public concern is in constant motion. Events, actors, and political forces are continually changing. To judge tomorrow by today is a mistake. State and local governments have played a key role in the evolution of energy policy in the United States. They will continue to play a role, with or without federal grant programs.

NOTES

1. These policy decisions are manifested in the Emergency Petroleum Allocation Act (PL 93-159), the Energy Policy and Conservation Pact (PL 94-163), the National Energy Conservation Policy Act (PL 95-619).
2. Each state's allocated share varied year to year depending on the appropriation level. No state was disqualified for failure to meet the stipulations of this program, which included mandatory thermal standards for buildings, mandatory lighting codes, right turn on red light, procurement standards for government, and a carpool/vanpool program.
3. State Energy Management and Planning Act of 1978, S3282; and Energy Management Partnership Act of 1979, S1280.
4. Harvey Ruvin, statement at Hearings before the Senate Committee on Energy and Natural Resources on S3283, 14 Sept. 1978, publication number 95-156, pp. 57-60.
5. Department of Energy, *National Energy Plan* (Washington, DC: U.S. Government Printing Office, 1981).
6. Ibid.
7. Senators Hatfield and Weicker filed S1166 in May 1981. This bill would have established an energy block grant program for states.

8. For example, in the House of Representatives, the responsible committees felt that states would forego the school and hospital grant program if a block grant were established. There was also concern about the viability of a low-income weatherization program if states had freedom to move monies across a broad agenda.

9. The proposed fiscal 1983 budget submitted by the Reagan administration zero funded all the major federal-state programs, albeit approximately $200 million in carry over funds would allow some of the programs to survive until Oct. 1983.

10. Nineteen states formally established energy offices to allocate fuels, while most of the remainder designated existing agencies to fill this responsibility.

11. In 1977, Department of Energy officials actively explored the feasibility of establishing a program to fund state public utility commissions to undertake a number of tasks including energy rate reform, forecasting, and energy facility siting, while simultaneously phasing out the EPCA-ECPA grants to state energy agencies. These negotiations were related to the development of the Residential Conservation Service.

12. In the latter part of the decade, many state legislatures enacted laws that required legislative approval for expenditure of federal funds. The level of specificity of that approval varied from state to state. However, it is clear that in the mid-1970s, state legislatures had less of a handle on the expenditure of federal monies than they possessed by the end of the decade.

13. The major catalyst for these changes was the budgetary constraints confronting Connecticut during the mid-1970s. These would not permit the luxury of an independent agency whose major purpose was to prepare for energy emergencies.

14. Council of Environmental Quality, *The Seventh Annual Report of the Council on Environmental Quality* (Washington, DC: U.S. Government Printing Office, 1976), pp. 75-76.

15. Council of Environmental Quality, *The Eighth Annual Report of the Council on Environmental Quality* (Washington, DC: U.S. Printing Office, 1977), pp. 130-132.

16. There were several bills submitted to establish a National Land Lease policy, the most visible being one drafted by Senator Henry Jackson of Washington. The Coastal Land Management Act, however, was the only major national initiative to come out of this process.

17. Council of Environmental Quality, *The Seventh Annual Report,* 1976, p.68-69.

18. The Occupational Health and Safety Administration was established in 1970, and the Consumer Product Safety Commission was established in 1972.

19. Council of State Governments, *The Book of the States, 1978-79* (Lexington, KY, 1978), p. 454.

20. Joseph Kalt, *The Economics and Politics of Oil Price Regulation* (Cambridge, MA: MIT Press, 1981), p. 238.

21. Paul Wasserman and Jean Morgan, *Consumer Sourcebook* Vol. 1 (Detroit, MI: Gale Research Company, 1978), pp. 34-67.

22. Council of State Governments, *The Book of the States,* pp. 452-3, 459.

23. Joseph Kalt, *The Economics and Politics of Oil Price Regulation,* n. 20, above, p. 286.

24. Ibid, pp. 262-264.

25. In the fall of 1979, the city of Fitchburg and ACTION organized an energy conservation campaign which reached 3000 out of 14,000 households and allegedly cut energy consumption by 14 percent. For details, see ACTION, "Community Energy Projects" (Washington, DC: ACTION, 1981), 40-42.

26. Attempts to replicate this program have been tried and several experiments may yet provide dividends. Seattle, Washington, and Fort Wayne, Indiana are possibilities.

27. John Alschuler, unpublished report for the Ford Foundation, 1980.

28. Jan Paul Acton and Ragnlild Mowill, *Regulatory Rationing of Electricity Under Supply Curtailment* (Santa Monica, CA: RAND Corporation, 1976).
29. Henry Lee, "The Role of Local Governments in Promoting Energy Efficiency," *Annual Review of Energy* (1981), 322.

Chapter 9
SELLING SAVED ENERGY:
A NEW ROLE FOR THE UTILITIES

Peter V. Davis

BARRIERS TO RESIDENTIAL ENERGY CONSERVATION

With the benefit of twenty-first century hindsight, the energy-related economic convulsions of the late twentieth century may well seem like nothing more than an inevitable adjustment to the end of the era of cheap energy. Historians are likely to point to the Arab oil embargo of 1973-74 as the event that reinstated energy efficiency as a key to individual and national economic competitiveness. Those who could not or would not make the changes in capital stock and lifestyle dictated by skyrocketing energy prices may appear to be as inflexible, and as doomed, as the dinosaurs. As historians look back, the idea that electric and gas utilities should take an active part in the adjustment process as peddlers of "saved energy" may then seem as natural as it now seems strange.

Historical inevitability can appear highly problematic right up until the time when trend becomes destiny. Despite significant economic incentives favoring active energy conservation efforts, it was by no means obvious in 1982 that the United States could overcome the complex barriers to a sharply reduced level of energy consumption. Nowhere were these barriers proving more intractable than in the residential conservation market. Ambitious public and private efforts to tap this market seemed to founder with distressing frequency on the jagged edges of market and political realities. Consumers who had been sufficiently frightened to give up their gas-guzzling automobiles by the millions in favor of more fuel-efficient models proved much slower to take advantage of opportunities to save energy in their own homes.

As the decade of the 1980s began taking shape, a new and potentially very effective group of players was emerging on the energy conservation scene. In state after state, political pressures expressed through federal legislation and state public utility commission rulings were leading the nation's electric and gas utilities to become promoters of energy conservation. Responding to the growing public outcry over skyrocketing rate increases, utility commissions began demanding that energy suppliers follow a "least-cost" strategy in meeting the future needs of their customers. Given the economic pressures embodied in soaring construction costs and record high interest rates, conservation was more and more frequently found to be the cheapest alternative available. Utilities were gradually being transformed from apostles of energy expansion to agents of energy conservation. Most utilities did not immediately welcome their new responsibilities. Many continued to regard conservation initiatives with all the enthusiasm of Samson contemplating a haircut. But others, perceiving the need to adjust to a new environment, took advantage of the chance to improve relations with their customers and to reduce the need for expensive new generating plant construction. For these latter-day converts to the conservation cause, devising means of dealing with the barriers to residential energy efficiency became a priority concern.

Not the least of these barriers was a dramatic shift in the national commitment to conservation as a key energy source for the future. This commitment, enunciated by President Jimmy Carter in 1977 and incorporated into the National Energy Act of 1978, had come to be viewed as something less than Carter's "moral equivalent of war" by 1982. Under President Ronald Reagan, the marketplace was to be the sole arbiter and expediter of energy efficiency in America. Federal funding for conservation that had been set at close to $1 billion annually was to be cut by more than 90 percent in fiscal year 1983. Only the legislative skeleton of the originally planned conservation program was to remain at the federal level.

Together with a temporary world-wide glut of oil, this comparative indifference to conservation as an area of public policy priority contributed to the revival of the notion that the energy crisis was over. The parallels with the optimism of the 1976-77 period, when experts predicted ample supplies and stable prices for at least a decade, were especially striking. Heating oil and gasoline were once again in plentiful supply in 1982, and spot crude oil prices were down sharply from their heights of the late 1970s. Analysts were publicly predicting that there would be no significant change in the price or supply picture for at least two years. "What energy crisis?" the public once again began to ask.

The market-oriented policy that produced this response ignores the significant social costs attached to continued reliance on imported oil for a major portion of U.S. supplies. As several observers have pointed out, these costs go far beyond the dollar value of the oil itself. United States dependence on imported oil increases the nation's balance-of-payments deficit and national security costs and adds to international instability. As a result, the real cost to society of imported oil has been put at about twice its nominal level (about $30 per barrel in 1982.)[1] From society's viewpoint, then, conservation investments costing less than the energy equivalent of about $60 per barrel appear worthwhile. All but some of the more exotic measures to improve residential energy efficiency can meet that test. For that matter, most conservation measures—including such items as caulking and weatherstripping, insulation, set-back thermostats, water heater blankets, high-efficiency burners, and vent dampers—have simple payback periods of less than five years even at current energy prices.

The question before us in this chapter, therefore, is not "What should the price of energy be to reflect its true cost to society?" but rather, "Why haven't homeowners made cost-effective investments in energy conservation, and what can utilities be expected to do about it?" In economic terms, the chapter focuses on market imperfections and their impact on the distribution of benefits from energy efficiency improvements among the citizenry at large. In human terms, the challenge is to find a means of *marketing* conservation as a cost-effective investment, providing *financing* to overcome the relatively high initial cost, and improving *quality control* to the point that conservation installers are viewed as reliable professionals by the public.

This policy agenda must be seen within the framework of a decade of energy price inflation. The national experience with rising energy prices has demonstrated that conservation energy is no more evenly distributed than reserves of coal or oil or natural gas. Just as large corporations have been able to gain control of most of the nation's conventional energy resources, so have they also been uniquely well positioned to tap the conservation gusher. Mustering technical talent to evaluate efficiency investments and capital to put cost-effective investments in place, companies like IBM, Dow Chemical, and Gillette have substantially reduced their energy use despite continued economic growth. The large automakers have responded to a combination of market pressures and legislative mandates by dramatically improving the efficiency of their products. Given the vast disparity in technical and financial resources between giant commercial and industrial firms and private citizens, it is little wonder that corporations have garnered a disproportionate share of the benefits of conservation energy to date.

The difference between the residential sector and the commercial and industrial sector is qualitative as well as quantitative. Business decision making is by its nature centralized, and large businesses are capable of implementing conservation programs involving thousands of workers and millions of dollars by administrative fiat. The central feature of the residential market, on the other hand, is its fragmentation. Millions of private individuals must independently decide to invest in conservation measures and to correct energy-wasting behavior. Except under wartime conditions, no government or public utility could legally enforce such requirements in the United States.

Consider for a moment the extent of the challenge in reaching the residential market, which accounts for 20 percent of all energy used in the United States. Just getting homeowners' attention can entail a massive publicity effort costing tens or hundreds of thousands of dollars. Once a sufficient segment of the market has been reached, the product must be custom packaged through a detailed energy audit. This sales tool, equivalent to the "foot-in-the-door" of the traveling salesman, generally costs $50-100 to administer, far more than most consumers are willing to pay without subsidy. Once a sale has been made, financing must be arranged. Then the product, consisting of a complicated and cumbersome combination of goods and services, must be delivered and installed in the customer's home. On being installed, the product becomes invisible. Its value is made evident to its purchaser only at the end of the month, when the gas or electric bill arrives or the oil tank is refilled. If energy prices have risen or the product has been poorly installed, savings may not be evident even then.

This scenario presents a difficult public policy challenge, to say the least. One must find ways of convincing the financially strapped homeowner to buy something invisible in order to displace the use of something else the homeowner does not want to think about. If equity is to be maintained, one must provide financing allowing everyone to purchase the conservation product and share in the benefits. If the program is to continue beyond the first few installations, one must ensure that defective workmanship will be relatively rare, or, at least, that it will be speedily corrected when it does occur.

In this chapter, we will examine the results achieved by three conservation programs established to cope with these difficult problems: the Mass-Save program in Massachusetts, the Pacific Gas and Electric (PGandE) program in California, and the Tennessee Valley Authority (TVA) program in Tennessee and six surrounding states. Each of these efforts has produced valuable insights into the prerequisites for successful conservation at the grassroots level. And each has helped to illuminate the magnitude of the task, given our complex and individualistic society and the imperfect state of our knowledge about conservation itself.

FIRST STEPS TOWARD EFFICIENCY

A Cyclical Crisis

The Mass-Save, PGandE, and TVA conservation programs cannot be seen in isolation. They must be viewed against the backdrop of a half-decade of federal legislative initiatives on the one hand and of radical shifts in the economic underpinnings of the electric utility industry on the other. Both of these resulted at least in part from the central energy event of the 1970s—the Arab oil embargo of 1973-74—and the new outlook it created. By the early 1980s, the price of oil had risen to about five times its 1973 level in real terms, dramatically increasing the value of energy conservation to individual consumers, to many utilities, and to the society at large.

The confused period following the oil embargo also made it clear how cyclical public concern about the long-term energy crisis can be. In the atmosphere of near panic created by the embargo, insulation became a first line of defense against the threat of fuel shortages and higher prices for homeowners in oil-dependent states. Insulation installers, many of them roofers and aluminum-siding dealers wearing different hats, appeared in profusion to meet the demand. It was during this period that the highly fragmented, largely unregulated insulation business experienced its first major wave of negative publicity about shoddy workmanship and shyster business practices. At the same time, many members of the general public continued to regard "conservation" as synonymous with "freezing in the dark."

Between 1974 and 1978, oil prices after inflation remained essentially stable, albeit at far higher levels than ever before. The average citizen, perceiving no further impact on his wallet, listened to expert predictions of a prolonged oil glut and went back to buying large, gas-guzzling cars. Oil imports continued to rise to record levels, peaking at more than 8 million barrels per day in 1978 (nearly half of total U.S. consumption). Far from being over, the energy crisis was just beginning to make its real impact felt through this debilitating oil dependence.

The public's complacency lasted only until the fall of the Shah of Iran in the winter of 1978-79, the event that precipitated the world's second oil shock. President Carter had been unable to seize the national attention on the energy issue, despite a barrage of speeches, programs, and proposals. The gasoline shortages and rapid price increases that followed the Iranian revolution succeeded where Carter had failed. Confronted with the prospect of spending hours in line to buy gasoline at more than twice the price they had been paying only a year before, Americans in the gloomy spring of 1979 began to perceive the fragility of the world energy supply system.

Congress, for its part, had not been oblivious to the need for action prior to the Iranian crisis. Having established a system of support to state energy offices in the Energy Policy and Conservation Act of 1975 and subsidies for the elderly and handicapped in the Energy Conservation and Production Act of 1976, Congress turned its attention to utility pricing and residential conservation practices in the comprehensive National Energy Act of 1978. One of its components, the Public Utility Regulatory Policies Act, required public utility commissions to consider six specific revisions in energy pricing practices, with the aim of bringing prices into line with costs wherever feasible. Another component, the National Energy Conservation Policy Act, required each large utility to establish a Residential Conservation Service, offering energy efficiency audits, referrals of conservation contractors, financing arrangements, and conservation information.

In requiring the utilities to provide the delivery mechanism for conservation services, Congress was simply taking advantage of popular sentiment. Surveys had shown that consumers tend to regard utilities as the most reliable source of information about energy, ahead of government at federal, state, and local levels. Utilities have the closest ties with residential consumers and most comprehensive data about these consumers' energy needs; their representatives are accepted visitors to consumers' homes; and their billing system is well established. But Congress was wary of the monopoly motives and monopoly clout of utilities in the fledgling conservation services market. Utilities were initially forbidden to provide more than $300 of financing or to perform insulation and weatherization services themselves. This provision was not removed until 1980, when the Energy Security Act gave expression to a new-found national consensus that the potential benefits of utility involvement in conservation outweighed the risks.

As the 1980s began, the challenge of doing something about continued energy waste in the residential sector was shifting to the utilities in response to the legislation of the preceding years. As it happened, a few forward-looking public utility commissions and some electric utilities were already beginning to move in the same direction on their own. They were doing so not only out of a recognition that the era of energy profligacy was over, but also because the economics underlying the business of producing electricity had undergone a fundamental transformation. Under these circumstances, conservation investments represented a rational response to changed conditions.

The policy shift from promotion of consumption to promotion of conservation was no less wrenching for being rational. Until the early 1970s, the electric utility industry was widely recognized as a declining-cost business, one in which each additional kilowatt-hour of electricity costs less to produce than the last. Larger generating plants were built to satisy increasing demands for power, and consumers were encouraged to heat, cool, cook, and clean the "modern, electric way."

Electricity prices continued to fall as a result, to the satisfaction of both the utilities and their contented customers.

This seemingly salutary trend came to an end about 1970. Rapidly accelerating inflation sent construction costs sky-high at just the moment when the utilities were discovering the limits to economies of scale in ever-larger power plants. In addition, concerns about the safety of a new generation of nuclear power plants were forcing their costs far above original projections. Investor-owned utilities became increasingly concerned about their inability to convince public utility commissions to increase rates fast enough to cover these rising capital costs. In this environment, building new plants with large amounts of borrowed money gradually came to be seen as inimical to the interests of shareholders and ultimately of the utilities as well.

Despite a certain amount of institutional inertia, the financial incentive to slash capital expenditures and reduce risks in this new energy environment brought a growing recognition of the value of conservation and load-management technologies in the late 1970s. Utility regulatory commissions in California, the Pacific Northwest, Minnesota, Wisconsin, New England, and the Mid-Atlantic states were at the forefront of this movement, often prodding utilities to be more aggressive in their conservation efforts. The political process played a vital role in these areas in forcing utilities to make changes in policy that would ultimately prove to be in their own best interests.

Long years of promoting the sale of cheap electricity (years in which growth was synonymous with increased profits) had led to substantial institutional inertia within the utility industry as a whole. It was extremely difficult for utilities to grasp the extent to which their world had been turned upside down by inflation and the end of economies of scale in power production. Political pressures to hold down rate increases ultimately led to forced conservation efforts among utilities that failed to perceive their own destiny. In a number of cases, a coincidence of political and economic interests provided a rare opportunity for utilities and the general public to work together in making the new conservation efforts succeed where past programs had failed.

Mass Save: "Conservation by the Barrel".

In Massachusetts, where oil accounts for half of all residential energy consumption and four-fifths of electric power generation, conservation can mean money in the bank for homeowners. In 1980, the state gave expression to this fact by requiring all 59 gas and electric utilities in the state to provide conservation services, instead of only the 10 largest as specified by federal Residential Conservation Service regulations. Mass-Save is a private, nonprofit corporation set up by the utilities to meet their obligations under federal and state laws. The organization was conceived as an innovative and cost-effective means of pooling utility resources and avoiding duplication in a tangle of varying utility jurisdictions. Yet this arrangement also placed a heavy burden on the organization to produce results.

Mass-Save opened its doors in the fall of 1980 with plans for a $4.2 million-a-year program of public information, auditing, and follow-up services to owners of existing homes using electricity and natural gas. By the end of the year, the operation was in full swing, complete with organization chart, board of directors, and an administrative staff hired entirely on a contract basis, supposedly to minimize bureaucratic inertia. In its first full year of operation, the organization established five regional offices and completed 60,000 residential energy audits. That represented a penetration rate of about 3 percent of the state's 2 million homes. In that first year, however, Mass-Save was the object of considerable controversy, much of it centering on a statewide surcharge imposed on energy bills to cover its cost. An attempt to force consumers to bear the full cost of the audits was barely beaten back in the state legislature.[2]

Mass-Save officials insist that audits are not the be-all and end-all of the program. "It is important to recognize that Mass-Save is not an audit program," the organization's annual report points out. "It is rather a program of encouraging energy conservation actions on the part of its customers." According to Mass-Save Executive Director John Roll, audits are regarded as the point of initial contact with a conservation client, to be followed by weatherization and financing referrals and inspection of the completed work. As of 1982, these aspects of the program had not been implemented statewide, and revised state and federal regulations made it doubtful they would be. The new rules made follow-up assistance largely optional for the utilities involved.[3]

Even Mass-Save's auditing effort is dependent for its success on attracting sufficient consumer interest. The organization kicked off its promotional campaign with a series of press conferences and the mailing of 1.6 million program announcements in early 1981. The response was immediate and impressive. By spring, 200 newly hired auditors were working overtime to plow through a substantial backlog of audit requests. It began to appear that the program would be a resounding success. Yet by the winter of that same year, audit requests had dropped off to a mere trickle, and a number of auditors had to be laid off. This, despite an unusually harsh winter in which outsize heating bills were a regular reminder of energy inefficiency.

A Mass-Save survey of about 600 customers in July 1981 pinpointed both strengths and weaknesses of the Massachusetts program. The survey found that nine out of ten homeowners believed conservation paid for itself and represented a good investment. Yet two-thirds indicated they thought conservation "cost too much," an apparent reference to relatively high front-end or capital costs. The average value of recommended improvements was about $4,000, yet only one in six customers would consider taking out a home improvement loan to pay for weatherization measures. Most consumers, the survey indicated, would rather reduce their energy bills by curtailing their energy needs than by investing in conservation.

The Mass-Save survey also reflected a finding common to many utility-sponsored conservation efforts: the tendency to preach to the already converted, a relatively narrow group of middle to high income, well-informed homeowners. The poor, the old, the less educated tend to be far less likely to take part in these programs. Factors that have been identified as contributing to their reluctance include the high percentage of renters in these groups; lack of understanding of weatherization; lack of faith in contractors; inability to obtain financing; and an emphasis on living for today rather than investing for tomorrow.[4] Massachusetts has responded to the needs of the poor with a combination of heating bill subsidies and a ban on utility shutoffs in the winter months, but it has yet to address the underlying problem in its auditing and information program.

Because Mass-Save was designed specifically to meet the requirements of state and federal laws relating to weatherization of existing homes, it makes no attempt to ensure energy efficiency in new homes. In Massachusetts, that role falls largely to local building inspectors charged with enforcing the state's Energy Code, a set of regulations approved in 1977 by the State Building Code Commission. The public interest group Common Cause picked the code as a model for the nation in 1980, but there has been some concern that the code may be limiting the energy efficiency of new housing. By appearing to constitute a state-recommended level of weatherization, it is felt, the relatively lenient code may actually be encouraging builders to make their products less energy efficient than the market would otherwise dictate.[5]

Pacific Gas and Electric Co.: "Conservation, California Style."

California has been an undisputed leader in tapping the conservation "gusher" as a substitute for conventional sources of energy like oil, natural gas, and uranium. Pacific Gas and Electric Co. (PGandE), the nation's largest private utility with 3.4 million electric and 2.8 million gas customers in central and northern California, has always prided itself on being responsive to the environmentally conscious, politically activist community it serves. Some observers have concluded that the company's survival as a privately owned entity in a bastion of the public power movement may have been due in large part to this ability to adapt to hostile surroundings.[6]

Despite its record of customer consciousness, which has earned it a national reputation for enlightened management in a generally stodgy industry, PGandE in recent years has been caught in the cross fire between two assertively conservation-oriented state regulatory agencies. On one side is the California Public Utilities Commission (CPUC), which has control over the rates the company can charge for electricity and natural gas. On the other side is the California Energy Commission, which was set up in 1975 to handle long-range energy planning, including energy facility siting. Staff members of both agencies privately concede that it may have seemed at times as if the two were trying to outdo one another in promoting conservation and renewable energy sources.

For PGandE, which had considered itself a leader in conservation since the early 1970s, the critical moment came in 1978. It was in that year that the CPUC adopted computer projections by the Environmental Defense Fund (EDF) showing that PGandE's construction plans could be scaled down drastically without creating serious energy shortages. In place of an ambitious building program including both coal and nuclear base-load generating plants, EDF proposed a far-reaching program of subsidies and incentives for conservation, cogeneration, and renewable energy. EDF claimed the substitute program could meet California's energy requirements more cheaply than the PGandE plan and still provide the company with an increased rate of profit, thereby leaving everyone better off.

Under the chairmanship of conservation advocate John Bryson, an appointee of vocally antinuclear Governor Jerry Brown, the commission ordered an EDF-style program put in place by PGandE. In so doing, the commission set in motion a train of events that would vastly expand the utility's interaction with its customers and fundamentally alter the nature of its business. The commission made it clear that future rate increases would depend on PGandE's success in getting the equivalent of half its additional energy supplies from conservation and renewable sources. By 1980, the company had settled on plans to add the equivalent of six large power plants to its system in the coming decade, with three of those to come from a combination of geothermal and hydroelectric sources, wind generators, and cogeneration. Under a state mandate, PGandE had embarked on what amounted to a giant conservation and alternative energy experiment, with the economic future of northern California potentially hanging in the balance.

In a report on its planned activities published at the CPUC's direction in 1980, the company noted, ". . . [T]he CPUC issued directives in PGandE's last general rate decision which have shaped much of our planning in terms of identifying conservation potential and goals. . . ."[7] The company was somewhat more direct in its report to stockholders in the same year: ". . . [W]e have taken a pragmatic approach in proposing plans to regulatory bodies for approval. We have proposed plans which strike the best balance we can between what we perceive to be society's desires, on the one hand, and the economic and engineering feasibility of providing energy supplies on the other."[8]

In striking that balance, PGandE has developed an impressive array of decentralized energy programs ranging from zero-interest financing of home insulation improvements to community-wide energy management and large-scale application of remote-controlled switches aimed at reducing reduced peak demand for electricity. Just listing all of these efforts, with brief descriptions of each, required a report of more than 100 pages in 1980. The utility planned to spend more than $200 million on the full range of alternative energy programs in 1982, including nearly $100 million on residential conservation.[9] These efforts go well beyond those required under the relaxed Residential Conservation Service regulations instituted by the Reagan administration, but they are still being required by the PUC of California, which remains more dependent on oil and gas than any other major state. According to the federal Department of Energy, PGandE and TVA were the only power producers in the country that opposed weakening the national RCS regulations prior to the approval of the revised standards. The stringency of California's standards and the success of TVA's conservation efforts undoubtedly played a part in these decisions.

The Tennessee Valley Authority: "Saving Energy and Cutting Costs."

The Tennessee Valley Authority produces more electricity than any other power system in the United States, and it is in no danger of "running out" of generating capacity in the near future. If anything, the authority expects to be able to provide somewhat more electricity than will be required within its service area for the rest of this decade. Whereas demand was growing about seven percent each year throughout the 1960s and was expected to continue increasing at about that rate through the 1970s, actual growth was only about one percent annually in the years following the Arab oil embargo.[10] TVA originally planned to build 17 large nuclear generating units to meet the growing demand. Four of those units were indefinitely deferred between 1979 and 1982 in recognition of the changed energy outlook, and four others have been cancelled.

At the same time, the agency has continued to expand its conservation and renewable energy efforts. TVA feels it can meet its customers' long-term energy needs more cheaply in this manner than by completing plants already under construction. In March 1982, the same month in which the three latest deferrals were announced, TVA expanded its decentralized energy program throughout the Valley region, which includes Tennessee and portions of six surrounding states. Under the expanded program, TVA's 2.5 million residential ratepayers are eligible for interest-free loans of up to $1,200 for a wide range of home improvement measures aimed at saving electrical energy. An additional $3,800 will be made available at TVA's cost of money (several points below the market rate). By the year 2000, TVA expects these and other alternative energy investments to reduce the need for new generating capacity by the equivalent of the three units most recently deferred.

How did this large New Deal agency, which gained international fame for its success as a producer of large quantities of cheap power, come to turn away from the goal of selling more and more electricity and toward a comprehensive conservation program? Agency officials say the roots of that decision lie in the authority's status as a publicly owned development agency committed to meeting its customers' energy needs at the lowest possible cost. Nearly half of the homes in the TVA region are electrically heated (three times the national average) yet attic insulation has only recently become standard in new homes. Large reductions in energy waste appeared possible with the right kind of conservation program. The key incentive to provide that program, however, came not from TVA's public service responsibilities, but from the changed economics of the electric power business. TVA, which had been a leader in taking advantage of economies of scale in ever-larger plants in the 1960s, discovered that those economies had come to an end in the 1970s. At the same time, inflation and safety requirements tripled the cost of new plants in only a few years' time. Every new addition to the TVA power system would increase rather than reduce the average cost of a kilowatt-hour to the consumer.

With the appointment in 1977 of long-time TVA critic S. David Freeman as one of three board members, and later as chairman of the agency, TVA moved rapidly to test the potential of conservation as a substitute source of energy. Directed by President Carter to make TVA a showcase of conservation and solar energy, Freeman wasted little time in firing up what has become the most successful TVA residential energy conservation effort, the Home Insulation Program. Through 1982, more than 650,000 free home energy audits had been conducted by TVA-trained energy advisors, a regional penetration rate of more than 20 percent. More than 290,000 consumers had received interest-free insulation and weatherization loans, repayable on monthly electric bills over a period of up to seven years. Post-installation inspections, provided free of charge, ensured that weatherization work met TVA quality standards before contractors received payment.

Designed to take advantage of the most readily available sources of "saved energy," the Home Insulation Program is the centerpiece of TVA's decentralized energy efforts. Like the PGandE efforts, which it in some ways resembles, the TVA plan includes a wide range of other programs, including promotional efforts aimed at cogeneration, wood heaters, solar water heaters, remote appliance switching, and heat-pump heating and air conditioning. The value of each of these devices to the power system and to the consumer is evaluated through an innovative methodology known as the "power credit," a form of cost-benefit analysis that allows conservation and alternate energy devices to be evaluated in comparison with conventional forms of power production.[11] Full-scale funding is provided only to those measures whose benefits to the power system exceed their costs. Despite advance preparation, TVA has discovered that effective conservation programs do not spring up overnight or without a lot of learning from experience.

"We have been on a very steep learning curve over the last four years," Freeman testified before a congressional committee in July 1981. "[It is] a curve that has demonstrated how much easier it is to talk about conservation and other kinds of decentralized energy than it is to implement them. Even the best information and months of careful planning cannot eliminate the possibility of failures and unexpected problems. And not all conservation and decentralized energy programs will cost as little or displace as much energy as initially projected. . . . [But] TVA has . . . created the organizational framework that will be required to meet the challenge of maintaining a balanced energy system."

CONSERVATION—SCALING THE BARRIERS

Marketing

Considerable progress has been made nationwide in the past few years in getting the fundamental concept of conservation across to the public. Most people now recognize that saving energy is not the same thing as freezing in the dark. As one Massachusetts official put it, "I think we've finally gotten through Conservation 101 anyway. People recognize that conservation is a necessity. Now we have to go on to Conservation 202, the lesson that conservation has become a paying proposition."[12]

For utilities attempting to get that message across to the residential conservation market, the central difficulty is the fragmentation we discussed at the outset: one must convince the financially strapped homeowner *individually* to buy something invisible in order to displace the use of something else the homeowner does not want to think about. How is this to be accomplished? Steadily rising prices, painful though they may be to some consumers, are generally seen as a prerequisite for success.

"The bottom line is that price is what makes the conservation machine go," commented Eric Hirst, a researcher at Oak Ridge National Laboratory in Tennessee, who has been evaluating a variety of utility conservation programs. "Without (rising prices), all the shouting about the need to save energy really doesn't amount to a hill of beans," Hirst said. Even with rising prices, accurate conservation marketing can be quite a challenge, he noted, because actual savings achieved vary so widely from program to program and even from house to house. "The plain fact is that we don't know how much energy a given set of conservation measures will save until they have been installed," Hirst said.

Of the three utility-sponsored residential conservation programs we have examined, TVA's appears to have had the greatest success to date in reaching its target audience. According to Hirst, TVA's 20 percent penetration rate for energy audits is the highest in the country, and its 45 percent success rate in convincing those audited to take out interest-free conservation loans is also unusually high. The role word-of-mouth advertising has played in attracting new business for the TVA program has been particularly noteworthy. Until 1983, TVA used no paid advertising to promote its program, and even public-service advertising has been limited in scope. Residential conservation in the TVA region has simply built on its own success in reducing ratepayer electric bills.

The Mass-Save program on the other hand has put considerable effort into attracting takers for its $10 audit program through bill-stuffers and public-service advertising. Initially, this appeared to be a useful means of reaching the barely tapped conservation market in the state. As the program entered its second year, the fall-off in audit requests had become a major headache for Mass-Save Director Roll. He ascribed the reduction in interest to "lack of money, lethargy, lack of concern, lack of knowledge" on the part of consumers. Of particular concern was a survey finding that only one in six of the state's residents even knew of Mass-Save's existence, indicating that word-of-mouth advertising had failed to reinforce the initial marketing efforts.

In the sheer scope of its conservation marketing techniques, PGandE appears to be a national leader. "Our concern here is that people may be hearing so much conservation advertising that they will simply tune it out," confessed one state utility commission staff member. PGandE has used a varied combination of bill-stuffers, paid and public-service advertising, and public-speaking efforts to reach its conservation audience. As of 1982, its audit penetration rate was still well below TVA's, but more than 350,000 additional audits were scheduled to be performed in 1982 and 1983. The utility's zero-interest loan program for weatherization improvements appeared likely to increase audit demand substantially.

Financing

"Financing is more of a psychological barrier than a real one," declared Mass-Save Director Roll. The financial barrier nevertheless appears to have had real effects in retarding the progress of residential conservation programs in America. With interest rates still in double digits, homeowners have been as reluctant to borrow for energy efficiency as for automobiles or houses, even in those cases where paybacks of two years or less are available. This in turn has fed the perception in the savings-and-loan and banking industries that people are not interested in making energy conservation investments.

"I think it's important to understand that lenders reflect marketplace attitudes. What they are reading in the marketplace is a general apathy about energy efficiency," said Harold Olin, director of architectural and construction research for the U.S. Savings and Loan League and a vocal advocate of loan programs to encourage conservation. "One problem is that everybody is terribly confused over what they can expect in the way of savings if they do retrofit. There has been a tremendous amount of variation in actual results reported." Olin said the league is attempting to devise an energy efficiency rating system that would allow mortgage lenders to take energy usage into account in determining loan eligibility when houses are sold.

From the point of view of the homeowner, unfortunately, energy conservation is a highly capital-intensive affair. Paying higher fuel bills generally costs much more in the long run, but the costs are incurred in relatively small bites. The average weatherization retrofit job costs about $1,000 if it is done right, and that outlay can seem quite imposing even if the money is borrowed and repaid in installments. The Mass-Save finding that two-thirds of surveyed homeowners considered the cost of conservation too high even though they believed most investments would ultimately be cost-effective is illuminating in this regard. So is the finding that only 15 percent of those homeowners would be willing to take out a loan to cover the cost of conservation improvements, at least at current interest rates.

"One of the really unfortunate aspects of the conservation program in this state is that we simply don't have any low-interest financing available right now," said Dan Schumm, a staff member of the Massachusetts Office of Energy Resources, which oversees the operation of the Mass-Save program. The state does have a number of banks willing to make "energy conservation loans" at about one percent below going interest rates. But Schumm said the number of banks participating dropped from about 150 shortly after the Iranian Revolution, when energy shortages were much in the news, to about 60 in 1982.

As originally proposed, the federal Residential Conservation Service regulations would have required utilities to play an intermediary role in arranging financing for their customers' conservation improvements. The revised standards make such services entirely optional. In Massachusetts, regulations for the state-mandated Energy Conservation Service have been pruned back to bring them in line with the federal rules. Utilities will be required only to provide "an explanation by the auditor to the customer of the cost-effectiveness of energy conservation investments."[13]

Those few utilities that have adopted conservation as a cost-effective "source" of future generating capacity are unlikely to be deterred by the relaxed regulatory requirements. TVA and PGandE, for instance, are both counting on conservation and alternative energy to reduce substantially the need for large new power plants. Financing residential energy-efficiency improvements is seen as a relatively cheap way of reducing the risk of future power shortages.

From the consumer's point of view, the "one-stop" aspect of the TVA program has proven especially attractive. Instead of having to deal with a separate bank or savings and loan association for financing, with all of the attendant headaches, ratepayers make all arrangements directly through one of the 160 distributors of TVA power in the region. The loan repayment schedule is simply incorporated into their monthly power bill. In many cases, consumers enjoy an immediate cash-flow improvement as a result. This reduces the often misunderstood concept of "payback" to the easily grasped idea that conservation really does save money.

Through 1982, more than $250 million had been lent to TVA ratepayers in this fashion, with a minuscule rate of default on repayment.[14]

In 1982, California's PGandE was in the process of expanding its own zero-interest financing plan to a statewide program after a trial run in one district of its service area. Existing low-interest loans were to be converted to zero-interest loans, in order not to discriminate against those who climbed on the conservation bandwagon early. Initial plans were to provide at least 250,000 interest-free loans during the program's second phase. Company officials said they do not expect any great difficulty in reaching that target.[15]

PGandE's loan delivery procedure is somewhat different from that employed by TVA. Like TVA, PGandE handles both billing and collection, but these are kept completely separate from the handling of electric and gas bills. This has been necessitated by the CPUC's regulatory requirements, according to PGandE.

Consideration was briefly given in 1981 to collecting the cost of the utility's conservation efforts through a surcharge on electric bills, raising the possibility of a political ruckus similar to that in Massachusetts, but the proposal was ultimately dropped.

Quality Control

In the absence of governmental supervision through registration or licensing, the fragmentation and low entry costs of the conservation services industry inevitably have bred abuses nationwide. Federal and state studies have named the industry as a favorite haven for the incompetent building contractor and the fast-buck artist. Public health scares over improper installation of urea formaldehyde insulation have contributed to the industry's low standing. Given that a poor weatherization job can substantially *reduce* the value of the largest investment most people ever make, it would seem that homeowners have been justifiably wary when dealing with aluminum siding installers turned conservation experts.

Just how significant a barrier public distrust of insulation contractors has been to residential conservation improvements remains unclear. At least one study, done for the Consumer Union Foundation in 1981, suggested that this factor has been very significant indeed.[16] While many "low-cost, no-cost" conservation measures can be installed without contractor assistance, relatively few homeowners appear to have confidence in their chances of getting their money's worth in those instances where professional help is required.

The original Residential Conservation Service regulations addressed these concerns by requiring that insulation auditors meet qualification standards, disclose any financial ties with contractors they recommend, and perform a postinstallation inspection to make sure the job was done right. The revised regulations delete mandatory quality control requirements, leaving any such measures to the discretion of individual utilities. Imposing mandatory requirements would be too burdensome to the utilities, as well as unnecessarily expensive, according to the Department of Energy.

In Massachusetts, where state rules are being relaxed to bring them into line with the federal standards in this and other areas, legislation to impose controls on the conservation installation industry has made little progress. This, despite a scathing 1978 study by the State Building Code Commission, which concluded that "the problems which this industry is presenting to the citizens of this Commonwealth are so clearly documented that something should be done before another heating season begins." In a random sample of 80 insulation jobs, the commission found a pattern of sloppiness, ignorance, and false labeling and advertising. More than half of all installations inspected showed one or more serious defects.[17]

Findings such as these reinforce the notion that something like Gresham's Law is at work in the conservation services business. Just as bad money drives out good, so do roofers and aluminum siding installers with little training in energy-conservation techniques drive out those intent on doing a good job. Price cutting takes an especially heavy toll in a market such as this, where the product is essentially invisible and consumers are generally not well informed. Without professional inspection, customers will continue to be at the mercy of the cut-rate installers, quality contractors will find themselves hard-pressed to obtain work, and conservation will continue to suffer from an unnecessary black eye.

This black eye is unnecessary as the success of the TVA inspection program in weeding out defective weatherization jobs demonstrates. Under the TVA system, the installer does not get paid until his work is approved, because TVA does not release its funds until that time. That about one in five of all insulation jobs does require some corrective action indicates that the inspection system has teeth. Yet about 1500 contractors from throughout the TVA region have agreed to participate in the program because it is the primary source of referral business in the region. Failure to maintain minimum quality standards can result in a contractor's being removed from the list of approved installers, a serious blow in a highly competitive market.[18]

THE FUTURE ROLE OF UTILITIES

If in fact Thomas Edison had it right a century ago when he insisted that utilities should be providers of heat, light, and power, not of kilowatt-hours of electricity or therms of gas, then the industry still has a long way to go in getting back to its roots. The varied utility conservation programs we have examined here illustrate some preliminary approaches to that process. As a first step, utilities must learn to take an active role in managing the way energy is used, for the benefit of society at large. The pitfalls, as we have seen, include difficult problems of marketing, financing, and quality control in the fledgling business of selling saved energy.

Despite very divergent histories and political environments, the utilities of Massachusetts, together with Pacific Gas and Electric Co. and the Tennessee

Valley Authority, have all found themselves thrust into this peculiar business of convincing people not to buy their product. After years of promoting increased sales of electricity and natural gas for every purpose under the sun, energy suppliers are making the slow and sometimes painful adjustment to a new reality. Expressed in the legalistic language of the National Energy Act, that reality seems to some almost un-American: we must seek to produce and consume less, not more. But some electric utilities are finding that it suits their economic as well as their legal environments. They are making a start, in the process, toward fulfilling the vision of their industry's founder: that of utilities as sellers of heat, light, power—and saved energy.

NOTES

1. Robert Stobaugh and Daniel Yergin, *Energy Future: Report of the Energy Project at the Harvard Business School* (New York: Random House, 1979) p. 61.
2. Linda Berry et al., *Review of Evaluations of Utility Home Energy Audit Programs* (Oak Ridge, TN: National Technical Information Center 1981).
3. Interview with Dan Schumm, Massachusetts Office of Energy Resources.
4. Bob James in an 31 Oct. 1981 memorandum to the Citizens Energy Corp. of Boston, Mass.
5. Gus Murby and Steve Blair, "Evaluating Home Builders' Response to Demands for More Energy Efficient Housing in Massachusetts," unpublished paper, Kennedy School of Government, Harvard University, 1981.
6. Marc Roberts and Jeremy Bluhm, *The Choices of Power: Utilities Face the Environmental Challenge* (Cambridge, MA: Harvard University Press, 1981), p. 130.
7. Pacific Gas and Electric Co., "Energy Conservation Activities: Plans for 1981-83," Dec. 1980, p. 2.
8. Pacific Gas and Electric Co., *Annual Report* (1980), p.3.
9. Pacific Gas and Electric Co., "Energy Conservation Activities" p. 1.
10. Tennessee Valley Authority, "Review of the TVA Load Growth/Plant Construction Situation," Jan. 1982, p. 8.
11. D.H. Walters et al., "TVA Methodology for Determining the Cost-Effectiveness of Conservation, Load Management and Renewable Energy Programs," unpublished paper, TVA Office of Power Planning Staff, 11 Feb. 1982, pp. 1-2.
12. Interview with Mary Beth Gentleman, energy advisor to Lt. Gov. Thomas O'Neill of Massachusetts.
13. Internal memorandum, Massachusetts Office of Energy Resources.
14. Tennessee Valley Authority, Division of Energy Conservation and Rates, "Program Summary," Oct. 1982, p.3.
15. Interview by telephone with John Kottinger, Finance Unit Supervisor, Zero Interest Program.
16. P.C. Stern et al., *Home Energy Conservation: Programs and Strategies for the 1980s* (Mt. Vernon, NY: Consumer Union Foundation, 1981).
17. State Building Code Commission, "The Massachusetts Study of the Retrofit Insulation Industry," Boston, MA, 1978.
18. Tennessee Valley Authority, n. 14, above, p. 2.

Chapter 10
ENERGY AND SECURITY: ACT TWO

Alvin L. Alm

Shortly after the 1980 election, the results of the Harvard Study on Energy and Security were presented to a distinguished group of public officials, business leaders, and the media. At that time, the threat of further economic damage and political instability from oil supply interruptions loomed large. Oil prices had already increased more than twofold, and the Iran-Iraq war scare was to increase prices even more. Some predicted that oil prices would climb until they reached the price of substitute fuels by the 1990s.[1] Considering the dramatic apparent changes in the world oil market and the relative lack of public interest today, it pays to ask whether the concerns expressed in December 1980 were real or ephemeral. Were they the product of hysteria, reflecting a streak of ill fortune that is unlikely to be repeated? Has the world energy system been fundamentally altered since the oil price shock of 1979-80? It is impossible to write an Act Two to the Energy and Security drama without resolving whether Act One was merely a passing fancy, soon to be replaced by new public concerns, such as battles over the budget and defense policy.

To understand the answer to this question, we must first review the damages which oil interruptions have inflicted upon us. Beginning with the 1973 Arab Oil Embargo, we can see a striking, unsettling change in our economic performance. The U.S. Consumer Price Index, which rose by a mere 3 percent in 1972, was increasing at an annual rate of 11 percent in 1974. Efforts to stem the oil induced inflation resulted in tight monetary and fiscal policies, which led to negative economic growth in 1974 and 1975. By 1976-78, on the eve of the Iranian Revolution, the inflation rate was hovering around 6 percent, only to shoot up to 11.3 percent in 1979 and 12.4 percent in 1980, as a result of the oil price shock from that episode.[2] Economic growth did not fall as dramatically as during the previous interruption, thanks to more accommodating fiscal and monetary policies. World-wide, the chief economist of the Organization for Economic Cooperation and Development (OECD) estimates economic growth losses totaling $300 billion for 1980 and over $600 billion for 1981 arising from the Iranian oil curtailments in 1979.[3] It is hard to conclude that energy has not been a major factor, in the industrialized democracies' economic performance over the last decade.

Despite such jarring figures, there has been a recent revival of optimism about the future. Declining oil prices and almost unbelievably low demand for OPEC oil have led some to conclude that energy security is a concern of the past. A new thesis has emerged that structural changes in the demand for oil will result in the withering away of OPEC. Such optimistic assessments assume either that oil interruptions are a phenomenon of the past or that they will somehow not inflict the same degree of economic damage again. It is as though the 1979 Iranian shortage was "the interruption to end all interruptions."

The structural thesis makes a number of assumptions about the future which may be incorrect. First is the assumption that most of the recent plunge in energy demand has taken the form of capital investments in conservation and substitute fuels, rather than curtailment of use and the other simple measures which are reversible. But most available evidence suggests that, except for the transportation sector, most energy shifts arise from better housekeeping and behavior changes rather than from capital investments. The structural thesis also discounts the effects of worldwide recession, currently high energy prices in Europe due to the strength of the dollar, and the role of destocking in reducing demand for imports. It further excludes the fact that some of the demand reductions attributed to recent conditions were well underway before the Iranian Revolution, such as fuel efficiency improvements in vehicles and substantial reductions in energy demand by industry. The 1979-80 oil price shock merely strengthened these downward pressures on demand for OPEC oil.

Worldwide recession is one major reason demand has fallen so far. As economic growth rebounds, the resulting upsurge in oil demand could be much sharper than expected, particularly since economic recovery will initially coincide with steadily falling oil prices. In 1976, for example, the worldwide recession had basically run its course and real oil prices were sliding. As a result, oil demand increased markedly among the IEA nations—rising 6 percent in 1976 and 3 percent annually over the next two years.[4] If history is any indication, the pattern could be repeated.

Because oil imports are the marginal source of oil and, in many instances, of energy supply, the amount of imports can oscillate dramatically. When world oil prices soared in the wake of past supply interruptions, governments, businesses, and private citizens responded by reducing oil consumption. Efforts were made to substitute nuclear power, coal, and natural gas and to cut demand whenever possible. Virtually all of the recent U.S. reduction in energy demand has been in the form of oil, and all of the reduction in oil demand has come from imports. The 6 percent decline in total energy consumption between 1979 and 1981 included a 13 percent decrease in oil consumption and a staggering 30 percent decrease in crude oil imports.[5]

Such leverage could work in reverse as well. Since domestic oil and natural gas supplies are fixed in the short run, and coal and nuclear power require not only long lead times, but also massive capital investment, any upsurge in energy demand increases from stationary facilities will be met with oil imports. Likewise, any upward shift in transportation demand will require more oil than currently anticipated. In many respects, the faster world oil prices fall, the faster they will ultimately rise, since lower prices will speed economic recovery and undercut substitutes, resulting in a sharp upturn in the demand for oil. In other words, supply and demand not only apply to the world oil market, but apply in both directions. Unless basic economic laws are repealed, the same forces that drove down demand for oil ultimately will drive it back up again.

A second aspect of the oil problem also remains. It is the threat of political upheaval, which translates into supply interruptions and economic chaos. The present oversupply or glut, while creating substantial spare capacity, could, over time, increase the likelihood of turmoil in the Middle East. As the real oil revenues of the OPEC countries continue to plunge, forcing back spending and jeopardizing development projects, new political, economic, and social tensions will emerge in these countries. Such tensions not only threaten domestic stability, but could even turn one exporter against another. When increased demand substantially reduces spare capacity, thereby recreating conditions prior to the Yom Kippur War or the Iranian Revolution, the West will again be vulnerable to even small, short-lived disruptions sparked by political upheaval.

Our mistaken belief that the oil problem has vanished is part of a national manic-depressive attitude toward energy security. During the manic phases, we delude ourselves into believing that oil interruptions will not strike again or that some magic elixir (whether huge new supply sources, fuel substitution, or structural demand reductions) will save us from future trauma. During the depressive phases, we contemplate spiralling energy costs, slower economic growth, and diminished national security. The press and those experts chosen by the press alternate between the two poles—confusing the general public, paralyzing businessmen, and creating an unstable environment for legislative action. It is no wonder that U.S. energy policy is so inconsistent and confusing.

The reaction to the Arab Oil Embargo was the first symptom of this malady. Shocked by the intensity of a modest supply reduction, we saw a quadrupling of world oil prices, rampant inflation, and worldwide depresssion. President Nixon responded to the crisis by proposing Project Independence, a goal of zero U.S. imports by 1980.[6] His successor, Gerald Ford, proposed a large corporation to finance synthetic fuel plants, utility power plants, and other energy facilities at the instigation of his Vice President, Nelson Rockefeller. The first depressive stage resulted in these policy responses, which were unrelated to the nature of the problem, and were physically or politically infeasible, or both. The Emergency Petroleum Allocation Act of 1974 included the price control and entitlement system, which was to stimulate a large increase in oil demand during the post-Embargo period. It was not a promising start.

As the economy recovered from the first oil price shock, the energy problem receded as an immediate political issue. The natural gas shortage during the winter of 1976-77 temporarily reversed the emerging complacency and emboldened a newly elected Jimmy Carter to place energy at the top of his national policy agenda. Emergency natural gas legislation was followed 90 days after the president's inauguration by the National Energy Plan and a call to action by the cardigan-clad president. The spring of 1977, however, brought warm weather, natural gas supplies were again plentiful, and no one could remember why President Carter's National Energy Plan had originally been castigated as too weak. Once snidely referred to as MEOW, for Moral Equivalent of War, most of the plan was suddenly labeled as too sweeping by the Congress. By summer, newspaper articles regularly referred to a new glut in world oil supplies, and characterized Energy Secretary Schlesinger as an alarmist.

In retrospect, 1978 was the calm before the storm. Stocks that had been built up during 1977 in advance of an expected OPEC price rise were drawn down rapidly during the first half of 1978, a clear reflection of the market's tranquil view of the future. That optimism appeared well placed, as the Natural Gas Policy Act (NGPA) quickly turned a gas shortage into a glut. By the fall of 1978, the manic stage had reached its highest pitch of intensity since the Arab Oil Embargo — that is, until the Iranian Revolution.

A year later, the second largest oil producer was effectively out of the market and world oil prices had more than doubled. The optimism of 1977-78 reverted to pervasive gloom. New projections showed continually rising prices until they reached those of oil substitutes, presumably synthetic fuels. Experts talked about a backward bending supply curve, arguing that high prices actually created incentives for major producers to maintain or even reduce production. Producers such as Saudi Arabia, Kuwait, and the United Arab Emirates were receiving revenues in excess of their needs, so they could always afford to cut back output to maintain prices. During much of 1979-80, policy makers were convinced that oil prices would have been even higher were it not for Saudi Arabia's moderation. Hence, the Carter administration was reluctant to resume filling the Strategic Petroleum Reserve (SPR) for fear that the Saudis would change course.

The depressive mood culminated with the outbreak of the Iran-Iraq war, which many experts predicted would cause another large price increase. A confluence of factors prevented such a spike, even though the war forced a net production cut of about 2.4 million barrels of oil per day by Iran and Iraq. Record high inventories had been built during the Iranian crisis. As oil companies saw demand slacken and interest rates tighten, they had strong incentives to draw down their inventories. This inventory drawdown occured at the same time that oil demand began a downward spiral; by the end of 1981, production from Iran and Iraq was no longer important in meeting world oil demand. These inventory reductions were the decisive, short-term factor in easing upward pressure on prices.

This happy turn of events, at least for oil consumers, has caused many to believe that the latest manic phase will be virtually permanent. Since OPEC's total production capacity is so great, being over 50 percent greater than current output, the optimists reason that energy security is a problem whose time has past. While their optismism could conceivably be warranted, it rests on two tenuous assumptions: that real oil price decreases will not again stimulate demand (which in turn would soak up excess capacity), and that the Middle East will not erupt into a conflict, which will interrupt oil supplies. A more realistic assessment is that oil demand *will* rebound once the West recovers from recession. Because virtually all of the increased demand will need to be supplied by OPEC production, much of the current spare capacity could vanish by the latter part of the decade. The dramatic downturn in demand for OPEC oil occurred quickly; it is not unreasonable to assume that it will increase just as fast. Once spare capacity is used up, political turmoil can be easily translated into a cutoff of oil supplies.

Predicting where and when the next supply interruption will occur is an intriguing, but not very productive exercise. However, recognizing that one *will* happen is vital. We know from history that the Middle East is in almost constant turmoil. Over the course of one year, we have witnessed the continuation of the Iran-Iraq war, civil war in Lebanon, the Israeli annexation of the Golan Heights, the assassination of Sadat, an attempted coup in Bahrain, the Israeli bombing of Iraq's Osirak nuclear reactor, Libyan adventures with all of her neighbors, and Israel's invasion of Lebanon. None of these conflicts has led to an oil interruption. In the future, the oil market will tighten and current alliances and political arrangements will change, potentially leading to a greater threat of oil interruptions. Using history as a guide, it would be unusually fortuitous if the oil consuming nations did not experience at least one major supply interruption in the next few decades.

Since publication of *Energy and Security* in December 1980,[7] the immediacy of the energy security threat has receded, but the long term threat has not changed. As long as oil continues to be the predominant world fuel, and as long as the industrialized nations continue to rely upon oil imports, vulnerability to oil interruptions will remain a serious threat to their security. Hence, it is imperative that action be taken now, before another disruption strikes.

Energy and Security was written when the energy security policy discussion was only beginning. At that time, the Strategic Petroleum Reserve (SPR) was not being filled, no legislation was pending on either extending allocation authority or moving to recycle oil revenues during an interruption, and little thought had been given to how the SPR would be used. The onset of the Iran-Iraq war provided for a limited test of consuming-nation cooperation, as the IEA established targets for stock withdrawals, but numerous issues remained to be worked out. During the course of 1981, consensus on the issues improved, and substantial progress was made in filling the Strategic Petroleum Reserve. However, not much progress was made on the majority of implementation issues.

The remainder of this chapter will deal with four of these issues. They are (1) ways of building strategic stockpiles faster given current capacity constraints, (2) management of the reserve, which is central to the nation's preparedness effort, (3) measures of recycling oil revenues, which will be necessary to avoid falling back on allocation and price controls, and (4) measures to coordinate the actions of major consuming nations.

BUILDING BUFFER STOCKS[8]

In contrast to controversy over emergency preparedness in general, virtually all agree on the importance of the Strategic Petroleum Reserve. A major emergency supply source can minimize the kind of panic buying that drove up prices during the Iranian Revolution. Several studies have shown the extent to which SPR draw downs would reduce the costs of an interruption to the U.S. economy.[9] A large reserve could also buy time during periods of international tension, improve chances for cooperation within the Western alliance, and perhaps deter politically motivated embargoes. And the SPR could minimize hardship during truly large interruptions.

However, despite such substantial benefits and strong, nonpartisan support, the combined insurance from both the SPR and private sector reserves is declining. Under current plans, the SPR fill rate will be limited by the fixed rate at which new salt dome capacity can be developed. Specifically, the average fill rate will be limited to fewer than 200,000 barrels per day, as compared to better than 300,000 barrels per day during the calendar year 1981. Assuming the need for at least 90 days worth of imports, or 500 million barrels, the United States will face a "window of vulnerability" until mid-1986 under the capacity-constrained fill rate. Moreover, the currently planned rate could be reduced still further if looming federal deficits lead to cuts in the SPR budget.

Constraints on the SPR program will be compounded by smaller private stockpiles in the near future. Inventories were increased to record levels in 1979-80 due to fear of shortages and higher prices. Today, lower real world oil prices and high interest rates provide oil companies and consumers a powerful incentive to maintain low inventories. Accordingly, major oil companies have been liquidating stocks for some time.

All of the above argue for reexamining U.S. stockpile options, particularly since the present political consensus may leave no other means of coping with an interruption. Four increasingly ambitious objectives can be distinguished:

• Speed up SPR fill to 300,000 barrels per day by overcoming capacity constraints.
• Overcome both capacity and budgetary constraints to achieve that target level.
• Create permanent private sector stocks.
• Establish a mechanism to involve oil companies in stockpiling decisions.

The most direct means of achieving the first objective is to purchase or lease above-ground storage space (steel tanks), which would hold additional oil until further salt dome capacity is developed. Leasing space could be cheaper, unless a long period of storage were forecast before transfer to salt domes. In order to achieve the 300,000 barrels per day target, interim storage will be needed from fiscal years 1983 to 1985, with a peak one-year requirement of 69 million barrels in 1985. In a May 21, 1982 report to Senator Bradley, GAO reports that:

> . . . Our inquiries at DOE and among industry sources also suggest that temporary storage in the form of steel tanks and/or tankers will probably be available at costs ranging from $1.20 to $3.65 per barrel per year. We estimate, therefore, that an interim storage program to meet the goals mentioned above (300,000 barrels per day) given DOE's estimates of future oil prices, would cost from about $0.7 billion to $1.1 million over 4 years. These estimates include storage costs and incremental debt financing of both storage and accelerated oil purchases.[10]

If budgetary constraints are a concern, the government could avoid the large, up-front costs of purchasing oil by leasing oil, as well as storage space, for a specified period—with the option to buy if an interruption were to occur. As with leasing storage space, the government could solicit bids, in this case for oil *and* space. Such a proposal offers insurance quickly without large, near-term budget costs. It also appears superior to the various incentives for private stocks, such as tax credits, which have been widely proposed. Such incentives are attractive in principle, but are extremely difficult to structure and administer in practice. To overcome both capacity and budgetary constraints, leasing is clearly preferable to tax credits.

Mandating private stocks is the one direct means of creating a permanent, private sector emergency reserve. Yet, a decisive objection is that virtually no one has viewed the option favorably, and the present administration is especially unlikely to do so.

A joint public-private corporation, which would store oil and manage draw downs during an interruption, represents a radically different option. Such a corporation would own and be responsible for managing between one-fourth and one-third of U.S. emergency reserves, purchased with government-guaranteed loans or with a portion of the SPR as collateral. Industry participants would cover operating costs, but would put up none of their own capital. Corporate management would consist of both industry representatives and presidential appointees.

By relying upon industry expertise and insulating corporate decisions from politics, many of the management pitfalls of a centralized reserve could be avoided. The corporation's stocks would constitute a flexible reserve at the outset of the interruption, which could be used to quell panic and blunt initial price increases, as well as to assure access to crude oil for the most directly affected refineries. The SPR would be available as a back up during large interruptions. Like mandating private stocks, the corporation suffers from lack of public interest and support. Nevertheless because it offers an interesting way to coordinate public and private actions during an interruption and to depoliticize initial stockpile withdrawal decisions, it has some interesting characteristics.

For the more immediate problem of building up U.S. buffer stocks, the preferable course is to establish a government commitment to fill the SPR at a rapid rate, barrels of oil per day, overcoming capacity constraints by leasing new space.

MANAGING THE STRATEGIC PETROLEUM RESERVE

The system established for managing the Strategic Petroleum Reserve will determine the extent to which its intended benefits are realized. The SPR's chief economic function is to moderate prospective oil price increases in disturbed markets. If the reserve is withdrawn after official OPEC prices have been raised, or not withdrawn at all during an oil interruption, prices will be higher than would have been necessary and the SPR will have failed partially or completely to achieve its purpose. Although it hardly seems possible that a $40 billion investment might not deliver its promised benefits, historically many strategic stockpiles have failed to achieve their price moderation potential.[11]

Often when people think about strategies for drawing down the reserve, as well as other emergency preparedness measures, they have in mind a discrete interruption scenario. They conceive of a scenario in which so many barrels of oil are lost over so many months and then the interruption stops. Under such conditions, management of the reserve would not be particularly difficult.

In the real world, however, government officials, oil companies, other private firms and individuals have no idea when an interruption will terminate, or whether the political turmoil giving rise to the interruption will spread. The Iranian Revolution, for example, created the conditions leading to the Iran-Iraq war. Also not known is whether oil companies, traders, and governments will each attempt to build stocks against an uncertain future or whether some form of cooperative framework will be possible. In the face of these uncertainties, firms and individuals will face strong pressures to build up inventories, thereby adding to the upward pressure on prices. The oil price shock of 1979 resulted chiefly from the panic stockpiling induced by the shortage, rather than from the shortage.

United States decision makers must also think how their stock withdrawal policies affect inventory management policies of foreign companies and governments. If U.S. inventory withdrawal was met with increased stockpiling in other major consuming nations, some of the price benefits could be lost.

Managing the strategic reserve is somewhat like the role central banks play in defending a particular currency. The managers should wish to stabililze world oil prices, and in this sense the analogy with central banks is close. They must also be concerned with trade-offs between short-run price stability and hedging against a more serious security problem later. Because the extent, duration, and potential spread of political turmoil are all unknown, decision makers face tremendous pressures to be conservative. From a practical point of view, they are more likely to be criticized for being profligate with a reserve during the early stages of an interruption than for not using it liberally enough. The economic damages from even small interruptions can be extremely large, which places a premium on quick and resolute action. Based on historical evidence, the probability of underusing the reserve is greater than that of overusing it, though guessing wrong in the opposite direction could lead to serious national security problems.

Although decison makers can support research, analyze options, play energy emergency war games, and the like, many of the decisions will depend heavily on the judgments made during the crisis. While true, two basics should not be improvised at the time: the overall strategy to be employed and how the oil would be distributed. Decisions must be made in advance on whether the reserve is to be considered a source of last resort, to be tapped only after a crisis reaches serious proportions, or whether the reserve should be used all along to reduce price pressures. Whether the reserve will be used to provide preferred crude oil access to some independent refiners at less than market prices is a second decision which must be made quickly. If, at the moment of a supply interruption, government officials are preparing options papers on these issues, they are in serious trouble.

The mechanism used for distributing oil depends upon whether the SPR will have any preferred claimants. If the answer is affirmative, then some mechanism for allocating supplies to distressed refiners must be devised. If the answer is negative, an auction system could be employed, allowing all U.S. refiners, and perhaps foreign refiners and traders, to participate on an equal basis. The latter approach has been advocated by the Reagan administration, but judging from voting on the Standby Petroleum Allocation Act, the Congress would opt for giving preferential treatment to some refiners during an interruption, if not creating a mandatory allocation program. If a decision were to be made to allocate oil through the marketplace, many alternatives would be available. The oil could be sold entirely by auction, or various schemes could be established to set aside some of the oil for special public needs and smaller refiners.

Creation of a futures or options market in SPR oil represents a particularly promising option to allocate supplies and stabilize markets.[12] For example, at the onset of an interruption the government might sell to oil companies and traders three month futures contracts for 25 million barrels and six-month futures contracts for another 50 million barrels. At the end of these periods, the oil would be delivered to particular buyers unless the futures contracts were repurchased by the government. Under the options alternative, the government would sell options for the same amount of oil and for the same period, but the government would set the price at which the option could be exercised. The difference between the option price set by the government and the amount actually bid for the options would represent the market's valuation of future prices. In both cases, if the interruption abates and supplies are no longer uncertain, the government need not discharge the oil. In the case of futures contracts, the government would buy the oil back. In the case of an options market, firms would not exercise the option.

A futures or options market would have many advantages for government decision makers. Since futures or option contracts could be sold prior to the interruption, market transactions could be initiated without making any declaration about the nature of the political event which precipitated an oil interruption, or about the potential for a more serious shortfall and higher prices. (Release of SPR oil, however, would be tantamount to U.S. government recognition of an impending crisis.) By allowing the market, rather than the government, to determine the future value of oil, the government can retain a greater flexibility during the early stages of an interruption. If options bids are so high as to give policy makers cause for concern, they can reopen the bidding with a greater quantity of oil, thereby reducing prices. Market prices for futures contracts, however, could not greatly exceed spot prices, since firms always have the option to buy in the spot market for future use or speculation. Under both options, a decision maker would not immediately distribute oil, leaving open the possibility that oil rights sold on such a market could be reclaimed for a dire emergency, such as war.

A futures or options market could be extremely effective in reducing panic during a supply interruption. While oil auctioned directly would be absorbed immediately in the system, a futures or options contract would guarantee that a certain amount of oil would be available in the future. Considering that data on secondary and tertiary stocks are nonexistent, and that even data on primary stock changes are initially anecdotal, the assurance that supplies of oil would be available at prescribed moments could exert a highly positive influence on market behavior. For any quantity of oil, a futures or options sale should give the "biggest bang for the barrel."

A futures or options market could address the claim that some independent refiners are unable to acquire crude oil. If they were able to purchase futures or options, they should not require special allocations from the government.

A futures or options approach could also be put in place during noninterrupted periods. For example, the government could continually roll over 3- and 6-month futures or options contracts during calm periods. With the small differences existing between cash and futures contracts during noninterrupted periods, the transactions could be closed out with cash rather than oil. Under the options alternative, the value of call options would likely be quite low for oil quoted above the current world oil price levels. Assuming no large upward swings in price, the options would not be exercised at their termination. Hence, either of the alternatives could be maintained in stand-by status, providing experience with the system and installing a mechanism which would not require further initial government action in the event of an interruption. Whether these advantages outweigh the cost of operating the market without significant physical transactions is an open question.

The futures or options market alternatives appear extremely promising. At this point, further research is necessary to determine whether they are superior to a direct auction and which of the two would be superior in terms of quelling market panic. In providing decision makers with greater flexibility and requiring less of a political commitment, they already appear to have some advantages over an auction and immense advantages over government allocation. Most likely, a management system relying on both competitive auctions and a futures or option market would make the most sense.

MANAGING MACROECONOMIC IMPACTS

The government record in managing domestic shortfalls has been far from satisfactory. During the shortages that followed from the Arab Oil Embargo and the Iranian Revolution, government regulations allocated crude oil to some independent refiners and gasoline supplies across the board, as well as diesel fuel to farmers. Coupled with the price controls then in effect, the government intervention made the shortage considerably worse.

Few close observers of the petroleum regulatory system have spoken kindly of using allocations as a method of coping with shortages. Most have advocated the market as a more efficient means of allocating scarce oil supplies. They point out that the microeconomic losses from inefficient government allocation are large. These market advocates, however, are unable to explain how to cope with the macroeconomic shocks from both large wealth transfers to OPEC for import purchases and in the case of domestic production, even larger transfers from consumers to oil companies and the government. Considering that such transfers could dwarf the entire tax and spending proposals of the Reagan administration, they are the Achilles heel of market-oriented solutions.

The macroeconomic management task is immense. During the Iranian Revolution, for example, the price of oil increased $15.80 from early 1979 to the end of 1980. Based on 8.6 million barrels per day (mbd) of production at that time, the extra revenues collected by the federal government could have been as high as $100 million a day, assuming that roughly 70-75 percent of additional oil revenues would be collected through the Windfall Profits Tax and the corporate income tax. Unless some provision were made to recycle such revenues, the "fiscal drag" on the economy could be serious.[13] The result would be equivalent to enacting a tax larger than President Reagan's combined reduction in income taxes and social security, at a time when OPEC has already enacted the equivalent of a stiff tax.

Moreover, the incidence of higher prices would be concentrated on those least able to afford it. Some low income families, including the elderly, would find an oil price shock of this magnitude devastating. Considering the macroeconomic and equity stakes, it is unlikely that a market allocation system is either economically sound or equitable without recycling.

Congress has thus far been unwilling to take recycling seriously. From a political point of view, powerful constituencies have clung to their privileged status first conferred in the Emergency Petroleum Allocation Act of 1973. Members of the House and Senate representing these constituencies enacted the Standing Petroleum Allocation Act, which would have authorized a somewhat scaled-down allocation program. Congress has clearly favored regulatory programs over market allocation systems and has been extremely cool to recycling.

Debate over a rebate system extends as far back as the Carter administration. Despite almost universal consensus that a market distribution system is preferable to government allocations, and a general recognition that recycling is probably at least a political *sine qua non* for a market-oriented system, only recently has substantial progress been made in designing a recycling system.

Politically, the two most difficult issues in need of resolution are what should be taxed and who should benefit from the program. Some would argue that not only should recycling revenues come from the Windfall Profits Tax, but also from a specific surtax to prevent oil company "windfalls" during an interruption. Others might support the concept of recycling, but oppose the notion of legitimitizing the Windfall Profits Tax. However difficult the revenue issues, they pale by comparison to the question of who benefits. Some members of Congress will advocate various formulas based on pinpointing need for assistance, which of course will be particularly applicable to their respective constituencies. They will argue that farmers, taxicab drivers, and other groups have exceptional needs and, hence, need larger rebates. While the problem is serious, it is not necessarily insuperable. In 1977, the House of Representatives did pass a rebate formula for President Carter's Crude Oil Equalization Tax, with only home heating oil and propane users receiving special treatment. That legislation, which never passed the Senate, would have provided equal reabates to households for a limited period until Congress could construct a permanent rebate system.

The implementation issues are less politically charged, but more complex. To highlight these issues, two different approaches to recycling are described. The first would rely primarily on the income tax withholding system to distribute rebates, supplemented by food stamps, supplemental security income, and aid to dependent children. The logic of this approach is that the payroll tax withholding system employed by businesses could readily be used to cover a large fraction of the population. No checks need be mailed; withholding allowances would simply be changed. The other programs could then be aimed at low income groups who do not have taxes withheld.[14]

Use of existing programs is superficially attractive. No new government bureacracy is required, the recycling program could be integrated into existing programs, and many federal agencies would get part of the bureaucratic action. There are also major disadvantages. Attempting to manage a recycling program through more than one federal agency would not be easy, raising the question of who would be accountable for a program administered across agencies. Using the income tax withholding system would require continual paperwork changes by hundreds of thousands of small businessmen.

The other general approach would be to manage the recycling program in the Treasury Department providing rebates directly to eligible parties. Most of the funds would be distributed to citizens on the basis of a per capita formula, while states would receive from 5 to 10 percent of the total revenues to meet extraordinary needs such as continuing public services. The bulk of eligible citizens would be identified from the income tax, social security, and welfare lists used by the federal government today. For citizens not listed as beneficiaries in any program, a registration system could be created.

The costs of this system are not overwhelming. Once the system was set up, each individual mailing of checks would cost about $40 million, which consists mostly of postage costs. Rebating once every quarter would cost about $160 million a year, and rebating every two months would cost $240 million annually. Considering the macroeconomic stakes and the past inconvenience arising from gasoline lines, and the real problems many Americans will face in adjusting to supply interruptions, such costs do not appear excessive.

It is too early to say which of the two systems is better. The centralized system would appear to provide for better accountability, place fewer burdens on small business, and be easier to implement. The system depending upon widespread use of the withholding system has the advantage of minimizing the problem of lost checks and fraud in delivery, at least in terms of those who receive benefits from the income tax system. Neither of these systems will be easy to implement, but compared to the option of government allocations, they should not lead to anywhere near the same level of dislocation.

ENERGY AND THE WESTERN ALLIANCE

The previous two supply interruptions created severe political strains among members of the Western alliance. During the Arab Oil Embargo, Japan altered its foreign policy almost overnight and Prime Minister Heath attempted to convince British Petroleum to allocate more supplies to Great Britain. Ironically, control and allocation of crude oil supplies by the multinational companies, defusing many of the potential political problems, prevented a major fissure in the alliance. The creation of the IEA exposed the conflict over oil policy between France and other industrialized powers, particularly over whether the West should cooperate with producing states or view them as adversaries. France refused to join IEA, although it cooperates with other major consuming countries through the European Economic Community.

During 1979, tension among the Western allies erupted at the Tokyo Summit, where hostility toward U.S. subsidies for distillate fuel oil evoked heavy criticism. Even earlier, the United States had been under fire for continuation of oil price controls. The United States, in turn, criticized the Japanese in 1979 for bidding up oil prices during the emergency. During the period through the Bonn-Tokyo-Venice Summits, energy policy dominated Western political discourse, though rarely in a calm and positive way.

The political tensions already experienced would seem small in the face of any large supply interruption. For example, the shortfall from the Iranian Revolution never exceeded 5 percent over a three month period. A truly large interruption could result in severe personal hardship and economic damage.

The present antidote for coping with such a large interruption is the sharing agreement of the IEA.[15] That agreement, supposedly the mainstay of Western cooperation during an oil interruption, suffers from a number of technical flaws which would make it difficult to implement. Even more serious, the agreement requires an extraordinary measure of cooperation to succeed. Under pressure from severe domestic energy shortages and economic chaos, it is far from certain that member governments would adhere to the IEA sharing plan. If they did not, the Western alliance could quickly fall apart, as each of the alliance partners attempted to gain preferential access to oil supplies.

Since the 1979-80 oil price shock, Western nations have been pursuing options to reduce dependence on foreign oil and to cope with crises below the IEA 7 percent shortfall trigger. At both the Tokyo and Venice summits, Western leaders stressed the need to develop alternative energy sources, including coal and nuclear power. After considerable debate, the summit leaders also agreed in Tokyo to abide by informal import targets, which were designed to put a lid on future imports. However, the quotas were ultimately rendered meaningless, as higher prices and recession drove import demand far below the summit targets. The market rescued the Western allies from a potentially explosive political problem.

Subtrigger interruptions have received substantial attention by the IEA and European Economic Community. Various proposals have been reviewed, ranging from consultation during subtrigger crises to centralized manipulation of some established amount of stocks, usually about five days worth. One such scheme, proposed by British Petroleum, would establish an entity to manage a specified portion of each participating nation's oil reserves—about five days reserves. Under this scheme, the corporation would buy specified amounts of oil from companies, who in turn could claim this oil if their supplies were disrupted by *force majeure*. Firms would also be free to buy and sell shares of the reserve, a feature that could result in the creation of a miniature spot market exclusively in the oil stocks held by the corporation.

Building larger and more flexible stockpiles is the logical next step to improve international cooperation. The IEA requirement that each country hold 90 days of imports is a misleading measure for nations producing a substantial amount of oil, such as the United States and Great Britain. This definition goes way beyond truly strategic stocks, including inventory necessary for day-to-day operations. Some consistent definition of truly flexible stockpiles would be highly desirable, even if the new measure resulted in stock levels below 90 days. Most of the major consuming countries, namely the United States, the Federal Republic of Germany, and Japan, are planning substantial levels of government-owned stocks, supplemented, in the case of the FRG, by stocks held by a public-private corporation.

A lingering concern about building large discretionary stockpiles is whether governments will be able to cooperate in managing them. If the major consuming nations pursue different inventory practices during a supply emergency, then the value of some of those inventories will be wasted. For example, if one nation discharges substantial amounts of its reserves to blunt world oil prices while a second builds up stocks, the action of the first nation may be effectively neutralized. If Switzerland works at cross purposes with the United States, little is lost because of the great difference in volumes. But if the United States and Japan work at cross purposes, the market could react tentatively and perhaps counter productively.

Lack of coordination during a supply interruption can also lead to serious political tensions. If some countries suspect that others are not cooperating to help ease market conditions, they will become resentful and may attempt some form of retaliation. The U.S. distillate subsidy of May 1979 was a major point of dissention at the Tokyo Economic Summit demonstrating how perceived lack of cooperation during an interruption can lead to political tension. Cooperation, on the other hand, makes a difference. Informal IEA coordination of stock draw downs during the early phases of the Iran-Iraq war at least resulted in a common policy, although at that time, oil companies had strong economic incentives to draw down inventories. Considering the large stakes, ways to coordinate stock withdrawal during oil supply interruptions must rank high on the list of energy security priorities.

Because the United States is the largest oil consumer in the world, it is a logical candidate for taking the lead in developing a framework for inventory management cooperation. Clearly, its policies in discharging the Strategic Petroleum Reserve will exert a substantial influence on future world oil prices. To commence negotiations, the major consuming nations need to understand what damages they have suffered from lack of coordinated action and, conversely, what benefits flow from cooperation. Such an understanding could provide the basis for undertaking negotiations on a joint management coordination system. Although such an agreement would be important, it is immediately more critical to build up larger stockpile levels. For it is unlikely that coordination will really work effectively unless the Western allies can feel comfortable about the capacity of their strategic stocks to withstand the buffeting of another supply interruption. High stock levels are the *sine qua non* for an effective emergency response; better management would make the system work better.

CONCLUSION: IS ACT TWO THE CLOSING ACT?

During the last few years, the energy security debate has become increasingly sophisticated. Academic research, conferences, and congressional hearings have led to an increased understanding of the world oil market, the dynamics of oil interruptions, and the effectiveness of various policy responses. Most major studies, such as those conducted by the National Petroleum Council, the Harvard Energy Security Program, Georgetown University, and others, conclude that there is a need to build strategic stockpiles and design a plan to use them, recycle revenues, and cooperate with our allies.

Two elements, however, have been lacking. Insufficient work has been conducted on the details of implementation, and the intellectual capital has not been transformed into political capital. Both deficiencies arise from a lack of serious national concern over the energy security problem, which, in turn, is related to the nations's manic-depressive attitude toward the subject. So much energy is expended in our depressive phases, whether through blaming OPEC and the oil companies or designing grandiose responses, that little psychic energy remains when the inevitable glut arrives. We have seen expert opinion change almost overnight from pessimism to wide-eyed optimism. It is no wonder that the public has grown tired of facing an energy crisis and happy to accept the advice of some experts that the problem has gone away. Lacking a consistent threat, the public moves on to other issues.

To make matters worse, many preparedness measures are boring as matters of public policy. Recycling of revenues or managing stockpiles are issues too complex to be characterized on a bumper sticker. Yet, without recycling, we may well be stuck with allocations and gasoline lines, as we were in 1973 and 1979. Without adequate stockpile management, we are likely to see a repeat of the substantial price increases which brought about the previous two economic downturns. And without international cooperation, we are likely to see considerable tension during the next oil interruption.

Energy security problems will be with us for the foreseeable future. The world will see gluts and tight markets, turmoil in the Middle East, and interruptions in the world oil market. We will see experts overshooting in both directions. The essential facts, however, have not changed. First, the Western nations will continue to be dependent upon oil imports, and in the 1990s, dependency on Persian Gulf oil will increase as U.S. and North Sea production declines and as marginal OPEC producers recede from the world oil market. Second, the West will be vulnerable to supply interruptions as long as it is dependent on oil from unstable areas. This vulnerability will grow again as spare capacity falls. Even if the United States and its allies are miraculously lucky and *never* experience another supply interrruption, the insurance policy proposed will have been worthwhile. An actuary, told that over $600 billion GNP losses were sustained in only one year from an oil supply interruption, would not consider that level of insurance excessive. To turn our attention from energy security because of the good fortune of benefitting from a temporary glut is like cancelling our fire insurance because our neighborhood escaped a serious fire over the last few years. Act Two of the Energy Security drama may ultimately turn out to be a tragedy, unless we learn to cope with the threat of oil supply interruptions as a *continuing* economic and political reality.

NOTES

1. See Energy Modeling Forum, "World Oil: Summary Report," Number 6, February 1982, p. 27.
2. Data on domestic inflation and economic growth are taken from U.S. Bureau of the Census, *Statistical Abstract of the United States: 1981* (102d edition), Washington, DC.
3. Sylvia Ostry, "A View from the OECD World" (paper presented at the 20th anniversary of the Atlantic alliance, October 20, 1981).
4. U.S. Department of Energy, *Monthly Energy Review* (Washington DC: DOE, April 1982), p. 92. International Energy Agency, *Energy Policies and Programmes of IEA Countries: 1980 Review* (Paris: International Energy Agency, 1981), p. 19.
5. Department of Energy, *Monthly Energy Review* (Washington, DC: DOE, April 1982), pp. 6,8.
6. See Federal Energy Administration, Project Independence Report, (Washington, DC: FEA, November 1974).
7. David Deese and Joseph Nye, eds., *Energy and Security,* (Cambridge, MA: Ballinger, 1980).
8. For a more complete discussion of the issues raised in this section, see Alvin L. Alm and Edward N. Krapels, "Building Buffer Stocks in a Bear Market: Policy Choices for Emergency Oil Reserves," *Discussion Paper Series,* Kennedy School of Government, Harvard University, March 1982, #H-82-01.
9. See, for instance, Congressional Budget Office, "The World Oil Market in the 1980s: Implications for the United States" (Washington, DC, 1980), p. 74. For estimates of optimum stockpile size, see J.L. Plummer, "Methods for Measuring the Oil Import Premium and the Oil Stockpile Premium," *Energy Journal* Vol. 2 (January 1981). Or H. Rowen and J. Weyant, "Oil and National Security: An Integrated Program for Surviving an Oil Crisis," *Annual Review of Energy* Vol. 6 (1981). Plummer finds an optimal stockpile size of at least 2 billion barrels for the United States; Rowen and Weyant report an optimal size of 1.0-1.5 billion barrels for the United States, and 2.0-3.0 billion for the OECD nations acting in concert.
10. General Accounting Office, Letter report and Honorable Bill Bradley on "Feasibility and Cost of Interim Storage for the Strategic Petroleum Reserve" (GAO/EMD-82-95).
11. For a discussion of U.S. strategic stockpiling policy in commodities other than oil, see Glenn H. Snyder, *Stockpiling Strategic Materials* (San Francisco: Chandler, 1966).
12. The benefits of a futures market in SPR oil are discussed in Shantayanan Devarajan and R. Glenn Hubbard, "Drawing Down the Strategic Petroleum Reserve: The Case for Selling Futures Contracts," *Discussion Paper Series,* Kennedy School of Government, Harvard University, forthcoming.
13. For a collection of in-depth analyses of links between energy price shocks and macroeconomic performance, see Knut A. Mork, ed., *Energy Prices, Inflation, and Economic Activity,* (Cambridge: Ballinger, 1981).
14. For a more complete discussion of this approach, see ICF, Inc. "Rebating Gasoline Taxes: Administrative Analysis, Analytical Framework and Issue Identification," October 1980, pp. 1-20.
15. For a more complete discussion of the IEA sharing agreement, and of the prospects for international cooperation generally, see Edward N. Krapels, *Oil Crisis Management: Strategic Stockpiling for International Security* (Baltimore, 1980). See also Robert Weiner, "The Oil Import Question in an International Context: Institutional and Economic Aspects of Consumer Cooperation," *Discussion Paper Series,* Kennedy School of Government, Harvard University, June 1981, #E-81-06.

PART IV

TOWARD A SOLUTION

In these final chapters, the authors look to past policy decisions for guidelines for the future. Harvey Brooks compares the success of the Apollo program created in the aftermath of the crisis triggered by the Soviet launching of Sputnik in 1957 with national energy policy planning of the 1970s. The former readily achieved its goals; the latter, admittedly a much more difficult mission, failed because of an absence of any real party discipline in the Congress, the presence of glaring media exposure in the Executive, and the rapid growth of competing "public interest" considerations. Reorganization, a hallmark of agency activity in the past decade—FEA, ERDA, DOE—was not sufficient; DOE failed not because of poor management but because of a failure of leadership at the highest level of the executive and the legislative branches of government. No president managed to convince the public that energy problems were real and demanded long-term planning. For future policy planning, Brooks demonstrates the need for a forum in which competing interests could be negotiated in order to arrive at social accommodation.

Continuing the theme that the energy problem is one which may recede temporarily only to return when economies begin to recover from the market-wide recession, Yergin analyzes the relevance of domestic policy for international relations. In arguing for the recognition of the political role oil plays in the interdependence of nations, Yergin demonstrates the need to implement policies which take into account *The Political Geology of the Energy Problem*. The authors argue that if American society and its government are to adapt to a new, uncertain energy reality, we will have to change not simply energy policy and government rigidity, but the very attitudes and values that have led to a lack of adaptation and a stalemate of policy implementation.

Chapter 11
HISTORY AS A GUIDE TO THE FUTURE

Harvey Brooks

INTRODUCTION

Two years ago a Department of Energy (DOE) study entitled "Energy Programs/Energy Markets" attempted to estimate the overall effects of the major federal energy programs mounted since the oil crisis of 1973. Using large scale economic models, it asked what the impact of all the then current programs would be in 1990 as compared with what would have been likely to happen in the absence of these programs. Of course, such a study constitutes a "thought experiment," subject to all the uncertainties of such exercises, since it is impossible to carry out controlled or parallel experiments with alternate policies in the real world. Thus "what might have been" is necessarily speculative, vulnerable to the inevitable simplifications and neglected variables inherent in the design of economic models. Nevertheless the conclusion is startling: the net effect of all federal energy programs is almost precisely zero. Total United States energy consumption will be about 2 percent less in 1990 than it would have been in the absence of these programs, while imports will be about 200,000 barrels per day, perhaps 3 percent, higher. By contrast the cumulative effect of energy price increases will have lowered U.S. energy consumption 20 to 30 percent by 1990, and oil imports will be at least 10 million barrels per day lower than if oil prices had stayed at their pre-1973 levels.[1]

Of course, the DOE study does not take into account the effects of energy R&D programs, environmental or macroeconomic policies on domestic energy supplies, nor does it estimate the impact of DOE-sponsored policy studies and research on public and political understanding of energy issues. These could be important for the energy supply/demand balance over the long run. However, government sponsored R&D could not in any case have been expected to have much impact on production or consumption by 1990. Environmental policies and regulation of electric utility rates have undoubtedly had some effect in reducing availability of energy sources, which might otherwise have displaced imported oil. These effects are probably small, at least up to 1990, and in any case make the effects of energy policy even more counter to original intent than indicated by the

DOE study. Commenting on this general picture Professor William Nordhaus of Yale has said:

> The conclusion seems therefore inescapable: Energy policy in the United States has been a drain down which we have poured enormous legislative, analytical and political efforts, yet it has produced mostly noise and fury.[2]

It is interesting and instructive to compare the U.S. political and social response to the October 1973 oil crisis with its response to a superficially similar crisis just 16 years earlier, the Soviet launching of Sputnik in October 1957. Just as the 1973 crisis resulted in the creation of a new national energy program and R&D apparatus (ERDA and, subsequently, DOE) so the 1957 crisis resulted in the creation of the National Aeronautics and Space Administration and the President's Science Advisory Committee (PSAC). Both crises led to the public enunciation of apparently clear national goals, in one case the achievement of "energy independence" by the year 1980, in the other the landing of American astronauts on the moon and their successful return to earth by the year 1970. The political instrumentalities created in each case were put together out of existing federal bureaucracies, but revitalized with new blood and galvanized with a strong rhetoric of presidential leadership. Space in 1957 and energy in 1973 also launched an extended national debate and soul searching about the goals and nature of American society, which had implications transcending the immediate causes of the crisis. Interestingly, both debates focused on our allegedly excessively materialistic goals and on our spiritual and ethical deficiencies as a society. The space program and the energy program were each viewed as both spiritual and material challenges, urging us to turn our backs on consumerism and the wasteful use of our resources, symbolized in each case by the automobile (tailfins in the case of space, "gas guzzlers" in the case of energy). During both periods there was a proliferation of congressional hearings and intense newspaper and media coverage of the crisis.

The parallel between the two crises seems to disappear at that point. The Sputnik crisis eventuated 12 years later in the achievement of the precise goal announced by the president in 1961, while in the energy crisis the goal of oil import independence receded rapidly into the future and eventually disappeared from sight. By almost any measure the space program was an extraordinary success, when judged against its own proclaimed goals. NASA is cited as one of the most successful federal agencies, a demonstration that the federal civil service bureaucracy can "deliver" with competence and alacrity when given clear and sustained political direction. Regardless of whether one subscribes fully to Nordhaus's gloomy summation, it would be hard to find many people, expert or otherwise, ready to pronounce DOE a resounding success, or to claim that U.S. energy policy has achieved any of its announced goals. Both the lay and the expert publics would be inclined to endorse the Nordhaus evaluation, tempered only by some reference to indirect educational and long term technology infrastructure benefits.

Nordhaus ascribes the failure to the contradictory policies of different presidents and competing congressional committees. While there is some truth in this, the space program also spanned four administrations, and was not entirely lacking in competing congressional jurisdictions. It experienced many vicissitudes, including a disastrous fire on the launch pad which killed three astronauts. It began with a searching and widely publicized debate between advocates of the lunar orbiter and earth orbit approaches to the mission, an internal debate that became embarrassingly public and involved important vested interests.

The question is why, despite the obvious parallels between the circumstances of the Sputnik and energy crises, the outcomes were so dissimilar. What were the differences between the two challenges that account for the apparent success of NASA and the apparent failure of ERDA-DOE? Was it the differences in the character of the problems addressed? Was it the differences in the competence of the bureaucratic managers responsible for the task? Was it the difference in the sustained commitment and dedication of the top political leadership? Was it due to the evolutionary changes in the character of and balance of power among American political institutions, which took place between 1957 and 1973 partly as a consequence of Viet Nam and Watergate? Was it due to misguided policy and underlying policy premises, or to ineffective execution or implementation of policy?

The remainder of this chapter will be an attempt to address, if not to answer, these questions. Our conclusion will be that all of the factors referred to played some part, but that differences in the character of the problem *interacted* with changes in our political institutions to produce the end result. Perhaps the greater social complexity of the energy problem, and the multiplicity of vested interests, would have been sufficient by themselves to produce failure. The energy issue was also peculiarly vulnerable to the political fragmentation and dispersion of political power, which had evolved in American society during the 1960s. It was undoubtedly the *combination* of social complexity with political fragmentation, which acted synergistically to frustrate the attempt to create an energy policy.

On the question of bureaucratic competence it is interesting to note that some of the same leading actors were involved in both the successes and the failures. For example, Robert Seamans was Deputy Administrator of NASA when some of the critical technical decisions were made, and he headed ERDA during the period when its major R&D strategies, later inherited by DOE, were established. There were many similar overlaps. As we shall also see, some of the techniques that were so successful in Apollo proved inappropriate for energy, and it is possible that the successful experience with Apollo may have actually set misleading precedents for dealing with the energy problem.

PROFESSIONALISM VERSUS POLITICS, POLICY VERSUS ADMINISTRATION

Political reform movements in the United States have almost always begun with an emphasis on "economy and efficiency" in government, usually with the underlying idea that the efficiently run business corporation was the appropriate model for the effective government agency. Thus the theme of management and technocratic efficiency has almost always emerged as an important ingredient of the national political response to crisis or external challenge. Failure was to be met by government reorganization to achieve managerial effectiveness in the pursuit of a newly perceived national goal. The creation of a new agency with its mission defined in strongly technocratic terms is the typical response. In the case of NASA the mission was to develop a new national space transportation capability. In the case of ERDA, and later DOE, it was to develop substitute systems for the production of energy to replace unreliable and expensive imported oil. The paradigm for the new agency in each case was the business corporation conceived as a strong technocratic organization, centrally managed, and capable of mobilizing national resources in an optimal way to achieve a clearly stated national goal. This paradigm fitted the Apollo goal reasonably well, but for the ERDA goal of energy independence it proved inappropriate.

As Professor Don Price of Harvard points out, the actual problems faced by government are less frequently those of efficiency and managerial effectiveness than those of achieving the compromises among conflicting goals necessary to satisfy competing interests and value preferences within the society. As Price observes, in government, waste is derived more from zealous pursuit of conflicting policies than from poor management.[3]

The optimum use of society's resources for reaching any stated goal is frequently frustrated by the consequences of single-minded pursuit of one particular goal. People will enthusiastically support the goal of energy independence, for example, until they gradually realize it may mean higher energy prices, more nuclear power stations, off-shore oil development, strip mining coal, or a massive transfer of wealth to the oil companies or to the Arab states. One of the reasons for the success of the Apollo program was the surprising absence of competing interests and goals on which the space effort impinged. It is true there was some competition for government funds, especially toward the culmination of Apollo, when Viet Nam and the War on Poverty were rapidly increasing their demands on the federal treasury, but the "fiscal dividend" resulting from the U.S. tax structure and economic growth was at that time still sufficient to keep the budgetary issue below the political boiling point, although the Reverend Abernathy and his followers did stage a protest demonstration on the occasion of the Apollo 11 launching to protest what they perceived as an ostentatious expenditure of tax funds needed for much more urgent social programs. There was also competition among the states to benefit from the economic multiplier effects that were believed to accompany the presence of high technology laboratories. The scientific community was similarly unhappy with the resources being absorbed by Apollo which it saw, probably inaccurately, as competitive with other more intrinsically worthwhile science. By and large the Apollo program was almost unique in that it was filling a vacuum, both literally and figuratively. On earth it produced significant economic benefits for a few favored regions and constituencies, but it had few environmental impacts, and it occupied both political space and real space to which nobody else laid claim. Furthermore, when Kennedy announced his political commitment to the Apollo goals before Congress, he had significant analytical work and technological planning behind him in the agency. Such doubts as remained pertained only to the cost and not to the feasibility of the goal. Moreover, since Apollo was a political and technological demonstration, economic considerations were distinctly secondary. The first successful demonstration did not have to be duplicated in hundreds of manufactured copies at a competitive cost with existing technologies in order to be considered successful.

By contrast President Nixon's declaration of the goal of energy independence by the year 1980 was not preceded by any professional analysis of the feasibility of that goal. Indeed, its feasibility was rather soon thrown into question by the first of a series of government energy studies, the *Project Independence Report,* prepared in late 1974 with the help of a model, the Project Independence Evaluation System (PIES) developed in-house by the newly created Federal Energy Administration (FEA).[4] Moreover, the emphasis of this report on the role of domestic energy prices in reducing consumption and stimulating production of alternate energy sources, and thus reducing oil imports, immediately antagonized consumer advocates, while its strong energy supply emphasis angered environmental groups, and its general conclusions undermined the administration's own announced goals. Over the next few years the discrepancy between the rhetoric of oil import independence and the reality of price controls and entitlement programs, which in effect constituted a subsidy for oil imports, became more and more painfully apparent. But the appreciation of such conflicts in objectives, since each of them seemed desirable by itself, took a long time to penetrate the consciousness of the U.S. public.

In one sense the goal of Project Independence was *technically* feasible, even on the short time scale projected, if it had been pursued single-mindedly using all the resources of the country for this one objective, without any reference to other social goals. To achieve it, however, would have required a reorganization of the national economy more analogous to wartime production than to business as usual. It would have required large public subsidies to consumers for investments in energy efficiency such as insulation, a rapid expansion of nuclear power and other substitute energy production technologies, and a government directed investment in retooling the automobile industry to force the introduction of energy efficient cars. Given the capacity of government to ration and redeploy resources for an

overriding national objective, the country could have achieved energy independence. The cost, however, would have been between one and two orders of
magnitude greater than that of the Apollo program and would have involved a
degree of government intervention in the allocation of materials and investments
which historically has been accepted politically only when the national existence
was believed to be at stake.[5]

The Project Independence exercise set a precedent for presidential declarations
followed by technocratic analyses which undermined their premises that was to be
repeated over and over again for the next several years. The discrepancy between
political preference and the real world led to the growth of a conspiracy theory of
the energy crisis, and a search for scapegoats, which was often encouraged by
politicians when confronted by the inconsistencies between the premises of their
policy pronouncements and the conclusions of technocratic studies. The favored
scapegoats were the multinational oil companies which, whether by intent or by
accident, clearly profited from OPEC price fixing in the crises of 1974 and 1979.
But the opprobrium was shared by OPEC itself, particularly its Arab members, by
the electric utilities, and by the U.S. auto makers with their "gas guzzlers". In the
words of one acute observer:

> The energy crisis fragmented society, unleashing forces pulling in many
> directions at once, alienating large segments of the population, pitting region
> against region, interest group against interest group, institution against
> institution, and business against business.[6]

Clearly one of the problems introduced by the energy crisis, and the political
response to it, was that the scope for assignment of incomes by a political rather
than an automatic self-regulating process was greatly increased. The rapid change
in the economic environment, produced by the unprecedented price rise of a basic
commodity, resulted in pressures for government to intervene in the "system of
equity" that had grown up around the production and consumption of energy, and
that had built up over many years stable expectations of both domestic producers
and consumers.[7] These interventions consisted of entitlement programs to insure
that all intermediaries in the distribution of oil see the same average price; of
special taxes (such as the mislabeled Windfall Profits Tax) to offset the large wealth
transfers (except those to OPEC), which would otherwise result from sudden price
increases; of detailed performance standards for energy using durable goods; and
of tax credits for consumer investments in energy conserving technology or
renewable resources. The political economist, Dan Usher, has pointed out that the
viability of democracies as stable forms of governance probably depends on the
fact that most income is allocated in accordance with impersonal and automatic
rules, which may be set politically in the first instance, but which are not subject to
political regulation in detail.[8] Price controls and entitlements, however, require
such political regulation because they involve detailed government judgments
regarding costs or regarding historical transactions. Once a process is established

for allocating income politically, it may become inherently unstable so that, on the one hand, "a system of majority rule creates irresistible temptations . . . . for the poor to expropriate the rich and, on the other, for any majority coalition to use its power to plunder the minority."[9] There is no question that the quite natural and understandable demand for offsetting the consequences of the OPEC price jumps has thrown a tremendous new burden on the political system of the United States at the very time when it is less well organized to bear such a burden than might have been the case 15 years ago.

In contrast to energy the Apollo program enjoyed two immense advantages. First it had many fewer redistributional implications, and, therefore, did not demand concomitant interventions in the existing "system of equity." Second, at the time the Apollo program was launched there were many fewer constituencies organized to register their concerns effectively in the political process. The environmental, consumer, and poverty constituencies were hardly visible in the early sixties, but had reached the peak of their influence and activism by the mid-seventies. Added to these natural advantages was the great political skill of James Webb, the administrator of NASA during the period of most rapid build-up of Apollo. Webb succeeded in satisfying the constituencies that did exist without compromising the technocratic efficiency necessary for achieving his primary goal. These constituencies were mainly the geographical areas that were represented by senators or congressmen whose political support for the program was essential to its success. Webb saw to it that these areas shared adequately in the economic benefits of NASA procurements and laboratories, without impairing the efficiency or effectiveness of the overall program.

The technical and economic analysis that underlay the energy program was probably more elaborate and demanding than that needed to support the management of Apollo. Thus from a technocratic standpoint it was as competent as that of NASA. Yet the issues of class equity and regional impact, which were at the heart of the citizen disenchantment with government and established institutions, were not addressed in any depth in these technocratic analyses. Perhaps they couldn't be. To much of the public and to many influential interest groups the very term "coherent national energy policy" became a code word for insensitivity to the distributional implications of the national policy. Thus rational analyses tended to be evaluated not according to their own terms of reference, but in relation to their implications for uncompensated redistribution of income or of health or environmental risks. The NASA professionals also ignored redistributional impacts, but they could better afford to do so not only because these impacts were small, but also because they had a shrewd political boss who knew how to take care of such distributional issues as remained without undermining the integrity of the professional analysis supporting the program. It is doubtful whether any leadership skill below the level of the president himself could have similarly juggled redistributional impact and professional coherence and self-consistency in respect to national energy programs. France appears to be the only country in which this has been done successfully. The French have set clear goals for energy conservation and the development and deployment of substitute energy sources, chiefly nuclear power. They have pursued these goals in a self-consistent and sustained manner, with little change of direction ever since the 1973 embargo.[10]

However, their success may be more due to the relative weakness of "special interests" in the political process than to political skill of top leadership.

This is not to say, however, that the technocratic approach of DOE and its supporting professional constituencies and analytical apparatus were wholly without effect. There was considerable movement in public and elite opinion between 1973 and 1981, and it is difficult to say how much of this was due to studies and how much simply to the march of events. There was certainly some convergence of initially highly polarized positions. For example, in 1973 most people in the energy industry and most policy makers believed that economic growth and energy consumption were very tightly coupled, and that the growth in energy consumption could not be curtailed without also curtailing economic growth and employment and without limiting the aspirations of the poorer segments of the population. No-growth advocates for the most part accepted this premise, but felt that reduced material consumption was an acceptable price to pay for a cleaner environment and for curbing the power of overblown energy oligopolies. They felt that the problems of the poor, both domestically and around the world, should be solved by redistribution rather than growth. Now both sides accept that the relationship between GNP and energy consumption has much greater flexibility in the long run than was once thought. They would probably differ most in their emphasis on price as the mechanism for curbing energy growth and encouraging substitution of energy forms with a larger resource base than oil and gas. The no-growth advocates have greater faith in political regulation and are more prepared to accept collective interventions in consumer choices.[11] In this, however, they are ambivalent in that they also seem to believe that the market would favor renewable resources and conservation investments if hidden subsidies for present energy technologies were eliminated.[12]

A consensus has also developed on deregulation of energy prices to permit domestic prices to come into equilibrium with world oil prices as set by OPEC. Differences in view regarding price have come to focus more on the degree to which special tax measures should be implemented to effect income transfers between the "winners" and "losers" from deregulation. There is also disagreement as to the extent to which even deregulated prices reflect the true costs of energy, both with respect to the internalization of environmental costs and with respect to the true marginal costs of oil imports. Various analyses have been carried out which attempt to estimate the "true" marginal cost of imported oil compared to the price actually paid for it by consumers.[13] However, most political conservatives do not accept the marginal cost concept, at least to the extent of taking it into account in decision making regarding government subsidies for conservation investments, synthetic fuels, or renewables.

There is little evidence of any convergence on the contentious issue of nuclear power, where the advocates and critics seem to be talking past each other, and disagree on the most elementary questions of economics and safety. Although the scientific community in fact appears to be overwhelmingly pronuclear, despite the articulate opinions of the minority critics, scientific opinion is perceived by the public to be nearly evenly split.[14] There is evidence that the falsely perceived division of the scientific community fuels public opposition to nuclear power.[15]

THE POLITICS OF SUBSYSTEMS

Because of the rise to influence of diverse new constituencies, the redistributional aspects of energy policy have received greater political attention than would probably have been the case if the energy crisis had developed at the same time as the Sputnik crisis. In the early 1960s there would have been a greater disposition of the public to accept the technocratic definition of the energy problem as it was first formulated in Project Independence and subsequently in the first two congressionally mandated "national energy plans" published in 1975 and 1976.[16,17] Indeed the sharp emphasis on conservation in the second of these reports as compared to the first already reflected the pressures from these new constituencies to a degree that would have been unlikely in an earlier era.

Perhaps even more important than the rise of new groups representing new perspectives and values on behalf of consumers and the environment were the changes in the structure of political institutions. These changes enabled new constituency interests, as well as the more traditional ones, to find effective political expression in the actual formulation of legislation and in the implementation of this legislation via the detailed "sublegislation" developed in numerous offices in the executive branch.

This new political configuration has been characterized by political scientists Dodd and Schott as "subsystem triangles" consisting of a specialized congressional subcommittee (and its professional staff), a subordinate bureau or office in an executive agency, and a special constituency interest—professional, economic, or advocacy—outside the government.[18] Both the formulation of new programs and the congressional surveillance and oversight of established programs tend to take place within these subsystem triangles, with the higher levels of the bureaucracy and the legislature merely ratifying the often suboptimized policies arrived at within these subsystems. Thus the subsystems may evolve policies for the breeder, solar energy, synfuels, or conservation as though no other energy option existed and without reference to, say, pricing policy, the tax code, or environmental regulation. With the erosion of bureaucratic discipline in the executive, and of congressional discipline through the shift of its business and its agenda control to its increasingly specialized subcommittees and their professional staffs, the pressure for consistency among the numerous subpolicies developed in different forums virtually disappears.

Within the executive, increased professionalization and specialization of staff also tends to insulate it from the overall policy discipline. This should, theoretically, be provided by the political appointees at the head of the agency, but they find it difficult because of their lack of control or mastery of the highly technical information that gives substance to policy. The autonomy of the professionals in executive offices is further encouraged by the short tenure of political appointees compared to professional civil servants and by frequent switches in broad policy, uninformed by detailed experience with the problems of implementation. There is thus a mismatch between the high level of generality of presidential policy guidance and political campaign commitments and the translation of this guidance into concrete regulations and programs. At the same time the Freedom of Information Act has provided increased public access to the ongoing processes of policy formation at the subsystem level. In practice this access is more frequently taken advantage of by a variety of special interests and stakeholders than by the general public. Thus while openness theoretically increases the accountability of public officials, this accountability tends to be expressed through continual buffeting in different directions by special interests or narrowly ideological perspectives.

Nowhere have the workings of subsystem politics been more apparent than in the operations of the Department of Energy. With its mission pieced together through countless separate and independent legislative initiatives, the department has struggled to be all things to all people and to appease hundreds of different public constituencies. Constantly shifting public perceptions of the "energy problem" were reflected in a proliferation of congressional committees and subcommittees, each competing for a piece of the action in energy policy, and each reflecting a slightly different mix of constituency interests ranging from large scale energy producers and breeder advocates to consumer groups or dedicated enthusiasts of particular technologies such as solar photovoltaics or other solar energy forms, fusion, or oil shale. The new department became a cornucopia for dispensing everybody's favorite remedy for the energy crisis, and, just as in the case of EPA before it, the mission of DOE became the accretion of hundreds of overlapping and sometimes conflicting statutory provisions and policy philosophies. As a result guidance for effecting trade-offs between conflicting goals was largely missing and instead was left to the play of contending lobbies and special interests, with the courts increasingly brought into the act to interpret vague and ambiguous legislative intent. Examples of the contending goals were:

1. the rate of expansion or substitution of energy supplies versus the level of protection of public health and the environment;
2. the desirability of energy conservation versus public resistance to higher prices or detailed government regulation of consumer choices and behavior;
3. holding down domestic oil and gas prices to avoid economic dislocation and hardship for particular groups and regions versus the hazard of further stimulat-

ing dependence on Persian Gulf oil imports through the *de facto* subsidization of
such imports through price controls and entitlements;

4. responding to public resentment against internal wealth transfer to domestic oil
   producers and multinational oil companies versus export of U.S. wealth to
   OPEC (on the whole the public seemed to prefer having the money exported to
   the Arab sheiks rather than contribute to the "obscene profits" of the Seven
   Sisters);
5. avoidance of risks to public health and the environment versus energy security
   and the diversification of U.S. energy supply sources;
6. reducing the risks of nuclear weapons proliferation versus the maintenance of
   good relations with our allies and our friends in the developing world;
7. reliance on the market to determine investments in energy supply and conservation versus the use of public policy and government regulation or targeted
   subsidies for this purpose;
8. our obligation to shape our domestic energy policies to make scarce and
   expensive oil available to assist economic development in the LDC's versus our
   concern for our own economic health and the protection of our own environment and safety.

The mandates given by Congress to the DOE contained only the vaguest
guidance regarding these difficult trade-offs, which were often not explicitly
recognized as such, as each piece of legislation was formulated in relation to its
own narrow goals and perspectives. The initiatives for making these trade-offs
could only have come from the president himself, but he never behaved or made
proposals in a way that suggested he was fully aware of the necessity for hard
choices among objectives, each of which almost everybody believed was desirable
in itself. There was never any indication as to which goals were to be sacrificed or
soft-pedaled in order to achieve other more important goals.

An important, and somewhat novel, element of the DOE cornucopia was the
"demonstration program"—something more than R&D, but less than a full
government commitment to override or anticipate the choices of the market
through actual construction of full scale commercial installations. Demonstration
programs are especially compatible with subsystem politics; indeed they may be
regarded as one of the most characteristic manifestations of these politics. They
permit satisfying many more diverse constituencies than would a more definitive
commitment to a particular policy orientation or to a chosen path of technological
development. They can constitute a more apparent commitment to action than
would an R&D program alone, and they permit a wider public to compete for a
share in the benefits of the "goodies" available. A typical example of this is the
case of various kinds of community demonstration programs for conservation
investments or renewables. In reality demonstrations are merely buying knowledge, and in this they differ little from R&D programs. Their benefit, if there is
any, must come from the shortening of lead times for future deployment at full

scale of new technologies or new regulatory policies should circumstances demand it. There is a good deal of recent literature that attempts to quantify the benefits derived from technological demonstrations, notably in the case of the now moribund synfuels program.[19] Perhaps, the political benefits of demonstrations are more obvious. The term "demonstration" has a connotation of real action, which is much more satisfying to various advocacy groups than an R&D program would be. However, the budgetary cost is also much higher.

The "demonstration" ploy was particularly effective and prominent in the field of renewable energy resources, especially solar energy, which became the focus of a rather influential lobby during the Carter administration. The influence of this lobby was enhanced by the presence of allies in the bureaucracy, especially in the Council on Environmental Quality, an office in the president's staff apparatus, which was itself a creature of the subsystem politics that accompanied the sequence of far-reaching environmental and safety enactments beginning with NEPA in 1969.[20,21] As a result of all these forces the budget in DOE for solar demonstration projects increased dramatically from 1975 to 1979, until, by the end of the Carter administration, the resources allocated to solar research, development, and demonstration became comparable with those devoted to fossil fuels and nuclear power. This development was brought to an abrupt halt by the Reagan administration, though signs of second thoughts were already beginning to be apparent in the last Carter budget, which evidenced particular skepticism in relation to demonstrations. The new administration rejected the demonstration philosophy more aggressively, suggesting that "demonstrations" were a task for the private sector. However, even this administration was unable to resist the pressures of subsystem politics when it came to the Clinch River Breeder Project, which was continued as an apparent exception to its "no-demonstrations" principles. The influence of subsystem politics also revealed itself in the failure of the new administration to deliver on its campaign promise to dismantle the DOE and return its constituent pieces to existing agencies.

WHAT HAVE WE LEARNED?

The question raised by the history of energy policy is whether the developments in both constituency politics and congressional and executive institutions that we have sketched will continue to condemn us to the lack of coherence in policy which has been so painfully apparent in the case of energy to date. In the absence of any real party discipline in the Congress, in the presence of glaring media exposure in the executive, and in the accessibility of both the executive and the Congress to a proliferation of regional, industry, and "public interest" constituencies, each competing to insure the protection of what it perceives to be its vital interests or values in the formulation of national energy policy, there are far too few incentives for the accommodation of these competing interests and values. This is true even when it is apparent that the nation as a whole, or the "public interest" in a real sense, is a net loser as a consequence of the failure of accommodation. In part, the problem is that there is no forum in which the competing interests can negotiate with each other to agree on a course of action, which keeps the national interest paramount while affording some, though by no means complete, protection to the various special interests affected.

Historically, this kind of accommodation has occurred most readily in times of crisis, but the various publics involved had to be convinced there really was a crisis. In addition the increased latitude delegated to the executive in times of crisis often tends to be withdrawn as the crisis subsides or simply becomes more familiar. Energy was particularly vulnerable to this problem, since the real threat to the national interest was long term compared to the more immediate threats to more parochial interests posed by various potential policy measures. In fact no president ever really succeeded in convincing the American public that the energy problem was a "crisis" in the sense needed to sustain a prolonged delegation of discretionary authority to the executive. Furthermore, the political leadership needs to do more than *say* there is a crisis. It must show by its proposed concrete actions that it really believes there is a crisis, and no president really did this during the entire period from 1973 to 1982. For example, President Carter's "moral equivalent of war" speech was not followed by concrete actions consistent with such a drastic view.

Reorganization proposals, the traditional American response to a perceived crisis, as in the case of FEA, ERDA, and DOE, are seldom sufficient by themselves. The purpose of reorganization is usually to give greater prominence and visibility to a national goal newly perceived as critical, but it is unrealistic to assume that when a new national goal emerges, older goals and their political constituencies will go away or remain silent. Many in the energy producing industry, for example, seemed to assume that the energy crisis would pull the teeth of the environmental and antinuclear movements, but it did no such thing. If anything the political strength of the antinuclear movement grew in both the United States and in all of Western Europe except France after the 1973 crisis.

Reorganization is form rather than substance; it can make the realization of substance easier or more efficient, but it cannot substitute for what Don Price describes as the need to "muster political support for the kind of discretionary authority required to deal with conflicting values and the determination of general political goals."[22] The reorganization to deal with energy was designed to produce the appearance of this kind of discretionary authority, but its substance was eroded by detailed legislative specification of various subsystem objectives, which were frequently in conflict with each other, and, which left little room for the negotiation of compromises or trade-offs free of media-generated pressures for action.[23] These trade-offs have to be negotiated in a much larger arena, with many more chips on the table, than is normal in the subsystem triangles that are the source of most policy initiatives.

Thus the problem of DOE was not primarily a problem of poor management, but a failure of political leadership at the highest and most general levels of both the executive and legislative branches—leadership which would have both the latitude and the courage to work out "deals" in which widely differing and apparently unrelated goals could be traded off against each other, and used to buy off losers for the benefit of a larger national interest. Such deals are, of course, repugnant to the professionals who inhabit the subsystem triangles, and who probably have to be by-passed if a break-through bargain is to be struck. To some extent the enactment of the Windfall Profits Tax in return for the deregulation of the domestic oil market is representative of the kind of deal that is necessary if subsystem politics is to be circumvented, but this deal came only after years of acrimonious debate.

In recent history it has been much easier to muster political support for the requisite "discretionary authority" in the foreign policy domain than in the area of domestic policy. Perhaps one of the classic examples is the inauguration of the Marshall Plan in 1947. To a considerable extent the Apollo program can also be viewed as a foreign policy initiative, and the record indicates that it was perceived as such by President Kennedy. Although the 1973 and 1979 energy crises were triggered by foreign policy events, energy policy was never viewed as a foreign policy exercise, and its foreign policy dimensions tended to be consistently underplayed in the national debate that accompanied the struggle to arrive at a "national energy policy." In fact energy can be regarded as a paradigm for a new type of challenge to American society in which the domestic and foreign policy aspects are much more inextricably intertwined than in the past.[24] To an increasing degree foreign policy initiatives may be expected to impinge on domestic constituencies, while other policies, which appear to be purely domestic, will have serious foreign policy implications and effects. This is one of the costs of world interdependence and an open international trading system.

Today we are beginning to see the same cluster of constituency interests and "subsystem complexity" in the political arena affecting the emerging national debate over international trade policy and the crisis of U.S. international competitiveness. The danger to the fundamental national interest that will occur if this national debate becomes submerged in "subsystem politics" is even more ominous than it was in the case of energy policy.

NOTES

1. Department of Energy, U.S. Energy Information Administration, *Energy Programs/Energy Markets*, Energy Policy Study, Vol. 16, 1980.
2. William Nordhaus, "Energy Policy: Mostly Sound and Fury," Business Section, *New York Times*, Nov. 30, 1980.
3. Don K. Price, *America's Unwritten Constitution* (Baton Rouge, LA: State University Press, forthcoming).
4. Federal Energy Administration, *Project Independence Report* (Washington, DC: USGPO, Nov. 1974).

5. Harvey Brooks, "Perspectives on the Energy Problem," *Proceedings of the American Philosophical Society,* 125 (Aug. 1981) p.249.
6. Martin Greenberger, et al., *Caught Unawares: The Energy Decade in Retrospect* (Cambridge: Ballinger, 1983) p.2.
7. Dan Usher, *The Economic Prerequisites to Democracy* (New York: Columbia University Press, 1981), p.ix. Usher defines a "system of equity" as "a set of rules for assigning income and other advantages independently of and prior to political decisions arrived at in the legislature."
8. Ibid., pp. 12-13.
9. Ibid., dustjacket.
10. Nicholas Wade, "France's All-Out Nuclear Program Takes Shape," *Science, 209 (*Aug. 22, 1980), pp. 884-889.
11. Harvey Brooks, "Energy: A Summary of the CONAES Report," *Bulletin of the Atomic Scientists,* 36 (Feb. 1980).
12. Amory B. Lovins, *World Energy Strategies: Facts, Issues, and Options,* (San Francisco: Friends of the Earth, 1975).
13. Energy Modeling Forum, *World Oil: Summary Report,* EMF Report 6 (Stanford University, February 1982) cf. especially, "The Value of Reducing Oil Imports," pp. 67-75.
14. Stanley Rothman and S. Robert Lichter, "The Nuclear Energy Debate: Scientists, The Media, and the Public," *Public Opinion* (August/September, 1982).
15. Stanley Rothman, "Contorting Scientific Controversies," Transaction/SOCIETY, 20 (July-Aug. 1983) 25-32.
16. Energy Research and Development Administration, *ERDA-48, Vol. 1, The Plan; Creating Energy Choices for the Future,* (Washington: GPO, 1975). U.S. Energy Research and Development Administration, *Public Meeting: The Midwest Perspective* (Washington: ERDA, 1976).
17. Office of Technology Assessment, *An Analysis of the ERDA Plan and Program,* October 1975.
18. Lawrence S. Dodd and Richard L. Schott, *Congress and the Administrative State* (New York: John Wiley and Sons, 1979).
19. James K. Harlan, *Starting with Synfuels: Benefits, Costs, and Program Design Assessments* (Cambridge: Ballinger, 1982).
20. Domestic Policy Staff, The White House, *Domestic Policy Review of Solar Energy, a Response Memorandum to the President of the United States,* TID-22834 (Washington, DC: DOE, Feb. 1979).
21. PL 91-190, *National Environmental Policy Act of 1969,* established Jan. 1, 1970.
22. Price, *America's Unwritten Constitution,* p. 127.
23. Ibid., p. 97.
24. Harvey Brooks and Eugene Skolnikoff, "Science, Technology, and International Relations," in *Science and Future Choice,* Vol. 2, ed Philip W. Hemily and M.N. Ozdas (Oxford: Clarendon Press, 1979).

Chapter 12
THE POLITICAL GEOLOGY OF
THE ENERGY PROBLEM

Daniel Yergin

The 1973 Arab oil embargo firmly established what had already become clear to a prescient few in the years preceding the dramatic events of 1973, that a growing world economy was in collision with an energy problem. But what to make of that collision? Its impact set off in the United States an intensive political debate that has continued for a decade. The center of contention has been a debate over price: How should prices be set? Who should set them? Who should benefit from them? And should domestic American prices reflect the world market conditions? It has been a debate not only about interests, as considerable as those interests may be, but also over competing versions of reality—about America's relation to the world, about the distribution of domestic economic and political power, and about the themes of abundance and constraint in our national culture.[1] When prices are level or declining, whether in real or nominal terms, the debate subsides, and there is no longer an energy problem, at least as far as much of the public is concerned.

This is an error of perception, for the major cost of the energy problem to date has been its charge on economic performance. In other words, as a society we have been paying for the energy problem in the form of double-digit inflation, stunted economic growth, and high unemployment. It has also been a major factor in the massive and precarious buildup of international debt. We may yet pay a heavy cost in terms of international politics, as well.

More than enough has changed in the decade since that initial impact to force us to review basic assumptions and think through anew the energy problem. There has been a considerable process of adjustment. Is it time now to shift from a cautious to an optimistic stance? Is the transition out of the era of expensive and insecure oil now complete? Or are we still in transit through a turbulent time and still vulnerable?

1. Even the definition of the energy problem is confusing. It means different things to different people, and certainly does encompass a multitude of matters—from the transportation of coal, to natural gas pricing, to nuclear waste disposal. But, in essence, it is a question about there being sufficient energy supplies to

power industrial society. This formulation places oil at the very center of the energy issue, but oil has to be considered on two levels.

First, the contemporary world is an oil-based civilization. This is a relatively recent development. In 1950, 57 percent of the energy needs of the industrial world were met by coal and 29 percent by oil. By 1973, 52 percent were met by oil and 22 percent by coal. The absolute magnitudes made this shift even greater, for oil consumption in the industrial world grew five times over during those years.[2]

In itself, this dependence on oil need not have been a problem. What has made it a problem is the asymmetry between oil consumption and the reserve base. That is, the industrial world consumes 80 percent of free-world oil. But low-cost reserves are concentrated in a politically unstable part of the world, the Middle East. The full significance of this dependence became apparent when U.S. oil production peaked in 1970, and then began to decline, and the United States became integrated into the world market as one of the two largest importers. Thus, the heart of the problem is what might be described as the "political geology" of oil—the intersection of politics, economics, and geology.

In terms of production, the significance of this political geology has declined over the last few years, as non-OPEC oil production has grown. Between 1973 and 1981, new production in Mexico, the North Sea, and Alaska added six million barrels a day to world production. In turn, OPEC's share of total free world production dropped from 67 percent in 1977 to 48 percent in 1982; and the Middle East's share dropped from 55 percent to 39 percent over the same period. (See table 12.1.)

The oil from two of the major new oil provinces, Alaska and the North Sea, is definitely not low-cost; it can cost 20 times more to produce than oil from the Persian Gulf. Moreover, despite optimism about the reserve base, future expansion both onshore and offshore in the north remains a daunting task, for these reserves are at the frontier in terms of technology, weather, and drilling conditions.

When we look at reserves rather than production, the impact of the political geology continues to loom large. About 70 percent of free-world proven reserves are to be found beneath the Middle East and North Africa. That means that 70 percent of world reserves are subject to that region's social turmoil, political upheaval, and military conflicts. The current American administration is trying to

Table 12.1 Shares Of Free World Oil Production[a]

%	1977	1982
OPEC	67	48
MIDDLE EAST[b]	55	39

a. Total free world oil production, excluding natural gas liquids, was 46.6 mbd in 1977 and 38.7 mbd in 1982.

b. Includes North Africa.

Source: Derived from *International Energy Statistical Review*

find ways to cope with this reality in its strategic policies, but seeks to downplay it, in its domestic energy policies.

This split, among other things, reflects the continuing saga in what became an overstated and unnecessarily overheated debate about government versus market. Clearly, a major mistake was made in controlling oil prices in the 1970s; those controls delivered a wrong message to consumers and producers and misled the American public by denying the integration of the United States into the world oil market. Though the controls are gone and hardly lamented, the residue of the political struggle, as well as a "rebellion" against government, has created a new distortion. The current administration says that "free markets" alone will solve the problem. But what does it mean by "free markets?" After all, these markets have major imperfections and costly externalities, and the costs of the two oil shocks have been very heavy.[3] The administration spokesmen complain that the Department of Energy has never produced a drop of oil, which was never its brief. Less often noted is that over half the budget of the Department of Energy has been earmarked to produce nuclear weapons.

Moreover, the Reagan administration has not been consistent in its dedication to free market principles. It seeks to heavily subsidize one energy source, nuclear power, while starving others that are actually in a more infant state. To its great credit, the administration has resumed the filling of the Strategic Petroleum Reserve, a most worthy and valuable task. Yet, given the administration's own basic premises, it takes some effort to justify what is obviously not a free market business, the filling of the strategic reserve, but what seems to most an obviously legitimate function of government. But it can be done, by turning the SPR into a device to prevent government intervention! In this spirit, W. Allen Wallis, Under Secretary of State for Economic Affairs, declared: "A strategic stockpile is necessary not because of any failure in the private sector. Companies would, I think, build stocks against potential shortages if they could be sure that they would draw the eventual benefits from disposal of those resources. Instead, corporate leaders justifiably fear that private stocks would be commandeered by government in periods of shortage."

Commandeering does not seem to be the problem. During a time of calm and slack in the world oil market—and a time of high interest rates, recession, and cost-cutting—companies tend to draw down inventories. During a period of interruption and panic, companies rush to build up inventories, to hedge against uncertainty, thus accentuating the panic and upward price push.[4]

Whatever the sins of government, real or imagined, the political geology of oil will continue to pose a major threat to world stability, and is still at the heart of the oil problem.

The oil problem operates at another level as well, and that is the longer-term issue of depletion. At some point, world oil production will peak, and then begin to decline. The "when" is a matter of enormous uncertainty. The timing of this event will be much affected not only by geology and advances in oil recovery, but also by the rate of world oil consumption, which in turn is conditioned by rates of economic growth, energy efficiency, fuel substitution, and technological innovation. M. King Hubert is the distinguished geologist who with remarkable accuracy predicted in 1956 that U.S. oil production in the lower 48 of the United States would peak between 1966 and 1971. Recently, he has offered two scenarios for world oil. If production increases at a modest rate, then peaking will occur around the year 2000. If world production remains flat at 20 billion barrels a year (55 mbd), then the peak would occur around 2035-2040, followed by depletion decline.[5]

Whenever it occurs, the peaking will obviously bring about a transition of some kind. Although still quite hazy, that transition will presumably be embodied in the aforementioned energy efficiency, substitution, and innovation. Unlike the disruption that can flow from the political geology of oil, depletion is unlikely to make its effect felt in a sudden moment. Rather, its approach will be much anticipated and much noted, and no doubt much signalled in rising real prices. It is unfashionable these days to give thought to longer-term questions of depletion, but it does provide the context of the longer-term energy problem, and will provide a challenge in the next century.

2. For many people, the energy problem is not a matter of causes, the political geology, but of effects and costs. In the first instance, this refers to those moments when there is a physical interruption of availability, preeminently experienced in gasoline lines. These are relatively fleeting moments. To the public, for the most part, the energy problem means higher prices at the gas pump and in utility bills. The change has been considerable. Gasoline cost 39 cents a gallon in 1973 and $1.26 a gallon in mid-1983. Correcting for inflation, that is a 67 percent increase in real terms. (See table 12.2.)

The real costs are in the economic consequences for the national economy— inflation, recession, unemployment. This connection between the oil shocks and the poor performance of the industrial economies is widely recognized in both Western Europe and Japan, but tends to be ignored in the United States.

We have had two case studies since 1973 of the connection. Since oil is so basic to our economy, a sudden jump in oil prices sends an inflationary shock wave

Table 12.2 Gasoline Prices

	Nominal Price	Real Price (1972 Dollars)
1973	$ .39	$.36
1983	1.26*	.60
World Energy Industry		

Source: *The Energy Decade; Weekly Petroleum Status Report*

*June

through the system. The price of oil products goes up, of course. So does the price of things that are made with oil, such as petrochemicals, or that depend on oil, such as airline travel. The price of things that we buy to reduce our oil consumption also goes up—be it natural gas, coal, housing insulation, or fuel-efficient Hondas. Meanwhile, people do not want to see their real incomes reduced by inflation, and so they scramble to play catch-up by seeking higher wages, and inflation begins to accelerate.

This inflationary surge has followed right on the heels of the price increase. The two peaks of inflation occurred in the latter part of 1974, a year after the 1973 embargo, and during the first part of 1980, a year after the second oil shock began.

At the same time, these two oil shocks had a depressing effect on the economy. For instance, after the second oil shock, our nation's annual bill for imported oil went up $50 billion. That is $50 billion of national income suddenly withdrawn from the economy, rather than being used to purchase goods and services at home.

When this happens, political leaders confront a dilemma, which to fight first, inflation or recession? This dilemma does not respect political ideology; it has to be faced whether your name is Jimmy Carter or Ronald Reagan—or Paul Volcker, or Francois Mitterrand, or Helmut Schmidt—or Helmut Kohl.

The general tendency has been to fight inflation first. So the brakes go on in the form of a tight monetary policy. Depending on how hard the brakes are hit, a slowdown turns into a recession. Certainly after 1979, it was necessary to pump the brakes in order to contain that second surge of inflation. But the policies that were adopted represented a considerable over-reaction, as though the inflationary surge were permanently built into our system. On the contrary, inflation would have slowed once the public became accustomed to the higher prices and oil prices themselves leveled out. But the causes of the inflation were misdiagnosed, and the brakes were stepped on so long and so tightly that we were thrown into a deep economic slump, the worst since the Great Depression, and it has proved to be a world slump.

Of course, no single set of factors can fully explain something as complex as the deep recession of the first three years of the 1980s. For instance, the tension in the economic program of the Reagan administration in its first two years, between tight monetary policy on the one hand and big deficits and loose spending policy on the other, aggravated matters, as has the rigidity in labor-management relations that developed in the past decade. But it is clear that the oil shocks, more than anything else, drove the world economy into the slump.

The bill for these shocks has been very heavy, and not just in terms of price at the gas pump. We found in the *Global Insecurity* study, that the two oil shocks had, by the end of 1981, cost the industrial world $1.2 trillion in lost economic growth and the account is not yet closed.[6] Consider what that means in human terms. A decade ago, unemployment in the industrial world averaged 9 million. By the end of 1982, 32 million people were out of work. That is a very basic indicator of the costs that the energy problem has imposed on economic performance. As Ulf Lantzke, director general of the International Energy Agency, expressed the matter: "There is still an oil gap; only now it is measured in the number of unemployed."[7]

Two other costs follow from the political geology of oil. One is the stress that falls on the Western alliance system as a result of the political and economic tensions, trade-offs, and suspicions that are created. "The disruptive impact," Robert Lieber has written, "has come from many directions, such as competitive bidding for oil supplies, opposing reactions to the Arab-Israeli conflict, differences over the export of nuclear power technology and facilities, tensions over policy toward Iran and Afghanistan, and disagreements over imports of Soviet gas."[8]

The other cost is the possibility of direct military conflict. It is hard to imagine a goose more golden in modern history than the oil reserves of the Middle East, whether it be a time of shortage or glut in the world oil market. For to control those reserves is to have a powerful handle over the entire world economy, and, thus, over world politics. Countries have gone to war for much less in modern times. The Middle East is highly susceptible to a very volatile mixture of oil and politics—with the axes of conflict running across national, regional, and superpower relations. The region has been described as the "New Balkans," evoking the geographic flash point that ignited World War I. Yet even that does not capture the full dimensions of the complexity. Imagine what the stakes might have been if the Balkans on the eve of World War I had been not only the stresspoint in the European states system, not only the vortex of competing nationalisms and imperial interests, but also the source of the bulk of Europe's coal! That in rough analogy is the situation in the "New Balkans," and it can hardly promote a sense of security.

3. There has been change over the last decade. The oil shocks of 1973 initiated a process of adjustment that was intensified in 1979. Changes in prices, availability, and perceptions have all had major feedback effects. We have already noted the growth of non-OPEC oil production. In addition, there has been a shift away from oil to other energy sources, and most dramatically, there has been a considerable improvement in energy efficiency, that is, energy conservation. The advance in conservation has demonstrated that there is much greater flexibility in the relation of energy use to over-all economic activity than a considerable number of skeptics had, throughout the 1970s, thought possible.

For instance, in 1976, the *Energy Report* of the Chase Manhattan Bank declared: "There is no documented evidence that indicates that the long-lasting, consistent relationship between energy and GNP will change in the future. There is no sound, proven basis for believing a billion dollars of GNP can be generated with less energy in the future." And as internal analyses of one of the major oil companies concluded: "There is no empirical evidence to indicate that the coupling of energy and economic growth can be uncoupled."[9]

How rapidly, thinking has shifted. What was seen in some quarters as the "off-the-wall" argument of *Energy Future* in 1979 is already in danger of becoming the conventional wisdom in the early 1980s.[10] For the industrial world was about 16 percent more energy efficient in 1981 than in 1973, as measured in terms of energy per unit of gross national product. Conservation provided the largest incremental contribution to the industrial world's energy supplies over that period, as indicated in table 12.3. All of this points to quite a considerable change—and shift.

For a decade and a half, the most immediate energy question mark has hung over supply: would there be enough energy to power industrial civilization? The question first began to be asked in the late 1960s and early 1970s in the context of the disappearance of spare oil capacity in the United States and a sudden tightening of some natural gas supplies, and then the peaking of United States oil production. It was driven home by the shortfalls of 1973 and 1979, brief and rather minor though they were found to be after the fact. Inadequacy of supplies—shortages and black-outs —this was the fear that provided the force behind the litany of projects announced around the world for nuclear and coal and liquefied natural gas. This concern was dramatically expressed first in the Project Independence proposals, 1973-75, and then in the crash plans for synthetic fuel development that emerged after the fall of the Shah in 1979. These proposals were actually driven by the fear of the danger of over-dependence on the Middle East, and the fear of a physical shortfall between world oil supply and demand. One particularly pungent expression of these concerns in the United States was a plan for synthetic fuels to fill a 15 million barrel a day "notional" shortfall by the end of the first decade of the next century.[11]

The focus was on supply because demand growth was assumed. Perhaps neither oil nor electricity consumption would grow at the high rates of the 1960s, but still, they would grow.

By the early 1980s, however, it became apparent that demand was behaving in a way quite different from what had been anticipated. In the United States, oil consumption was thirteen percent lower in 1982 than in 1973—although the economy was eighteen percent larger in real terms. Most oil companies were taken by surprise. Three comments illustrate the confusion and predicament of those for whom this discovery has unexpected, but very significant implications.

Table 12.3   Incremental Addition to OCED Energy Balance 1973-81 (mbdoe)*

North Sea Oil	2.3
Alaskan Oil	1.6
Nuclear Power	2.5
Coal	3.6
Conservation	12.9

Source: Derived from *The Energy Decade;* World Energy Industry; *British Petroleum Statistical Review, 1981*

*million barrels a day of oil equivalent

"If you should gain the impression that we feel somewhat less confident than usual about forecasting near-term economic and energy trends, you are absolutely correct," the president of Exxon observed. "Forecasting oil demand these days is a bit like solving Rubrik's cube—except that there are no pamphlets available to let one pick out the right answer."

At about the same time, a top official of an OPEC national oil company made a similar point: "Never have so many forecasters had to change their forecasts so often."

"Uncertainty clouds the estimates of future demand for energy and oil, dependent as they must be on assessments of future economic conditions and the energy/ oil intensity of gross national product," observed a director of the Royal Dutch Shell group. "The climate of uncertainty affects investments in, and future supply of, alternative energy sources and non-conventional oil, investment in energy conservation, the geopolitics of OPEC and the Gulf States, and the production and fiscal policies of a wide range of oil-producing governments. . . . To put it bluntly, we simply do not know what will happen—not even between now and the year end."[12]

Whereas the supply interruptions and price hikes of 1979-80 had created a crisis for consumers in 1979, as well as an intoxicating boom for those in the business of supplying energy, the bizarre behavior of demand in 1981 and 1982 created a crisis for those who are in the energy supply business. (Consumers were too busy with other economic ills to spend much time celebrating the declining real price of oil.) For instance, the entire infrastructure of the oil industry (its tankers and fleets and oil refineries and gas stations) was based upon a certain notion of growing demand. The change in that trend has made a healthy chunk of this infrastructure, as the British say, redundant, and has forced the industry into a painful process of rationalization and reorganization.

The oil-exporting countries were for the most part even more convinced that the boom would go on forever, and the 40 percent drop in demand for 1979-82 has proven deeply traumatic and painful for them. For instance, Nigeria's fourth national development plan, for 1981-85, envisioned oil production of 2.2 million barrels a day, with oil prices escalating to $55 a barrel by 1985—bringing $44 billion in revenues that year. Instead oil revenues fell from about $27 billion in 1980 to about $16 billion in 1982.[13] The $16 billion is just $6 billion more than was earned in 1978, and even less when adjusted for inflation. The fall in revenues, and even greater fall in anticipated revenues, has necessitated austerity and a sharp retrenchment in imports and in government spending. These conditions, in turn, have promoted unemployment, economic stagnation, and social and political discontent.

Thus the energy question mark has shifted to the other side of the equation. Now the most critical question concerns what has happened, and what will happen, to energy demand.

4. Let me first offer what has become known as the "structural" case. It says that Middle Eastern oil will meet a smaller part of the over-all demand than was the case in the 1970s, that oil in turn will meet a smaller part of total energy demand than was the case in the 1970s, and that the uncertain day of oil's peaking will have been pushed farther into the hazy future.

The structural case argues that the two oil price shocks, as well as other increases in energy prices, have had a profound impact on energy demand and supply, that continued improvement in energy demand is automatic, and that we have indeed entered a new era. In essence, according to this view, the energy problem is over, the double earthquakes of 1973 and 1979 have done their work, significantly shifting the terrain. To state the case in a pithy form, we can close up the blast furnaces, and get back to work on our home computers.

5. The structural argument is a sensible and very legitimate case. Obviously, much structural change has happened—and is happening. I am certainly convinced that there is a great deal of flexibility between energy use and economic activity. Even if we cannot completely uncouple energy and economic growth, barring major technological change, we can certainly greatly loosen the link. But, on the basis of what we know today, I find myself skeptical of the argument that the structural change has been as thorough-going as one might initially have anticipated.

It proved unwise to try to generalize the future of energy and oil at the top of the petroleum boom in 1980, when oil companies were being minted daily in the United States on the premise that oil was going to $100 a barrel. Many people in the energy industries made that error, and have been scrambling to pay off their bank loans ever since. Similarly, it seems unwise to generalize energy trends in both the developing and developed worlds from the depths of a recession. That error may have to be paid off not in the form of individual and corporate debts, but once again through poor economic performance in the future.

In addition, we have no historical experience with oil in the $30-a-barrel range. As late as 1979, it was something not expected until the year 2000.

Given all this uncertainty, any generalization must be tentative, until we have some recovery and some history. Certainly we have seen a great deal of adjustment. But how much is permanent, how much is temporary, and how much that looks like adjustment is actually the effects of recession? In other words, the basic issue is to assess the relative weight of structural changes versus cyclical change.

A number of factors lend support to the notion that cyclical factors are also important. First, energy-intensive industries have been in a deep slump. The American steel industry in the latter part of 1982 was operating at less than 40 percent capacity, as was the Japanese aluminum industry.[14] Perhaps these industries will never come back, but if that is the case, then there will be other grave economic problems that have yet to be recognized. Second, structural change depends upon investment, but high interest rates and then a painful recession— and cost-cutting and pessimism—have retarded investment over the last couple of years. Third, the pattern of oil prices has a direct impact on investment, both for energy supply and for conservation. In *Global Insecurity,* we describe this as a pattern of "jagged peaks and sloping plateaus."[15] The sloping plateaus, the decline in the real price and consequent shifts in expectations and rise in uncertainty undercut the entire range of energy-related investments, as became very clear in 1982.

The OPEC countries are the suppliers of last resort. Most other oil around the world is produced at or near capacity. OPEC makes up the balance of demand. Thus, it is the swing producer.

Oil analyst Bijan Mossavar-Rahmani has called this process the "OPEC multiplier."[16] It is the mechanism by which any swing in energy demand is magnified in demand for OPEC oil, the world's residual energy source. The forces that drove OPEC production down so quickly could work in the opposite direction, driving it up rapidly and bringing us back to a tight oil market again in a half a decade or less.

What might bring this about? Energy demand would be stimulated both by a renewal of economic growth and by a further drop in the real price of oil. Both would lead to a renewed demand for oil as Mossavar-Rahmani writes, "Indeed, it is illogical to believe—as some analysts insist—that higher prices decrease demand permanently, but that lower prices will not increase it. . . .To believe the structural thesis, that energy demand is a one-way street, one must also believe a great deal of uneconomic behavior will occur. But the rapid recovery of world energy demand in the mid-1970s, resulting from renewed economic growth and falling real oil prices, suggests otherwise."

OPEC oil might well end up meeting the bulk of that demand growth because of the slowdown in and long lead times for nonoil energy developments, and because of the lack of the kind of surge of non-OPEC oil that occurred in the late 1970s.

Once again, the world might face a tight oil market; once again the market would become susceptible to political instability; and once again, the world might experience another oil shock, even as it is still healing from the last one. Imagine what a third shock might do to such industries as automobile and steel.

Of course, events might not develop like this. Perhaps the swing away from oil will prove more thorough and more durable. Perhaps economic recovery will be very weak because fear of inflation leads to restrictive monetary policies in the industrial world, and a fearful, international banking system constrains liquidity to the developing world—and thus constrains their economic growth.

6. There are no absolutes here. Rather, it is a question of the balance between cyclical factors and basic structural change. There has been a great deal of adjustment. We just do not know the extent and the thrust, the momentum. There is, however, an extreme version of the structural case, really a distortion, that denies that there is any energy problem, that denies that there is any question or doubt about the powering of industrial society.

Let us call those who make this case the Panglossians—in honor of the ever-optimistic tutor of Voltaire's *Candide*. No matter what calamity befell the innocent

Candide, be it shipwreck or public torture, the happily deluded Pangloss was there, in spirit if not always in flesh, to proclaim that this was the best of all possible worlds, and that everything that happened was for the best.

The Panglossians devote themselves today not to philosophy but to energy analysis. For they say not only that there is no energy crisis, but there probably never was one, and never will be one. Admittedly, while the energy question can be fascinating in its intricacies and scale, the public's experience with it has not been exactly fun. Thus, there is something quite appealing, even seductive, in having the Panglossians come forward and, with a wave of their wand, banish the problem.

Probe beneath the attractive surface, and you find that it rests upon an incomplete and quite confusing foundation. Thus, their arguments do not provide a solid undergirding for analyzing the issues and challenges. Indeed, their arguments, while soothing, can be quite misleading. A few examples follow.

The Panglossians informed us that the energy crisis is "largely a media event."[17] Unfortunately, this arresting declaration was made in January 1979, the very month that the Shah lost his job. Over the next 15 months, the price of oil increased two and a half times over. Whoever thought the media was that powerful!

High oil prices will "bring forth an avalanche of supply."[18] It's not what we have seen so far. The United States is producing 10 percent less oil today than in 1970, when domestic oil went for $3 a barrel. Even in real terms, the price of oil has still increased about four times over what it was in 1970.

The Panglossians make the mistake of assuming that price drives supply, clear and simple. But other factors also affect supply—technology, politics, and, of course, geology. Cheaper, larger reserves tend to be found and produced earlier than the smaller pockets of reserves. And constraints on supply, as Robert Stobaugh has emphasized, also drive price.[19]

Table 12.4   United States Oil

	1970	1982	1983
U.S. oil production (mbd)	11.2	10.2	10.2
Domestic oil price** (nominal)	$3.39	$31.77	$28.77
Domestic oil price (real $1972)	$3.53	$16.40	$13.39

Source: *Energy Decade;* World Energy Industry; *Statistical Review, 1981; Weekly Petroleum Status Report.*

*May 1983

**Refiner acquisition cost

"What about the second half of the decade?" the Panglossians ask about the 1980s. "For this period, we can no longer rely on the development of known oil fields. . . ." In other words, uncertainty increases. Yet that does not bring any caution to their predictions: "However, there are some solid reasons for making the projections optimistic." And what are they? "The main reason is that the 1979-80 rise in oil prices has already given major impetus to the search for new supplies."[20] So it may have seemed in 1980. Within two years, however, the drilling boom in the United States and around the world collapsed, suggesting that the "main reason" for optimistic projections is no longer operative.

"There are now," the Panglossians announce, "substantial commercial prospects for non-natural gas manufactured from coal . . . ," otherwise known as synthetic fuels.[21] Again, within two years, the synthetic fuels effort has almost completely collapsed, and those "commercial prospects" have once again disappeared into the haze.

Chinese oil production "will have growth at a 10 percent rate" in the 1980s.[22] There is a good deal of optimism about Chinese offshore oil, which may begin to flow in the 1990s. Meanwhile, Chinese oil production was lower in 1982 than in 1978.

"Around the world," say the Panglossians, "residential and commercial uses of light fuel are also switching to cheaper substitutes, principally to natural gas."[23] That was certainly the case three years ago. In 1982 , however, industrial fuel users in the United States have begun to switch away from natural gas to what in some regions is a cheaper fuel—oil. Meanwhile, coal-conversion projects are stalling or stopping altogether in the United States, Western Europe, and Japan.

Dr. Pangloss also sometimes forgets what he has written and gets confused. In 1980, in the pages of *Fortune,* he boldly called on the U.S. government to be "implementing energy policies designed to encourage conservation and foster production." Two years later, once again in the pages of *Fortune,* he strongly denounced such policies. The Panglossians regularly announce the death of OPEC. For instance, in March 1982, one declared, "OPEC is 100 percent dead. Nothing can save them."[24] There is no question but that many oil-exporting countries and OPEC itself have been thrown into deep crisis by the huge drop in demand for OPEC oil. Pressures and tensions are very great within the organization, and the stresses may for a time, or even permanently, prevent its members from acting in a cohesive manner. Still, despite their differences, the OPEC countries do have a profound commonality of interest, and a great deal to lose from not acting together. In 1982 OPEC managed, however raggedly and with a good deal of cheating, to turn itself into a true cartel, allocating production cutbacks among its members. The system looked like it might collapse by early 1983, but the OPEC nations managed to revise the system in March of 1983. In the face of the precipitous decline in its production since 1979, OPEC has—at least at this writing—been able to stabilize the price—albeit after a $5 a barrel reduction. In addition, the new importance of non-OPEC producers puts further stress on the OPEC price structure.

For a corpse, OPEC has done pretty well. But its ability to maintain its prices—and its cohesion—will continue to be under pressure for some time. The longer the world slump goes on, the longer demand for OPEC oil will be down—and the more difficult for it to hang together.

Four basic problems cloud and confuse the Panglossian analysis. First, the Panglossians generalize permanent energy trends from the bottom of a deep recession. Every responsible energy analyst recognizes that a combination of recession and conservation are at work; the debate, as we have already indicated, is over the mix. The Panglossians seem to forget the recession.

Second, they appear to ignore the costs of the two oil shocks and what a third might cost. A recognition of those costs would seem to call for a certain prudence. Instead, as the examples above make clear, the Panglossians show a systematic bias, always selecting the most optimistic assumption, even if the facts of the matter are ambiguous or do not support it, and discounting the uncertainties and risks. It's as though they let wish dominate analysis.

Third, they do not recognize the powerful feedback effects in the entire energy economy. They make a reasonable assumption when they say: "It is pretty safe to predict that world oil prices in 1985 will be lower in real terms than the unified official price of \$34 a barrel" agreed upon by OPEC countries in late 1981.[25] The producers overshot the market, and oil prices are likely to continue a decline that began in 1981, for a time. But the Panglossians fail to see the implications of that downward-sloping plateau. For such a decline inhibits oil exploration and development; undercuts the rationale for such alternative energy developments as coal, synthetic fuels, and renewals; stimulates demand; and reduces conservation. In other words, it accentuates the cycle, and sets the stage for another jagged peak.

Finally, the Panglossians accept a lot at face value. They assume that everything that is announced will be built, that all expectations will be met, that politics and confusion will not get in the way and everybody will have plenty of capital to invest in conservation and alternatives and research and development, in short, that everything will turn out for the best.

The last 10 years, however, have proved less than the best of all possible worlds, and the Panglossians' assertions about the future are hardly reassuring. But then Pangloss himself was a master of self-delusion. Even the earthquake that destroyed much of Lisbon in 1755 was, he said, "for the very best end . . . everything is for the best."[26]

Of course, surprise has followed surprise in the energy field, and no one can claim a consistent monopoly of wisdom. And the Panglossians do force a review of the basic assumptions. But, we are living with the consequences of earthquakes as destructive in their own way as that which struck Lisbon—earthquakes in the price, availability, and security of energy supplies. Based upon what we know today, and the costs already borne, there is a great deal to be said for prudence and caution in announcing a successful transition to a new energy era, at least until there is sufficient evidence. The turbulent era of expensive and insecure oil that dawned in the early 1970s does not yet appear over. The political geology of oil will continue to have a major say over the fortunes and the future of the world economy. The rest of this decade and the next still looks to be a race between crisis and adjustment—a time of uncertain power.

NOTES

1. See Daniel Yergin, "America in the Strait of Stringency," in *Global Insecurity: A Strategy for Energy and Economic Renewal*, ed. Daniel Yergin and Martin Hillenbrand (Boston: Houghton Mifflin, 1982) pp.114-24.
2. World Energy Industry Information System (San Diego, Calif.); William Liscom, ed., *The Energy Decade 1970–1980* (San Diego, Calif.: World Energy Industry, 1982); and United Nations, *World Energy Supplies, 1950–74*, Ser. 5, No. 9 (New York: United Nations, 1976).
3. On externalities and market imperfections see Robert Stobaugh, "After the Peak: The Threat of Hostile Oil," in *Energy Future: Report of the Energy Project at the Harvard Business School*, ed. Robert Stobaugh and Daniel Yergin (New York: Vintage, 1983); also Ibid., chap. 9.
4. W. Allen Wallis, "Coping with Energy Vulnerability in the US and Japan," remarks to US-Japan Energy Policy Conference, 17 Nov. 1982; for inventory behavior, see Alvin Alm and Edward Krapels, "Building a Buffer in a Bear Market: Policy Choices for Emergency Oil Reserves," Harvard Energy Security Program Paper #1, March 1982.
5. M. King Hubbert, "The World's Evolving Energy System," *American Journal of Physics* 49 (Nov. 1981), 1025-26. The cumulative world production is estimated at 2000 billion barrels, of which about half has been discovered, and 20 percent consumed.
6. Yergin and Hillenbrand, *Global Insecurity*, pp.3-7. Also see Ibid., chap. 3, 5, and 7.
7. Ulf Lantzke, "Energy Vulnerability and the Industrial World," paper presented at the twentieth anniversary of the Atlantic Institute, Oct. 1981, p.9.
8. In Yergin and Hillenbrand, *Global Insecurity*, n. 1, above, p. 320.
9. Chase Manhattan Bank, *Energy Report From Chase*, internal company memorandum, Sept. 1976.
10. Stobaugh and Yergin, *Energy Future*, ch. 6.
11. Exxon USA, *The Role of Synthetic Fuels in the United States Energy Future* (Houston: Exxon USA, 1980)
12. *Wall Street Journal*, 24 Feb. 1982, p. 2; L.C. Van Wachem, Presentation to Financial Analysts in the Hague, Royal Dutch Shell, 7 Oct. 1982.
13. *New York Times*, 26 Nov. 1982, p.D1.
14. Presentation by Toyaki Ikuta, President of Japan Institute of Energy Economics, to Atlantic Council U.S.-Japan Energy Policy Conference, Washington, DC, 17 Nov. 1982.
15. See Yergin and Hillenbrand, *Global Insecurity*, n. 1, above, pp.51-57.
16. Bijan Mossavar-Rahmani, *The OPEC Multiplier: The Rebound of The Producers?* (Cambridge, MA: Cambridge Energy Research Associates, Nov. 1982).
17. S. Fred Singer, "OPEC's Price Reduction," *The New Republic* (6 Jan. 1979), 11-12.
18. William Brown, "Gloom and Doom on Energy," *Fortune* (20 Sept. 1982), p. 153.

19. See Richard Nehring, *Giant Oil Fields and World Oil Resources* (Santa Monica: Calif. Rand Corp., 1978); Robert Stobaugh, "World Energy to the Year 2000," in *Global Insecurity,* ed; Yergin and Hillenbrand and his chapters in *Energy Future,* n. 3, above.
20. William M. Brown and Herman Kahn, "Why OPEC is Vulnerable," *Fortune* (14 July 1980), 69.
21. Ibid.
22. Ibid.
23. S. Fred Singer, "A Crisis for OPEC," *New York Times,* March 31, 1981, A19.
24. For the contradictory views on energy policies, see Ibid, and William Brown, "Doom and Gloom on Energy," *Fortune* (20 September 1982). For OPEC's 100 percent death, see William Brown's comments in the *New York Times,* 16 March 1982, p. D 1.
25. William Brown, "Can OPEC Survive the Glut?" *Fortune* (30 Nov. 1981), 89.
26. Voltaire, *Candide and Zadig,* ed. Lester G. Crocker (New York: Pocket Books, 1962) pp. 18-19.

ABOUT THE AUTHORS

Graham Allison is Dean of the Faculty of Public Administration, John F. Kennedy School of Government, Harvard University.

Albert Carnesale is Professor of Public Policy and Academic Dean, John F. Kennedy School of Government, Harvard University.

Alvin A. Alm is Director of the Harvard Energy Security Program and Adjunct Lecturer at the John F.Kennedy School of Government, Harvard University.

Harvey Brooks is Benjamin Peirce Professor of Technology and Public Policy and Professor of Applied Physics on the McKay Endowment, Harvard University.

Peter V. Davis, at the time this was written, was a candidate in the Master of Public Administration Program, John F. Kennedy School of Government, Harvard University and is currently Supervisor of Research and Speech Staff for the Tennessee Valley Authority.

Roger Kasperson is Director of the Center for Technology, Environment and Development, Clark University, Worcester.

Henry Lee is Executive Director of the Energy and Environmental Policy Center and Adjunct Lecturer at the John F. Kennedy School of Government, Harvard University.

Douglas MacLean is Senior Research Associate at the Center for Philosophy and Public Policy, University of Maryland.

Michael Rice is a Senior Fellow of the Aspen Institute with a special interest in issues of communication and society.

Richard E. Sclove is a Research Associate, Department of Political Science, Massachusetts Institute of Technology.

William Colglazier, Jr. is a Postdoctoral Research Fellow at the Center for Science and International Affairs, John F. Kennedy School of Government, Harvard University.

Daniel Yankelovich is President of The Public Agenda Foundation, and Yankelovich, Skelly and White, Inc., New York City.

Daniel Yergin, formerly Associate Director of the Harvard Energy Security Program and Adjunct Lecturer at the Kennedy School of Government, Harvard University is Director of Cambridge Energy Research Associates.

Dorothy S. Zinberg is Lecturer in Public Policy and Director of Seminars and Special Projects at the Center for Science and International Affairs, John F. Kennedy School of Government, Harvard University.

INDEX